The Politics
of Kinship

The Politics of Kinship

Race, Family, Governance

MARK RIFKIN

DUKE UNIVERSITY PRESS *Durham & London* 2024

© 2024 DUKE UNIVERSITY PRESS
All rights reserved

Designed by Matthew Tauch
Typeset in Garamond Premier Pro by
Westchester Publishing Services

Library of Congress Cataloging-in-Publication Data
Names: Rifkin, Mark, [date] author.
Title: The politics of kinship : race, family, governance / Mark Rifkin.
Description: Durham : Duke University Press, 2024. |
Includes bibliographical references and index.
Identifiers: LCCN 2023017379 (print)
LCCN 2023017380 (ebook)
ISBN 9781478030003 (paperback)
ISBN 9781478021049 (hardcover)
ISBN 9781478059004 (ebook)
Subjects: LCSH: United States—Race relations. | Indians of North America—Government relations. | Kinship—Political aspects—United States. | Families—United States—History. | Family policy—United States. | African American families—Government policy. | BISAC: SOCIAL SCIENCE / Ethnic Studies / American / Native American Studies | SOCIAL SCIENCE / Ethnic Studies / American / African American & Black Studies
Classification: LCC E184.A1 .R484 2024 (print) | LCC E184.A1 (ebook) | DDC 305.800973—dc23/eng/20230907
LC record available at https://lccn.loc.gov/2023017379
LC ebook record available at https://lccn.loc.gov/2023017380

Cover art: Coyote Park, *Group Scene*, 2022.
Acrylic on plywood. Courtesy of the artist.

CONTENTS

vii   *Acknowledgments*

1   Introduction: Enfamilyment, Political Orders, and the Racializing Work of Scale

43   ONE. Kinship's Past, Queer Interventions, and Indigenous Futures

93   TWO. Indian Domesticity, Settler Regulation, and the Limits of the Race/Politics Distinction

145   THREE. Marriage, Privacy, Sovereignty

199   FOUR. Blackness, Criminality, Governance

257   Coda: Inside/Outside State Forms

271   *Notes*
343   *Bibliography*
379   *Index*

ACKNOWLEDGMENTS

The idea for this project originally came from a conversation, a very long time ago, with Eric Cheyfitz, and while it has gone through numerous changes since then, I am grateful for his suggestion that I return to and expand my engagement with notions of kinship.

Thanks so much to Courtney Berger, Laura Jaramillo, and everyone at Duke University Press for a great experience. I would also like to thank the anonymous readers for their incredibly helpful feedback. This project was aided by a research assignment from UNC-Greensboro and the time and funds made possible by the Linda Arnold Carlisle professorship in Women's, Gender, and Sexuality Studies. Portions of the book were presented at Amherst College, Berea College, the University of Chicago, and the University of Pennsylvania, and I would like to thank all those who invited me as well as all those who attended my presentations and provided feedback. Parts of chapter 1 previously were published as "Beyond Family: Kinship's Past, Queer Worldmaking, and the Question of Governance" in *Queer Kinship: Race, Sex, Belonging, Form* (edited by Elizabeth Freeman and Teagan Bradway), and parts of chapter 2 previously were published as "Making Peoples into Populations: The Racial Limits of Tribal Sovereignty" in *Theorizing Native Studies* (edited by Audra Simpson and Andrea Smith) and "Around 1978: Family, Culture, and Race in the Federal Production of Indianness" in *Critically Sovereign: Indigenous Gender, Sexuality, and Feminist Studies* (edited by Joanne Barker). Thanks to Duke University Press for allowing me to draw on those essays.

There are numerous folks whose presence in my scholarly world over the long haul makes this work possible. Among them are Hoku Aikua, Chad Allen, Aimee Bahng, Joanne Barker, Nancy Bentley, Lisa Brooks, David Chang, Eric Cheyfitz, Pete Coviello, Jean Dennison, Rod Ferguson, Beth Freeman, Ashley Glassburn, Mishuana Goeman, Alyosha Goldstein, Lisa Hall, Grace Hong, Shona Jackson, Daniel Heath Justice, Dana Luciano, Scott Morgensen, Diane Nelson (whom I miss very much), Rob Nichols, Beth Piatote, Joseph Pierce, Audra Simpson, Riley Snorton, Kyla Tompkins,

Kiara Vigil, and Priscilla Wald. I would also like to thank those at UNC-Greensboro who have been great supporters over the last lots-of-years. Thanks to Risa Applegarth, Danielle Bouchard, Sarah Cervenak, Daniel Coleman, Asa Eger, Jen Feather, Tara Green, Gwen Hunnicutt, Janine Jones, Karen Kilcup, Derek Krueger, Lisa Levenstein, Christian Moraru, Jenn Park, Gene Rogers, Scott Romine, María Sánchez, Amy Vines, and Karen Weyler.

In addition to the folks above, there are also those beyond the university who keep reminding me of the inestimable importance of family and friendship. Thanks to Tiffany and Will Allen, Sheila and Alex Avelin, Zivia Avelin, Laura and Jim Baxley, Keith Brand, Craig Bruns, Ali Cohen, Kevin and Justin Dichter, Lori and Steve Fineman, Mike and Rebecca Hardin, David Horowitz and Courtney Allison, Steve and Dianne Horowitz, Debbie and Andy Johnson, Drew and Elizabeth Johnson, Steven and Erica Johnson, JJ McArdle, Alicia and Bobby Murray, David Peck and Abby Kornfeld, Stefanie Peck, Toby and Brian Pecker, Sarah Johnson Saunders, Lisa Smith, and Jon Van Gieson.

To Erika Lin, for being my other lifetime partner.

I'm deeply grateful to Neal and Sharon Rifkin and Gail Dichter for everything.

To Rich Murray, for being there, being funny (and sweet and nice), and loving me unconditionally.

Introduction

Enfamilyment, Political Orders, and the Racializing Work of Scale

CHILD-STEALING HAS been a historical staple of racialization in the United States. In perhaps the most spectacularly egregious example of this pattern in recent memory, the Trump administration adopted the policy (often denied as such but still enforced) of rending migrant families at the border, leading to the detention of at least 4,500 children over a three-year period and possibly thousands more. This horrifying, unspeakably cruel, and deeply traumatizing denial of migrant humanity, though, came into view as part of mass-mediated discourse in ways other routine modes of institutionalized child-stealing do not. Every year Black and Indigenous children are taken into government custody, separated from their parents by the state at rates that are, respectively, approaching two and over three times their presence in the US population. These numbers represent almost 6,000 Native children and over 53,000 African American children annually.[1] Such state intervention may appear as, in Elizabeth Povinelli's terms, a "quasi-event," one that does not appear as a crisis per se while being part of an extended state-sanctioned project of wearing down racialized populations;[2] it illustrates a sustained set of dynamics in which the government's terrifying and sickening actions on the border can be seen less as exception than as a particularly concentrated example of the status quo of how whiteness operates through structural violence. In understanding these patterns, commentators often have emphasized the horror of dividing families on the basis of race. Justice, then, lies in refusing to use racist distinctions, demeanings, and discriminations, such that families can remain intact.

Appeals to the affective units and densities of feeling associated with *family* aim to endow a sense of shared humanness that can serve as a basis for repudiating institutionalized racial distinctions. Yet, in doing so, a range of structuring assumptions about what constitutes personhood, privacy, and political authority are employed that de facto can normalize the racializing dynamics of liberal governance. What if the issue lies less in the nonrecognition of family than forced incorporation into the category of "family"? What if such inclusion helps drive the very ideological and institutional processes of race-making that result in diminished possibilities and life chances for those belonging to populations constituted as non-white? What if "the family" serves as a principal vehicle through which to draw the line between those who count as persons and those who don't, not because they can't access the rights of "family" but because they are subject to this category through which the racializing construction of (non)personhood occurs? A naturalized vision of what might be called kinship acts as an ostensibly neutral frame of reference that effaces not only the politics of how kinship is defined and deployed (i.e., who is included and excluded), but also the ways kinship itself serves as an ideological matrix through which the content, contours, and character of "politics" is constituted. If we think of kinship less as a means of remediating racialization than as a discursive and institutional mode through which processes of racialization are (re)produced and regulated, antiracist and anticolonial intellectual work might turn away from affirming the capacity of people of color to be what we might describe as *enfamilied* and turn toward an analysis of how family/kinship serves as a mechanism for producing depoliticizing narratives of ingrained deviancy around which racial population-making takes shape. Since the late nineteenth century, the concept of kinship largely has functioned as a way of translating non-liberal social formations into the categories, differences, and scale structures of liberalism.[3] "Kinship" allows social units and networks that do not fit liberal mappings of the public-private distinction and that exceed the nuclear family unit to be cast as excessive, backward, and/or socially dysfunctional versions of liberal home and family, albeit ones that do not seem to know their proper place and character. The specific contours and content of such supposed failures have served as ways of delineating and typifying kinds of racialized persons, of constituting racialized populations. Particular racial groups appear as such in being targeted for state intervention and management due to their ostensibly characteristic inabilities to live out liberal forms of privacy, intimacy, and care, as those dynamics categorically are contradistinguished from the work of governance.

What would happen, though, if we were to understand the very forms cast as racialized aberrance, due to their supposed failure to enact liberal norms of enfamilyment, as, instead, *political orders*? What might such an act of *redescription* make possible? The construction of racial nonpersonhood through presenting non-white populations as constitutively incapable of performing proper forms of family and homemaking is less an expression of the secure dominance of liberal governance than its anxieties, contingencies, and instabilities in the face of what might be characterized as alternative political orders. In "The State Is a Man," Audra Simpson addresses the ways that the murder of Indigenous women on lands claimed by Canada and the United States can be understood as part of a broader assault on Indigenous governance. She observes, "An Indian woman's body in settler regimes such as the US, in Canada is loaded with meaning—signifying other political orders, land itself, of the dangerous possibility of reproducing Indian life and most dangerously, other political orders."[4] When Simpson speaks of "other political orders," more than referring to the jurisdiction of Indigenous polities over their territories, unbound from settler legal and administrative oversight/intervention, she is invoking other conceptions of what constitutes the shape and stuff of governance, such that the gendered, heteronormative, and privatizing frameworks at play in the liberal state do not provide the paradigm for governance (in terms of its modes of operation, its normative principles, or its scalar structure). Leanne Simpson (no relation) further develops the notion that Indigenous bodies signify or point toward the existence of other political orders into the idea that Indigenous bodies *are* such political orders. She argues that "Indigenous bodies, particularly the bodies of 2SQ people, children, and women, represented the lived alternative to heteronormative constructions of gender, political systems, and rules of descent. They are political orders," later adding that "within Nishnaabeg thought, every body is a political order and every body houses individual self-determination."[5] This (re)framing radically reimagines political scale by understanding intimate life and everyday connections as immanently bearing within them the structuring dynamics of governance, as shaping collective processes of decision-making, resource distribution, placemaking, belonging, etc., that *are* the substance of self-determination (in both an individual and a political sense). While these analyses speak specifically to Indigenous peoplehood and modes of life,[6] the conception of *political order* that they articulate might serve as a means of thinking about the kinds of collective practices that become racialized as expressions of failed/aberrant kinship. More than solely pointing to the failure of the settler-state fully to acknowledge the sovereignty of Native governments, the attention to Indigenous political orders seeks to open up possibilities for expanding the kinds of processes, networks, regularities of practice, and webs of interdependence that can be seen *as governance*. The ideologies of enfamilyment that historically have been central to liberal governance, and that remain so, cannot accommodate these formations *as politics*. Or rather, liberal governance may be said to depend on recoding such politics as *kinship*—as properly belonging to a private sphere in which such forms appear as racialized deviance.

While articulated within Native studies as a means of characterizing Indigenous peoplehood, the notion of political orders might be drawn on as a way of rethinking, of redescribing, the dynamics of racialization in the United States more broadly. A familiar strategy within Native intellectual and political discourses is to insist that Indigenous peoples are political orders rather than the population constructed through racializing figurations of *Indianness*. Doing so seeks to leverage the ways racialization recasts Native polities as collections of non-white persons who can then be treated as *domestic* subjects of the settler-state's jurisdiction, rather than as their own autonomous, self-determining political entities with rightful governance over their lands and waters.[7] However, if that insistence often serves as a way of separating politics from race as a definitional frame for understanding Native peoplehood, the imbrication to which that very confusion points can operate as a lens through which to characterize the ideological work of racialization itself. To cast modes of governance as, instead, a function of racial genealogy not only denies that these matrices of collective self-ordering can count *as a politics* but presents them as a function of racial inclinations, as expressive of a pathologically deformed private sphere—as emanating from aberrant, excessive, and disordered kinds of kinship and homemaking. In this way, forms of governance that do not fit liberal frameworks historically get presented as evidence of privatized racial incapacity, as symptomatic of an ingrained inability to be a proper subject. This dynamic, though, might be seen not only as pertaining to Indigenous peoples but as also at play with regard to other kinds of racialization enacted within the US (settler-)state, recognizing that the contours of those racializations may differ as well as the kinds of political orders to which they point. More than defining groups as outside enfamilied personhood, the dynamics of racialization recode patterns of collective life that do not fit liberal geographies and scalar dynamics as if they were immanent tendencies that testify to inherent racial difference.

The Politics of Kinship argues that the institutionalized matrix of family/kinship serves a central function in organizing and normalizing forms of racial distinction that themselves provide a principal means through which the contours of politics and governance are defined. Sociopolitical formations that contest the terms of the liberal state are recast as expressions of an ingrained, privatized, corporealized deviance. This approach might be seen less as a strong argumental or exclusionary claim ("it's really this and definitely not that . . .") than as an experiment with how characterizing something in other terms constellates it with concepts, frames, and analyses other than those that previously have been used, thereby reconfiguring the problem-space in which whatever so considered takes intellectual shape. David Scott defines a problem-space as "an ensemble of questions and answers around which a horizon of identifiable stakes (conceptual as well as ideological-political stakes) hangs," further suggesting that distinctions among problem-spaces include their "tropes, modes, and rhetoric" and the "horizon in relation to which [they are] constructed."[8] In drawing on Indigenous formulations of "other political orders," the book aims to reconfigure the problem-space for analyzing racialization in the United States, which tends to cluster around how bodies are interpellated as nonpersons (and how populations are made through such interpellations), rather than foregrounding what kinds of collective forms are disavowed through those interpellations. I want to suggest that highlighting the question of governance in other-than-liberal terms—attending to social formations that conventionally would not be understood as enacting governance and conceptualizing them *as political orders*—shifts extant ways of understanding how racialization operates by attending to the conversion of modes of collective life and self-organization into the terms of (wrong) enfamilyment, thereby making those other modes (which denaturalize and potentially upset the terms and structure of liberal governance) a legitimate target for state interventions of various kinds. I characterize this process of reframing as *redescription*; as a method it aims to reorient how we conceptualize phenomena and relations among them, in this case the terms of the title—race, family, and governance. This taking up of Indigenous formulations to think Native and racialized non-native modes of collective life seems particularly pressing in light of both the tendency within Indigenous studies, often implicitly, to circulate a narrative of Indigenous exceptionality (as not defined by race, as other than national minorities), which can be diminishing of other social struggles, *and* the tendency in other areas of critical ethnic studies and progressive/broadly leftist scholarship to treat Indigenous intellectual frames as parochial and thus largely irrelevant for thinking about anything not specifically focused on Native people(s). I center Indigenous analytical coordinates and priorities while, in the process, immanently shifting them so as to articulate with non-Indigenous struggles and freedom dreams, thereby also redescribing those collective formations in ways that seek to emphasize the immanent potentials of governance within them and the ways racializing discourses of enfamilyment work to forestall and foreclose those potentials by casting other forms of life and political will through their narration as perversion in family/kinship—as an ingrained inability to sustain the private sphere in proper, natural ways.

Race-Making as Family-Making

Liberal modes of rule depend upon a particular scalar imaginary in which the personal is fundamentally distinguished from the political. Scale is less an indicator of size than about how entities, institutions, spaces, and processes are conceived and function in relation to each other, particularly the extent to which one is understood as "inside" (subordinated, coordinated, or regulated) by the other. Scale, then, expresses the kinds of connections between such entities, institutions, spaces, or processes.[9] In addition to not serving as the site for generating public policy or for collective decision-making and resource distribution beyond the "family," the sphere of the personal/domestic/intimate is envisioned as organized around natural principles that lie beyond and before those of governance but that should animate governance as its legitimating core and ethical horizon. In this frame, government exists to protect and capacitate forms of family/domesticity/privacy that themselves are decidedly not scenes of governance and are not conceptualized as having meaningful lateral relations outside the political institutions to which they have ceded limited kinds of authority. The scale of the personal nestles within that of political institutions, which extend over a number of aggregated households/families, and that unit of political authority itself is nestled within a larger one, expanding in scope until the unit encompasses the entire nation. In the United States, that political scale goes from the municipal, to the county, to the state, to the federal government, with each level having its own set of powers and superintendence over the level(s) below—with each level also largely understood as lacking lateral relations with other units at that level unmediated by the level above. However, as Elizabeth Maddock Dillon suggests, the personal sphere that appears as outside and prior to political institutions arises as a back-formation within those very institutions through "state of nature" fictions that normalize the form of the private sphere. She argues that there is "a recursive loop between privacy and publicity in which the intimate sphere 'prequalifies' certain subjects for participation in the political public sphere," and marriage (and, by extension, the modes of privatized family organized around it) "plays a pivotal role in defining the private subjects of the liberal state who will thenceforth have the capacity to emerge from privacy into public recognition, and to defend the sanctity of 'privacy' against a seemingly exterior public sphere."[10] Within this liberal dialectics, defining family and belonging to one—being the subject of kinship—situates persons within the political architecture of liberal governance while also serving as evidence of the extent to which someone can be a proper political subject, whether they emerge from the *kind* of home, family, and matrix of intimate bonds that "prequalifies" one to be a rights-holding citizen.

This recursive dynamic, through which the naturalized realm of family illustrates the capacity to participate in political life while also normalizing the scale structure of state jurisdiction, further depends upon processes of racialization. The forms of bourgeois homemaking that lie at the heart of liberal ideologies of governance were never free from accompanying sets of discourses and institutional practices that disqualified from enfamilyment those deemed to be too backward and brutal to enact liberal subjectivity and sentiment. As Imani Perry argues, Euro-patriarchy entailed the production of racialized populations who were legally subordinated as propertyless nonpersons: "the economic liberalism of which [John] Locke was a foundational thinker—and, specifically the doctrine of personhood—entails a system whereby the subject before the state or the law was made into either a patriarch, his liege (woman) [and, one might add, his children], or someone outside legal recognition, whether slaves or what in that time were termed 'savages' but whom we can also term 'nonpersons' in the juridical sense." Those racialized beings/groups stood outside the boundaries of civilized homemaking, or at least could not be included as family members but only as the subjects/objects of state-sanctioned discipline. Their collective inability to participate in liberal life was marked by "deviant forms of gendering and sexuality" that symptomatized both their "exclusion from the rights and recognitions of legal personhood" and the particularity of the racial status that made them thus ineligible for inclusion.[11] Simply expanding the concept of family, such as through appeals to supposedly more flexible and less nuclear notions of kinship, does not undo the distinction between personhood and nonpersonhood, as it turns on racially saturated understandings of depoliticized property, privacy, and intimacy.

The concept/category of family serves as a principal vehicle for ongoing race-making due to its unique capacity as an ideological and institutional template to naturalize the sociopolitical architecture of liberalism as integral to human reproduction itself and to contain nonliberal formations and modes of life within the scale structure of liberalism as deformations of the private sphere, potentially dangerous but not fundamentally challenging the validity of the political infrastructures of liberal governance.[12] Put another way, the ideological matrix of "family" cannot readily be severed from the work it has done and continues to do in providing the material of which racial distinctions are made and through which racial hierarchies are articulated, explicitly and implicitly. Family and its privatizing norms, including kinship as its ostensibly more porous and malleable supplement, serve as vital parts of the "assemblages," in Alexander Weheliye's terms, through which race continually is (re)produced. Notions of enfamilyment provide much of the conceptual infrastructure through which various forms of non-whiteness are marked as socially aberrant and dangerous in ways that treat nonliberal modes of collectivity and self-governance as expressions of deformed and dangerous private tendencies—as kinds of wrong personhood that arise due to ingrained racial tendencies.[13]

More than simply differentiating between classes of persons who can be seen as enfamilied (as bearing liberal intimacy) and those who constitutively cannot, the racial making of the terms and boundaries of kinship illustrates the insecurities that surround that process as well as the roles kinship is called on to perform in redressing forms of political crisis—in containing, regulating, effacing, and dismantling alternative political orders. In this vein, Ann Laura Stoler's work provides a powerful model for tracing the ways middle-class norms, liberal frameworks of governance, and distinctions between citizens and nonpersons arise out of and in response to dynamics of political instability and disarray, rather than being brought to processes of racialization as preformed paradigms. Stoler argues that Michel Foucault's *History of Sexuality* not only does not engage with the forms of racialization and colonialism that were occurring during the period in which he suggests "sexuality" emerged as a coherent biopolitical formation in Europe, but that the very kinds of normative articulations among bodies, sensations, home, family, health, gender, and reproduction that discourses of sexuality make possible were occurring earlier in the colonies in ways inseparable from the making of forms of racial identification and distinction.[14] She suggests that turning to the colonies reveals the importance of "focus[ing] not on the *affirmation* of bourgeois bodies ... but on the uncertainties and porous boundaries that surrounded them," which she terms "their precarious vulnerabilities." Such a shift in scholarly attention away from the metropole highlights the production of the kinds of racial distinctions necessary for both justifying and enacting colonial rule: "Much of the anthropology of colonialism ... has taken the categories of 'colonized' and 'colonizer' as givens, rather than as constructions that need to be explained." Attending to that construction means that the production of such difference is "not about the importation of middle-class sensibilities to the colonies, but about the *making* of them." Understandings of the distinctions between the normal/healthful and the perverse/savage, then, were not brought *to* sites of colonial governance but were generated *within* them as part of seeking to regulate varied populations (whose difference from each other is not an a priori given), shore up forms of institutional authority, pursue particular political and economic agendas, and map out who would have access to what forms of political subjectivity. As Stoler argues, "who would be a 'subject' and who a 'citizen' converged on the sexual politics of race"; thus, "colonial discourses of sexuality were productive of class and racial power, not mere reflections of them," earlier noting that "an implicit racial grammar underwrote the sexual regimes of bourgeois culture."[15] Following Stoler's argument, "sexuality"—including modes of and relations among household-making, erotic relationships, everyday care, reproduction, and childrearing—provided a means for producing and defining racial difference as part of seeking to control forms of association, exchange, alliance, cohabitation, and political status/belonging.

Such enfamilied differences between viable political subjects and racialized nonpersons, then, arise out of existing policy quagmires and knotted difficulties of governance as a continually vexed and incomplete effort to stabilize imperial order. Viewed from this perspective, racial identities remain always in process, made and remade largely through recourse to "middle-class sensibilities" and the "sexual regimes of bourgeois culture" that themselves take shape around the frustrations, failures, and incoherencies of rule that racialization aims to redress/manage. In the context of the United States, we might consider how whiteness and various categories of non-whiteness such as blackness, Indianness, Asianness, and Latinness function as ways of addressing shifting political and economic difficulties/crises within US governance.[16] The biopolitical production of racial populations crucially animates and secures the sovereignty of the state by ideologically transposing challenges to its jurisdictional frameworks into an account of pathological bodies and families. This way of approaching the matter of population draws on Foucauldian frames while directing attention more explicitly back to questions of collective self-governance and how alternatives to the state are managed through modes of racialization.

Race marks the distinction between those seen as able to participate in life-affirming projects of state regulation and those seen as pathologically unable to do so, as posing problems for the health and well-being of citizen-subjects—who illustrate their aptitude, competence, and deservingness by embodying the norms that undergird policy. As Foucault observes, "the death of the other, the death of the bad race, of the inferior race (or the degenerate, or the abnormal) is something that will make life in general healthier: healthier and purer," and in this sense, the "bad race" are "enemies who have to be done away with," less in the sense of being "adversaries in the political sense of the term" than as "threats ... to the population."[17] In being defined as separate from the national population/public and as threats to that collective's well-being, this race (or set of races—presented as representing varied kinds of threat due to varied kinds of normative failure) itself is a distinct population, a designation/identity that does not count as "political." To be a population is to be a biologized aggregate *rather than* a collective subject engaged in struggle over what can constitute legitimate forms, frameworks, and principles of governance.[18]

Not simply envisioned as biologically transmitted, race marks immanent aberrance with regard to norms of enfamilyment, ingrained tendencies that make racialized subjects a collective problem that needs to be regulated/contained/eliminated for the good of the "general population."[19] Those norms serve as the vehicle for transposing modes of collectivity into failures of racialized flesh.[20] We might suggest that, as a mode of rule, governmentality sustains state sovereignty through the ideological conversion of alternative political orders into aggregations of pathological bodies. In this way, discourses of race perform a (re)scaling of bodies, in which such bodies signify synecdochically as part of a (biological) population rather than as actors in alternative networks and processes of governance.[21] The very activities that could be understood as participation in other political orders—arrangements of decision-making, resource distribution, place-making that do not fit the terms of enfamilied social organization (and that often are collated under the concept of kinship)—are seen as expressive of ingrained, pathological tendencies toward disorder within what should be the private sphere.

Turning back to Stoler's account of the ways processes of racial (re)definition operate as means of managing running "uncertainties," what problems arise in the operation of institutions of governance and in the determination of both policy objectives and means of achieving them? How do racializing discourses of sexuality seek (and often fail) to manage such tensions and incoherencies? And what other social and political possibilities emerge and need to be regulated, denigrated, and disavowed through such racializing discourses of sexuality (including charges of failed, aberrant, and antisocial family/kinship)? Foregrounding the always-in-process character of racial categorizations draws attention to the ways liberal articulations of family and the private sphere, particularly within law and policy, are dynamically responsive to perceived challenges to the form of state governance. In this sense, race serves as a flexible and multifaceted discursive technology for recasting threats to the structures, scales, and regularities of liberal political economy as deformations of proper kinship, (re)constituting the contours of normative family in the process. Seen in this way, ideologies of family/kinship operate as a malleable translational and regulatory matrix through which to manage ongoing challenges to state grids of political intelligibility: *family* is never separate from the metapolitical process of struggling over what constitutes *politics*, or the principles and scope of governance. Attending to the ongoing imbrication of race-making in efforts to differentiate normative from pathological family formation and domesticity underlines the roles played by shifting notions of family in the (re)making of the sovereignty of the liberal state, not just as the ostensibly private sphere around which such governance is organized but as pointing toward the presence of other social networks and formations—other political orders—that are contained and disciplined through their racialization as expressive of failed/deviant/backward/excessive family.

The concept of kinship, though, often implicitly reinforces such racializing enfamilyment by presenting patterns of collectivity as expressive of personal relations and modes of intimate life, de facto reinscribing a liberal paradigm of governance even in the process of seeking to denaturalize it. Since the late nineteenth century, the concept of kinship has functioned as a way of indexing the existence of kinds of human sociality that do not necessarily fit the form of the nuclear family. Yet, as discussed further in chapter 1, it does so in ways that largely reinstate that social form in the process of noting divergences from it, using the nuclear family as the frame of reference through which to categorize and characterize other configurations of care, provision, affection, and everyday life. The linkage of kinship with *family*, *intimacy*, and the *personal* in recent historiographic efforts to address race and patterns of social life that precede the state's claims to what currently is US territory (or that occur in spaces that were at the time on the national periphery) illustrates this dynamic. In her excellent award-winning study *Empires, Nations, and Families*, Anne F. Hyde addresses how relationships among persons and groups in the trans-Mississippi West in the late eighteenth and early nineteenth centuries defied the terms of European imperial policy and incipient forms of US national jurisdiction. She observes, "Family connections across national and ethnic lines allowed business and diplomacy to flourish in these places," later adding, "This flexible and stable system, based in families who had the ability and desire to make powerful kinship links to other families, solidified over the entire period, protecting people against change and insulating them for a very long time against the rigid demands of American conquest."[22] Hyde casts *kinship* and *family* as interchangeable terms, understanding both as a function of "personal connections."[23] What seems to bind this mosaic of relationships is familial connection, juxtaposed with the formal realm—the "demands"—of law and policy. Yet, those bonds themselves generate a "stable system," which leaves one wondering as to the character of that formation. This portrayal presents the networks of trade discussed and the immanent patterns and normative principles that shaped those networks as a function of de facto private relations, distinguished from the inefficacious claims to jurisdiction by various national and imperial powers. The usage of "kinship" in this way speaks to a conceptual aporia in the argument. Hyde characterizes these overlapping matrices of interaction as both an ungoverned borderland and as largely Native in character.[24] She at points references Indigenous peoples as offering "an alternative vision of political space" to that at play in official Euro-American frameworks of governance,[25] but in much of the study the concept of kinship does the work of marking differences from liberal social forms, including networks that did not conform to (Anglo) racial divisions, while also deferring discussion of the kind of political order in which those relationships were enmeshed and for which they helped provide an infrastructure. Moreover, these social formations are not dependent on whiteness as a mode of securing the social organization (and political scale structure) of liberal governance; or, perhaps more accurately, whiteness as a means of installing and defending liberal political economy gains shape and force through its articulation as against these competing formations. When combined with its continued conjunction with "family," the characterization of such matrices and their attendant political economies as organized around "kinship" underplays the ways the absence of meaningful authority by Euro-American powers speaks to the existence of other political orders not dependent on the privatizing and racializing matrix of "family."

Such invocations of kinship implicitly enact a scalar imaginary in which particular kinds of proximity, engagement, and/or interdependence appear as a function of the personal/private—de facto defined as against the public/political. Certain sorts of interaction, say sexual or with regard to childcare, are presumed to exist in an *intimate* realm (even when the writer seeks to understand the connections between such scenes and phenomena deemed more macrologically political or economic).[26] In her magnificent study *Wicked Flesh*, Jessica Marie Johnson explores Black women's efforts to forge livable worlds and networks of relation for themselves and their children across a range of sites in the eighteenth and early nineteenth centuries within the networks of transatlantic enslavement—primarily on the islands off of what is now Senegal, in the Antilles, and across the Gulf Coast of what is now the United States. In telling this story of socialities made under the shadow—or perhaps in the maw—of the political economies and ordinary brutalities of enslavement, Johnson consistently uses versions of the phrase "intimacy and kinship" to name the kinds of connections Black women made in order to carve out spaces of freedom (whether legally recognized as such or not): "Understanding the role intimacy and kinship played in black women's lives highlights black women's everyday understanding of freedom as centered around safety and security for themselves and their progeny"; they were "determined to build community and make generations, imagining futures that were, if not beyond bondage, at least buttressed against harm, they cultivated, protected, and defended kinship networks."[27] What, though, does *intimacy* do in figuring the construction of modes of community that, as Johnson later notes, "form[ed] maps of kin between towns and countryside" in defiance of imperial policy imperatives and census tabulations?[28] As in Hyde's account, the juxtaposition of the "networks" in question with the terms and priorities of imperial institutions of governance creates the sense of alternative modes of sociality operating through their own immanent principles that do not comport with those of official law and policy. Yet, the running conjunction of intimacy and kinship seems to position the latter term as expressive of ordinary scenes of interaction and care that qualitatively differ from the work of governance. In this way, the figure of kinship can have topological effects, positioning the phenomenon described within the realm of *family* in ways that potentially underdescribe the challenges such modes of collectivity pose to dominant paradigms of governance. To break out of this cycle, what is needed is a richer and more textured conception of what constitutes a political order.

Political Order as Analytic

If liberal frameworks presume that governance necessarily takes a particular form, the idea of alternative *political orders* not only can help draw attention to interwoven liberal ideologies of scale, personhood, and social reproduction but can refigure what constitutes political form and processes of governance, refusing the narration of collective being and becoming as inherently subordinate to state categories/mappings, expressive of unreasonable/deviant inclinations, or a kind of confusion about the proper boundaries of intimate life. Audra Simpson suggests that anti-Indigenous gendered violence is an extension of an institutionalized "death drive [by the settler-state] to eliminate, contain, hide, and in other ways 'disappear' what fundamentally challenges its legitimacy," "polities" that "serve as alternative forms of legitimacy and sovereignties to that of the settler state." The imposition of heteropatriarchal principles and geographies is an integral part of this effort to displace, deny, and dismantle Indigenous polities that maintain "other life forms, other sovereignties, other forms of political will" to those of the liberal (settler-)state.[29] Building off of this analysis, Leanne Simpson argues, "we must understand that colonizers saw Indigenous bodies—our physical bodies and our constructions of gender, sexuality, and intimate relationships— . . . as a symbol of Indigenous orders of government and a direct threat to their sovereignty and governmentality."³⁰ The racialization of Indigenous bodies through their portrayal as expressing a backward, degraded, and deviant Indianness works to efface Indigenous governance as such, recasting it as failed gender, sexuality, family-making, and homemaking. In doing so, this routine and pervasive translation of political orders as race indicates the ways Indigenous sovereignties actively challenge the terms, mappings, and legitimacy of the state that claims them and their lands. The force of such translation further suggests the limits and insecurities of settler governance, the need for the ongoing management and attempted foreclosure of competing formations. These kinds of Indigenous feminist (re)formulations illustrate how the concept of political orders can do the following: point toward kinds of collectivity whose existence is not organized by the state or around its terms; indicate the presence of "orders of government" not structured around a rigid public/private distinction, particularly the heteropatriarchal norm of the nuclear family; and illustrate how everyday bodily experience—enmeshed in webs of relation with other persons, places, and nonhuman entities—immanently bears modes of governance, which, again, is not inherently distinct/disjunct from "intimate relations." Although articulated in ways that are about the specificity of Indigenous sociopolitical forms, particularly as against settler insistence that Native peoples be recognized through institutionalized state discourses, this (re)framing of *the political*, I want to argue, can serve as a vehicle through which to rethink the broader work of racialization within liberal governance. While not seeking to diminish Indigenous articulations of sovereignty or necessarily to equate them with other kinds of collective processes, the use of the concept of political order in this way—to index and conceptually displace the scale/jurisdictional structure of liberal governance and its racializing mobilization of ideologies of enfamilyment—might direct attention toward "the possibility of other possibilities" for non-Indigenous (or mixed Indigenous and non-native) modes of collectivity.³¹

The concept of alternative political orders primarily has been developed by Indigenous intellectuals as a way of addressing modes of Native sovereignty and self-determination that exceed or defy interpellation into state jurisdictional grids and modes of racialized (non)personhood. As Audra Simpson notes with regard to the work of settler conceptions of *Indianness*, "Here we see the biopolitical project of recognition, which sees governable populations based on bodily attributes rendered as 'races,' trumping a prior and ongoing, if not strangulated, political order of sovereignty."³² Racialization operates as a means of translating Indigenous governance into a non-"political" idiom that enables its strangulation—through which peoples are recast as "populations" in order to insert them into existing settler legal and administrative templates. In marking and tracing that dynamic, though, Simpson points toward the presence of political formations that do not fit into the terms of liberal governance. She characterizes such Indigenous collective self-understandings as "feeling citizenships": "These are alternative citizenships to the state that are structured in the present space of intracommunity recognition, affection, and care, outside the logics of colonial and imperial rule." Simpson further notes that they "may not be institutionally recognized, but are socially and politically recognized in the everyday life of the community" and emerge from emplaced "web[s] of relations."[33] In addition to obeying their own principles separate from those institutionalized by the state, these modes of belonging emerge out of and are sustained through everyday relations, lived webs of connection. More than merely an aggregate of interpersonal networks or semipublic associations, such citizenships bespeak the existence of non-state political orders—matrices of collective decision-making, resource distribution, placemaking, and care in which there is not a bright-line distinction between private and political domains and in which governance does not necessarily attach to institutional apparatuses that are disjunct from the domestic sphere.

The use of "feeling" as a way of characterizing belonging and processes of political meaning-making itself indicates the central role of affective connections in the ongoing remaking of these formations, in contrast to liberal notions of disinterested distance and generic, serialized personhood. As Laura Harjo suggests with regard to Mvskoke (Creek) collective life, "prevailing governance structures, as well as the resources that a community may assume are necessary to build communities intentionally, can become entrenched with formality," adding, "formality can reproduce normative settler colonial governance structures that shift power from the collective of everyday folks to the elites, putting decision-making in the hands of a few." Liberal conceptions of the political as a distinct sphere, and of other political orders as expressions of illiberal forms of racial/cultural particularity, enact governance-as-formality, separating it from networks of everyday interaction through which "a network of relationality" is built. Juxtaposing "the politics of normative governance systems" with "the poetics of Mvskoke community," Harjo understands Indigenous polities as potentially enacting governance through processes of decision-making and collective practices of engagement that do not operate at a differentiated scale from those kinds of routine relationships that would be understood from a liberal perspective as private.[34] Or, more pointedly, from within the perspective of liberal institutions such networks would appear as excessive distensions of bourgeois privacy, producing aberrant (racialized) subjects unable to embody the ideals of proper personhood.

Understanding these forms of collectivity as political orders underlines principles of governance organized around sites and kinds of ordinary interaction, as opposed to a differentiated and formalized sphere with its own distinct rules and processes, and that conception of governance, or the potential for those relations/networks to count *as governance*, entails revising notions of scale implicit in liberal ideas of "the political." Harjo notes that "scale requires us to examine the processes that created the geopolitical units," indicating that lived Indigenous experiences of political form have more to do with "relational processes" than territorial grids.[35] From this perspective, clearly demarcated spheres of privatized domesticity do not sit next to each other as semi-isolated units encompassed within the delimited area over which a given government exerts jurisdiction (operating on a separate set of principles than those at play in the serialized domestic units). The idea of a political order, then, opens up possibilities for considering the kinds of relational processes that might enact modes of collective self-ordering, in ways divorced from the scale structure of dominant conceptions of governance in which there are a limited number of kinds of "geopolitical units" pegged to the nation-state form and the relations among states.[36]

This (re)framing of what governance can be calls for an account of political decision-making not restricted to an institutionalized structure, suggesting it can occur in a range of spaces that do not necessarily have constitution-like, impersonal procedural rules that are meant to guide the process. Historically, among the forms that Indigenous governance has taken on the lands currently claimed by the United States, there are many peoples who have a clan system of one kind or another in which decisions about leadership and the distribution of resources occur through these genealogically inflected ensembles, and while those social entities sometimes are also residential in character, clans (or other genealogically inflected kinds of collectivity) often extend beyond residence, such that there are ties among different residential groups (town/village/band/camp) and, reciprocally, residential connections that tie together members of disparate clans.[37] These connections can create overlapping kinds of association, identification, and interdependence that produce complex, layered processes of decision-making that cannot easily be broken into modular and hierarchized units of jurisdiction, nor can the dynamics of deliberation, debate, negotiation, and consensus within and across these processes be narrated in ways divorced from the situated imbrications in which they are enmeshed. This is not to say that Native peoples do not have constitutional modes of governance, especially given the history of Indigenous entanglement within colonial systems and the need both to signify their political autonomy to settler-states and to enact their sovereignties in ways that effectively can defend that landed autonomy.[38] Rather, it is to say that Indigenous theorizations of political form—of the existence of political orders that differ from the organizational structures and normative principles of the (liberal) state—seek to counter the dismissal of other modes of governance as excessive, backward, and/or dangerous deformations of liberal privacy.[39]

Such other political orders appear as deviant personhood when viewed against the background of liberal ideologies of justice and public order, which employ a series of implicit conceptions of the contours and character of the sphere of (privatized) social reproduction in ways that shape the terms of the supposedly irreducible personhood at the heart of citizens' *political* interaction with each other. In *Liberalism and Empire*, Uday Mehta argues that "the exclusionary basis of liberalism ... derive[s] from its theoretical core, ... not because the ideals are theoretically disingenuous or concretely impractical, but rather because behind the capacities ascribed to all human beings exists a thicker set of social credentials that constitute the real bases of political inclusion." Mehta further characterizes such credentials as what is taken to be an "anthropological common denominator."[40] This point might be reframed as the idea that liberal governance presumes the existence of certain ostensibly extrapolitical modes that create and sustain the conditions for being a viable social/political subject, modes that provide the unstated but necessary infrastructure for the operation of political institutions and the kinds of personhood whose recognition legitimizes such institutions (the kind of recursive preauthorization Elizabeth Maddock Dillon discusses, as noted earlier).

For example, John Rawls, perhaps the premier theorist of liberalism as a necessary normative frame for good governance, indicates that a just form of political order requires "a basic structure," which refers to the "main political and social institutions and how they fit together as one system of cooperation." These institutions ensure that the processes of "care, nurture, and education" that produce "free and equal citizens" are themselves secured; in doing so, they "shape citizens' character and aims, the kinds of persons they are and aspire to be." The dynamics of social reproduction, then, are not ancillary to the shaping of the subjectivity of citizenship and what equality and freedom mean. Rawls insists that "the political" is "distinct from the personal and the familial, which are affectional . . . in ways the political is not," but he also observes that "the political constitution, the legally recognized forms of property, and the organization of the economy, and the nature of the family all belong to the basic structure."[41] The *family*, therefore, is not simply a site of social reproduction having nothing to do with the shape of political institutions and subjectivity; rather, its form is part of the "basic structure," enabling the training of citizens who can understand themselves as serially segmented, politically equivalent, and self-possessed.[42] In this way, these personhood-generating and personhood-sustaining familial spaces testify to an unacknowledged yet crucial scale structure within political liberalism. The extrapolitical needs to be organized in a particular segmented, subordinate—enfamilied— way in order to produce the free, equal citizens who can recognize each other as such within/as the political sphere. The normative model of ideal liberalism, then, takes shape around a political/private distinction and an attendant scalar imaginary that are embedded in conceptions of citizen-personhood, which are de facto essential both to liberalism as a political order and to understanding liberalism as the model of a just political order. International movements to mark and contest the relation between enfamilyment and capitalist political economy (particularly in terms of the unwaged work of social reproduction), such as Wages for Housework, also challenge the privatizing scalar logic of liberal personhood, and my discussion here resonates with such critique and movement work.[43] However, my argument seeks to view "the family" less as a central site of extraction (in which social reproduction produces necessary value without being compensated) than as a means of transposing alternative configurations of sociality (in which social reproduction and governance may not be understood as contradistinguished) into a normative frame in which such configurations can be cast as (racially) excessive, deviant, and dangerous.

Within the dominant liberal framing of what governance should be, what happens to modes of social reproduction—and their associated kinds of personhood—that do not fit this paradigm? How does this normative model engage forms of collectivity, identification, and relation that exceed or contest the terms of the "basic structure"? Since they do not conform to the parameters of liberal public reason, such social dynamics do not themselves count as political formations but, instead, are either dangerous deformations of the "background culture" or distinct "cultures," necessarily contained within the scope of public institutions and, therefore, subordinate in scale and character to the jurisdiction of liberal legal and political processes. Rawls notes that political power should not be used to "repress comprehensive views [extrapolitical belief systems] that are not unreasonable."[44] Modes of collective worldmaking not organized around enfamilyment and the scale structure it naturalizes, though, contradict the "basic structure" of liberalism and, as such, constitute a challenge to the social geography that provides the infrastructure for ideals of equality, freedom, and the domain of the political. In this way, they are "unreasonable" and justifiably can be targeted for state restriction.[45] The *unreasonable* within normative liberal theory—not exactly equivalent to but resonant with figurations of savagery, backwardness, and animality—serves as an implicitly racializing way of repudiating the political character of social forms that do not conform to enfamilied notions of personhood and proper political subjectivity.

As opposed to this dismissive orientation, one might see efforts to recognize cultural plurality within the liberal state as more promising. However, the category of the *cultural* itself does a good deal of work in normalizing the privatizing scalar imaginary at play in liberal notions of equality and the attendant (racializing) delimitation of what can count as a *political* claim or a mode of governance. Developing a deliberative approach that seeks to value voices and concerns outside the political sphere as such, Seyla Benhabib presents culture as providing a means of naming collective articulations, experiences, and social forms whose significance for/within governance and broader public debate would be sidelined within a stricter conception of political liberalism.[46] Such an approach, though, raises the question of why particular movements or assertions of collectivity would be understood as "cultural"? How does that categorization position them in relation to liberal notions of the state? Benhabib argues that such recognition of culture occurs within political institutions themselves, organized around forms of "constitutional and legal universalism": "at the end of the day, the ideal of government based upon the consensual agreement of equals prevails as a foundation for all democratic theory and practice."[47] Cultures exist within the state and, thus, not only remain subordinated to the laws of the state but cannot themselves contravene those modes of personhood—and, therefore, also social reproduction—privileged as the basis for liberal governance. Moreover, the welfare of the citizenry as a whole functions as the background for assessing the value of such cultural claims. When discussing the decision of a Canadian court to allow oral testimony from the Gitxsan people about their traditional territories, Benhabib observes, "What lent legitimacy to the Canadian court's decision was precisely their recognition of a specific group's claims to be in the *best* interests of *all* Canadian citizens."[48] The delimitation between the political and the cultural, then, enacts a double foreclosure with regard to scale and the question of what can count as a political order: the cultural cannot contravene modes of privatized social reproduction that produce the citizen as such; and cultural principles, authority, ethics, and relations are necessarily contingent on the naturalized jurisdictional structure of the state. These a priori conditions, viewed as normative necessities, disavow the potential for a political order that is not the (liberal) state. In the process, the cultural works to cast all modes of collectivity other than the state as potentially immanently bearing unreasonableness.[49] The understanding of extrapolitical identity as potentially a danger to the liberal polity due to ingrained collective tendencies toward uncivilized or regressive behavior—here cast as "culture"—provides one of the most common historical trajectories in mobilizing discourses of race. The absence of the term race does not save or exempt such formulations from that dynamic (a point addressed more extensively in chapter 2, with regard to the invocations of "culture" in US federal Indian policy).[50]

The reformulation of political scale at play in conceptualizations of Indigenous political orders reorients ideologies of personhood at play in liberal governance, refusing the racializing effects of narratives of deviant enfamilyment. Within many Indigenous theorizations of political form, personhood is neither generic nor serialized, but instead is conceptualized as enmeshed within flexible and shifting networks that are the substance of governance. As noted earlier, Leanne Simpson characterizes Indigenous bodies as political orders, but rather than suggesting the kinds of privatizing atomization at play in liberal form(ul)ations, including the separation between the political sphere and social reproduction, this vision of personhood presents political matters as at play in ordinary experiences of embodied connection. Moreover, it speaks to the ways that state interventions into Indigenous sovereignties have sought to break forms of everyday engagement as part of installing settler ideologies, mappings, and administrative systems as the de facto norm. Simpson observes, "The removal of Michi Saagiig Nishnaabeg bodies from the land, from the present, and from all of the relationships that are meaningful to us, politically and otherwise, is the meta relationship my Ancestors and I have with

Canada." She adds, "A great deal of the colonizer's energy has gone into breaking the intimate connection of Nishnaabeg bodies (and minds and spirits) to each other and to the practices and associated knowledges that connect us to land, because this is the base of our power."[51] Focusing on bodies in this way allows for an attention to how Indigenous forms of collective placemaking and processes of negotiation over the shape and direction of collective life are enacted through intimate relations. Additionally, it brings into relief the role of heteronormativity in naturalizing settler frameworks—how interwoven understandings of gender, home, couplehood, family, and desire produce a vision of domesticity that itself works to break up Native social networks by inserting an atomizing and privatizing unit of propertyholding as the supposedly necessary form of social reproduction and extrapolitical life. If political orders dwell within and emerge from ordinary phenomenological and corporeal experience, then there is no normatively scripted private realm that provides the implicit infrastructure for specialized institutions of governance or that produces a kind of person out of that realm who therefore can serve as the normative subject of such political institutions. Without that implicit scalar distinction, bodies can be viewed as always already immersed within networks of governance in ordinary interactions. That immersion means that persons are less easily typed as belonging to groups (call that categorization race or culture) whose groupness is thought to entail them immanently bearing ingrained extrapolitical tendencies: tendencies that lead to failures of liberal social reproduction and that therefore disqualify one from being a proper (serialized) citizen-subject.

One of the running concerns within Indigenous studies, though, has been to distinguish between Indigenous peoples and national minorities in order to avoid the collapse of the former into national citizenship and the attendant normalization of the domestic space and jurisdiction of the nation-state. Insisting on Indigenous peoples' status as political entities that exceed the terms and contest the legitimacy of the settler-states that assert authority over them, this scholarship has sought to mark the boundary between kinds of political claims and imaginaries that take the existence of the nation-state as their de facto frame of reference and those that challenge its right to exist based on the presence of prior and ongoing Native sovereignties. As Jodi Byrd argues with respect to the idea that full citizenship can serve as a horizon of Indigenous reparation, "remediation of the colonization of American Indians is framed through discourses of racialization that can be redressed by further inclusion into the nation-state," and this (set of) maneuver(s) enacts a "conflation" that "masks the territoriality of conquest by assigning colonization to the racialized body," such that "American Indian national assertions of sovereignty, self-determination, and land rights disappear into U.S. territoriality as indigenous identity becomes a racial identity." Racialization, then, transposes matters of governance—sovereignty and self-determination—into qualities of bodies, thereby positioning the problem as exclusion from national belonging and national resources rather than as the seizure of Indigenous territories for/as the nation-state and the associated disavowal of Native polities. Thus, as Robert Nichols suggests, "A distinction is required then between a politics of antidiscrimination and a politics of antiusurpation," since the framing of antidiscrimination "construes the normatively favored solution to the problem of racism as a more expansive, universalist redescription of personhood or humanity, realized through a deeper integration of racialized subjects under the legal protection of (unproblematized) colonial sovereignty."[52] These analyses mark the ways that race works as an ideological framework through which to convert questions of jurisdiction, dispossession, and colonial occupation into issues with regard to the status of non-white bodies/populations *within* the nation-state.

While broadly affirming this line of argument, we might approach it as itself potentially conflating two distinct points, and we might endorse one of those points and reframe the other. Those two points might be stated as follows: as a conceptual and discursive framework, race can translate social formations as if they were the immanent qualities of bodies/populations in ways that allow political orders to be cast as wrong kinds of corporeal tendencies and policed as such; and, therefore, Indigenous peoples need to be distinguished from other racialized groups in order to counter that colonial translation—to recognize them as polities rather than a race (Indians). I want to suggest that the first point facilitates a reorientation of the second. If racialization effaces matters of sovereignty, enacting a "process of minoritization" that "mak[es] racial what is international,"[53] that dynamic might be rethought as one in which other racialized groups also are caught. Part of the point of this kind of argument is to underline that Indigenous peoplehood precedes and is irreducible to racializing ideologies of Indianness, such that antidiscrimination efforts under US law do not so much counter as extend forms of structural violence.[54] Even as other racialized groups may not appeal to modes of peoplehood that predate racialization (and themselves need to consider the dynamics of settlement that produce the space of the nation they inhabit), racialization can be seen as imposing models of normative personhood that work to break up networks of collective self-organization that exceed the privatizing parameters of liberal governance. In this sense, processes of minoritization render the social formations of communities of color—which themselves arise within conditions of institutionalized racism yet are not reducible to those conditions (explored more fully in chapter 4)—as aggregate expressions of individualized deviance emerging from ingrained racial inclinations. In other words, rather than turning away from other racialized groups, understanding antiracism as generically reinforcing the legitimacy of state structures, Indigenous refusals of minoritization might open toward such other struggles: by foregrounding the ways race serves as an ideological matrix through which to disavow the character of political orders as governance; and by opening the potential for seeing social formations among other racialized populations *as* political orders (albeit ones whose relationships to Indigenous peoples and territories may be complex and not always politically aligned).

In this way, the concept of a political order as I use it here, drawing on and extending Indigenous studies theorizations, is itself less a rigorously defined normative category than something of a conceptual placeholder through which to refuse the normalized terms of liberal governance and to draw attention to modes of collective self-ordering that do not fit those terms. The argument is largely a negative one that seeks to mark the political violence of the racializing dynamics through which social forms are denied the status of governance and subordinated, effaced, assaulted, and/or dismantled on that basis. In calling these formations *political orders*, I am less making a claim about desirable modes of collectivity per se than seeking to explore what becomes visible and thinkable once one marks the liberal state's racializing vision of what constitutes legitimate governance, including the role of ideologies of enfamilyment in that process of racialization. The anonymous readers for this project—to whom I am very grateful for their time, care, and insight—asked me versions of the following, though: if I'm suggesting that Indigenous studies intellectual frames and strategies are useful in thinking about non-Indigenous modes of sociality, collectivity, and placemaking, including what I might term in this vein Black political orders, why not indicate how Black studies framings and strategies, for example, could be useful in engaging Indigenous social formations and governance? In response, I would say that part of what I'm seeking to suggest is that ways of approaching the scale, character, and dynamics of governance developed within Indigenous studies open up rich intellectual and political possibilities (in ways not usually substantively taken up outside of Indigenous studies' contexts), while, reciprocally, I'm seeking to develop within Indigenous studies more capacity for engaging racialization and modes of landed collectivity by non-native people(s). Engaging Indigenous studies formulations, then, opens toward a reconceptualization of what kinds of relations can constitute sites and processes of governance, refusing an axiomatic public/private distinction (and the use of *culture* as a way of supplementing liberal imaginaries by distinguishing modes of collectivity from *politics* as such) in ways that also reimagine scale—the spatial domains and mappings of governance (and how within liberal ideologies those ostensibly distinct domains nest within each other as part of the extension and exertion of national/state jurisdiction).

Racialization as Primitive Accumulation

What I've been suggesting is the importance of addressing how ideologies of familial normality and deviance provide powerful forms through which to translate nonliberal political orders as expressions of racial pathology. Reciprocally, I've been suggesting that the ongoing remaking of racial categorization in the United States is animated by such translations, giving shape to how concepts like blackness and Indianness are mobilized by dominant institutions as part of a continuing process of seeking to manage the running legitimacy crises of the state. In doing so, I've largely been drawing on formulations from Indigenous studies, while suggesting their wider applicability in understanding the work performed by processes of racialization—the conversion of political orders into population types. That strategy, as I've suggested, though, runs counter to some of the tactics employed within Indigenous studies to refuse domestication within the settler-state (including within my own earlier work).[55] Such analyses seek to distinguish discussion of the dispossession of Indigenous peoples, and the erasure or subordination of their existence as polities, from an antiracist vision of full inclusion into citizenship as the trajectory of remediation. However, if one recalibrates a sense of the work that race does—not simply differentiating and hierarchizing kinds of bodies but recasting processes of collective self-organization as expressive of failed/aberrant personhood (incubated in failed modes of enfamilyment)—then the theorization of dispossession with regard to Indigenous peoples might be expanded to address the state disavowal, management, and disciplining of forms of governance by other racialized groups.⁵⁶ Further, attention within Indigenous studies to the translation of Native geographies and political systems into the terms of the liberal state in order to facilitate expropriation—what has at times been discussed under the rubric of "primitive accumulation"—can open toward an understanding of racialization as doing similar kinds of work with reference to the social formations of non-Indigenous collectivities. In this way, continuing processes of racial population-making, including racial governmentality and racial capitalism, can be seen as dependent on translating political orders as signs of biopolitical deviance.

Indigenous critiques of race as a mode of colonial ascription/inscription can enable a broader engagement with how the biopolitics of racialization in the United States (and, arguably, other Anglophone settler-states) depends on and enacts a metapolitical constriction of what can count as governance, a dynamic that productively might be theorized as primitive accumulation. In Marxian analysis, that concept conventionally refers to the breaking up of *the commons*—land available to all in usufruct ways— into privately owned units. This segmentation and expropriation helps launch capitalism by leaving those who relied on the commons for sustenance with no means of providing for themselves, thus precipitating them into systems of wage labor, exploitation, the extraction of profit from their work, and the privatization of social reproduction. Scholars in Indigenous studies, though, have sought to recast the concept such that it refers less to a particular period in capitalism's emergence than to processes of colonial interpellation and seizure that are crucial to settlement and that remain ongoing. In *Red Skin, White Masks*, Glen Coulthard observes that "Marx's historical excavation of the birth of the capitalist mode of production identifies a host of colonial-like state practices that served to violently strip . . . noncapitalist producers, communities, and societies from their means of production and subsistence," thereby "set[ting] the stage for the emergence of capitalist accumulation and the reproduction of capitalist relations of production by tearing Indigenous societies, peasants, and other small-scale, self-sufficient agricultural producers from the source of their livelihood—*the land*." However, that process of accumulation has not ended, since settler governments such as Canada and the United States continue to pursue "state access to the land and resources that contradictorily provide the material and spiritual sustenance of Indigenous societies on the one hand, and the foundation of colonial state-formation, settlement, and capitalist development on the other." The ongoing role of such expropriation and displacement requires shifting the critical lens from a focus "on the *capital relation* to the *colonial relation.*" Doing so foregrounds the dispossession of particular peoples from their territories and refuses the notion that colonialism can be remediated by inclusion into a national frame, by envisioning Native people(s) as citizen-subjects who should receive more of the resources of the state and/or by casting the land of the nation-state as a "commons" that should equally be shared by all citizens. Theorizing primitive accumulation as a persistent part of settler colonial governance, then, "interrogate[s] practices of settler-state dispossession justified under otherwise egalitarian principles and espoused with so-called 'progressive' political agendas in mind," including recognizing that "the 'commons' not only belong to somebody—*the First Peoples of this land*—they also deeply inform and sustain Indigenous modes of thought and behavior that harbor profound insights into the maintenance of relationships within and between human beings and the natural world built on principles of reciprocity, nonexploitation and respectful coexistence."[57] Primitive accumulation, therefore, does not simply prepare the way for capitalism: it remakes the meaning of the land and people's (and peoples') relation to it such that the "modes of thought and behavior" in "Indigenous societies"—Indigenous political orders—are replaced by state jurisdiction, the legalities of property ownership, the privatization of social reproduction, and the atomization of peoples into an aggregate of state citizen-subjects.

The "colonial relation" refers not only to the seizure of the land and the effects of that occupation on the materiality of Indigenous modes of life, but also to the recoding of the meaning of collective territoriality in terms of the political economy of the settler-state. In this way, primitive accumulation might be thought of as having two parts to it that are related to each other although not identical: divorcing Indigenous peoples from land-based modes of life such that the state can claim and exploit their territories as part of the nation and incorporate Native persons as subjects of the state; and translating existing Indigenous sociopolitical forms into the terms of state legal and administrative frameworks such that the only mode of legitimate governance, the only political order, is that of the state itself. As Robert Nichols argues, colonial dispossession, especially as enacted by the settler-state, "combines two processes typically thought distinct: it transforms nonproprietary relations into proprietary ones while, at the same time, systematically transferring control and title of this (newly formed) property. It is thus not (only) about the *transfer of* property but the *transformation into* property. In this way, dispossession creates an object in the very act of appropriating it." The system of meanings and relations in which the land was inscribed before are not the same as the ones afterwards; or, put another way, as far as the state is concerned, the nonproprietary relations that may still actively be present can only be engaged through the prism of proprietary ones. The problem with conventional figurations of primitive accumulation, then, is that "the framing of the problem of expropriation and exploitation . . . proceeds as though the movement into a capitalist system of private property and markets arises out of a zero point in time, that is, as though no previously existing normative order exists," rather than reckoning with, for example, Indigenous modes of collectivity and landedness—including the force of their erasure/disavowal/translation by the liberal state and the implications of this translation/transposition for Indigenous peoples when seeking to stage normative political claims (which then appear as if they were assertions of property within the ideologies of the liberal state).[58]

Yet, as Coulthard and Nichols insist, this transposition is not singular, a moment in time now past, but is continuous and is a central feature of the colonial relation as it structures political institutions, possibilities, debates, and ideologies in the present. The assertion of Native peoples' *priorness* is a major part of Indigenous struggles to contest the legitimacy of the settler-states that assert authority over them.[59] With respect to this discussion of primitive accumulation, though, before and after less index a strictly temporal phenomenon (chronologically earlier and later) than mark a logical relation: the ongoing transposition of one formation into another. Approached in this way, the issue is less priorness as such than the non-acknowledgment of Indigenous modes of social organization on their own terms, including collective governance and placemaking, in ways that work to naturalize the paradigms, parameters, and geographies of the state. While there certainly is the matter of Indigenous priorness and the construction of states over top of peoples who did not consent to their existence, to have this *before* be the sole underpinning to Indigenous normative assertions can result in the following: denying the legitimacy of Native peoples who emerged after contact with Europeans or after the construction/independence of the states that now claim Indigenous lands; locking Indigenous legitimacy/authenticity into an historically static image (what is truly "Indigenous" is what is taken to have been present before significant contact with settlers); and, perhaps most importantly for my argument, obscuring the potential for understanding the political formations of other racialized groups as just that—political orders.[60]

If priorness is what makes possible the existence of modes of political collectivity irreducible to the state, then non-Indigenous people of color can only be envisioned as, ultimately, subjects of the state or participants in supranational or transnational movements/formations. Such an approach leaves little room for considering how other situated communities might be engaged in forms of self-governance distinct from state processes (whether using the idioms of nationhood or not) and how the racialization of those groups/communities/collectivities might be shaped by efforts to demonize and dismantle those networks (as discussed in chapters 3 and 4). I am not so much endorsing a model of *internal colonialism* as seeking to suggest that following principles of critique in Indigenous studies might enable attention to how the sociopolitical formations of non-native people of color also may contest the jurisdictional structures and legitimacy of the US state (the "internal" of domestic space), including drawing attention to the ways interwoven liberal discourses of racialization and enfamilyment position other modes of governance as indications of racial deviance.[61] In his study of the ongoing history of Black community in Tulsa (a topic to which I'll return in the coda), Jovan Scott Lewis suggests the importance of engaging with "sovereignty" as a central concept within understandings of Black geographies and collectivity. Attending to "the meaning that land has for Black people," Lewis indicates the importance of "pursu[ing] a deeper sense of placemaking" than he suggests has been the case in contemporary theorizations of blackness (especially in relation to questions of settlement), what he describes as "*sovereign belonging*": "the exercising of nonfreedom, of violence, has occurred primarily through rending Black people's relationship to place."[62] Such emplacement and the quotidian networks of governance through which it is produced, maintained, and lived—as well as efforts to rupture the relationship to place through atomizing and racializing narratives of failed home and family—are precisely the dynamics capaciously foregrounded by the Indigenous studies frames on which I draw. This mobilization of the notion of a political order to rethink what constitutes governance, and to draw attention to the racializing translation of such governance as enfamilied deviance, also has significant implications for understandings of scale: if the modes of collectivity of non-native racialized groups need not be routed through the nation-state, then the kinds of nationalisms that have tended to position themselves as applicable to all members of a particular racialized population within the boundaries of the nation-state (such as Chicano nationalism or Black nationalism) need not be the implicit referent when discussing, for example, Black, Chicanx, Latinx, Asian, or other political orders.

Without equating Indigenous peoples and other variously racialized groups, or implying that they cannot take part in forms of oppression against each other, I want to emphasize that race may be conceived less as that which differentiates them (Native nations are political entities and other racialized populations are . . . something else) than as, at least in part, a shared modality of primitive accumulation through which modes of collective life—call them political orders—are positioned definitively as not governance and as an obstruction to the proper ordering of liberal life, space, and progress in ways that facilitate continuing dynamics of subjugation, occupation, dispossession, exploitation, and extraction. Again, this is primitive accumulation less as proletarianization or insertion into capitalist systems of production and reproduction than as a metapolitical denial of the legitimacy, or even existence, of other political orders. The translation of forms of collective governance as racialized bodies/populations does facilitate capitalist extraction and economies of dispossession.[63] However, employing the notion of primitive accumulation also draws attention to the normative order(s) such translation seeks to supplant, highlighting the presence of other political formations and the active role of race in disavowing and disciplining them—in rendering them as collective failures or incapacities in performing proper enfamilyment. That continuing process is crucial in addressing the running legitimacy crises of the liberal state—part of managing, in Stoler's terms quoted earlier, the "uncertainties," "porous boundaries," and "precarious vulnerabilities" of state categories, practices, and mappings. In this way, the critical orientation I'm articulating is politically aligned with but differs from the concept of racial capitalism. The latter offers greater attention to processes of production, financialization, and the management of capitalist systems of labor and exchange, the ways capital accumulation depends on "producing and moving through relations of severe inequality among human groups"; yet this highlighting of dynamics of valuation, accumulation, and circulation can deemphasize the "terms of relationality" and modes of "collective-making" that need to be broken up in order to enable such fungibility and extraction.[64] The two framings give rise to differently configured problem-spaces, and instead of arguing for the adoption of one over the other as an explanatory framework, my aim is to increase the critical tools available for conceptualizing racialized social formations as political orders—as enactments of governance—while marking the ways institutionalized and interlocking liberal ideologies of politics, scale, and family have worked to deny their existence as such.

Opposition to the dynamics of racial governmentality, though, would seem to involve liberating racialized persons from populational aggregation. From this perspective, a formulation like "bodies are political orders" can sound like another project of governmentality, and the idea of "political orders" itself can appear as just another conscription, normalizing in its own ways. This kind of analysis of oppositional nationalisms often has been offered within women of color feminisms and in queer of color critique. One of the principal charges against what have been termed *minority nationalisms* is that they produce conceptions of collective unity that depend on a heteronormative vision of generational inheritance and a notion of shared culture in which women are positioned as the ones responsible for transmitting it through domestic relations, and thus of maintaining forms of purity in terms of both reproduction and cultural life.[65] As Grace Kyungwon Hong suggests in her reading of Audre Lorde, we need "to reckon with the ways in which the 'institutionalized rejection of difference' happens *within* African American communities [and other minority nationalisms] through the very strategies of race-based collectivity that were instituted to protect these communities from the privations of being 'surplus people.'"[66] While contesting the terms of state exclusion and economic exploitation, these stagings of collectivity can draw on forms of biopolitical affirmation that aim to present racialized populations as undeserving of being rendered as surplus or social enemies. If "access (or lack thereof) to gendered and sexual respectability becomes the dividing line between those who are rendered deviant, immoral, and thus precarious and those whose value to capital has been secured through a variety of norms," then the mobilization of such signs of respectability serves as part of a collective antiracist project that is also deeply normalizing, pointing toward "revolutionary nationalism's investments in heteropatriarchy" as well as underlining how the articulation of collective history and identity in those nationalisms "suppresses knowledge of the gender and sexual heterogeneity that composes social formations."[67] This kind of intersectional analysis raises questions about the presumption of inherent unity within the racial collective, instead drawing attention to the ways these forms of racialized peoplehood and movements "are themselves made up of diverse and heterogeneous entities" such that "they are themselves always already coalitional" in ways that contest the sense of political singularity that they may seek to project, a sense that also potentially haunts the figure of the political order.[68]

Moreover, to the extent that the political order is envisioned as territorial in character, as extending over a determinate space that provides a significant part of the character of the collective as such, it can overlook both the significance of movement and migrancy for racialized persons/groups in the United States as well as the heteropatriarchal ideologies that structure legal processes of immigration and that, therefore, can play a large role in shaping the dynamics in immigrant families and communities. The Immigration and Nationality Act of 1965 ended the previous country-quota limits, creating a system organized around skilled workers and family reunification. As Chandan Reddy observes, "Federal immigration policies such as family reunification extend and institute heteronormative community structures as a requirement for accessing welfare provisions for new immigrants by attaching those provisions to the family unit."[69] In addition to often facilitating forms of heteropatriarchal coercion (such as the need to work for relatives or stay in an abusive relationship for fear of losing access to legal residence), this emphasis on nuclear family relations of generationality contributes to a normative reproductive understanding of immigrant cultures and communities as diasporic offshoots of the national culture of the country-of-origin (itself seen in relatively homogenizing terms), also creating the kind of pressures on women to be the bearers of purity just discussed. In contrast to this doubly inflected vision of a true home (household and nation), Gayatri Gopinath offers a queer diasporic imaginary through which "the dispossessed powerfully contest these forms of regulation through alternative imaginings of emplacement, dwelling, housing" that speak to "how all spaces of 'home' and dwelling are shot through with contradictions and fissures"—a critical geography organized not around "homecoming" but "dwelling in those off-center spaces and of staying lost, and thereby perhaps even stumbling into new worlds of possibility."[70] These moves toward a deterritorialized sense of identity, relation, solidarity, and coalition can seem targeted toward the apparent enclosure of something like a political order and the effort to present emplaced collectivities as comprising networks of governance. In the recent collection "Left of Queer," David Eng and Jasbir Puar argue for "an antinational, nonnational, and no-state queer theory oriented to the art, to borrow a concept from James C. Scott, 'of not being governed.'"[71]

However, if racialization enacts a disciplining and terrorizing biopolitics of (failed) family and group identity from which people of color would seek escape, what forms of collective worldmaking lie beyond such state projects of policy, management, and legitimation? Turning briefly to Scott's analysis can offer a sense of why a concept of political orders is important in struggles to live otherwise. In *The Art of Not Being Governed*, Scott argues that the "tribal" entities that historically have lived in Zomia, the hill regions of Southeast Asia, need to be understood less as residual formations representing pre-state societies than as the result of efforts over the longue durée to escape the power of centralizing states. He contends that "this pattern of state-making and state-unmaking produced, over time, a periphery that was composed as much of refugees as of peoples [who] had never been state subjects. Much of the periphery of states became a zone of refuge or 'shatter zone,' where the human shards of state formation and rivalry accumulated willy nilly." What historically largely have been taken to be autonomous modes of social life existing outside the jurisdictional field of state formations, Scott argues, instead should be seen as expressive of efforts to evade the reach of such administrative networks, which "means that all those who had reason to flee state power, for whatever reason, were, in a sense, tribalizing themselves. Ethnicity and tribe began, by definition, where sovereignty and taxes ended." The "patchwork of identities, ethnicities, and cultural amalgams that are bewilderingly complex" across the hill regions—what Scott later refers to as a "crazy-quilt pattern of constantly reformulated identities and locations"—was itself the result of "a 'state effect,' or, more precisely, an effect of state-making and state expansion."[72] He further compares these dynamics to those among Indigenous peoples on lands claimed by the United States and suggests that "indigenism" as a category of international discourse and law represents a state-based formulation on which populations such as those in Zomia draw in order to create distance from states that would enclose them.[73] Within this framework, all political formations ultimately are a function of states, and what may seem like other political orders exist merely to create distance from the exercise of direct state authority. Thus, this vision of what it is to be "ungoverned," on which Eng and Puar draw, implicitly defines governance entirely in terms of states and the effort to evade their power, such that there are no other normative frameworks or principles at play in those modes of sociality that reject state rule but simply a reconstellated series of maneuvers derived from the states they seek to evade. In some sense, only states matter here, and the only substantive political project "lies in the daunting task of taming Leviathan, not evading it."[74] The state foundationally orients collective life from this perspective, since what may appear like non-statist forms are really just negations of the state whose existence provides the terms of their self-articulation.

As against such an ontologizing of the state, the notion of political orders offers a way of addressing modes of collectivity without reducing them to an epiphenomenon of state-ness, providing a means of thinking possibilities for situated governance effaced and disavowed through racialization while also decentering the (liberal) state as the commonsensical background against which to conceptualize what governance is/might be. Bearing in mind feminist and queer refusals of the potentially heteronormalizing and homogenizing dynamics of oppositional nationalisms, the concept of political orders (drawn from formulations in Indigenous studies in ways discussed earlier) need not be understood in genealogical-reproductive terms, as a generationally enduring entity with a rigorously defined geographic scope or foundationalizing narrative of an original, proper, collective home-space. Rather, as an analytic, political order draws attention to the ways everyday matrices of relation contribute to and constitute processes of collective decision-making, resource distribution, placemaking, and belonging in ways that remain irreducible to state imperatives. Separateness from the principles, categories, and privileged geographies of liberal governance is not a matter of purity (figured in cultural and/or reproductive terms) or unbroken lineage/transmission, but of foregrounding the immanent integrity of ordinary networks that enact alternatives to enfamilied personhood and liberalism's privatizing scalar imaginary. In discussing the ways racially marginalized populations are seen as inimical to the promotion of (liberal, biopolitical) life, Hong asks with regard to the social formations cast as "social (non)existence" in dominant discourses: "Is it (im)possible to build a politics around them?"[75] I want to suggest that the notion of political orders, Indigenous and otherwise, offers a way of tracking the work of racialization in deeming such socialities and modes of worldmaking pathological and deviant—the work of racialization as primitive accumulation—and a way of marking how those so dismissed, disciplined, targeted, and assaulted take part, in Roderick Ferguson's terms (discussing the forms of collective life that "urban development" has sought to dismantle), in "non-normative and insurgent forms of creativity" that "produce alternative and in some cases radicalized households and communities."[76] Why not understand—*resdescribe*—such creativity *as governance*? Or, put another way, what possibilities for attending to the importance of minoritarian, marginalized, racialized, and effaced forms of everyday collective self-organization might be opened in doing so? How might characterizing and theorizing such formations *as political orders* offer potentials for contesting the terms, mappings, and normalizations at play in racial population-making—whether or not such a formulation is explicitly articulated by those participating in such formations?

In presenting this argument, I aim to challenge the de facto self-evidence of liberal ideologies of family (including their normalization in common uses of the concept of kinship), the dynamics of racialization that sustain such ideologies, and the scalar geographies of political form for which such racializing ideologies provide a vital infrastructure, as well as to open additional possibilities for thinking the contours and character of governance absent its fusion to the state. In seeking to expand Indigenous studies frames in order to address non-Indigenous political orders and to rethink how we conceptualize processes of racialization, though, I want to be clear that any engagement with such political orders and modes of placemaking and collective self-determination needs to grapple with Indigenous peoples, territories, and sovereignties. My approach does not offer a *substitute* for attending to Indigenous landedness and projects of reclamation, resurgence, and land and water protection. Rather, I seek to generate additional intellectual tools and strategies for recognizing, negotiating, and further capacitating the array of political orders on the lands claimed by the United States. Some are genealogical and generationally expansive, and some are not; some contain persons from a range of racialized groups, some do not; many have rich and complex overlaps; many have contested boundaries and fraught relations; and persons may belong to different ones simultaneously, sequentially, or recursively, over the course of a life.[77] Instead of approaching these networks as an ungoverned/ungovernable negation of dominant state forms, as evasion/escape (a point to which I'll return in chapter 4), this book is an exploration of how to consider them as projects and experiments in the making of governance—a *bewilderingly complex* profusion of political formations and processes of collective self-organization irreducible to the liberal frame of family.

Organization and Chapters

The organization of this book is less a progression than a refraction, an effort to illuminate these questions, relations, and potentials from a range of intellectual and methodological perspectives. While my approach is broadly historical, in the sense that I both tend to understand patterns in genealogical terms (their being is shaped in many ways by their processes of becoming) and seek to illustrate how patterns emerge and consolidate (but also change) over long stretches of time, I do not offer a history *per se* of family, race, or governance. Instead, each chapter takes up the presence of nonliberal political orders and the ways they are managed through racializing ideologies and discourses of enfamilyment; each is less a case study than an elaboration of how the ideas sketched thus far play out within a particular domain or set of concerns. Together, the chapters provide an accounting from varied angles of how discourses of family/kinship translate what might be (re)described as nonliberal modes of governance into racialized deviance in ways that legitimize and naturalize the privatizing geographies, jurisdictional scale structure, and overriding "domestic" sovereignty of the United States. Reciprocally, the chapters illustrate how the concept of political orders offers possibilities in marking the presence of forms of collective self-organization that do not obey and need not inherently be understood through liberal frameworks. The first two chapters address how the concept of *kinship* emerges through (mis)translations of Indigenous peoples' ways of enacting self-determination, the continuing force of such racializing translations and notions of enfamilyment in contemporary Indian policy, and how Native intellectuals have refigured kinship as a means of attending to Indigenous political orders whose contours and character do not fit settler templates. The final two chapters more explicitly move beyond indigeneity to consider how the notion of political orders most explicitly developed within Indigenous studies productively can redescribe the dynamics and stakes of other processes of racialization in the United States. This concept provides a means of rethinking the significance of legal debates over marriage and privacy (particularly their relation to ideas about and insecurities within the staging of national sovereignty) and of reframing understandings of institutionalized narratives of Black pathology and criminality, seeing them as a means of regulating and/or foreclosing Black political orders. The coda takes up the case of *Oklahoma v. Castro-Huerta* (2022) as a way of thinking through issues of recognition and multiple, intersecting regimes of racialization as they play out in Black and Indigenous political orders in Tulsa.

Chapter 1 offers a genealogy of the kinship concept that traces the work it does in translating social formations into liberal terms. *Kinship* often is invoked, critiqued, and praised, as if we inherently know what it means—its contours, character, and relation to other domains of life. However, by what means do we know that the relations, dynamics, or formations we're talking about are "kinship"? Or, put another way, what kinds of heteronormative and colonial presumptions are at play in such commonsensical attributions? The architecture of liberal political economy—in its constitution of a private sphere understood as qualitatively distinct from and outside the sphere of proper governance—provides the frame of reference for the modes of relation named as kinship, and in this way, invocations of kinship remain haunted and shaped by this privatizing imaginary, even when they seek to contest liberal norms and envision alternatives. We can see this dynamic quite clearly by turning back to the work of Lewis Henry Morgan, whose writings in the latter half of the nineteenth century launched the anthropological discourse of kinship around which the uses noted above largely continue to orbit in unacknowledged and politically constraining ways. More than positioning the nuclear family as the self-evident frame through which to define kinship, Morgan's texts illustrate how the characterization of varied kinds of sociopolitical relations *as kinship* depoliticizes them: they appear as expansively extended "personal" relations rather than modes of "political" organization. While seeking to challenge normative notions of enfamilyment, queer intellectual and activist citations of kinship tend to carve out spaces of exception without necessarily challenging the broader infrastructure of liberal governance in its sealing away of alternative lifeways and political orders into the private sphere. In order for the concept of kinship not to reinforce those privatizing and racializing dynamics, it explicitly needs to engage the metapolitical question of what constitutes governance and to refuse the ideological architecture of the liberal state, which requires the differentiation of a sphere of privacy/family/property that stands outside the workings of politics as such. In this vein, Indigenous intellectuals' deployments of kinship have worked not simply to expand the scope of its reference (to include other forms of "family") but to break down the distinction between scales that characterize liberal notions of politics. Such Indigenous analyses refigure kinship in ways that shift the social imaginaries at play in dominant and most oppositional invocations of it, challenging the concept's depoliticizing, privatizing, and insulating tendencies in ways that open toward models of radical relational governance and the potential for recognizing other extant political orders.

Chapter 2 addresses contemporary Indian policy, specifically its reliance on a conception of indigeneity as racialized enfamilyment. Within federal Indian law, Indianness is presented as a *political* status rather than a *racial* one, as tied to belonging to the sovereign collective of the tribal nation as opposed to an individual quality separate from matters of governance.

This kind of distinction also has been important within Native studies arguments that Indigenous peoples are polities, not racial/ethnic minorities within the (settler-)state. However, federal policy also consistently represents Indians as a racial population, with tribes as collections of enfamilied persons whose identity arises through the "special" status accorded them under US law. Through this ideological transposition, the US government inserts Native peoples into the matrix of federal jurisdiction, translating Indigenous governance as de facto a "cultural" collective passed intergenerationally through racial genealogies in ways that enable sovereignty to be cast as quasi-political. The understanding of Indianness as the transmission of racial substance and of Native kinship systems as unique, culturally specific forms of family (the logic at play in Morgan's framework) take part within an understanding of indigeneity as a form of inheritance, which is intrinsically distinct from anything that could constitute true political sovereignty. Within this policy imaginary, Indianness represents the innate/ingrained characteristics of a racialized population, even in the absence of an explicit discourse of racial difference in situations where the United States seems to acknowledge the distinctness and political autonomy of Indian tribes. Indigenous governance is made to pivot around some version of the privatized family, delimiting the scope of Native peoplehood through its repeated linkage to the scene of (racial) procreation and liberal conceptions of political scale. These dynamics can be seen at play in three of the watershed changes in Indian policy adopted in the same year (1978), judicial and legislative determinations that seem in many ways rather disparate yet that all remain cornerstone parts of federal Indian law. Attending to the Supreme Court decisions in *Oliphant v. Suquamish* and *Santa Clara Pueblo v. Martinez* and the enactment of the Indian Child Welfare Act (ICWA) illustrates the ways racializing discourses of family are central to the current administrative architecture through which the United States acknowledges continuing Native collective presence while seeking to accommodate it to, and to validate the persistence of, the geopolitics and jurisdiction of settlement. By contrast, Native feminist work has addressed the ways Indigenous governance and peoplehood emerge through everyday matrices of interdependent relation that cannot be conceptualized as merely an extension of the private sphere. Building on the reorientation of kinship discussed in chapter 1, we can see how such work provides analytical frameworks for conceptualizing Indigenous governance in ways not routed through a liberal imaginary or scale structure and distinct from the matrix of Indianizing enfamilyment.

Turning from indigeneity per se but retaining the critique of state frames at play in the articulation of Indigenous political orders, chapter 3 focuses on the ways legal discourses of marriage and family in the United States position the family unit as an always already racialized entity that anchors national sovereignty against deviant and dangerous alternative collectivities. I chart a twofold pattern at play across the history of US law: the simultaneous citation of the private/domestic/familial sphere as defining the condition of possibility for and the character of state sovereignty and as itself beyond political contestation; and the characterization of alternative formulations of collective life—other political orders—as racial tendencies, for which the inability to sustain a properly contoured private sphere serves as evidence of a racial incapacity that threatens the integrity of national life. Legal articulations of family and privacy provide sites for tracing dominant formulations of liberal sovereignty and for tracking how various kinds of racialization are crucial to the (re)making of bourgeois domesticity. This chapter addresses three different sets of legal negotiations stretching from the late nineteenth century through the early twenty-first century—three kinds of legal conflict that illustrate this matrix of privacy, sovereignty, and racialization. These three controversies are with regard to Mormon polygamy prior to Utah statehood, the emergence of the right to privacy in the late 1960s and early 1970s, and the evolving legal status of queer sex and relationships from the 1980s through the 2010s. Centering discussion on relevant Supreme Court cases, I aim to show how US law defines the terms and boundaries of the private sphere in ways that naturalize the jurisdictional architecture of liberal governance by positioning the principles of enfamilyment as separate from the work of political institutions and presenting countervailing social forms as expressive of racialized aberrance. These examples also further illustrate how the reconfiguration of the private in the name of equity and inclusion does not itself displace the work of the personal sphere in the making of liberal sovereignty, instead often reaffirming and reanimating the modes of racialization through which alternative matrices of governance are disavowed as perverse forms of failure and threat.

In chapter 4, I address how the ongoing construction of the contours and meaning of racial blackness through association with criminality takes shape around attributions of a collective, ingrained inability on the part of Black people to fulfill normative conceptions of home and family. Black persons and households are cast as bearing within them immanent inclinations toward excessive publicness that engender social disorder, and historically, discourses of Black criminality have been bound to depictions of Black people as unable to form and maintain proper families. As a number of scholars have shown, Black people may be seen as *heterosexual* while still falling outside the boundaries of the *heteronormative*. Regardless of the matter of object-choice, African Americans' formations of desire, care, association, procreation, childcare, and residency have been presented as aberrant, degraded, and menacing. However, what if those patterns taken to be deviant and dysfunctional, such as the movement of persons and resources within networks that exceed the nuclear household, were instead understood as expressive of modes of governance? If we rethink those matrices of collective worldmaking as governance, then the racialization of such social formations as evidence of ingrained, destabilizing tendencies toward deviance (and the attendant criminalization of blackness as a danger to private property, the family, and legal structure) comes to look more like an effort to crush competing political orders so as to legitimize liberal economies, mappings, and modes of state violence. This approach, though, runs against the grain of Black intellectual formations that emphasize the importance of turning toward ungovernability—that understand governance as always already a form of capture and an extension of a fundamentally antiblack regime of property. More than providing information on specific Black social networks/matrices that can be understood as enactments of governance, the intellectual gambit of this chapter is to address the stakes of characterizing Black social forms as political orders. Doing so involves staging the current intellectual blockages to doing so (the ways they often are figured as "kinship" and/or as prepolitical, such that they need to be given proper institutional form in order to constitute a politics) and addressing how redescribing them in this way shifts existing accounts of the character and contours of antiblack racialization and policy. For this reason, I return to what may seem like familiar historical scenes—the first years of Reconstruction and the Freedmen's Bureau, the Moynihan moment of the 1960s, and the emergence of Black Lives Matter in the 2010s—in order to read them differently, highlighting how discourses of criminalization transpose alternative Black political orders into racialized narratives of failed enfamilyment.

* * *

Returning to the scenes with which I began—the long history and urgent presentness of the seizure of immigrant, Black, and Indian children—such state action is unquestionably racist and denies the feelings, intimacies, and legitimate autonomy of people of color, understanding them as threat, disorder, and pathology that in various ways endangers the well-being of the nation. Parents of color are seen as incapable of raising persons who can participate as proper subjects, and those very a priori assumptions of deficit with regard to home and family help illustrate the inextricable enmeshment of enfamilyment in the ongoing (re)making of race in the United States. For this reason, we should question *family* as a horizon of humanization for those deemed non-white. Toward what relations do we implicitly point in such bids for recognition? How are those social matrices misrecognized through their interpellation in liberal ideologies and mappings? How might we see supposed failures of domesticity less as requiring a more capacious vision of family than as enactments of governance otherwise? Reading such formations *as political orders* opens toward a rethinking of what constitutes political life, how we understand matters of scale, and how processes of and contestations over racial identification are bound up in both. In her work on the ungendering dynamics of blackness within institutions of enslavement and their aftermath, Hortense Spillers addresses the "kinlessness" that has shaped African American life, the nonrecognition of Black people as having familial bonds. With regard to normative (white) gender, Spillers remarks, "we are less interested in joining the ranks of gendered femaleness than gaining the *insurgent* ground as female social subject. Actually *claiming* the monstrosity."[78] The same might be said with regard to recognition of kinship/family, not by ignoring matters of intimacy, affect, and everyday embodiment but by refusing axiomatically to understand governance as existing in a separate sphere from those experiences and networks of relation. Largely drawing on Indigenous studies strategies, I aim to provide a wide-ranging genealogical engagement with the role of race and family as crucial ideological and institutional means through which the state has regulated, disavowed, and sought to dismantle alternative genres of governance within the United States.[79] In doing so, *The Politics of Kinship* seeks to expand intellectual possibilities for engaging with other collective modes of living and projects of self-organized thriving beyond liberal personhood, perceptual frames, privacy, and structures of political scale.

ONE

Kinship's Past, Queer Interventions, and Indigenous Futures

WHAT IS KINSHIP? This term often is invoked, critiqued, and praised, as if we inherently know what it means. While arguments certainly erupt over the concept's flexibility and relative utility in describing a given set of interpersonal arrangements, modes of collective life, and normative principles, those conversations tend to assume we already are aware of kinship's de facto scope and scale and can get on with the business of debating its relative elasticity and merit in designating a particular social configuration. Perhaps the easiest way to express this set of presumptively shared meanings is to say it has something to do with being a "relative," intergenerational transmissions/transitions, and forms of sustained interpersonal care. However, even as that apparently mutual frame of reference provides a basis for folks to take up pro and con positions in relation to it, particularly as a vehicle for envisioning and pursuing social justice and especially in the orbit of projects (intellectual and political) that name themselves as *queer*, this largely unremarked upon set of background assumptions leads to profound misrecognitions around the work that the concept of kinship performs and that it could perform. Attending genealogically (pardon the pun) to how kinship comes to be a means of talking about kinds of relationships and social formations draws attention to the ways the concept functions as a racializing and imperial placeholder. It translates formations of collective governance, placemaking, decision-making, and resource distribution into the terms of the liberal private sphere, as a (distended, perverse, pathological) version of nuclear homemaking. It normalizes the scalar dynamics and infrastructure of liberal governance in ways that misrepresent, diminish, and contain the (largely Indigenous) socialities and sovereignties it emerged to name. Absent the definitional dependence on normative liberal family formation as the implicit point of reference, kinship is incoherent as a concept. Moreover, its transposition of social dynamics into that frame allows for those dynamics to be cast as outside of *politics* as such, largely through racializing narratives of aberrance.

By what means do we know that the relations, dynamics, or formations we're talking about are *kinship*? Or, put another way, what kinds of heteronormative and colonial presumptions are at play in such commonsensical attributions? Queer, feminist, and anthropological analyses tend to invoke kinship to name a nexus of interactions and interdependencies constellated around the concept of family. In *Queer Phenomenology*, Sara Ahmed discusses how sexuality comes to be "oriented," particularly in relation to the reproduction of "the father's line," and she suggests, "The table in its very function as a kinship object might enable forms of gathering that direct us in specific ways or that make some things possible and not others. Gatherings, in other words, are not neutral but directive. In gathering, we may be required to follow specific lines. If families and other social groups gather 'around' tables, what does this 'gathering' do?"[1] In a related vein, Juana María Rodríguez observes that "under the logic of neoliberalism the mainstream LGBT movement attempts to secure individual rights through the valorization of normative kinship," adding, "Kinship, in all its varied forms, is at its core about creating boundaries of inclusion and exclusion, tribe and nation."[2] In these instances, "kinship" seems to refer to a kind of relationship or matrix of connection modeled on the nuclear family form as that very form is being rejected. The bundling of patterns of desire, care, childrearing, reproductive genealogy/lineage, and household formation creates an *artificial unity*,[3] and formulations of kinship regularly invoke and reproduce that de facto unity, even when they seek to critique or reorient it. In *What Kinship Is—and Is Not*, Marshall Sahlins apparently refuses the alignment of kinship with procreation as such, arguing that "kinfolks are persons who participate intrinsically in each other's existence: they are members of one another." He further notes, "The work of language and culture is to delimit and differentiate the human disposition for transpersonal being into determinate kinship relations by specific criteria of mutual being."⁴ As part of a volume dedicated to thinking about modes of relation that would stem current population densities, Adele E. Clarke insists, "We need to generate new kin interventions, new concepts and practices for making kith and kindred, as well as attending and attuning to how people and peoples *already* make and value other-than-biogenetic kin in non-imperialist ways"; as against defining kinship through "familial metaphors," she argues that "'making' also refers to the daily actions that transform partial relations into deeper ones, kinship crafted through the exchange of things, sharing activities, and other practices. This second sense of 'making' is how kinship is sustained over time."⁵ However, even as these formulations seem to repudiate heteronormative accounts of the necessity of nuclear reproductive units, and to do so forcefully and unequivocally, they also implicitly reinstall that dominant social model as the center around which revisions conceptually pivot. What could "making kin" mean absent the implicit appeal to liberal homemaking as the referential field that delimits the sort of relations that "kin" indexes? The various forms of connection, care, solidarity, enmeshedness, and mutual belonging toward which Sahlins and Clarke gesture still all constitute expressions of a thing called *kinship*. The reason for that linkage, though, remains unclear. The "familial metaphor" remains controlling as the dominant configuration of family—the artificial unity of heteronormative Euro-American liberalism—ostensibly is being set aside.

This conceptual and political conundrum cannot help but inhabit the effort to employ kinship as a comparative frame. As David Schneider suggests of anthropological efforts to distinguish the principles at play in non-Euro-American social contexts, in which kinship supposedly provides the basis for social cohesion and organization but in ways disjunct from the nuclear family, they make "a complex series of implicit assumptions about the 'idiom of kinship' which, because they are unstated, are not open to easy review or evaluation," and he asks, "If each society had a different social convention for establishing a kinship relationship . . . by what logic were these all considered to be kinship relations since each constituted a different relationship?" He suggests that the "genealogical grid" provides the ground for understanding other modes of relation as "kinship." In this way, he argues, normative Euro-American notions of biological relatedness serve as the unexamined background by which kinship can serve as metaphor or idiom in characterizing other arrangements and social formations. The genealogical grid, though, is less, as Schneider suggests, a way of figuring "real or putative biological bonds or their culturally defined equivalents" than a naturalization of nuclear family homemaking by de facto casting it as the necessary unit/unity through which human reproduction occurs.[6] In other words, the issue is less how the pervasiveness of, in Schneider's terms, a "folk theory" of biology ethnocentrically obscures understandings of other social systems (although there is that) than how the architecture of liberal political economy—in its constitution of a private sphere understood as qualitatively distinct from and outside the sphere of proper governance—provides the frame of reference for the modes of relation named as *kinship*. Invocations of kinship remain haunted and shaped by this privatizing imaginary, even when they seek to contest liberal norms and envision alternatives.

We can see this dynamic quite clearly by turning back to the work of Lewis Henry Morgan, whose writings in the latter half of the nineteenth century launched the anthropological discourse of kinship around which the uses noted above largely continue to orbit in unacknowledged and politically constraining ways.[7] More than positioning the nuclear family as the self-evident frame through which to define kinship, Morgan's texts illustrate how the characterization of varied kinds of sociopolitical relations *as kinship* depoliticizes them: they appear as expansively extended "personal" relations rather than modes of "political" organization. The liberal private sphere serves as the horizon and frame of reference through which "kinship" gains meaning in Morgan's writing, even as the concept seems like it expansively incorporates a wide range of social configurations that qualitatively differ from those normatively enacted by/under the liberal state. Those other formations are classified as "kinship" in order to mark the ways they have failed to become the slimmed-down and more cleanly organized model of the nuclear family, shaped as it is both by its contouring around private propertyholding and by its distinction from the "territorial" logic organizing "political society." In this way, *kinship* provides the means through which to differentiate the state form from other political orders that, instead, appear as the private sphere before it knew its proper boundaries and its difference from properly formed political institutions.[8] As a topos of political thought, then, kinship works to distinguish proper governance from genealogy, enacting a mode of primitive accumulation by translating non-statist forms as expressive of (failed/backward/excessive) notions of home and family.

In addition to providing an important way of historicizing what kinship has meant as it has moved through intellectual and administrative circuits over the last century and a half, Morgan's work offers an illuminating allegory through which to describe certain racializing entanglements within liberal thought and political economy that have been significant from the nineteenth century onward, albeit in shifting ways. The absence of liberal enfamilyment, in Morgan's logic, signals a disruptive and potentially dangerous relation to other people and households as well as to the jurisdiction of the state—a kind of wrong personhood. Modes of what is treated (and, thereby, depoliticized) as spheres of intimacy and domesticity that are other than heteropatriarchal and nuclear are portrayed as expressive of innate or ingrained tendencies that signify one's immanent status as criminal, savage, and/or irredeemably alien. Queer intellectual and activist citations of kinship tend to carve out spaces of exception to this ideology of enfamilyment—largely with regard to forms of what has been termed "stranger sociality"—without necessarily challenging the broader infrastructure of liberal governance in its sealing away of alternative collectivities and political orders into the private sphere, a dynamic in which such worldings are already racialized in their failure to engender proper forms of personhood and are understood as perverse and threatening in their destabilization of the distinction between public and private life. In order for the concept of kinship not to reinforce those privatizing and racializing dynamics, it explicitly needs to engage the metapolitical question of what constitutes governance and to refuse the ideological architecture of the liberal state.

If the concept of kinship tends to pinion nonliberal social formations to heteropatriarchal notions of the family in ways that cast such formations as other-than-"political," can the invocation of kinship also mark the potential for modes of collective life and governance that do not follow liberal principles and are unintelligible, or cast as racialized aberrations, within them? Indigenous intellectuals' deployments of kinship have worked not simply to expand the scope of the term's reference but to break down the distinction between scales that characterize liberal notions of politics. While liberal political economy seeks to differentiate the domestic unit from the workings of the public sphere, especially in order to seal it off from the dynamics of politics as such, Indigenous uses of the kinship concept displace such distinctions, thereby theorizing and envisioning alternative modes of personhood distinct from racializing discourses of enfamilyment. Everyday dynamics of interdependency provide principles for more encompassing processes of collective belonging, decision-making, resource distribution, placemaking, and diplomacy. Such Indigenous analyses refigure kinship in ways that shift the social imaginaries at play in dominant and most oppositional invocations of it, challenging the concept's depoliticizing, privatizing, insulating, and racializing tendencies in ways that open toward models of radical relational governance.

Distending the Family

Although having no degree in what would become the field of anthropology, Lewis Henry Morgan developed an elaborate narrative of the intertwined evolution of family, property, and civilized governance that would help set the terms for scholarly and administrative engagements with non-European peoples for over a century. While employed as a lawyer in Rochester, New York, Morgan became acquainted with Ely S. Parker, a Tonawanda Seneca chief, through Parker's participation in a club Morgan cofounded called the Grand Order of the Iroquois. Drawing on the Parker family as informants, Morgan wrote an account of what he took to be traditional Haudenosaunee life and governance—*League of the Ho-dé-no-sau-nee, or Iroquois* (1851)—that began to set out what would become his theory of the role of *kinship* as a crucial mode of social organization across human history.[9] In his writings over the course of the late nineteenth century, particularly *Ancient Society* (1877), Morgan develops a model for explaining the presence of various permutations of what he characterizes as "marriage" and "family" among peoples around the world, situating such differences within a teleology of progressive becoming that eventuates in the interdependent emergence of private propertyholding, the nuclear family, and the state. Morgan's formulations were immensely influential within the realms of policy and various academic fields, but rather than suggesting a causal link between his texts and the broader dynamics of liberal ideology and policy this book seeks to address, I want to draw on Morgan's prominence as a means of offering a condensed sketch of the work the concept of kinship performs in normalizing processes of what I have characterized as *enfamilyment*. In Morgan's analysis, all social formations can be figured within a distinction between "personal" and "political" modes of organization, in which those that do not fit Euro-American bourgeois homemaking can be slotted into the former category. Doing so specifically presents those other social formations as failing (yet) to be *political* in ways that allow them, when engaged within liberal ideologies and governance, to be treated as aberrant and/ or dangerous anachronisms, distensions, and deformations of the private sphere. Morgan's writing illustrates, then, how *kinship* conceptually operates as an extension of *family*, serving as both a container for nonliberal modes of sociality and governance and a means of racializing them in their potentially disruptive divergence from the paradigm of heteropatriarchal propertyholding.

In *Ancient Society*, Morgan provides his most complete articulation of his theory of civilizational emergence, and his taxonomies of "family" and "marriage" provide the intellectual infrastructure for the text's account of human development. He positions his observations with regard to non-European peoples, particularly Indigenous peoples whose lands are claimed by the United States, as a window into earlier periods of what would become Euro-American modernity. In the preface, he indicates that "the history and experience of the American Indian tribes represent, more or less nearly, the history and experience of our own remote ancestors when in corresponding conditions." He later notes, "A council of Indian chiefs is of little importance by itself; but as the germ of the modern parliament, congress, and legislature, it has an important bearing in the history of mankind."[10] The forms of life at play in "American Indian tribes," then, gain meaning by being understood as earlier versions of the forms that structure the Euro-American present.[11] This conjectural history takes shape around the model of the bourgeois household, which by the late nineteenth century already had become dominant in the United States.[12] In a rather stark instance of this approach, Morgan asserts that "modern society reposes upon the monogamian family. The whole previous experience and progress of mankind culminated and crystalized in this preeminent institution."[13] Not only has all of human history been building toward heteropatriarchal, couple-centered homemaking, but that mode of family actually functions as the definitional core of "modern society." If one wants to understand how civilizational progress works, one has to focus on the process by which this type of family comes to exist and gains prominence. Reciprocally, this unit—in which intimacy, romance, childbearing, childrearing, household formation, subsistence, placemaking, and interpersonal care are fused—acts as the background, as the frame of reference, through which to interpret all other social formations. As Ahmed suggests, "a background is what explains the conditions of emergence or an arrival of something as the thing that it appears to be in the present."[14] Monogamous, privatized couplehood conditions the emergence of all other social formations onto the scene of Morgan's analysis by providing the principal, if at times implicit, way of interpreting the dynamics and significance of the various modes of relation that come to be characterized as kinship. The couple-form grounds the figuration of what family is (in a somewhat torsioned way as both conceptual origin and evolutionary horizon), and the deployment of the concept of family translates all other configurations of collective life as antiquated and obsolescent versions of this central "institution" of liberal life.

More than temporally displacing Native peoples to the properly superseded past of mankind, this set of intellectual procedures treats *family* as itself a transhistorical and transcultural signifier through which to engage what might otherwise be understood as a wide range of kinds of social arrangements lacking much resemblance to each other. In drawing on family and marriage as conceptual constants, Morgan de facto presents the nuclear family unit as a neutral means through which to explain, categorize, and compare all other arrangements of housing, reproduction, collective belonging, and nonliberal systems of governance. He suggests, "With respect to the family, the stages of its growth are embodied in systems of consanguinity and affinity, and in usages relating to marriage, by means of which collectively, the family can be definitely traced through several successive forms." At various points, he provides a taxonomy of stages of human evolution (levels of "savagery" and "barbarism" before culminating in civilization) in which sexual intimacy, procreation, allocation of children among groups, forms of housing, and the relation between those prior dynamics and processes of collective decision-making and resource distribution are wildly disparate.[15] Yet, they all can be narrated "with respect to the family," taking "the family" as an inherent unit of knowledge-making and an unquestionably relevant framework for social order.[16] "Marriage" gets used in the text to designate a wide array of kinds of sexual connection and living arrangements, ranging from monogamous couplehood to groups of brothers and sisters (at opposite ends of the evolutionary spectrum), but the term still appears as if it indexes a coherent idea/institution/set of practices, as if all of these widely divergent configurations could be viewed as (developmentally staged) versions of the same thing.[17] *The family* can be traced across social difference because it provides the basis for *systems of consanguinity and affinity*, in ways regulated by *marriage*. If the variously shaped matrices of relation that Morgan designates as family all can be designated as such due to their relation to *consanguinity*, to what exactly does this latter notion refer? Returning to Schneider's critique discussed earlier, by what logic are all of these forms versions of the same thing?

Morgan's answer to this question involves recourse to what he casts as the facts of reproduction, but his discussion of how those natural relations are elaborated and extended in early stages of human development (which he argues are still present among non-European peoples) indicates that liberal notions of privatization provide the framework in which the narrative of biological necessity takes shape.[18] He distinguishes between ways of defining one's "kindred," *classificatory* and *descriptive*, which are the "two ultimate forms" and are "fundamentally distinct": "Under the first, consanguinei are never described, but are classified into categories, irrespective of their nearness or remoteness in degree to *Ego*; and the same term of relationship is applied to all the persons in the same category"; while "in the second class consanguinei are described either by the primary terms of relationship or a combination of these terms, thus making the relationship of each person specific."[19] To the extent that "consanguinei" refers to blood relation, "nearness" and "remoteness" indicate degree of shared biological connection. Thus, "the primary terms" (descriptive) are those that correctly indicate relations of reproduction (such as using the term "father" only for one's genitor and "mother" only for one's genetrix), while classificatory terms stretch descriptive terms to encompass a class of persons that goes beyond the term's "primary" referent (referring to one's genitor and his biological brothers all as "father" or one's genetrix and her biological sisters as "mother," for example). As a basis for figuring primary or descriptive relation, "Each person is the centre of a group of kindred, the *Ego* from whom the degree of relationship of each person is reckoned, and to whom the relationship returns. His position is necessarily in the lineal line, and that line is vertical. Upon it may be inscribed, above and below him, his several ancestors and descendants in a direct series from father to son." If descriptive and classificatory systems are "fundamentally" disparate, and these two forms "yield nearly the exact line of demarkation [sic] between the barbarous and civilized nations," how do they both belong to the categories of "family" and "marriage"?[20] Given the great qualitative difference—and, in Morgan's terms, developmental gulf—that separates them, how can they be understood as versions of the same thing? Morgan suggests that the descriptive form actually underlies all forms, such that the genealogical grid centered on a given individual ("Ego") and radiating outward, but oriented lineally up and down, provides the basis for understanding "kindred" (or kinship) in all modes.

The logic here is the following: since all social formations remain predicated on human reproduction, the basic unit of such reproduction provides the *primary* terms through which to engage (and compare) all other configurations.[21] Inasmuch as classificatory terms/systems mark relations among "consanguinei," they must in some sense refer back to and gain meaning from the descriptive/primary terms, an implicit link that provides the conceptual justification for employing the terms family and marriage across significant discrepancies in the shape, arrangement, and practices of the relationships so designated. As Schneider observes, in order for this transit of terms to make sense (including the use of the terms *kinship* or *kindred* to characterize the various formations being described), "the biological relationship" must be "treated as the reference point, the fixed position against which all cultural aspects take their meaning," a presumption he later describes as the de facto "Doctrine of the Genealogical Unity of Mankind" in which "the features that define the genealogical grid" serve as the constants that enable comparison.[22] This putative continuity serves as the background for the transhistorical, transcultural use of family and marriage as terms that can be referred back to a "primary" unit, relation, or social function that ostensibly exists in some form everywhere.

However, while certainly characterized and legitimized through reference to what are cast as the requirements for sexual reproduction, the concepts of family and marriage within liberal ideologies are not reducible to biological processes or functional roles in procreation. At one point Schneider notes that the use of kinship as a comparative concept depends on "the assumption of the primacy of the nuclear family and the extension of all kinship out from the nuclear family," such that the nuclear family is cast as "in some sense basic to, or structurally prior to, and fundamental to the rest of the sociocultural system" that extends those primary relations in classificatory ways. The nuclear family, though, does a great deal more work in envisioning proper modes of social organization, personhood, and political life than merely serving as the Euro-American unit for reproduction. Morgan's text illustrates how the grounding of kinship in the nuclear family abets a racializing and colonial imaginary in which nonliberal modes of governance constitute a deformation of the private sphere that is antithetical to the proper operation of the liberal state. In laying out the logic of the genealogical grid and of the definition of "kindred" via consanguineous connection with "Ego," Morgan notes, "A brief reference to our own system of consanguinity will bring into notice the principles which underlie all systems," indicating that what he presents as the core of civilized society can provide a set of "principles" through which to apprehend the other social systems (and stages) he chronicles. Earlier, in discussing the "monogamian family," he indicates, "It was founded upon the marriage of one man with one woman, with an exclusive cohabitation; the latter constituting the essential element of the institution. It is pre-eminently the family of civilized society, and was therefore essentially modern. This form of the family also created an independent system of consanguinity." Later, he adds that this monogamous unit "assured the paternity of children and the legitimacy of heirs" in ways that "fell back upon the bare facts of consanguinity."[23] Defined as a married couple who have their own household, the prototypical form of the family takes shape around the legal dynamics of nineteenth-century marriage, bourgeois propertyholding, and generational transmission of privatized inheritance, such that *consanguinity* as a concept depends on this model of nuclear homemaking, insulation, and ownership.

The nuclear unit's status as "independent," then, has less to do with its supposedly necessary role in procreation than with its legal and spatial distinction from other such units, enclosed as they all are within their own private spheres contradistinguished from the broader collective dynamics of the public/political realm (a point to which I will return shortly). Even when Morgan is talking about social configurations in which what he terms "the family" takes on what he characterizes as "governmental" functions, he still describes those expressions of family/consanguinity/kindred as "domestic institutions," including among the "barbarous" and "savage" segments of "mankind," and he also refers to "the marriage relation" as fundamentally "personal" in character.[24] Since consanguineous relations definitionally are contained in the realm of the "domestic" or the "personal," all social connections and networks patterned in some fashion after the "facts" of biological connection must themselves be domestic and a form of family. In discussing what Morgan terms the "gens," a term borrowed from Latin usage, he defines this unit of social life in the "barbarous" stages of human development as "composed of consanguinei, under a chief of their own election," and he later adds, "A gens . . . is a body of consanguinei descended from the same common ancestor, distinguished by a gentile name, and bound together by affinities of blood." He suggests that this unit was the principal form of social organization among Native peoples in what is now the United States, often referred to as "*tribe* and *clan*," which are "equivalent" to gens. Groups of gens, or "gentes," also could gather "under the government of a council of chiefs," and that council "had a natural foundation in the gentes of whose chiefs it was composed." Morgan further characterizes such "groups of persons" as forming "organic unities." While addressing the gens as a "unit of a social and governmental system," Morgan continually presents this mode of sociality as familial in character, including through the use and repetition of terms like "consanguinei," "natural," and "organic," which imply an expansion from a reproductive core that defines the character of this configuration of collective belonging and its modes of decision-making.[25] The concept of the gens remains rooted in the "facts" of nuclear homemaking that provide the paradigm for what "consanguinity" (as well as its attendant "affinities") means. Morgan indicates that "gens" has the "primary signification of *kin*" and that it is "a very ancient social organization founded upon kin."[26] The term *kin* and its permutations, then, index extended formations of family among less-than-civilized peoples, in which relatedness bleeds out beyond the domestic lineality that defines its proper descriptive boundaries. The conceptual modularity of *the family* as a comparative framework—with its *primary* terms of relation as the basis for understanding (and anatomizing) other modes of marking "kindred"—arises from the privatized autonomy attributed to it within liberal ideologies and norms.

In addition to illustrating the ways the concept of kinship (and social systems supposedly organized around it) depends on liberal notions of "the family," Morgan's analysis suggests the stakes of that defining context, the ways it demeans and contains nonliberal formations by depoliticizing them—casting them as irrelevant and/or anathema to the operation of state law and policy. The crystallization of the monogamian family as the fruit of "successive stages" of human evolution pairs with the emergence of "political society" as the basis for defining the achievement of civilization. Political society is "founded upon territory and upon property, and may be distinguished as a state (*civitas*). The township or ward, circumscribed by metes and bounds, with the property it contains, is the basis or unit of the latter, and political society is the result." Unlike "a gentile society," in which "relations were purely personal," the state has a public character divorced from "personal" relations, one organized around the extension of afamilial modes of jurisdiction over a clearly delimited territory, such that all persons living within that area are subject to its authority irrespective of any "domestic" connections among them. Not only are these modes of governance "fundamentally distinct," Morgan declares, "It is impossible to found a political society or a state upon gentes."[27] States are organized around "territorial" relations, not "personal" ones, and the gens and other non-statist modes of governance ultimately depend on *kinship* as the infrastructure for social order in ways that remain tethered to or tainted by familial association. The governance present in *kinship* systems cannot truly count as governance, because it remains bound up in properly domestic relationships and modes of affiliation.[28] It lacks the *impersonal* character of laws extending uniformly over a determinate place and its populace; it lacks the capacity for afamilial publicness that characterizes properly *political* relations. Within this framing, not only do kinship-based socialities extend fundamentally domestic/familial principles beyond their proper sphere of operation, they fail to produce the kind of *independence* among family units that normatively shapes political process and personhood in the state—the kind of privatized intimacy that qualifies one to be a properly public/political subject.[29] In this way, the kinds of decision-making, resource distribution, placemaking, and modes of belonging present among gens-based societies, and other formations organized around *kinship*, remain incompatible with "modern" (liberal) governance. They deform the domestic into a quasi-public by failing to appreciate/understand both the proper limits of familial affiliation and the necessity for a distinction between such private/personal networks and matters of (the) state.

Morgan, however, observes that tribal governance, which he understands as a "barbarous" example of gens-based social organization, has distinct territorial dimensions, in ways that would seem to cloud the distinctions upon which his definition of the state depends. He notes, "Each tribe was individualized by a name, by a separate dialect, by a supreme government, and by possession of territory which it occupied and defended as its own." He further suggests, "Their territory consisted of the area of their actual settlements, and so much of the surrounding region as the tribe ranged over in hunting and fishing," defining "the domain of the tribe" which was "recognized as such by other tribes, and defended as such by themselves."[30] The definition of Native modes of governance as personal *rather than* territorial (and the attendant distinction Morgan makes between "tribe" and "nation"), then, seems to falter, raising the question of why tribal governance (putatively kinship-based councils of gentes) cannot count as properly political. This apparent paradox underlines how Morgan's invocation of territory envisions a particular kind of geography, one ordered around private property. He asserts that "governments and laws are instituted with primary reference to its creation, protection and enjoyment," earlier arguing that the "dominance" of the pursuit of private property "marks the commencement of civilization" and "led mankind to overcome the obstacles" that had delayed the "establish[ment of] political society."[31] In order for governance over a territory to count as impersonal, it must be shaped by and in the interest of the division of the territory into privately held units, which are not enmeshed in extended networks of affiliation (with such networks themselves understood as deviant distensions of "the family").[32] Political forms of governance arise in the existence of a disjunction between the institutions of governance and the atomized assemblage of property holders whose rights in their privatized territory the state exists to protect. Prior or other forms of kinship threaten to rupture the modes of familial household individuation that lie at the core of private propertyholding while also creating bloated units that disrupt the nested, impersonal hierarchies and geographies of *political* order—the structure of state jurisdiction. As supposedly achieved through the process of human evolution, the insulated domestic or personal sphere therefore indicates not simply the natural unit of reproduction but a key part of the scale structure of civilized political economy, in its distinction from the public logics and processes of the state and in families' spatial distinction from each other. The possession of property by individual(ized) families enables the differentiation of public and private presented as lacking in social systems organized around *kinship*.

When considering units of such propertyholding and the normative justification for the emergence of property and the state, the monogamian family becomes central as both an organizing unit and as the means of legitimizing the existence of privatized forms of ownership and personhood. In Morgan's narrative, property arises as a function of the recognition of the proper (patriarchal) autonomy of "the family," in its descriptive core consisting of a married couple and their children. He suggests that "after tillage had led to the ownership of houses and lands in severalty, an antagonism . . . ar[o]se against the prevailing form of gentile [within the gens/clan] inheritance, because it excluded the owner's children, whose paternity was becoming more assured, and gave his property to his gentile kindred."[33] The importance of transmitting inheritance from a man to his children (particularly his sons) leads to the shift away from belonging to a gens—a kinship network—and toward an exclusive understanding of the "natural" unit of consanguinity as the basis for social reproduction. Of course, the heteropatriarchal orientation of family and marriage appears clear in the presumption that the one having real property to transmit to future generations necessarily is a man.[34] More than simply enabling men's lineal passage of wealth to reproductively defined heirs, this shrinkage, according to Morgan, promotes a range of positive outcomes, which themselves validate the system of private property in which the monogamian family is definitionally enmeshed and that it helps crystalize. The prior arrangement of the "syndyasmian family," in which there was a "communal household" among multiple reproductive units and in which the "principle of communism in living was practiced," illustrated "an admission that the family was too feeble an organization to face alone the hardships of life." However, as "the formation of families consisting of single pairs" facilitated greater "industry and frugality" and "increased protection of life," "the more stable such a family would become, and the more its individuality would increase." The nuclear family comes to serve as a more stable means for promoting the well-being of its members than the "communal household," and as its "individuality" increases, separating from other reproductive units, "It marks the peculiar epoch in human progress when the individuality of the person began to rise above the gens, in which it had previously been merged, craving an independent life, and a wider field of individual action."[35] Note, though, that the "individuality of the person" arises from and remains contingent on the "individuality" of the family as an institution. Such enfamilyment serves as the crucible for producing kinds of individual personhood consistent with civilized norms.

The possession of private property, therefore, expresses relations of intimacy and care that already are incipient within *the family* as a necessary part of human life, rather than, say, property being envisioned as inscribed within racializing institutional matrices of settler colonial expropriation, enslavement, imperial economies of force and seizure, and differential valuations of labor. The racial and colonial dynamics that enable the existence and sustaining of the liberal conception of family propertyholding—an ideal that in the United States has been and remains animated by whiteness and white privilege—disappear behind the image of the family as a privatized crucible for engendering proper personhood and personal relations. Not only does "monogamy" express and engender a particular "moral development," it also makes possible a "passion of love" that was "unknown among the barbarians." Moreover, it creates circumstances in which "the wife is necessarily the equal of her husband in dignity, in personal rights and in social position."[36] Privatized familial homemaking provides the basis for generating moral subjects who also understand the kinds of values and norms protected and enabled by political institutions. In this way, proper enfamilyment also acts as the condition of possibility for producing political subjects—ones who can participate in and support the life of the state in ways that enable it to fulfill its purpose and rightful aims (which, in Morgan's terms, largely consist of enabling private propertyholding and the intergenerational transmission of attendant wealth). The family, therefore, serves necessary public functions in its apolitical domesticity, namely by inculcating proper modes of enfamilied personhood that enable someone to form their own family, to understand the value of a *personal* sphere distinct from governance, and to take part in processes of governance in ways that preserve that distinction (which itself promotes moral development, health, and well-being). Property appears as part and parcel of these relations and distinctions, as a necessary corollary of the work of enfamilyment, and thus as pre- or apolitical instead of as the result of racializing and imperial policy regimes that create the conditions for white zones of privacy and ownership.

One might argue that Morgan's evolutionism and the civilizational hierarchy in which he situates his account of kinship indicates his work's limited utility in understanding liberalism, kinship, or the relation between them. Beyond the question of whether stripping out Morgan's developmental language and staging actually alters the racializing and imperial character of the kinds of qualitative distinctions he makes (such as by employing notions of relative "complexity" to categorize social systems in their reliance on "kinship" versus "state" forms),[37] what I want to highlight is the ways the concept of kinship largely continues to require treating the nuclear family as a de facto descriptive core, such that "family," "marriage," "blood-relation," and "relative" can be treated as coherent and linked ideas through which to understand a wide range of disparate practices, principles, and formations as if they could be characterized as versions of the same thing. Morgan's text provides a powerful condensed illustration of how kinship's definitional entanglement with liberal ideologies of nuclear homemaking further reiterates a distinction between public and private spheres, even as those networks of care and governance characterized as *kinship* seem to thwart that division. Put another way, a careful reading of Morgan's work suggests the ways that kinship appears as a comparative way of talking about familial-based modes of governance only against the background of liberal political economy. In addition, this reading draws attention to the issue of how other modes of governance that differ in their operative principles, internal infrastructural relations, and scalar dynamics from those of the liberal state, especially when they appear within the claimed jurisdiction of such a state, can be discounted as expressions of a nonpolitical (or not-yet-political) kinship network or, even worse, as expressions of wrong forms of home and family. If kinship gains meaning in relation to *the family*, then characterizing social networks and formations, of whatever scale, within the claimed boundaries of the liberal state *as kinship* preserves the sense of them as ultimately private in character, as expressions of kinds of relations qualitatively distinct from those that organize the state and that form the basis for true and rightful political subjectivity.

In addition to preserving the public/private distinction by implicitly situating kinship in relation to domesticity, the use of kinship to characterize nonliberal modes of sociality largely reinforces the ideological dynamics of enfamilyment, particularly in the racializing depiction of digression from those norms as potentially dangerous forms of deviancy. The concept of kinship enables nonliberal dynamics of social organization and governance to be translated into liberal terms as a deformation of the family. Such a distension of kinds of relation considered to be personal/domestic might be cast in relativistic terms as fine for other people(s) elsewhere, but when such formations occur within the liberal state, they appear as ruptures of properly private space, as dangerously spilling across the boundaries of familial independence in ways that threaten the political geographies of the state and its normative commitments to atomized property claims (and the kinds of moral subjects such propertyholding supposedly produces). In this way, the dependence of kinship on the nuclear family for its definitional coherence means that, even when used to mark extra-nuclear modes of relation, it implicitly normalizes ideologies of enfamilyment, with the configurations characterized as kinship operating as supplement/exception. In *The Empire of Love*, Elizabeth Povinelli engages the work performed with and for liberalism by the distinction between what she terms "the autological subject" and "the genealogical society"; she suggests that the former involves "discourses, practices, and fantasies about self-making, self-sovereignty, and the value of individual freedom," as contrasted with "social constraints" associated with "various kinds of inheritances." She further argues that "the intimate event" mediates the relation between the two, providing a sense of privatized intimacy that does not limit, but instead facilitates, liberal selfhood: "the intimate event derives much of its ideological force from something that co-emerged with it—discourses about genealogical society," which provide a vision of "illiberal, tribal, customary, and ancestral" attachment that serves as the "opposite" of "liberal adult love."[38] As I've suggested through my reading of Morgan, though, normative individual and political selfhood depends on ongoing processes of enfamilyment in childhood and adulthood, and other modes of relation—among intimacy, decision-making, resource distribution, belonging, and placemaking—appear less as the opposite of liberal domesticity (as the crucible of personhood) than as excessive extensions of familial arrangements beyond their descriptive sphere.[39] Morgan's writing, therefore, underlines the work the concept of kinship performs in transposing modes of sociality and governance into liberalism's privatizing imaginary. Reciprocally, tracing that process of translation and depoliticization opens possibilities for tracking the ways the failure to conform to normative narratives of enfamilyment provides a basis for racializing attributions of failed personhood, social menace, and political delinquency to non-white populations. Their supposed inability to have proper domesticities can be presented as bespeaking immanent and irremediable tendencies toward criminality, backwardness/savagery, and/or unassimilable alienness.[40]

The itineraries of kinship serve as a means of marking the racializing dynamics of enfamilyment, the process by which liberal privacy takes form and is reproduced through attributions of kinship (as perverse, disorganized, and dangerous) to other matrices of collectivity and placemaking. In his analysis and critique of what he terms "queer liberalism," the pursuit of normative home and family by LGBT people, David Eng argues that "intimacy" can be understood "as a racialized property right—one predicated on a long U.S. history of racial subordination and the legal protection of white privilege—[that] now serves to constitute normative gay and lesbian U.S. citizen-subjects as possessive individuals." He further suggests that this turn "demand[s] a more thorough investigation of the degree to which (homo)sexuality and race constitute and consolidate conventional distinctions between the time and space of civilization and barbarism."[41] More than speaking to the political implications of certain strategies within contemporary rights movements, the understanding of familial intimacy as racialized and racializing is the flip side to Morgan's account of kinship. The notion of kinship transposes alternative formations of personhood and governance into signs of barbarous tendencies. In doing so, it helps enact and secure a biopolitics of enfamilyment that normalizes whiteness as the basis for privatized property rights, positioning a racially coded ideal of domestic life as necessary to maintaining the scalar structure and subjectivities (public and private) of the liberal state.[42] A kinship imaginary may be understood as crucial to ideologies of liberalism in 1) normalizing the distinction between the familial and the political in ways that fuse nuclear family homemaking and privatized propertyholding to each other as the natural/inevitable basis for proper governance, while 2) allowing what might otherwise be understood as alternative modes of governance to be cast as alien, backward, and/or criminal (mis)understandings of personal/domestic life—collective inclinations that express forms of racial incapacity that disqualify members of such populations from being proper national subjects and that require remediating state intervention.

Zones of Queerness

Queerness often is narrated as beyond kinship, as lying outside of the enclosures of dominant conceptions of home and family. Intellectual gestures of this kind speak to the ways same-sex desire historically has been cast as antithetical to heteronormative domesticity and morality while also contesting more recent efforts to seek what often has been characterized as homonormative inclusion within liberal institutions and social forms.[43] Legalized same-sex marriage stands as perhaps the paradigmatic instance of such desired belonging. As against the pursuit of the rights to bourgeois homemaking, others have insisted on the ways queerness does and should stand outside the privatizing formations of, in Povinelli's terms, the "intimate event" of liberal enfamilyment. Scholars and activists argue against the privileging of the institution of marriage, the presumption that sexual life should be directed toward monogamous couplehood, the fusion of eroticism to intimacy, and the de facto equation of normality (in its various registers) with whiteness. They seek to develop and chronicle forms of queer worldmaking that displace these ideals and that open other avenues for enacting collective life. In this way, such conceptual, cultural, and political work might be understood as harboring a deep ambivalence toward the concept of kinship. Such work disowns normative formations of intimacy, couplehood, and privacy (for which *kinship* sometimes provides an encompassing name) while also wanting to gesture toward modes and spaces of relation whose coordinates do not match those of bourgeois domesticity—kinds of alternative worlds, principles, and practices for which *kinship* sometimes also serves as the index.[44] This paradoxical doubleness might be understood as a function of the kinship imaginary that I've been describing, in which kinship registers nonliberal social and political formations but translates them into liberal geographies and ideologies of privatization as distended (and racialized) kinds of family. Queer analysis inhabits this conceptual oscillation, the political desire for possibilities beyond enfamilyment emerging as an ambivalence toward kinship as topos/frame. However, such analysis often reiterates the problems of that paradox by similarly positioning the forms of worldmaking it seeks to highlight as something of an exception within liberal geographies of enfamilyment, rather than engaging more directly with potentials for recognizing modes of nonliberal governance.

To the extent that intellectuals cast queerness as a break from the enclosures of family, it appears as opposed to kinship, as a rupture within social geographies organized (legally and normatively) around kinship.[45] This staging of queerness often works in the interest of seeking to promote and secure forms of sexual freedom. Perhaps the most classic statement of such a position within queer studies appears in Lauren Berlant and Michael Warner's crucial and oft-cited essay "Sex in Public." They argue for the need to foreground "queer zones and other worlds estranged from heterosexual culture" that support modes of sexual and intimate relation that do not conform to the terms of liberal couplehood and family formation organizing so much of public and political discourse in the United States. They contest the ways sexuality continually gets consigned to or territorialized as the proper province of the privatized home, in which it can be dissociated from questions of what can constitute a viable and valuable public. They observe, "Intimate life is the endlessly cited *elsewhere* of political public discourse, a promised haven that distracts citizens from the unequal conditions of their political and economic lives, consoles them for the damaged humanity of mass society, and shames them for any divergence between their lives and the intimate sphere that is alleged to be simple personhood."[46] The kinds of normatively privatized existence generated through liberal political economy work to legitimize and depoliticize the structures that shape everyday relations, naturalizing systemic patterns of inequity and exploitation while presenting deviations from this privileged model of social reproduction as expressive of individual pathologies. As opposed to this vision of erotic life as properly contained within the social architecture of heterohomemaking, Berlant and Warner insist on the importance of attending to queer modes of "world-making" that exist through forms of what can be described as "stranger sociality."[47] Such forms and spaces of queer engagement and desire cannot be constrained within a conception of "community," which itself tends to be "imagined through scenes of intimacy, coupling, and kinship; a historical relation to futurity is restricted to generational narrative and reproduction." They further argue that "making a queer world has required the development of kinds of intimacy that bear no necessary relation to domestic space, to kinship, to the couple form, to property or to the nation."[48] Kinship helps name kinds of enclosure that work to delimit who can serve as the object of eroticism and sexual play and where such sociabilities of pleasure can occur. The refusal of kinship here operates in the service of remapping the terrain of intimacy such that it need not definitionally be located within or tend toward the couple-form or the bourgeois household.

If repudiating kinship points toward a different kind of spatiality than that organized around normative domesticity, what or where are the "zones" in which such envisioned queer worldmaking occurs? As other scholars have noted, particularly feminist and queer theorists of color, the sorts of spaces often paradigmatically (if implicitly) imagined as the sites for stranger sociality remain unavailable to numerous subjects whose desires, pleasures, and intimacies might be understood as queer. As Juana María Rodríguez observes, "The inability to recognize the alternative sexual cultures, intimacies, logics, and politics that exist outside the sight lines of cosmopolitan gay white male urban culture is never benign," and she adds, "the spaces of sexual exploration and expression so common in the narratives of urban gay male sexuality—sex clubs, bathhouses, public bathrooms, rest areas, and parks—are places that can prove deadly to female-bodied people, female-presenting people, and others perceived as psychically vulnerable," as well as exacting greater costs from communities-of-origin for participation in such "alternative sexual formations." Similarly, L. H. Stallings argues, "Unfettered mobility as a privilege of masculinity allows the public spaces of bathhouses, parks, gyms, and nightclubs to serve as an oasis for single, partnered, and married men who wish to escape social constraints geared toward sexual domestication. Because historically women have not been allowed such physical mobility without the threat of violence or criminalization, cruising has not figured heavily into the sexual imagination of women until quite recently. Yet the physical dangers and risks linger."[49] Access to stranger sociality is not evenly distributed, in terms of race, class, gender, nationality, etc. The public, and largely commercial, spaces of urban queer cruising and consummation remain inaccessible to many who do not have the resources to enter, who would be denied entry on the basis of their identity/identities, and/or remain at greater risk of violence (including, and perhaps especially, by the police). Understanding queer worldmaking as a rejection of the privatizing and heteronormalizing matrix of kinship (such as in Rodríguez's suggestion, quoted earlier, that "kinship, in all its varied forms, is at its core about creating boundaries of inclusion and exclusion, tribe and nation") contests geographies that normalize a public/private distinction that fuses intimacy to the family household, but, conversely, the matter of the *where* of such worldmaking remains somewhat vexed.[50]

While raising questions about the public (nondomestic) sites of sociality and pleasure conventionally understood as bearing queer potential, work in queer studies often continues to gesture toward a space for that which does not conform to the demands and principles of heteronormative privatization—something like a *zone*, even if one whose precise location or boundaries remain unspecified. Heteronormativity itself creates kinds of spaces from which queerness is barred or in which queerness appears as a kind of aberrant, disorienting intrusion. In *Queer Phenomenology*, Ahmed suggests that "the queer orientation might not simply be directed toward the 'same sex,' but would be seen as not following the straight line" of heteropatriarchal reproduction. In addition to creating a sense of vertical integration across time, dominant notions of familial belonging and inheritance generate spaces of familial relation that organize place. Ahmed observes that "heterosexuality functions as a background, as that which is behind actions that are repeated over time and with force, and that insofar as it is behind does not come into view."[51] As a background, heterosexuality implicitly orders the spaces through which people move as well as how they do so, contouring individual actions, inclinations, and life trajectories in ways that reinforce the centrality of the bourgeois family and home as a nexus for personal choices and movements. In this way, even as hetero-lineage functions as a form of temporal imagination—the generational unfolding of familial (or kinship) relations—that temporal narrative helps produce a lived geography of what I have called *enfamilyment*, in which participation in heteronuclear family households constitutes not just a basis for social belonging but for mapping the terrain through which liberal subjects move. Not only, in Ahmed's terms, does "the queer couple in straight space hence look as if they are 'slanting' or are oblique," but the aggregation of such domestic-familial spaces provides an imagined cartography in which queer bodies/desires—those that do not reproduce the genealogical space-time of heteropatriarchy—appear as perennially out of place, as lacking any proper place. The turn toward "bodies that have been made unreachable by the lines of conventional genealogy" enacts forms of "queer orientation" that opens spaces and lines of connection that exceed the "cramped space of the family."[52] Queerness exists outside, or perhaps athwart, such space. If the heteronormative family provides an organizing ideological framework for mapping social space, the question of where and how to locate queerness remains ambiguous, or the site of ambivalence. Does queerness, whatever it might mean, exist in a delimited kind (or kinds) of elsewhere from nuclear homemaking, or is there another geography, a *queered* one, that exists alongside and that disrupts the privatizing imaginary of nuclear homemaking?

Queer critiques of the force of heterofamilial worldings run up against the tensions between articulations of queerness in its more minoritarian form (attending to modes of sociability and sexual expression that deviate from normative straightness) and a more encompassing vision (challenges to institutionalized heteronormative social formations and ideologies in their entirety, regardless of any individual's object-choice or sexual practice).[53] This conflicting set of investments shows up in the intimations of a kind of space whose queerness remains definitionally distinct from the enclosures enacted by kinship-based visions of social life. Queerness can name a particular sort of space/place that enables modes of relation that do not conform to the dictates of enfamilyment, such as in José Esteban Muñoz's understanding of queerness as necessarily sutured "to the concept of ephemera." He argues, "We can understand queerness itself as being filled with the intention to be lost. Queerness is illegible and therefore lost in relation to the straight minds'[sic] mapping of space. Queerness is lost in space or lost in relation to the space of heteronormativity," and he earlier suggests the need to "carve out a space for actual, living sexual citizenship."[54] If heteronormativity occupies or organizes space in ways that displace the possibility for "sexual citizenship," then queerness emerges in noninstitutionalized, or underinstitutionalized, ways that temporarily convert spaces into sites for enacting dynamics of desire, intimacy, collective belonging, and interpersonal connection that are both "defiantly public" and provide "glimpses" into "an ensemble of social actors performing a queer world."[55] Being *public* works to evade the constrictions of heteronormative mappings of *privacy*.

Yet, the provisional and transitory eruption of spaces of queerness, utopic in their simultaneous ephemerality and gesture toward the potentials of a "queer world" to come,[56] does not undo or remake heteronormative space, even as such queer spaces provide opportunities for experimenting with subjectivities that offer alternative possibilities for being and becoming beyond those provided within dominant arrangements of kinship. These are places in and through which, in Ahmed's terms, to touch those barred within and by "straight space." In a similar vein, Stallings advocates for what she describes as "*funky love*," which "can be defined as publically radical configurations of family, love, and relationships where monogamy and marriage are not situated as the ideal praxis."[57] Recognizing the ways that liberal ideologies of enfamilyment construe Black subjects as deviant regardless of object-choice,[58] she champions arrangements of desire, care, and intimacy not bound to heteropatriarchal homemaking and the couple-form. However, even as she traces the racializing violence of heteronormative constructions of gender, home, and family, she less envisions a replacement of such social mappings as such than highlights modes of "erotic maroonage" that provide for some an alternative to dominant conceptions of marriage: "rather than all-out rebellion against domestication—that is, marriage rooted in monogamy—we get temporary flight from the institution or a group of fugitives banding together to create independent nonmonogamous communities, even within the institution of marriage."[59] While multivalent and historically dense, the topos of maroonage suggests a separate space to which those refusing normative enfamilyment can take flight, albeit one that is only "temporary."[60]

In these alternative queer mappings, publicness serves as a counterpoint to the privatizing imaginary that often gets associated with kinship, but the continued imagination of something like a space of queer worldmaking apart from the constrictions of heteronormative domesticity implicitly territorializes queerness as a particular sort of site. It appears to indicate a kind of place in which to perform versions of selfhood, sexual relation, and collectivity that do not obey the dictates of liberal personhood and intimacy. However, that de facto localization tends to leave the structures and dynamics of enfamilyment themselves undisturbed, in the sense that queerness is envisioned as occupying an elsewhere distinct from "straight space." This way of talking about alternatives to heteropatriarchal formations of home and family seems to replicate the dynamics at play in anthropological discourses of kinship. Inasmuch as kinship is used to characterize a kind of formation whose difference is calculated in relation to the *descriptive* paradigm of the nuclear family, it provides a supplement through which to name divergences from liberal norms while continuing to center such norms. Similarly, understanding queerness as a kind of site/space/zone, even a *public* one, can serve as a way of marking distinctions from dominant processes of enfamilyment while still allowing the latter to serve as the background against which liberal political economy takes shape and against which queer deviations can be marked as such. Thus, even when queerness does not refer to same-sex desire as such, when it references modes of pleasure and intimacy that do not conform to hetero-monogamy and/or the couple-form irrespective of object-choice, understanding queerness as occupying a kind of space still can position it as an exception, such that queer worldmaking occurs in places understood as apart from the "straight space" that contours most of social and political life in ways that de facto give queerness a minoritizing cast. Thus, even as these accounts may disown *kinship*, they can position queerness to do a similar kind of ideological work.

As suggested thus far, the envisioning of a kind of queer space outside or beyond the dynamics of kinship often functions in the service of arguing for modes of sexual freedom understood as incompatible with the privatizing contours of liberal enfamilyment, but queer intellectual work also often aims to recast normative configurations of homemaking, to envision how queerness might occupy the space of kinship in order to argue for alternatives to bourgeois domesticity. Critiques of LGBT efforts to approximate liberal norms enact a conflicted relation to the concept of kinship—disowning the tendency to desexualize queer lives in order to legitimize them as worthy of state recognition while also embracing the potential for marking the existence of non-nuclear family and household formations.[61] Rodríguez suggests, "the mainstream LGBT community is enmeshed in expensive political machinations to secure the rights of same-sex marriage through media campaigns that sanitize our lives in order to make us palatable as subjects worthy of the rights of citizenship, even as it fails to recognize the multiple vectors of violence and injustice that also constitute our lives as queer subjects" while "projecting an image of hypernormative domesticity worthy of political respect and validation." She later notes, "the mainstream LGBT movement attempts to secure individual rights through the valorization of normative kinship" by accepting "the logic of neoliberalism." In a similar vein, Eng insists that "we need to ask how a constitutive violence of forgetting resides at the heart of queer liberalism's legal victory, its (re)inhabiting of conventional structures of family and kinship."[62] Eng foregrounds the erasure of processes and violences of racialization in the vision of acceptance through marriage equality, what Jasbir Puar has referred to as "the ascendancy of whiteness," in which the approximation of normative domesticity enables qualified access to the privileges of whiteness at the expense of an erasure of ongoing forms of racism (including attributions of sexualized deviance to people of color, regardless of object-choice, in ways that license heightened state surveillance, intervention, and containment).[63] The pursuit of the right to marriage, such arguments suggest, stages inclusion within heteronormative social arrangements as the horizon of aspiration in ways that not only present the aim of queer social movements as their own ultimate depoliticization but that efface the dynamics of oppression that have been enacted and continue to be enacted through the vision of the nuclear family as the privatized ideal of national life and personal subjectivity. The invocation of "normative kinship" and "conventional structures of family and kinship," though, suggests the potential for championing modes of kinship that would be more responsive to forms of desire not centered on conjugal couplehood and configurations of intimacy, care, and interpersonal relation that do not conform to the nuclear model.

In this way, kinship marks both that which queerness must critique and evade and that which it must engage and champion. Queerness names what exists beyond the bounds of kinship *but also* ways of inhabiting the space of kinship differently. In *The Cultural Politics of Emotion*, Ahmed argues that "queer lives do not suspend the attachments that are crucial to the reproduction of heteronormativity, and this does not diminish 'queerness,' but intensifies the work that it can do. Queer lives remain shaped by that which they fail to reproduce," and she adds, "the closer that queer subjects get to the spaces defined by heteronormativity the more *potential* there is for a reworking of the heteronormative." The places called "home" and the relations understood as "family" can be sites for queer engagement, refiguring the kinds of *attachments* from which queers often have been understood as excluded by understanding them as, instead, bearing nonheteronormative meanings and configurations. Rather than replicating the dynamics of normative or conventional kinship, kinship can be queered. Ahmed argues that queerness is less about displacing norms than "*inhabiting norms differently*. The inhabitance is generative or productive insofar as it does not end with the failure of norms to be secured, but with the possibilities of living that do not 'follow' those norms through," a process of "*working on* the (hetero)normative."[64] Such *reworking*, then, might include, as Rodríguez suggests, attending to "multigenerational extended families who cohabit because of economic need, cultural conventions, or their own desires; families whose social and sexual networks extend beyond one couple or one household; 'unstable' households that are in a state of flux with people entering and existing as space, money, and need dictate; or families that are denied the ability to live together due to immigration policies, economic need, or practices of institutionalization."[65] The process of taking up possibilities for reformulating and recomposing home and family positions queerness as dwelling within what might otherwise be understood as the enclosing domain of the domestic in order to extend it beyond "heteronormative formulations of kinship," seeking "to destabilize familial norms" in ways that offer "alternative structure[s] of family and kinship" that expand who can be the subject and object of "feeling[s] of kinship."[66] In these instances, kinship indexes modes of relation, desire, intimacy, care, and interdependence that do not conform to the parameters of heteropatriarchal homemaking and that contest the genealogical imaginary at play in liberal ideologies.

However, in addition to illustrating the tensions and torsions around how to conceptualize the relation between queer critique/worldmaking and kinship, as that from which queerness seeks to separate itself and as that which queerness should inhabit and reshape (sometimes in the same argument), these queer engagements indicate how the kinship imaginary can supplement liberal political economy and its organizing racializations, by implicitly reaffirming the sense of a zone that can be differentiated from *political* institutions, decision-making, and subjectivities. If queerness can take up residence in "the spaces defined by heteronormativity" or "straight space" in order to remap it/them (as contrasted with seeking inclusion, such as by achieving access to state-recognized marriage), that generalizing impulse does not evade the following dynamics (discussed in the previous section): the ways kinship tends to transpose the arrangements and matrices it ostensibly references into the scale structure of liberalism—as forms of distended domesticity, distinct from properly political relations; and the racializing processes by which people of color variously are portrayed as failing to be properly enfamilied due to ingrained inclinations that also mean they cannot participate as legitimate political subjects as well as bear tendencies toward violations of privacy and property. Queer efforts to expand the possibilities for acknowledging *kinship*, then, do not undo the heteronormative principles at play in liberal political economy, because, as I have been arguing, the concept of kinship itself largely reaffirms the descriptive centrality of nuclear family homemaking as the frame of reference in which other social configurations appear as non-political deviations—preserving the sense of a space apart that does, or fails to do, the subject-making work of enfamilyment. In this way, the generalizing work of challenging heteronormative geographies, social statuses, and distributions of resources implicitly flips back into a minoritizing marking of exceptions and difference within what de facto remains a liberal mapping of the structural position of domesticity.[67]

This set of problems in seeking to *queer* kinship can be seen at play in the "Beyond Same-Sex Marriage" statement. Issued in 2006 by a collection of queer activists and intellectuals, it sought to reframe public discussion around priorities for queer political struggle, shifting from a focus on marriage equality to a broader notion of what kinship can entail.[68] It presents its aim as "seek[ing] to offer friends and colleagues everywhere a new vision for securing governmental and private institutional recognition of diverse kinds of partnerships, households, kinship relationships, and families," and it further notes, "To have the government define as 'legitimate families' only those households with couples in conjugal relationship does a tremendous disservice to the many other ways in which people actually construct their families, kinship networks, households, and relationships."[69] Here, as in Morgan, kinship gains meaning through being in relation to "household" and "family," marking versions of the connections associated with them while gesturing toward other formations that do not fit a nuclear model. The statement challenges the privileging of the monogamous couple-form as the presumptive standard for social life specifically due to the role of that ideal in promoting and validating various kinds of harm done to a range of groups, especially through public policy. The authors argue, "The Right's anti-LGBT position is only a small part of a much broader conservative agenda of coercive, patriarchal marriage promotion that plays out in any number of civic arenas in a variety of ways—all of which disproportionately impact poor, immigrant, and people-of-color communities," with the aim of minimizing governmental provision of resources to those groups and "transfer[ring] responsibility for financial survival to families themselves." In articulating what they call "the principles at the heart of our vision," the writers also call for "access for all to vital government support programs, including but not limited to: affordable and adequate health care, affordable housing, a secure and enhanced Social Security system, genuine disaster recovery assistance, [and] welfare for the poor" within a broader ethos that includes the "recognition of interdependence as a civic principle."[70] The argument for bracketing the pursuit of marriage equality as a principal goal of LGBT struggle, then, is in the interest of advocating for a more expansive conception of modes of interdependence that transects liberal ideologies of privatization based on property and self-possession.

Contesting the nuclear family model correlates with a large-scale reapportionment of the means of social reproduction that breaks with the principle of enfamilyment as the practical and normative basis for the distribution of resources. As Lisa Duggan suggests of the statement a decade later, "we were making this critique trying to say that we need to understand ... that marriage is embedded in these race and class relations of inequality" and that marriage brings "populations into a set of property relations ... that people ... have been defying." Yet, while seeking to contest the racializing ideologies of property normalized through marriage, the statement's invocation of kinship repeatedly turns those concerns back toward a private sphere, albeit an expanded one. At one point, the statement insists, "Many of us, ... across all identities, yearn for an end to repressive attempts to control our personal lives," and in a list of possible configurations of "kinship networks," the examples all consist of some version of living in a single "household" or being in a version of "partnership," whether romantic or not.[71] As with Morgan, these various permutations of relation all can be understood *as kinship* by virtue of being personal/domestic: they take shape against the de facto background of the nuclear family as the descriptive model, defined as *personal* relations and spaces in contrast to *political* dynamics and logics of governance based on depersonalized spheres of jurisdiction (territory).

I do not mean to diminish the value of the statement's intervention into public discourses and activist aims, calibrated as it is to take part in a public policy debate pitched to the existing terms of US governance. However, I do want to underline the minoritizing and exceptionalizing work that kinship does here, situating nonnuclear modes and matrices of relation within a liberal structural and scalar imaginary. Kinship constellates with *home* and *family* to index zones of privatized intimacy, desire, care, and interdependence distinct from public processes of political decision-making. This invocation of the kinship imaginary seeks to relativize what can constitute legally recognized and protected forms of privacy in ways that also can be understood as aiming to open up the heterogenealogical presumptions at play in the definition and transmission of property (in Ahmed's terms quoted earlier, the integrity of "the father's line"). This pluralization of *family*, though, does not foreground or contest the racial dynamics in which proper enfamilyment serves as a condition of possibility for being seen as a viable political subject (one not subject to discipline and containment for immanent criminality, savagery, or alienness), nor does it undo the process of translating nonliberal principles and patterns of governance—political orders—as a set of private/familial relations that need to be nested within liberal governmental mappings in ways that do not ultimately disrupt or challenge the dynamics of state jurisdiction (itself supposedly organized around impersonally protecting enfamilied propertyholding). Put another way, queer invocations of kinship as an alternative frame through which to displace nuclear homemaking tend to reiterate the territorializations at play in liberal political economy—as in nineteenth-century formulations of the kinship concept, discussed earlier.

What drops out is the question of governance. By this term, I mean not what the government can do with regard to issues and formations otherwise coded as private/personal/domestic but how relations and modes of social organization understood in liberal terms as private/personal/domestic can provide the basis for governance, in ways that do not have to fit within the jurisdictional scale structure of the liberal state. In *Unapologetic: A Black, Queer, and Feminist Mandate for Radical Movements*, Charlene A. Carruthers argues, "Governing is not synonymous with becoming part of the governments we live under—or duplicating them. Governing happens whether we like it or not and whether we're involved or not," and she adds, "Governing is the process of making decisions that impact groups of people. How are we governing in our organizations and communities?" She suggests that "governance" entails "making collective decisions about how our lives are lived," creating a "space" for "liv[ing] out the project of collective liberation."[72] She seeks to indicate the ways that individuals and groups need not turn to the state as the sole site for generating new plans for shaping collective decision-making, resource distribution, belonging, and placemaking. Instead, governance involves collective efforts to develop ways of shaping "how our lives are lived" that may or may not involve engagement with the existing institutional networks and protocols of the state and that certainly do not need to take the normative, jurisdictional, and procedural principles of state policy as the basis for "making decisions." While Carruthers is not addressing kinship per se, her emphasis on the need to develop and to attend to existing processes of governance (even when not currently self-characterized in those terms), while understanding challenges to existing political and economic formations as involving such work, displaces the propensity within queer engagements with kinship to envision zones of difference carved out of liberal social mappings (either as queer spaces distinct from those of kinship or nonnormative reconfigurations of relationships conceived of as kinship). Such a shift also potentially brackets enfamilyment, and its racializing dynamics, by refusing the de facto distinction between a private sphere and a political one. Taking up Carruthers's framing of the character and horizon of activist and intellectual labor as *governance*, in ways that resonate with Indigenous theorizations of political orders discussed in the introduction, moves beyond the forms of conceptual and political containment and the liberal scalar structure at play in the kinship imaginary.

Kinship beyond "Kinship," or What's in a Political Order?

I've been talking about the ways that a kinship imaginary, as it emerges in proto-anthropological discourse in the late nineteenth century and operates as a way of framing social/cultural difference in the twentieth and twenty-first centuries, presents social formations in terms of a *descriptive* model of nuclear homemaking—an interpretive prism that normalizes liberal geographies of governance, ideologies of property, and racializing figurations of enfamilyment. I have further suggested that work within queer studies that has sought to set aside normative arrangements of home and family tends to get caught within the logics and binds of that imaginary. This model of kinship largely arises through nineteenth-century efforts to characterize the social formations of Indigenous peoples, presenting them as something other than sovereign and self-determining polities. However, Indigenous intellectuals have taken up the concept of kinship in ways that refuse and refunction this dynamic. They do so by explicitly articulating how the kinds of attachments and belonging that have been labeled as kinship operate as part of matrices of governance, of what has been termed *political orders*. In doing so, this intellectual work displaces the personal/political distinction on which the kinship imaginary hinges. Indigenous theorizations of kinship refuse ideologies of enfamilyment, in particular the reifying of isolated household units as the basis for personhood and for political subjectivity; the positing of a qualitative break between private/domestic and public/political domains; the nestling of the former under the authority of the latter; and the organization of social life and political process around the atomizing and exclusionary principles of property. Native intellectuals' ways of inhabiting the kinship concept highlight webs of ongoing relationality, responsibility, and accountability that animate all engagements—with other persons, other peoples, and non-human entities, including lands and waters.[73]

Within this framing, there is no separate domain of governance operating at a qualitative remove from the principles, ethics, and relationships of quotidian interdependence. Such Indigenous framings of governance do not necessarily depend on an institutional matrix that has its own operative principles at odds with but putatively meant to defend an apolitical or prepolitical zone of privatized, insular, propertied intimacy—a zone which could not exist as such absent state law and policy but which is cast as merely being recognized, rather than actively constituted, policed, and disciplined by state action. There is neither the narration of racialized aberrance based on improper enfamilyment nor a carving out of queer exceptions within geographies of privatization. Reciprocally, Indigenous analyses organized around kinship do not cast the work of governance as a negative pole against which to define freedom, as merely the corrupting province of the state. Instead, governance is continuous with and happens through the modalities, principles, and sites of everyday engagement. For convenience's sake, we can anatomize Native (re)conceptualizations of kinship beyond the kinship imaginary into three lines of analysis: illustrating the ways intimate experiences of heteronormativity are part of ongoing histories of racialization and colonialism that have worked to manage and foreclose Indigenous peoplehood and political orders; challenging and undoing the scale structure of liberalism, in which home and family are a private sphere nestled within an overarching jurisdictional architecture that itself is apersonal; and offering an ethics of relation that extends from interpersonal intimacies to diplomacy among nations, providing principles that transect the enclosures of property.[74] I want to foreground such (re)framings of kinship for their ability to mark and contest liberal ideologies of governance, including the racializing work of enfamilyment at play in mappings of the personal/private/domestic.

Native theorizations of kinship help illustrate the connection between felt experiences of wrong enfamilyment and histories of racializing intervention by the state that have worked to demean, discipline, and foreclose alternatives to settler political economy. Often Indigenous formations of peoplehood and political orders are narrated within non-Indigenous institutions and discourses as *culture*, marking them as expressions of collective inclinations in ways that distinguish them from the political work of governance. Audra Simpson argues, "We must be mindful, however, that in its theoretical and analytic guises 'culture' is defined in anthropological terms most consistently by its proximity to difference, not its sovereignty, its right to govern, to own, or to labor," and within that conception of "difference" lies the presumption "that you are a savage, that your language is incoherent, that you are less than white people, not quite up to par, that you are then 'different,' with a different culture that is defined by others and will be accorded a protected space of legal recognition *if* your group evidences that 'difference' in terms that are sufficient to the settlers' legal eye."[75] This designation of Indigenous peoplehood and worlding as "culture," and thus subordinated to the workings of settler sovereignty and law, turns on a notion of kinship that recodes formations of collective life as nonpolitical webs of quasi-familial attachment. As Povinelli observes, a condition of a group being seen as having a "culture" is being characterized as a genealogically constituted network: "The lack of choice in the domain of genealogical classification effectively mirrors thick public presumptions about culture and determination."[76]

Yet even as Indigenous polities get recast as cultures, the settler-state works to break up the genealogical matrices that ostensibly provide the infrastructure for such collective cultural identity. If kinship designates deviations from the liberal family, such deviations can themselves be experienced as personal failure, perversion, and pathology. Kim TallBear observes, "I was suffocating all my life under the weight of the aspirational ideal of the middle-class nuclear family, including (hetero)normative coupledom with its compulsory biological reproduction," and she earlier notes, "the clearly unsustainable nuclear family is the most commonly idealized alternative to the tribal and extended family context in which I was raised." Despite living in a nonnuclear arrangement, TallBear describes how she came to view those arrangements of home and family as expressive of an inability to achieve the ideal of health and well-being with which she and the people around her had been taught to identify, despite its running alienness to the actual circumstances in which they lived. That personal sense of wrongness emanates directly from the imposition of "a system of compulsory settler sexuality and family that continues building a nation upon Indigenous genocide," one that aims to "free up land for settlement" by *whitening* "red people."[77] TallBear shows how quotidian Indigenous modes of connection can come to be experienced by Native people as a racialized incapacity to attain proper enfamilyment.[78]

In this way, kinship less provides a way of describing nonliberal *cultural* forms than a way of indexing how the jurisdictional imperatives of the state come to be felt as a hierarchical difference among kinds of families. The need to clear land for white settlement and to break up Indigenous modes of placemaking and governance is lived in personal and intimate ways as the insufficiency of Native social networks, as the need to understand them in relation to the "middle-class nuclear family." The routinization and normalization of that process of comparison *is* the work of the kinship concept in the everyday operation of settler colonialism. However, TallBear inhabits and works that relation in reverse in order to foreground the violence both performed and effaced by ideologies of enfamilyment. Her analysis jumps between scales to illustrate how private feelings of familial lack—or the affective underside of Indian *difference*—serve as a site for registering the ongoing disavowal of Dakota modes of governance. She observes, "Prior to colonization, the fundamental social unit of my people was the extended kin group, including plural marriage. The Dakota word for extended family is *tiospaye*," later adding, "Despite colonial violence against our kin systems, we are in everyday practice still quite adept at extended family."[79] The "extended kin group" was the matrix of political placemaking and decision-making—a unit of governance. The lived network of "extended family," then, marks the ways Dakota social relations exceed heteronormative settler frames while also highlighting the continued existence and efficacy of processes of collectivity that provide the infrastructure for peoplehood: "I grew up with an implicit mandate that our tiospaye must caretake kin across the generations as part of caretaking the oyate, i.e. the 'tribal nation' in 20th-century parlance." Thus, when Tall-Bear asserts, "I grew up in a very pro-kinship world," the referent here for kinship is not simply a larger or differently configured version of liberal notions of homemaking but a sociopolitical matrix in which politics and family are not contradistinguished domains. The feeling of having failed at enfamilyment—the affect generated by an inability "to paint a white, nationalist, middle class veneer over our lives"—itself testifies to the ongoing colonial work of remaking Native people(s) as racialized subjects and the continuing presence of dynamics of decision-making, resource distribution, placemaking, and collective belonging that contest such liberal subjectification and that enact alternative political orders, practices that are irreducible to cultural identity/aberrance.[80]

TallBear traces the connection between intimate experiences of racialized insufficiency and pathology and the longue durée of the state's imposition of liberal political economy as part of projects of colonial remapping, and in doing so, her analysis raises a differently configured version of the tension between minoritizing and generalizing frameworks discussed earlier with regard to queer (re)formulations of kinship. In this case, by *minoritizing* I do not mean being positioned as a minority within the nation-state but an account of kinship that emphasizes the particularity of Indigenous peoples and their governance over their lands and waters, rather than one in which principles articulated by Indigenous intellectual formulations are understood as widely applicable to non-Indigenous groups as well. While pointing to the relay between the historical and continuing force of state intervention and personal experiences of familial "failure," TallBear both engages Indigenous specificity and offers formulations that extend beyond indigeneity. She notes, "Perhaps our kinship arrangements are actually culturally, emotionally, financially, and environmentally more sustainable than that nuclear family, two-parent model we are so good at failing at, and that's why we are 'failing,'" and she adds that "focusing on actual stories of relation—on being in good relation-with, making kin"—could "spur more just interactions" by "promiscuously re-aggregating relations."[81]

These principles arise out of her experience as a Dakota person while aiming to speak to processes of enforced nuclearization and attributions of racialized failure and incapacity that exceed those of Native people(s). Her refiguring of such putative inability as the potential for "kinship arrangements" that displace liberal ideologies of enfamilyment—that recast "kinship" in ways that breach the distinction between family and politics—resonates with other accounts of racialized insufficiency. For example, Rodríguez points toward the ways "racialized excess" gets "read as queer," regardless of sexual object-choice. In discussing scholarly and official accounts of Black aberrance in the early to mid-twentieth century, Roderick Ferguson notes that "African American communal and corporeal difference became the symbol of the nonheteronormative perversions of industrializing and urbanizing economics," the sign of tendencies toward wrong enfamilyment. Addressing the potential limits of queerness in engaging forms of racialization, Cathy Cohen foregrounds how the "'nonnormative' procreation patterns and family structures of people who are labeled heterosexual have also been used to regulate and exclude *them*," highlighting the "roots of heteronormativity in white supremacist ideologies" in which the "institution of heterosexual marriage" has operated as a way to "designate which individuals were truly fit."[82] This dominant understanding of blackness as pathologically excessive with regard to liberal models of home and family aims to foreclose what Stallings has described as "the funking of love and eros that black people had been developing and working through for centuries in response to racism and capitalism,"[83] and Cohen further has traced how such notions of racialized deviance come to shape the self-assessments of Black youth. She observes, "Much of the data from the Black Youth Project indicate that our black respondents hold quite conservative opinions about social issues when compared to other racial and ethnic groups," later adding that "while they recognize, for example, the lack of choices many black youth face in terms of opportunities for progress and mobility, they are quick to blame individuals and their parents for their poor choices and seemingly deviant behavior."[84] Following TallBear's lead, though, these varied racializing attributions of failure, and the attendant internalization of such narratives, can be interpreted as indicating not so much the need for a more expansive conception of kinship as the importance of understanding the very practices marked as failure as themselves expressive of networks of belonging and governance that contest liberal ideologies and imaginaries.

The question of how intimate experiences of (wrong) enfamilyment are shaped by the racializing frames of state policy opens onto the dynamics of scale. How are domestic units defined through their location within the encompassing geography/geographies of state jurisdiction(s)? How does that infrastructural imaginary provide the background for delimiting particular networks of relation as *home* and *family* while casting matrices of relation that defy or exceed those boundaries as a deformation of the domestic—as racialized aberrance that can be narrated as a threat to state jurisdiction?[85] Within liberal ideologies, private space remains organized around units of social reproduction, the family, that also are units of propertyholding. Personhood arises from maturation and participation in such a unit, and governance consists of the exertion of authority over a particular territorial expanse in which such units are situated, while itself remaining distinct and detached from such units—following impersonal principles that, nonetheless, exist to protect those personal spaces and the norms that shape them. Absent that nested structure of governance, though, the domestic makes no sense as a way of thinking about a kind of unit. A scalar and infrastructural imaginary animated by continuity, rather than disjunction and privatization, offers a very different picture of the dynamics and aims of governance. Addressing the logics and politics of scale within dominant US mappings of social life, Mishuana Goeman argues for the importance of being able to think "conduits of connection rather than impermeable entities," which she further describes as a sense of "scale based on connection."[86]

In *Speaking of Indians*, Ella Deloria explores the implications of such a rescaled vision through the topos of kinship. A Yankton intellectual who studied with Franz Boas, Deloria takes up the terms of anthropological discourse (although, notably, in a largely non-Boasian idiom) to highlight how within Dakota thought the kinds of collective processes that are characterized as the stuff of politics within liberalism cannot be differentiated from the realm of the familial, or the space of social reproduction.[87] In this way, she refuses the categorical distinction of the genealogical and the governmental that animates liberal geographies. Early in her discussion of "A Scheme of Life That Worked," Deloria notes that, prior to direct US intervention into intra-tribal social organization in the late nineteenth century, "Kinship was the all-important matter. Its demands and dictates for all phases of social life were relentless and exact," adding, "By kinship all Dakota people were held together in a great relationship that was theoretically all-inclusive and co-extensive with the Dakota domain."[88] The text offers no explicit definition of kinship as such, drawing on the term's accrued meanings while often figuring it in ways that have little to do with genealogical units of any sort. As a "great relationship" holding together "all Dakota people," it provides the principles through which collectivity itself is defined and lived. Moreover, the territory encompassed within Dakota peoplehood cannot be distinguished from the contours and character of that "all-inclusive" relationship. There is no jurisdictional mapping that exceeds and encloses the "phases of social life" to which kinship here gestures. The singularity of "relationship" suggests that kinship expresses something less like Morgan's notion of "gens"—an internal category of division/differentiation that does (distended) double-duty as a genealogical marker and a component of governance—than the means by which Dakota sociality occurs and by which place is generated out of that shifting matrix of modes of connection. The notion of kinship here marks processes of interaction and enmeshment; as Daniel Heath Justice argues, "kinship is best thought of as a verb rather than a noun, because kinship, in most indigenous contexts, is something that's *done* more than something that simply *is*."[89] In Deloria's framing, the philosophies and practices that constitute such doing transect the liberal distinction between the public and private, enacting a scalar imaginary that moves from the individual (as responsible social actor) outward but that does not posit a break in which a different set of principles, actors, and institutions—*political* ones—take over in order to help actualize a kind of relation and space— the personal/private/domestic—that is envisioned as qualitatively distinct from the workings of governance.[90] Deloria indicates that "kinship held everybody in a fast net of interpersonal responsibility," and she soon thereafter observes, "that was practically all the government there was."[91] If "kinship" indexes forms of "interpersonal" engagement, those patterns of behavior and conceptions of interdependent vulnerability and accountability provide the materials for continually generating a broader "net" that itself is the matrix of "relationship" that defines Dakota belonging and placemaking. Governance is the workings of that net in action, at all scales and in the movements among them—within a dwelling, among persons and dwellings in the tiospaye, in relations among tiospayes, etc.

This scalar imaginary envisions a social infrastructure in which the political arises out of and is embedded within embodied experience, itself understood as inherently relational.[92] If in liberal ideologies public personhood and political subjectivity depend on normative enfamilyment, an insulated space and set of affects that ostensibly trains individuals to take up impersonal principles and relations in order to protect norms of privatization and property, kinship in Indigenous intellectual work defies such segmentation. Offering an account of Michi Saagiig Nishnaabeg self-determination that resonates with Deloria's discussion of kinship as an encompassing relationship and mode of living, Leanne Simpson argues, "within Nishnaabeg thought, every body is a political order and every body houses individual self-determination." She later underlines the importance of attending to "the generative and emergent qualities of living in our bodies as political orders."[93] To describe the Indigenous "body" as a "political order" means understanding everyday forms of lived sensation, feelings, and connections with other physical and noncorporeal entities as themselves enactments of governance. Persons are not atomized units (or ones who emerge from families that themselves are discrete units) who live within a polity that encompasses them and to which they belong in a serialized way by institutionalized criteria, such as genealogical inheritance. Instead, personhood involves complex and shifting reciprocities and responsibilities with other beings, and those relationships both constitute one as a person and position the body as a site from which the connections that constitute political life—the collective being and becoming of the polity—emanate. In this vein, Simpson observes, "Nishnaabeg life didn't rely on institutionality to hold the structure of life. We relied upon process that created networked relationship"; through such processes of networked relation, "Governance was *made* every day."[94] As in Deloria's discussion of Dakota kinship, a nested jurisdictional logic of scale is replaced by a series of overlapping yet nonequivalent commitments of varied scope (in terms of persons/beings involved and geographic reach).

Liberalism normatively territorializes the individual within the family (what I have termed enfamilyment), and articulations of kinship tend to enlarge or reconfigure that space while holding constant the scale structure of political institutions and their geographies of authority. Ideologies of property, which as Morgan's account suggests can be understood as grounding ideas of home/family, require that familial households operate as discrete units, and a similar logic shapes the levels of political scale: they enclose discrete units and are themselves discrete units enclosed within the level above them. Approaching political scale as a series of discrete entities nested in ever-larger units understands scale as a function of property, as inherently divisible units that are somewhat interchangeable in their relative equivalence operating in ways delimited by the (jurisdictional) level they occupy—with the family as the smallest and foundational social unit. This scalar imaginary is atomizing and hierarchical (what we might call the "straight line" of state jurisdiction, echoing Ahmed's figuration of heteropatriarchal inheritance). It allows for little lateral connection among units, or such lateral relation itself appears as anomalous and potentially disruptive of both the insular discreteness of units and units' subservient integration through the exertion of authority at the next-highest level. As Goeman suggests, though, "Rather than think of these scales as disconnected, we need to think of the social processes that 'freeze' them";[95] conversely, an alternative account of governance involves envisioning such scales as fluid in relation to each other. Understanding the body as immanently bearing and enacting a political order in everyday interactions and conceptualizing governance as a collection of overlapping networks that form a "great relationship"—one that is, in Deloria's terms, "all-inclusive" of peoplehood and "co-extensive" with the "domain" of a people—reconceptualizes political scale in terms of permeability, enmeshment, and continuity.[96] It is less a matter of defining strict boundaries between inside and outside (including seeking to contain deviant and pathological excess) than determining the principles, processes, and practices by which to negotiate shifting thresholds and intensities of responsible relation among a range of intersecting, yet not necessarily equivalent or nested, kinds of belonging and forms of accountability.[97] Governance, then, *is* that negotiation.

The idealization of the nuclear family form not only engenders the racialized policing of failures to live that norm, as TallBear suggests, but naturalizes the personal/private/domestic sphere and the jurisdictional scale structure of liberalism, thereby breaking up possibilities for modes of governance—political orders—organized around permeable and shifting networks. Deloria takes pains to elaborate how the imposition of the nuclear family disrupts Dakota political processes and geographies by introducing artificial forms of disjunction and enclosure. She notes that for Dakota people prior to the imposition of allotment policy, "The family unit of parents-and-child was not the final and complete idea it is elsewhere. It was an integral part of the larger family, the *tiyospaye*, bound together with blood and marriage ties."[98] Here the tiospaye appears as an extended, "larger" family, meaning a series of relationships defined by "blood and marriage." In this way, Deloria's account seems to echo Morgan's definition of kinship through comparison to a "descriptive" core of nuclear homemaking, such as in her use of the phrase "social kinship" to describe relationships that do not fit dominant Euro-American definitions of "family." In differentiating Dakota kinship from "the parents-and-child" unit, though, she employs the concept of family in ways that stretch it beyond recognition, turning it into a way of registering a series of networks that do not map neatly onto each other. She observes that "the father-mother-child unit was not final and isolated; it was only one of several others forming the larger family, the *tiyospaye*," which "denotes a group of families, bound together by blood and marriage ties, that lived side by side in the camp-circle. There was perfect freedom of movement. Any family for reasons valid to itself could depart at any time to visit relatives or sojourn for longer or shorter periods in some other Dakota camp-circle. There was no power to hold them back." She adds, "Those camp-circles were peripatetic villages, periodically on the move over the vast Dakota domain." In addition, she indicates that "all the families of a *tiyospaye* operated as a single unit in practically all activities. Men often hunted in company; women did their work, especially fancywork, in pleasant circles."[99] In these moments, she describes nuclear units as distinct, the entire tiospaye as a "single unit," groups of relatives that could constellate with people in other tiospayes (and potentially join them), and shifting and mobile relations among tiospayes in ways that constitute the "Dakota domain" as such.

Persons and "families" can combine and recombine in a range of ways at and across various scales (in terms of determinate groups or households within a tiospaye, the tiospaye as itself a singular entity, connections with persons or groups among different tiospayes, and the connections among tiospayes as semi-discrete entities), such that none of these kinds of engroupment are fixed. *Family* itself for Deloria has variable referents demographically and geographically, and relations at what can be considered a larger scale (in terms of number of persons or geographic expanse) do not encompass and coordinate dynamics at a smaller scale. Instead, there are a collection of intersecting and crosscutting webs of relation. Decision-making, resource distribution, collective belonging, and placemaking occur in all of them in ways that are neither normatively segmented from each other nor regulated through the hierarchical management of units envisioned as otherwise serially insulated. Deloria also notes that through the workings of these interpenetrating and diverse networks of relation, which she terms kinship, "everyone was literally in the public eye," which she suggests created forms of mutual responsibility that she refers to as "government."[100] Being "in the public eye" in this way is not differentiated from an enclosed, familial privacy. The imposition of enfamilyment through US policy, then, fragments these intersecting networks of governance, while also casting a range of collective issues as merely privatized problems, responsibilities, and failings. Within this remapping and rescaling of governance, the kinds of concerns often cordoned off as reproductive politics or reproductive labor—attaching to the composition of households and families and care of children—are not separable from a sphere of governance/politics as such.[101] As Deloria observes, "Many Indians cannot yet feel complete with just their little family, their spouse and children." Christopher Pexa suggests of Deloria, "Her defining of kinship against the liberal ideal of the individual thus refuses convergences of race, class, and gender around heterosexual, monogamous marriage and the nuclear family," in ways that also understand "peoplehood" as "a fluid sort of relationality" that is "not statist."[102] The body bears political orders because it is always enmeshed in ongoing matrices of relation with a range of persons, groups, and nonhuman entities/collectivities through which lived personhood cannot be differentiated from participation in the politics of governance.

I should clarify that I am not suggesting that the processes of generating political networks I have been discussing, often characterized as kinship by Indigenous thinkers, serve as the only means of enacting Indigenous peoplehood. Many Native nations have governmental structures that operate in ways similar to Euro-American models, and even if we might understand such dynamics as overdetermined by continuing forms of "colonial entanglement," in Jean Dennison's terms, Indigenous peoples' employment of such modes of governance should not be dismissed as inauthentic.[103] Moreover, settler-state disregard for the jurisdiction of Native nations itself serves as a significant part of continuing projects of colonial expropriation. Rather than casting Native accounts of kinship—like Deloria's—as the proper mode of indigeneity, I'm turning to such formulations as a way of highlighting nonliberal social mappings and visions of governance that refuse the following: categorical and scalar distinctions of the familial from the political; understandings of individual subjectivity as emanating from a privatized space of enfamilyment; and normative commitments to property and its exclusions and insulations, through which other modes of relation appear as racialized excess. As Shiri Pasternak argues, such forms of Indigenous governance can be understood as an "exercise of jurisdiction as an *ontology of care*," and attending to such governance as an exercise of jurisdiction, although operating in ways quite different than that of the state's, can help highlight how "a set of exhaustive administrative regimes" seek to "undermine, erase, and choke out the exercise of Indigenous jurisdiction," including by understanding it as a cultural anomaly and/or by translating into the terms and scale structure of liberal geographies and propertyholding.[104] In her analysis of the elite imposition of forms of bourgeois normativity in Hawai'i during the Kingdom period, J. Kēhaulani Kauanui points to the value of Indigenous principles of relation beyond "family" as enabling "a reconfiguration of sovereignty outside of its dominant Western meaning," adding that such ways of conceptualizing governance "can serve as epistemological and ontological resources for rethinking our current conditions."[105]

This conception of governance is meant less as a program than as, borrowing from Rodríguez and Carruthers, a gesture or a lens through which to reframe what *kinship* and *governance* are and how the two can be thought in transformational relation to each other.[106] While continuing to foreground the importance of Indigenous peoples' sovereignty and self-determination, the broader employment of these principles of governance—often articulated by Indigenous intellectuals as "kinship" but distinct from the kinship imaginary at play in Morgan (which I've suggested largely persists in other invocations of the notion of kinship)—works toward displacing ideologies of enfamilyment, including their heteronormalizing and racializing geographies of privatized enclosure.[107] As TallBear argues, "*Decolonization is not an individual choice.* We must collectively oppose a system of compulsory settler sexuality and family that continues building a nation upon Indigenous genocide and that marks Indigenous and other marginalized relations as deviant," a process of radical reimagination that "includes living or supporting others in living within nonmonogamous and more-than-coupled bonds."[108] From this perspective, the possibility for supporting non-straight and non-couple-centered sexual cultures emerges neither from their separation from the space of kinship nor an expansion of kinship as a sphere of life within liberal political economy. Instead, reenvisioning governance—the politics of shaping and enacting, in Carruthers's terms, "collective decisions" and "the project of collective liberation"—allows for a vision in which persons can constellate with other persons and groups in ways that do not require the production of stable, determinate households (of whatever size and configuration) as the units for propertyholding, self-provision, and regulation by *political* institutions, ostensibly acting in the interest of the "public" good.

Rather than seeking to fit within liberal mappings (of personhood, identity, enfamilyment, jurisdiction), this reimagination of governance promotes an attention to existing and possible practices of collectivity and the lived and malleable connections among them—of a variety of kinds of alternative political orders. Such reenvisioning foregrounds the question of how those forms of belonging and interdependence function as *political* processes, rather than segmenting them off as familial or cultural. How does the United States already contain within it political orders whose existence is not recognized as such (Indigenous and otherwise)? How do we understand those formations and modes of life that legally and administratively are cast as excessive, deviant, pathological, and criminal as, instead, lived political orders? How does doing so separate the question of governance from that of citizenship and the apparatuses of the liberal state? As Melanie Yazzie argues, attending to Indigenous "practices of making kin" can "encourage people to imagine collective forms of belonging and accountability that do not reproduce liberal ideas about citizenship and nationalism like those that give shape to US settler nationalism."[109] In this way, reconceptualizing governance as overlapping and intersecting networks of responsibility seeks to orient away from the institutionalities and scale structure of the state as the de facto background; to open pathways for envisioning redistributions and alternative coalescences of affects, resources, and placemaking; and to offer normative frames for political life—for processes of governance—not dependent on the logic of property. Moreover, redescribing existing formations, Indigenous and not, as political orders opens up capacities to think in more varied ways about what governance can entail.

In this vein, Indigenous theorizations of kinship further present an ethics of relation that provides a basis for negotiation among persons and collectives at all scales. Less indicating a particular format for relating or a specific kind of political infrastructure, the concept of kinship as employed by Indigenous intellectuals speaks to organizing principles of social life that refuse liberal mappings of personhood, privacy, and possession and that expand what "social life" might mean beyond connections among human beings. In his analysis of the work of Indigenous literature,

Justice asks, "How do [Indigenous people(s)] learn to be human after centuries of settler colonial assaults on the health and well-being of the very Indigenous kinship structures and social values that have determined our distinctive humanity?" He later refers to "our distinctive kinship practices and understandings," which "have been primary sources of our strength and resistance" while being "primary targets of settler-state policy and practice, with devastating results."[110] Kinship here indexes Indigenous distinctiveness, in terms of both lived modes of sociality and philosophical precepts through which to understand right conduct and the violence of settler interventions. This tracing of Indigenous specificities (a minoritizing frame, as discussed previously), though, sits alongside a more generalizing impulse to offer ways of conceptualizing kinship that highlight the value of an emphasis on reciprocal, responsible relationships for reorganizing dominant sociopolitical formations. Justice observes that "to be a *good* relative, to be fully *kin*, we must put that relatedness into thoughtful and respectful practice, individually and collectively, and take up our responsibilities to one another and to the world of which we're a part."[111] Even as the term relative seems to mark the kind of kinship imaginary at play in nineteenth-century (proto)anthropology, as in Deloria's use of "family," it foregrounds ways of understanding what being in relation means, as having ongoing "responsibilities" of various kinds that animate the character and conduct of connection. In this way, to be a *relative* less refers to some permutation of family in Morgan's sense than to be involved in the doing of relating in ethical ways. Using the topos of kinship to emphasize the presence and value of complex, layered, and overlapping networks of ethical relation based on responsibility and reciprocity also works to counter the racializing discourses of excess and danger that continue to attach to articulations of kinship as an enlarged or reconfigured sphere of the personal/private/domestic (implicitly situated within the scale structure of liberal political economy).

Such relations are not simply enacted but envisioned, self-reflexively taken up as a basis for conduct. As Justice argues, "Relationships are storied, imagined things; they set the scope for our experience of being and belonging," including "the ways we understand our obligations to the diverse networks of relations and relationships," and he further notes, "kinship, like empathy, is as much an act of imagination as it is a lived experience." That imagination promotes webs of networked responsibility while also challenging the segmenting and privatizing work performed by liberal geographies and imaginaries in favor of what Justice terms "cartographic kinscapes."[112] These mappings also include ongoing engagements with other-than-human beings. Justice indicates, "the range of relatives to whom we are responsible extends far beyond our biological relatives and, indeed, the category of the human itself"; that process of accepting responsibility involves the "recognition of other-than-human personhood," which itself arises from "deep histories with the land and profound familiarity with its varied peoples and their ways."[113] While most directly speaking to Indigenous principles of political order and diplomacy, these formulations gesture toward a broader ethos of what can be understood as a politics of relation or a relational theory and practice of politics (as opposed to one organized around insulated jurisdictional units and hierarchies). In this way, Indigenous reformulations of kinship such as Justice's can be interpreted as providing a more expansive frame of reference for what Ruha Benjamin has characterized as "cultivating kinfulness," a process that can be seen as less about the boundaries or affects of *family* than the guiding principles that might orient conceptions of what the making and operation of governance can entail.[114] Theorized via the rubric of kinship, this vision of political order dislocates personhood from enfamilyment while emphasizing relative-making as an important act of critical and political imagination, refusing property claims to exclusionary possession in favor of principles of ongoing ties and formations of interdependence—ones that do not necessarily neatly nestle into each other within an ascending scale structure.

Rather than relying on invocations of home and family in developing critiques and imagining alternatives, intellectuals and activists can draw on such cartographic kinscapes as a way of orienting and coordinating movements for change, including in strategic projects of advocacy within the existing policy infrastructure of the state. In challenging the notion of *population* as a way of understanding and countering forms of resource scarcity and environmental devastation, Michelle Murphy argues for the importance of taking as a "starting point the *affirmative making of the conditions that support collective life* in the face of persistent racist, colonial, and heteropatriarchal life-negating structures." She further suggests that such an affirmation involves mapping "densities of relations" that enable expropriative, extractive, and exploitative social patterns, seeking to untangle and redistribute such densities in ways that shift from an "infrastructure" based on privatized ownership and consumption to one that emphasizes "conditions of becoming with the many."[115] Indigenous efforts to inhabit and refunction the concept of kinship can aid in that work by shifting away from liberal political economy (with its scales and spheres) as the de facto orienting background. Instead, such theorizations offer an expansive conception of governance and its operative principles, suggesting pathways for taking up Carruthers's challenge to rethink what governing is and does. Although not addressing engagements with law and policy (in fact, arguing against turning to the state), Leanne Simpson offers a powerful articulation of why theorizations of kinship that highlight nonliberal modes of governance can be of service when engaging the state. She argues that "*how* we live, *how* we organize, *how* we engage in the world—the process—not only frames the outcome, it is the transformation. *How* molds and then gives birth to the present. The *how* changes us. *How* is the theoretical intervention."[116] She specifically is speaking of lived relations with Indigenous lands and other Indigenous people that continually reconstitute governance through experiential engagement, rather than bureaucratic apparatuses, but her emphasis here on the "how" of theorizing and pursuing campaigns for change and transformation highlights the potential of Indigenous theorizations of kinship and political orders for integrating a range of otherwise disparate issues within a shifted, nonprivatizing conception of what governance is (a different mapping than current exploitative, extractive, and expropriative "densities"). In other words, even when seeking to engage state law and policy, being guided by a vision of networks of relation (including with nonhuman entities) provides conceptual tools through which to vision across such apparent divisions in order to devise legal and administrative interventions and programs of advocacy.

* * *

Indigenous intellectuals inhabit and deploy the concept of kinship in ways that reorient it, helping highlight the often implicitly privatizing work the concept does within liberal political imaginaries. By foregrounding questions of governance and the inadequacy of family as a way of characterizing the networks of interdependence, responsibility, and accountability they address, these approaches theorize nonliberal sociopolitical dynamics and formations. Even while using terms like "relatives" that might imply a familial framework, Indigenous articulations of kinship refuse insulating ideologies that wed intimacy to property and that position the political as both an impersonal space apart and a nested jurisdictional surround that encompasses the private sphere. Instead, kinship comes to name an alternative way of envisioning governance in which enfamilyment is not the racializing means of (pre)qualifying for personhood and political subjectivity. From within the dominant kinship imaginary I've discussed, though, Indigenous formulations might be understood as a vision of governance operating through a kinship idiom—a way of talking about non-liberal social forms offered by later anthropologists working within the broad framework established in Morgan's writings. However, following Schneider, I have argued that kinship needs to be understood as having a clear referent in order for it to serve as an *idiom* for something else. As suggested in my reading of Morgan, what grounds the referential field of kinship is the nuclear family form and associated geographies of property, against which kinship can appear as a civilizationally backward or relativistically acceptable extension of the private/domestic beyond its (proper/logical/natural) "descriptive" bounds. Moreover, the idea that kinship and governance are logically disjunct—such that an idiom of the one needs to be smuggled into the separate domain of the other—retains the organizing distinction, visible in Morgan's work, between personal and political spheres: kinship becomes a deviation from a paradigmatic model of what politics *is* that is modeled on the liberal state. Thus, while Indigenous intellectuals use the term *kinship*, I want to suggest such usage breaks with the imperial and racializing work the concept performs within liberal imaginaries, including when such imaginaries serve as the background for cultural relativism or oppositional efforts to reimagine home and family.

Non-native queer efforts to grapple with kinship have tended to run into the translation that concept enacts. If kinship potentially provides a way of recognizing a wide range of social configurations, it also remakes them as a version of family, indexed to nuclear homemaking as (savage, perverse) deviations. Queer intellectual and activist work has sought to distance itself from these privatizing implications, arguing for the value of stranger sociality and sexual cultures not cast as versions of *home* and *family*. Conversely, such work also has sought to access the alternative imaginary of domesticity, intimacy, desire, and social reproduction that the concept of kinship seems to offer. The shuttling between these two positions with respect to kinship (sometimes in the same argument) illustrates an ambivalence that is less about non-native queer political projects per se than the dynamics of the kinship concept as it has emerged out of nineteenth-century formulations. The goal of envisioning forms of sociality and collective life outside of and beyond "straight space" gets sidelined by the difficulty of situating such queer constellations within the geographies of liberal political economy. Or, perhaps more to the point, these queer critiques of liberalism, capitalism, and property get blunted by the difficulty of not de facto reinstalling liberal imaginaries as the background against which queerness (whatever its contours and character) gains meaning as deviation or exception. *Kinship* does a good deal of work in this regard: it dislocates intimacy, desire, and social reproduction from the scene and sites of governance/politics in ways that direct queer energies toward disowning the domestic (as the space of normative constriction) or distending/reforming it, rather than seeking to dismantle that distinction between public and private, which legitimizes property-holding, privatization, and the scale structure of state jurisdiction. The matter of governance—its forms, processes, subjectivities—tends to slide from view, except inasmuch as state enactments bear on the construction of the supposed sphere of kinship.

To contest, in Eng's terms, the ways that intimacy functions "as a racialized property right" involves more than expanding the parameters of kinship, since enfamilyment continues to serve as a matrix of racialization through which to define and regulate the kinds of collectivities and modes of personhood, placemaking, and resource distribution that can exist in the territory claimed by/as the US state. Turning to the question of governance broadly stated, as Carruthers suggests, requires a revisiting of the kinship imaginary and the ways it orients horizons of critique and sociopolitical transformation. Indigenous appropriations of the kinship concept mobilize it toward registering the presence and tracing the operation of nonliberal modes of governance—*political orders*—that neither segment off a privatized domesticity (however configured) nor remake such modes as cultural difference across a relativist divide (existing in an elsewhere/elsewhen separate from the liberal state). Instead, the topos of kinship takes part in Indigenous critiques of the principles, interventions, mappings, and institutional frameworks enacted by the liberal state. In this way, Native articulations of kinship offer valuable intellectual avenues through which to highlight both the violence of ideologies of enfamilyment and the possibilities for acknowledging nonliberal social forms *as governance*. Drawing attention to the racializing and imperial translations enacted through the kinship imaginary, the ways it tends to reinstate liberal geographies and ideologies of enfamilyment as the organizing background, opens the potential for reformulated conceptions of jurisdiction, belonging, and relation. Such a shifted political imaginary includes Indigenous peoplehood while also engaging non-Indigenous movements and modes of collectivity that might not otherwise be understood as enacting practices of governance. Redescribing such non-Indigenous formations as *political orders* in ways that draw on Indigenous revisions of kinship opens avenues for linking what may seem to be disparate kinds of social projects and for expanding the sense of actually existing alternatives to the liberal state and its enfamilied infrastructures.

TWO

Indian Domesticity, Settler Regulation, and the Limits of the Race/Politics Distinction

IN THE LEAD-UP to the reauthorization of the Violence Against Women Act (VAWA) in March 2013, the US Senate and House of Representatives both passed versions with very different provisions with respect to sexual assault and domestic violence by non-natives on reservation.[1] Specifically, the language of the Senate version, which was included in the enacted law, allowed for tribes to have limited criminal jurisdiction over the non-Indian "romantic" and "intimate partners" of women living in Indian Country in cases involving dating and domestic violence, as well as enabled tribal governments to issue and enforce protection orders.[2] These provisions were absent in the House bill, which instead required that Native women seek protection from federal courts. In a speech on the Senate floor, Senator John Kyl (R-AZ) described these provisions as "blatantly unconstitutional," adding that the section "breaks with 200 years of American legal tradition that tribes cannot exercise criminal jurisdiction over non-Indians."[3] He went on to say, "All tribes require either Indian ancestry or a specific quantum of Indian blood in order to be a tribal member. Even a person who has lived his entire life on the reservation cannot be a tribal member if he does not have Indian blood." In a similar vein, Senator Chuck Grassley (R-IA) argued, "Constitutional problems are made worse because the bill gives tribes criminal jurisdiction as part of their claimed inherent sovereignty."[4] These comments speak to a much larger problem within contemporary federal Indian policy, namely how the matter of Indigenous governance—and its contours and limits—is routed through conceptions of *Indianness*, the reproductive transmission of an otherwise undefined racial substance via "ancestry" or the passage of "blood." To attempt to extend the jurisdiction of Native nations further, to include those who are "non-Indian," then, supposedly would unconstitutionally subject them to the rule of a racialized clique to which they can never belong. Maintaining the distinction between *Indians* and *non-Indians* as the central axis by which to define the limits of Native sovereignty substitutes the reproductive transmission of racialized substance—having "Indian blood" or "Indian ancestry"—for the geopolitical dynamic of Indigenous peoples continuing to exist on territory forcibly incorporated into/as the settler-state. Turning the matter of the bounds of Native governmental authority into the question of who counts as Indian transposes the issue into a different register, one that makes Indigenous political orders dependent upon biological difference and a heteronormative logic of reproduction. Making indigeneity into Indianness, then, involves the ideological work of enfamilyment.

Even though the final act does offer possibilities for tribal jurisdiction over "non-Indians" unavailable in the House bill (replicating the language that had been in the Senate version), it does not escape the orbit of the racializing reproductive assumptions guiding the arguments made by the Senate bill's detractors. The law notes that the persons that would be prosecutable under this act must be "in a social relationship of a romantic or intimate nature" with the alleged victim or "a current or former spouse or intimate partner." While such categories do not fit exactly the contours of the nuclear family unit, especially since the act pertains to "dating" as well as "domestic" violence, the model here still appears to be that of marital pairing, extended backward to courting and forward through divorce. This delimitation of the potential authority exerted over "non-Indians" seems to take couplehood as the axiomatic frame. Why, though, would romantic partnering provide the prism for thinking about how legally to redress violence against Native women by non-natives?[5] The key to answering this question may lie in the repeated description of the powers of Native governments under this law as "special domestic violence criminal jurisdiction." What makes it "special" is that the statute offers forms of authority "that a participating tribe may exercise under this section but could not otherwise exercise," due to the 1978 US Supreme Court ruling in *Oliphant v. Suquamish* that tribes could not exert criminal jurisdiction over "non-Indians."[6] In other words, this law creates a limited exception for kinds of violence that can be understood in relation to the nuclear family unit. In this way, the statute preserves the presumptively reproductive distinction between non-Indian and Indian (a term which itself is nowhere defined in the statute),[7] while allowing for cases in which non-Indians enter into the romantic-familial orbit of the propagation of Indianness. More than signaling a particular Republican reluctance to expand tribal jurisdiction or a Democratic championing of Native self-determination, the debate over VAWA points toward the ways that notions of racialized enfamilyment—of an Indian domestic sphere—lie at the center of official narratives of Indigenous governance.

The categories of *Indian* and *tribe* can be understood as generated within US political discourses and institutions, as (mis)translations of Indigenous political orders. Representing Indians as a racial population enables the US government to insert them into the matrix of federal jurisdiction, defining them not as polities whose existence precedes and exceeds that of the settler-state itself but instead narrating tribes as collections of enfamilied persons whose identity arises through the "special" status accorded them under US law, a status that largely is imagined as a quasi-political acknowledgment of Native peoples as *cultural* collectivities. As discussed in the previous chapter, the representation of collective practices and formations as (failed) family, including through rhetorics of kinship, normalizes liberal governance and helps render it commonsensical, both by casting alternative frameworks as (excessive and deviant) versions of the private sphere and positioning the family within a particular scalar imaginary in which proper governmental institutions exert jurisdiction over it in a concentric hierarchy (such as in the movement from municipal to state to federal authority). In addition to naturalizing the nuclear family unit as the self-evident atom of social existence, ideologies of enfamilyment enact processes of privatization, racialization, and depoliticization that cross-reference each other in the alignment of procreation with the replication of social identities understood as inherently beyond governmental creation or control, as having a quasi-organic existence properly free from political interference. In this vein, Indigenous peoples can be narrated as a population defined by reproductively transmitted Indianness. The understanding of Indianness as the transmission of racial substance and of Native kinship systems as unique, culturally specific forms of family both take part in a heteronormative understanding of

Native identity and of indigeneity itself as a form of genetic or genealogical inheritance, which therefore is intrinsically distinct from anything that could constitute true political sovereignty. Through non-native discourses of kinship, Indigenous principles of geopolitical organization—the contours and character of peoplehood—are presented, instead, as characteristics that attach to a (racially imagined) population, such that *tribes* appear as collections of *Indians* rather than as autonomous Indigenous political orders. Attending to how that process works within contemporary policy can shed further light on the ways racialization functions as an enfamilying mode of primitive accumulation (translating forms of governance as collective difference and deviance, as discussed in the introduction), as well as how attending to Indigenous theorizations of nonliberal governance can provide models for engaging with—*redescribing*—non-Indigenous social formations as themselves political orders.

This process of creating an *Indian* population not only subjects Native peoples to a biopolitical regime but reaffirms the obviousness of the territoriality and jurisdiction of the settler-state. An attention to the ways Indian family, racial identity, and tribal identity are intertwined within the discourses of federal Indian law and policy helps in tracking the process of normalizing US jurisdictional frameworks. Within this policy imaginary, Indianness represents the innate/ingrained characteristics of a racialized population, even in the absence of an explicit discourse of racial difference in situations where the United States seems to acknowledge the distinctness and political autonomy of Indian tribes. In translating the geopolitics of Indigenous self-determination into the itinerary of racial reproduction, contemporary US Indian policy defines the political dimensions of Native sovereignty through reference to a reprosexual logic.[8] An implicit emphasis on the generational inheritance of biological Indianness—the understanding of peoplehood through ideologies of enfamilyment—translates place-based indigeneity into a matter of lineage, itself not a basis for asserting authority as a proper *political society*, in Lewis Henry Morgan's terms discussed in chapter 1. That representation of Indigenous peoples as if they were extended families, and therefore necessarily something other than full polities, extends to endorsements and even expansions of Native sovereignty. Thus, the attempt sometimes made to separate the "political" from the "racial" with regard to Indian affairs, to insist that Native peoples are political entities under US law rather than a racial group, effaces the ways the recognition of Native governance within contemporary US Indian law and policy becomes utterly incoherent without supplementation by discourses of racialized enfamilyment as the basis for conceptualizing Indian particularity.

Moreover, even while pointing to the political status of Native nations, based on prior treaties and (qualified) acknowledgment of the ways Indigenous peoples' governance precedes and exceeds that of the United States, differentiating between political and racial understandings of Indian tribes can cast Native peoples as exceptional in ways that reinforce the commonsensicality of applying liberal modes of racialization to other groups. Their social forms, such as the struggles for Black self-determination discussed in chapter 4, themselves appear other-than-political, as expressions of racial identification rather than enactments of governance—political orders.[9] In attending to and highlighting Indigenous sovereignty, scholars need to be careful not to reinforce the depoliticizing work of racializing enfamilyment I've been tracking, including the ways it circumscribes indigeneity. Addressing the knotty conceptual and legal process of (re)producing Indianness as a category requires less jettisoning the racial as a false mode of designation than tracing the ideological dynamics by which indigeneity becomes understood as a function of the genealogical passage of Indianness, a transmission that de facto is segregated from the sphere of politics as such. In this way, Indigenous governance is made to pivot around some version of the privatized family, delimiting the scope of Native peoplehood through its repeated linkage to the scene of (racial) procreation and liberal conceptions of political scale.

Rather than suggesting that all of contemporary Indian policy follows a singular logic or set of principles, though, I aim to trace patterns of translation that cut across seemingly opposed political positions, thereby indicating some of the ways the possibilities for Indigenous self-determination and for envisioning what constitutes Indigenous political orders are managed and stymied in the current conjuncture. These dynamics can be seen at play in three of the watershed changes in Indian policy adopted in the same year (1978), judicial and legislative determinations that seem in many ways rather disparate yet that all remain cornerstone parts of federal Indian law. Attending to the Supreme Court decisions in *Oliphant v. Suquamish* and *Santa Clara Pueblo v. Martinez* and the enactment of the Indian Child Welfare Act (ICWA) illustrates the ways racializing discourses of family are central to the current administrative architecture through which the United States acknowledges continuing Native collective presence while seeking to accommodate it to, and to validate the persistence of, the geopolitics and jurisdiction of settlement. While the specific ends/effects of these three are quite different and can be described as taking up rather varied political perspectives, all of them hinge on a shared narrative of indigeneity as dependent on enfamilyment, in which tribal belonging and Indianness appear primarily as a genealogically transmitted cultural formation that may be recognized by the United States for certain purposes but that is not fundamentally political in character—a kind of distended private sphere whose legal acknowledgment has decided limits. As against this institutional matrix, in which Native political orders remain tethered to and internally organized by racializing ideologies of family, Native feminists have addressed how Indigenous governance and peoplehood emerge through everyday matrices of interdependent relation that cannot be conceptualized as merely an extension of the private sphere. In doing so, they provide analytical frameworks for engaging Indigenous political orders—and potentially non-Indigenous political orders—in ways not routed through a liberal imaginary or scale structure.

Indians, Not Territories

Oliphant v. Suquamish not only continues to serve as good precedent in federal law, it provides a grounding logic through which Indigenous sovereignty is understood as inapplicable in vital respects to non-natives because it is cast as not-quite-political in character. The decision turns on the question of what constitutes an Indian tribe as such. The case involves the prosecution of Mark David Oliphant for assaulting a Suquamish police officer on the Port Madison Indian Reservation on August 19, 1973.[10] After being released on his own recognizance from the tribal jail, Oliphant petitioned the US District Court for a writ of habeas corpus, arguing that the tribal court had no jurisdiction over him as a non-Indian. The district court denied the writ, the appellate court affirmed that decision, and the Supreme Court reversed it. While putatively focused on defining the position of "non-Indians" in relation to Native governments, the majority opinion, written by Justice William Rehnquist, rehearses a version of the history of federal Indian policy in order to present the exertion of criminal jurisdiction over those outside the category of "Indian" as fundamentally incommensurable with the "tribe" as a kind of entity under US law.[11] The decision uses Indianness as a placeholder to bridge forms of political and conceptual incoherence, positioning it as a quality that self-evidently attaches to certain bodies and not others. Indianness provides a principle of uniqueness that depends on a kind of belonging differentiable from the fact of inhabitance in a given space. As Philip Frickey observes in "A Common Law for Our Age of Colonialism," "in *Oliphant* there was no contention that the reservation had been diminished," therefore "the Court had to limit tribal territorial sovereignty by limiting the sovereignty rather than the territory." Additionally, N. Bruce Duthu argues that the case "gutted the notion of full territorial sovereignty as it applied to Indian tribes."[12] Indian and non-Indian appear as commonsensical categories that do not arise from the law itself. Instead, they bear inherent orientations and qualities that the Court merely recognizes and that provide an immanent and obvious set of limitations to the scope of tribal authority. The decision articulates a vision of Native sovereignty as itself turning on the possession of a purposively ill-defined Indianness whose contours and character are implicitly racial and that is passed through family lineages that themselves are taken as the extra-political, natural basis of personal identity. In this way, heteronormatively envisioned racial belonging provides the scalar infrastructure for thinking about Indigenous jurisdiction.

In addressing the question of tribal authority, the decision does not so much examine existing precedent as offer a broad (re)assessment of the character of tribes in relation to the US government. As against well-established judicial and administrative principles for understanding Native nations as continuing to possess an inherent sovereignty over all matters not explicitly ceded to or prohibited by the federal government, *Oliphant* creates the doctrine of what would come to be known as *implicit divestiture*. Tribes' occupation of lands within US borders necessarily means that they cannot exercise certain kinds of authority.[13] Approaching the question of whether tribes have the power to try non-Indians in this way, though, leaves the decision with something of a logical and ethical conundrum. How precisely did Indigenous peoples who occupied their lands prior to the emergence of the US nation-state and in ways not subject to the latter's control come to be under the jurisdiction of the federal government? The opinion insists, "Upon incorporation into the territory of the United States, the Indian tribes thereby come under the territorial sovereignty of the United States and their exercise of separate power is constrained so as not to conflict with the interests of this overriding sovereignty."[14] The supposed obviousness of the contours of US domestic space leads to the conclusion that everything within it must be subject to the "territorial sovereignty" of the nation, and no form of "separate power" that *conflicts* with that "overriding" jurisdiction can be deemed valid. In other words, the unilateral declaration by the settler-state that Native peoples and their lands have been *incorporated* into an alien political entity without their consent counts as the means for determining the legitimacy of Indigenous governance.[15] Later, the decision ameliorates this description a bit by indicating that the constriction of Native peoples' authority arises as a result of "the tribes' forfeiture of full sovereignty in return for the protection of the United States," suggesting that the diminishment of sovereignty results from decisions made by "the tribes" rather than the enforced colonial inscription of settler territoriality over Indigenous polities.[16] However, this narrative remains in tension with the decision's earlier derivation of the US government's "overriding sovereignty" as necessarily following from its projection of political contiguity "within" its borders, a process that appears independent of Native choice. The claim that tribes *forfeited full sovereignty* retrospectively posits a moment of Native agency in order to provide a legitimizing gloss for the a priori imposition of "territorial sovereignty" by the settler-state over the lands it claims as its domestic space. In seeking to argue that the bare fact of tribes' inhabitance on territory "within" the United States necessarily limits their sovereignty,[17] the decision runs headlong into the central aporia of federal Indian policy, namely that the "conflict" between the "separate power" of Native peoples and the settler-state's effort to superintend them cannot be resolved in constitutional terms and that the geopolitical existence of the state rests on an extraconstitutional and ongoing process of imperial arrogation.[18]

The decision seeks to manage this fundamental and irresolvable problem by recasting the specific impasses in legitimizing US jurisdiction as the content of Indianness. Citing the language of the appellate court's decision, the opinion finds tribes' exertion of criminal jurisdiction over non-Indians to be *"inconsistent with their status."*[19] What precisely is that "status"? If tribes lack "full sovereignty," are they polities? If they are not, how could they consent to forfeit sovereignty (including through land cessions in the treaty system)? Moreover, if they were polities for the purposes of ceding authority to the United States, are they something else now? If so, what, and how exactly did they become so? *Oliphant* displaces these troubling questions by treating Indianness as a kind of status that can provide continuity across time and that can have sovereignty-effects without being understood as properly political (as competing or in "conflict" with the geopolitical claims of the settler-state). While acknowledging that Indians form collectives that possess sovereignty in some fashion, such that it can be ceded to the United States, the decision argues that the very kinds of juridical processes that would indicate their ability to try non-Indians have been lacking historically. Rehnquist asserts, "Until the middle of this century, few Indian tribes maintained any semblance of a formal court system. Offenses by one Indian against another were usually handled by social and religious pressure and not by formal judicial processes."[20] Rehnquist's language here certainly presents Native peoples as "relatively lawless, unsophisticated, and uncivilized."[21] Perhaps more notable than the general cast of his comments, and their racist intimations of Indian barbarism, is the way they do not so much indicate tribes' inability to produce order as the absence of specifically *legal* means to do so. If tribes address "offenses" by exerting "social and religious pressure," the principles guiding that effort and the formations through which such discipline is enacted do not constitute "a formal court system." The opinion suggests that whatever specific configurations and processes *social* and *religious* might designate, they are not of the same kind as the political and constitutional structure of the United States and other recognized nation-states. Rather, they illustrate a communality that cannot make comparable geopolitical or legal claims to that of the "territorial sovereignty" of the United States. In the words of Lewis Henry Morgan, discussed in the previous chapter, they are "kinship," not "political society." *Indian* serves as a mediator in naming the kind of entity they are and the (limited) "separate power" they exercise, providing a way of substantializing the incommensurability of settler and Indigenous framings as a set of attributes that characterizes the latter. The inherently diminished "status" of tribes, then, appears to derive from their Indianness.

However, in this formulation, is Indian a racial category? Can it be juxtaposed to a more properly political way of designating Native peoplehood under US law? As part of developing its argument about the necessary immunity of non-Indians from tribal justice systems, *Oliphant* cites an earlier case, *Ex Parte Crow Dog* (1883), to bolster its claim about the difference that Indianness makes in the construction and operation of systems of governance, including criminal jurisdiction. In that case, federal authorities had prosecuted and convicted a Lakota man for killing another Lakota man; he appealed to the Supreme Court, arguing that the US government had no jurisdiction over Native-on-Native crime in Indian Country; and the Court found in his favor, leading to the enactment of the Major Crimes Act (1885), which formally created such jurisdiction.[22] Quoting from the Supreme Court opinion in *Ex Parte Crow Dog*, Rehnquist states that in it "the United States was seeking to extend United

States 'law, by argument and inference only, . . . over aliens and strangers; over the members of a community separated by race [and] tradition, . . . from the authority and power which seeks to impose upon them the restraints of an external and unknown code,'" and Rehnquist's quotation continues, "It tries them, not by their peers, nor by the customs of their people, nor the law of their land, but by . . . a different race, according to the law of a social state of which they have an imperfect conception."[23] *Ex Parte Crow Dog* actually found for inherent Native sovereignty, but *Oliphant* inverts that decision to illustrate that non-Indians should not be subjected to rule by "a different race" and "tradition" about which "they have an imperfect conception." More specifically, the particular way the opinion invokes *Ex Parte Crow Dog* suggests that the understanding of Indianness as a racial category crucially supplements *Oliphant*'s portrayal of tribal identity, endowing the latter with a sense of innateness and generational continuity over time that makes it impermeable/unintelligible to those who do not always-already belong while casting that belonging as something other than the exercise of full political sovereignty. To be subject to a tribe's "tradition"/"code"/"social state" entails bearing a "status" that immanently prequalifies an individual for such incorporation into the "community." The geopolitical torsions involved in narrating Indigenous peoples' "status" in relation to US jurisdiction are transposed as the inherent/racial terms of belonging to a tribe—having "status" as a member.

Although precedent at the time *Oliphant* was decided defined Indian as a *political* rather than a *racial* designation (specifically *Morton v. Mancari* [1974] and *U.S. v. Antelope* [1977]), those decisions and *Oliphant* cannot maintain such a distinction, as the two seemingly disparate kinds of categorizations fold into each other in articulating the reason for the "special" status tribes bear under the overarching sovereignty of the United States.[24] In *Morton*, non-Indian employees of the Bureau of Indian Affairs (BIA) claimed that the clause of the Indian Reorganization Act (1934) providing for Indian preferences in BIA hiring maintained an illegal and unconstitutional form of race preference. The Court found that "the preference, as applied, is granted to Indians not as a discrete racial group, but, rather, as members of quasi-sovereign tribal entities whose lives and activities are governed by the BIA in a unique fashion," adding that "the preference is reasonably and directly related to a legitimate, nonracially based goal."[25] The decision has been understood as indicating that designations of Indianness in federal law do not prima facie refer to racial identity, instead presumptively indicating a "tribal" relation.[26] *Antelope* addressed the claim by two enrolled Coeur d'Alenes that their prosecution for murder under the Major Crimes Act as Indians constituted racial discrimination. Following the precedent in *Morton*, the Court found that "federal legislation with respect to Indian tribes, although relating to Indians as such, is not based upon impermissible racial classifications," instead noting that "classifications expressly singling out Indian tribes as subjects of legislation are expressly provided for in the Constitution and supported by the ensuing history of the Federal Government's relation with Indians."[27] While opposing racial identity to tribal belonging, the concept of "tribal entities" itself fudges the question of what exact status Native peoples occupy in relation to US law. *Morton* grounds the supposed displacement of racial meaning in "the unique legal status of Indian tribes under federal law and upon the plenary power of Congress, based on a history of treaties and the assumption of a 'guardian-ward' status, to legislate on behalf of federally recognized tribes."[28] Tribes have a "legal status" that previously entailed the negotiation of diplomatic agreements having the highest constitutional status—treaties—*and* that status now licenses the exertion of virtually unlimited Congressional authority—plenary power.

Here, again, we see the legitimacy problem raised by the construction of the settler-state over existing Indigenous polities presented as a *uniqueness* that attaches to "tribes" as a "special" kind of entity within US law. However, both decisions defer the question of what defines tribal identity. If tribes are not fully sovereign polities (referred to in the decisions as "quasi-sovereign" and "once-sovereign"), what are they?[29] *Antelope* refers to "Indian tribes" as "unique aggregations." What precisely do they "aggregate"? *Antelope* speaks of the US "relation with Indians," and *Morton* invokes the federal government's "unique obligation toward the Indians."[30] In attempting to signify the kind of "entity" tribes are, all three decisions end up citing Indianness as determinative. If "tribe" names a polity, what makes that polity "special" (somehow less sovereign than the United States. and necessarily subordinated to the "overriding" authority of the latter)? The tribes' definitional Indianness partakes of something not-quite-political that must give way in the face of, in *Oliphant's* terms, the apparently self-evident "territorial sovereignty" of the United States as the polity exerting jurisdiction over Native peoples' lands. Brian L. Lewis suggests that "*Morton* and *Antelope* created a legal fiction that Indian status is not based on race or ancestry."[31] Rather than arguing that these decisions invent a "political" category for what previously had been "based on race," or conversely that "political" identification is preferable to "racial," I want to suggest that a racial imaginary grounded in heteronormative ideologies of enfamilyment crucially supplements the legal notion of *tribe* by positioning Indianness as an inherited, innate, and immutable characteristic that is not itself political in character. Racial Indianness provides a means of differentiating tribes from other populations, but in ways that do not undermine the authority of the US government to superintend them and to assert the a priori internality of Indigenous territory with respect to the settler-state—to insert tribes into the scale structure of US jurisdiction as subordinate, not fully *political* entities.

This ostensibly nonracial mobilization of racially conceived Indianness as a way of tethering tribes' authority to US sovereignty appears perhaps most insidiously in *Oliphant*'s claims about the need to protect non-Indians. More than simply recirculating a racist image of needing to save whites from the dangers of Indian savagery, the opinion develops an implicit account of what non-Indianness is that has broad ramifications for understanding the character of Native sovereignty and Indigenous political orders.[32] The opinion observes, "Protection of territory within its external boundaries is, of course, as central to the sovereign interests of the Unites States as it is to any other sovereign nation," additionally observing that "the United States has manifested an equally great solicitude that its citizens be protected by the United States from unwarranted intrusions on their personal liberty." The decision further claims, "By submitting to the overriding sovereignty of the United States, Indian tribes therefore necessarily give up their power to try non-Indian citizens of the United States except in a manner acceptable to Congress."[33] A series of transferals and translations occur here, with the Court asserting the following: the "external boundaries" of the US nation-state are clear, with Native peoples lying within them; the "sovereign interests" of that nation in such exclusive jurisdiction manifest as the "personal liberty" of its citizens; non-Indians must be insulated from "intrusion" on such liberty, because to do so, absent Congressional plenary permission, would be tantamount to refuting US sovereignty within its national borders. The concept of protection transits from US national territory to non-Indian persons, appearing as an embodied quality of the latter. As N. Bruce Duthu suggests, the decision posits a "nationality that clung like a protective cloak to these settlers."[34] It may be helpful, though, to approach non-Indian status less as a cloak than a form of innate and immutable inheritance. Rehnquist indicates that "many of the dangers that might have accompanied the exercise by tribal courts of criminal jurisdiction over non-Indians only a few decades ago have disappeared," further heightening the sense of a preexisting bodily coherence potentially *endangered* (even if less so now) by Native presence.³⁵ In this way, the decision restages the question of national territoriality as a set of extrapolitical somatic properties that the government must defend, rather than a set of legal attributes assigned by the state as part of managing/displacing the legitimacy crisis that subtends its jurisdictional claims over Indigenous peoples and political orders.

In referring to Mark David Oliphant as well as Daniel B. Belgrade, whose case was folded into the consideration of Oliphant's, the decision notes, "Both petitioners are non-Indian residents."³⁶ What does it mean to *reside* in Native territory? Or, more precisely, how is such residence emptied of significance by the decision's portrayal of non-Indianness as a constitutive *lack of relation* that defines non-Indian legal personhood as a given and unchangeable insulation from Indian spatiality?³⁷ Within the decision's logic, non-Indian persons bear their non-Indianness as an extralegal quality of which the state takes notice, particularly in *protecting* them from capture by Indian institutions. If the non-Indian body gains meaning in its difference from the Indian place it occupies, it is understood as bearing qualities or an identity that emanates from elsewhere than the space of residence and the relations and imbrications that follow from such residence. From whence does non-Indianness arise? To say that the issue is that non-Indians cannot become members of a tribe because tribal members must be Indians does not address this question, instead deferring it through the supplemental and unacknowledged citation of racial genealogy as the de facto framing principle. Seeking to provide a context for the argument that exceeds the strict language of treaties, statutes, and congressional documents, Rehnquist insists "the intricate web of judicially made Indian law, cannot be interpreted in isolation but must be read in light of the common notions of the day and the assumptions of those who drafted them."³⁸ While certainly not cited, one of those "common notions" stretching from the nineteenth century through today and given greater judicial force by *Oliphant* would be the conception of Indianness as a reproductively transmitted substance that only can be gained by birth from an Indian parent or parents.³⁹ In discussing the relation between the (re)construction of racial identity and notions of reproductive union and inheritance, of enfamilyment, Sara Ahmed addresses "the production of whiteness as a straight line rather than whiteness as a characteristic of bodies," observing, "we can talk of how whiteness is 'attributed' to bodies *as if* it were a property of bodies; one way of describing this process is to describe whiteness as a straightening device. We can ask how whiteness gets reproduced through acts of alignment, which are forgotten when we receive its line." She adds, "Genealogy itself could be understood as a straightening device, which creates the illusion of descent as a line."[40]

Non-Indianness in the decision is not described as itself a kind of racial identity (namely, whiteness), but it does appear in the decision as a form of descent. Non-Indians appear to inherit their non-Indianness in ways that precede and exceed any judicial determination, aligning the non-Indian body with other-than-Indian bodies and spaces. The non-Indian body supposedly bears such an orientation/tendency immanently rather than as a result of the *straightening* effects of the decision itself. The opinion implicitly construes the vertical line of racial lineage—the genealogical transmission of identity/belonging via chains of enfamilyment—as necessarily insulating the non-Indian from the horizontal spatiality of tribal jurisdiction. Ahmed further observes that "a white body might be barred from access to non-white bodies given the 'reachability' of such bodies: a prohibition only makes sense when something can be reached."[41] In this case, the issue is the "reachability" of non-Indian, specifically white, bodies to Native jurisdiction. In prohibiting tribal prosecution of non-Indians, the Court presents non-Indianness as if it were "a property of bodies" rather than a legal device by which to carve out zones of jurisdictional incapacity within Native political space.

This implicit heteronormative citation of racial reproduction as the means of characterizing the limits of tribal authority reciprocally contributes to defining the positive contours and content of that authority and of tribal identity itself. The positing of an exemption for non-Indians denies the territorial and geopolitical coherence of Native peoples, positioning them as less than fully sovereign and as not quite properly political entities. It does so by invoking and evoking, in the decision's language quoted earlier, "common notions" of race as reproductively transmitted, thus defining *tribe* as a "special" category. If non-Indianness is a trait that attaches to particular bodies irrespective of jurisdiction or political discourses, Indianness reciprocally attaches to bodies in a similar fashion, emanating from a reproductive process that implicitly is cast as extrapolitical and as providing the scalar core of *tribal* governance while also presenting such governance as not-quite-governance due to its fundamentally familial/reproductive/racial character. Unlike other polities understood as having a determinate territorial existence over which they exercise sovereign authority, tribes are a "unique" kind of legal entity, and if they at times exert "quasi-sovereign" powers, they ultimately have a "status" that is not "inconsistent" with US claims to "overriding sovereignty" within its "external boundaries." The decision achieves that noncontradiction by denying tribal authority over non-Indians. This insulation of the non-Indian, and attendant radical circumscription of Native governance in scope and character, appears as if it were merely a recognition of the ultimately extrapolitical character of *Indianness* as an inherited, enfamilied status. Put in Morgan's terms discussed in the previous chapter, racial reproduction lies at the *descriptive* core of Indianness even as the tribe potentially operates as a *classificatory* extension of that nonpolitical/prepolitical (set of) relation(s). The recognition of Indigenous political orders by the state, then, is pinioned to this Indianizing racial imaginary.

Delineating the Racial Enclave

The ability to determine who belongs to a polity may be the most crucial marker of its autonomy—a fundamental condition of its exercise of sovereignty and the recognition of that sovereignty by others. In enacting such self-definition, Native nations illustrate their inherent right to govern themselves and to delineate their authority. *Oliphant* understands such belonging in terms of an innate Indianness that provides the basis for distinguishing the legitimate exercise of tribal jurisdiction from unconstitutional overreach. By contrast, *Santa Clara Pueblo v. Martinez*, decided in the same session as *Oliphant*, does not rely on an evident rhetoric of Indian racial identity, and it seems to work from the assumption that Native peoples should be treated as such—as independent political entities whose organizing structures should not be superintended and regulated by the United States. Within an interpretive frame that equates racialization with racist denigration or that dichotomizes race and politics, this case appears as the opposite of *Oliphant*. However, if one attends to the ways the decision narrates federal jurisdiction, its dual emphasis on Congress's plenary power and tribes' cultural difference (especially as formulated through reference to kinship) comes to the fore. Rather than being at odds, these lines of discussion crucially supplement each other, presenting limited tribal autonomy as a gift granted by the government to Indians due to their anomalous cultural-cum-racial formations. The decision translates and manages Native political orders, but in an affirmative mode that often characterizes contemporary forms of settler power. The raciality of

Indianness as an inherited identity/status provides the grounds for operationalizing a sense of tribal difference that enables the decision to exempt tribes from usual federal principles—to affirm tribes' *specialness* in ways that also reinforce the superintending sovereignty and authority of the United States. At the conceptual heart of this apparently political account of Native nations' autonomy lies Indianness, itself a function of ideologies of enfamilyment in which it appears as a not-truly-political deviation from proper privatization: one tolerated for certain purposes by the federal government. The shadow role of the transmission of racial Indianness in giving coherence to the decision illustrates how federal recognition of tribal authority continues to tether Indigenous peoplehood to a liberal scalar imaginary, in which racializing enfamilyment marks the space of what cannot count as true governance.

The case itself concerns Santa Clara Pueblo's membership code. Passed in 1939, under a constitution adopted through the provisions of the Indian Reorganization Act (1934), it specified that the children of member fathers and nonmember mothers would be part of the community, but that the children of member mothers and nonmember fathers would not.[42] The original plaintiff, Audrey Martinez (the respondent in the Supreme Court case on appeal), was a recognized member of Santa Clara Pueblo who had married a Navajo man and whose children, who had grown up and continued to reside on the reservation, had no claims to tribal citizenship or landholding under the 1939 act. She sued to have that act declared null and void under the provisions of the Indian Civil Rights Act (ICRA). Passed in 1968, that law made most of the provisions of the Bill of Rights applicable to Native peoples, requiring that tribal governments extend these protections to their citizens.[43] Among them is the Fifth Amendment's "equal protection" clause, and Martinez sued under this provision, alleging that the Santa Clara Pueblo code violated her rights on the basis of gender. The case began in the United States District Court for the District of New Mexico, in which the justices found that the court did have jurisdiction but that the ability of the Pueblo to define its own membership was "basic to the tribe's survival as a cultural and economic entity."[44] The Court of Appeals for the Tenth Circuit also found it had jurisdiction to hear the case, but it reversed the lower court's decision, ruling that a main intent of the ICRA was to protect American Indians (who were also US citizens from 1924 onward) from the arbitrary exercise of tribal authority. Given that the distinction made by the Pueblo was based on sex, the justices held that it required greater judicial scrutiny and that the tribal interests served by the requirement did not outweigh its discriminatory impact. The Pueblo appealed that decision to the Supreme Court. Rather than ruling on the merits of Martinez's claim, though, the Court found that federal courts did not have jurisdiction to hear the case in the absence of the Pueblo's agreement to have the matter tried. The opinion argued that the ICRA included a provision for federal court oversight only with respect to habeas corpus petitions, extending more broadly to criminal prosecution, but not for what might be termed civil matters. In the absence of clear congressional intent to extend federal jurisdiction, the Pueblo's sovereign immunity from suit still holds, so even though the ICRA applies to all acts by tribal governments, possible violations of a noncriminal nature cannot be remedied through the federal court system.

The decision seems to offer a portrait of tribal autonomy that fully recognizes Native peoples' existence as polities in ways that are not dependent on the positing of an underlying (racial) Indianness; yet, the line of thought privileging inherent sovereignty seems at odds with the opinion's running reiteration of Congress's plenary power over Indian affairs.[45] The majority opinion, authored by Justice Thurgood Marshall, emphasizes the ways Native governments are separate from those of the United States. The decision quotes from earlier cases that describe tribes as "distinct, independent political communities, retaining their original natural rights" and as a "separate people, with the power of regulating their internal social relations." After indicating the ways Indigenous peoplehood precedes the Constitution, the decision finds that the ICRA had a double purpose. While "strengthening the position of individual tribal members vis-à-vis the tribe," the law "also manifest[s] a congressional purpose to protect tribal sovereignty from undue interference," so courts should be loath to "interfere with a tribe's ability to maintain itself as a culturally and politically distinct entity."[46] Yet, in equal measure, Marshall highlights Congress's plenary authority in Indian policy. Dating from *U.S. v. Kagama* (1886), this doctrine holds that essentially Congress can do whatever it will with respect to Native peoples without any of the restraints present in other aspects of US law. Not only does Marshall rehearse the narrative of this unfettered absolutism, he often invokes it in the same sentence in which he affirms tribal independence from US rule. In addition to quoting from *Kagama* early in the decision, he observes of tribes' sovereign immunity that "this aspect of tribal sovereignty, like all others, is subject to the plenary control of Congress," and in outlining why such immunity cannot be presumed to have been abrogated, he indicates the need for "a proper respect both for tribal sovereignty itself and for the plenary authority of Congress."[47] The two appear consistently yoked to each other in ways that suggest the projection of tribal authority from congressional will, but in a displaced way. Describing Native sovereignty as "the powers of local self-government," the decision immediately adds, "however, Congress has plenary authority to limit, modify, or eliminate the powers of local self-government which the tribes otherwise possess," noting that the ICRA is in part "an exercise of that authority."[48] While Native sovereignty is characterized as distinct from and anteceding US control, it structurally appears as a potentially temporary pause in the exercise of unrestricted/unrestrictable Congressional power.[49] There appears to be a direct proportion between the Court's insistence on the distinctness of Native sovereignty and the complete and utter subordination of that sovereignty to congressional whim and fiat.

Rather than being antagonistic, the Court's portraits of Native politics and US jurisdiction are interwoven and interdependent, suggesting that the term *sovereignty* means something radically different when applied to Native peoples. Marshall emphasizes the importance of "a tribe's ability to maintain itself as a culturally and politically distinct entity," but what sort of differentiation is being made through the term "distinct"?[50] While in one sense it can refer to the separateness of a tribe as its own polity not incorporated within that of the United States, a meaning toward which the decision sometimes gestures ("separate sovereigns pre-existing the Constitution"), "distinct" also can indicate an "entity" of a different sort than that of the United States. That slippage, across which tribal sovereignty is stretched, is signaled by Marshall's description of tribes as occupying an "anomalous" position within US governance.[51] They are cast as an exception to the usual dynamics of federal law, in the sense of occupying a position that crosses the threshold between law and some other kind of "entity." This placing of Native peoples within a legal limbo resonates with the assertion in decisions from that same session that certain political powers are at odds with the *status* of Indian tribes, such as in *Oliphant*.

If tribes are "distinct" yet, returning to *Santa Clara Pueblo*, not "possessed of the full attributes of sovereignty,"[52] what sort of "entity" are they? Or, put another way, how does the Court manage the logical and legitimacy crisis of US jurisdiction by presenting the autonomous governance enacted by Indigenous political orders as US engagement with the special qualities of tribes? Status is cast as being derived from the characteristics of tribes themselves rather than expressing the geopolitical torsions produced by settler colonialism. In justifying the existence of a tribal sovereignty irreducible to the will of Congress, *U.S. v. Wheeler*, decided in the same session, observes that tribes "have a significant interest in maintaining orderly relations among their members and in preserving tribal customs and traditions," and in *Santa Clara Pueblo*, Marshall notes "the often vast gulf between tribal traditions and those with which federal courts are more intimately familiar."[53] More than acknowledging the potential discrepancy between Indigenous peoples' modes of governance and those of the United States, the trope of tradition provides a content for tribe that appears to explain why it occupies an exceptional "status" within the law. If *Oliphant* emphasizes the dangers of Indian difference for criminal jurisdiction, *Santa Clara Pueblo* highlights such difference as tradition. The priorness of Native peoples binds the United States to recognize *in* the law what is not *of* the law, a kind of "entity" not fundamentally legal/governmental in character, but the production of that categorical distinction also seeks to preserve the (territorial) realm of law from mediation by the presence of tribal entities. Tradition marks tribes as a kind of collectivity that can exercise some political/legal functions, but one that is not ultimately political/legal in nature: as partaking of attributes of sovereignty but not occupying it in the ways the United States does while doing so contingently at the discretion of the United States.[54]

Given that the traditions of various tribes may differ, what do tribes share such that they all can occupy the same status? In addressing the ICRA's effort "to protect tribal sovereignty," the opinion in *Santa Clara Pueblo* observes that the law "provides that States may not assume civil or criminal jurisdiction over 'Indian country' without prior consent of the tribe,"[55] and later, Marshall reminds that the Court "repeatedly" has found that "Congress' authority over Indian matters is extraordinarily broad."[56] While the decision uses the term Indian in colloquial and somewhat commonsensical ways, the very obvious ordinariness of the concept allows it to do a great deal of uninterrogated work. Indianness binds *tribes* to each other, providing cohesion for this category in ways that allow the term tribe to indicate something other than a fully sovereign polity (or the disjunctive incoherence of settler jurisdiction itself). As in *Oliphant*, the figure of the Indian in *Santa Clara Pueblo* covers over the conceptual chasm generated by the difficulty of fitting Native peoples into the United States' own narrative of its territorial identity and jurisdictional authority. Unlike in *Oliphant*, though, here it appears in the service of affirming a tribe's jurisdictional authority, the ability of the Pueblo to set its own membership criteria (or at least not to be sued in federal court for doing so in ways that substantively violate federal law).

In light of *Santa Clara Pueblo*'s recognition of Pueblo *traditions* within a legal frame that understands itself as affirming Indian as a *political* category rather than a *racial* one, one might want to affirm the sovereignty recognized in *Santa Clara Pueblo* as a win for Native peoples. If one wanted to argue for politics over race, *Santa Clara Pueblo* could be celebrated as a rejoinder to *Oliphant*'s constriction of sovereignty. However, *Santa Clara Pueblo* is constituted out of the elements of *Oliphant*, just in a different key. *Oliphant* notably distinguishes between "Indians" and "non-Indians" rather than between Indians and whites. Reading *Santa Clara Pueblo* within that frame, the Indianness that surrounds and makes intelligible the acknowledgment of tribal sovereignty takes on a different cast. *Santa Clara Pueblo*'s insertion of tradition in the breach between the representation of US sovereignty and of Native political orders positions tradition as the kinder, gentler conceptual companion to congressional plenary power, presenting such power as a necessary corollary to the uniqueness of tribes rather than the preeminent sign of the imperial illegitimacy of settler rule.[57] Scholarly discussion of *Santa Clara Pueblo* has tended to cluster around four positions: the decision honors patriarchal tradition over the protection of women's rights; it respects tradition, or at least tribal autonomy, in ways that bolster Native sovereignty against settler imposition; it reaffirms as tradition a set of patriarchal practices largely instituted by US policy or in direct response to government mandates; and/or it accepts a dichotomy between universal rights and relative cultural distinctiveness that denies the complexity of Santa Clara Pueblo's history—the existence of multiple, changing traditions and a layered and shifting field of self-governance.[58] These approaches, though, do not examine the ways that, in the decision, the rhetorical and ideological condition of possibility for recognizing Native sovereignty is Congress's "authority to limit, modify, or eliminate [tribes'] powers of local self-government."[59] Tribe designates a kind of *entity* completely at the mercy of Congress, which can decide at what point some (set of) practice(s) denominated as "tradition" can enter into the field of politics—of/as sovereignty—from the nonpolitical sphere of social life in which it otherwise resides. The threshold the Court repeatedly posits, in *Santa Clara Pueblo* and elsewhere, for that Congressional act of will is the line between matters *internal* to the tribe and *external* to it (also at play in *Oliphant*). That distinction transposes anxiety about the topology of US jurisdiction into the process of determining the boundaries of tribal authority—or the line at which tribal cultural customs can become transmuted into (a simulation of) sovereignty.

However, while sounding like a geopolitical differential, internal/external and, thus, tribal identity in the Court's portrayal of it turns on racial Indianness and, by extension, the scalar logic provided by ideologies of enfamilyment. If *Morton v. Mancari* insists on the political character of Indianness as a designation in federal law, later cases like *Santa Clara Pueblo* create a conception of the tribe as a kind of collective entity that is defined by its inherent Indianness. More than serving as a ready-to-hand way of characterizing Indigenous polities within US law, Indianness marks the kinds of persons who can count as being inside of tribal authority (as in the demographics of jurisdiction at play in *Oliphant*). Indianness appears less as a way of designating political entities whose existence precedes and exceeds the constitutional structure of US (colonial) governance than as an immanent characteristic of certain bodies, such that tribes occupy a "special," "peculiar," "anomalous" place in US law. As Dan Gunter argues, the US government employs a "technology of tribalism" in which Native peoples "in order to obtain tribal status ... must demonstrate instead that they have a European sense of tribal identity."[60] While he is addressing the formal process a group must go through to gain status as a "federally recognized tribe," his observation is broadly applicable to the *tribalization* of peoplehood, which translates the geopolitics of indigeneity into the biopolitics of shared Indianness. The guidelines instituted by the BIA for such recognition, also adopted in 1978, testify to the circular, self-identical, and seemingly innate quality of being *Indian* that appears to precede and undergird identity as a tribe: "tribal existence" depends on, among other things, "Longstanding relationships with State governments based on the identification of a group as Indian"; "Identification as an Indian entity by anthropologists, historians, or other scholars"; "Repeated identification and dealings as an Indian entity with recognized Indian tribes"; and proof of existence as a coherent group can involve evidence of significant rates of marriage among group members.[61] One knows a tribe as such because it fits the characteristics of an "Indian entity," but more than referring to a specific (stereotypical) ensemble of elements, *Indian* here marks a conception of racialized enfamilyment. While particular qualities can be added or subtracted, they all signify as if they pointed back to a subjectivity/identity that provides a decisive and self-evident means for adjudicating who is and who is not Indian—the apparently commonsensical line between internal and external. The name given to this assemblage that makes it *not race* is *tradition*, but as argued above, tradition is inapplicable to "non-Indians," defining inside/outside in other-than-territorial terms and casting that distinction as a *unique, special, peculiar* tribal deviation from governance and law as such (meaning liberal frameworks for determining what constitute such relations).

The issue of tribal membership can occupy this not-quite-political space of *anomaly* due to its linkage to kinship, which provides a key intermediary concept between race and sovereignty. Although not directly conveying a notion of racial inheritance, and in many ways rejecting such a logic of identification by tying belonging to patrilineal descent rather than blood quantum, Santa Clara Pueblo's membership requirements that are at stake in the case link tribal identity to reproduction in ways that allow them to be read as a variation within dominant, liberal notions of family. The fact that the Pueblo's code departs from the standard of nuclear couplehood does not disqualify it from being recognized by the United States, but instead helps testify to Indian cultural *distinctiveness*. The idea that Indian identity is acquired at birth is not challenged by the Pueblo's rules: they draw on the kind of biologization at play in discourses of race without the Court having to mandate racial blood as the gradient of belonging (still implicit, though, in the accepted and a priori distinction between Indian and non-Indian). Lucy A. Curry observes, "In the arena of 'intra-tribal' matters, including membership, marriage, and family matters, tribal activities go unobstructed, whether or not the Indian involved is a member."[62] This comment suggests the ways federal law and the courts construe the tribal through reference to an Indianness that itself exceeds the specific dimensions of any given tribal polity. Indian in *Santa Clara Pueblo* continues to signify within a heteronormative nexus formed by the association of reproduction, marriage, household formation, and privacy, which provide the context for determining what kinds of persons will count for the purpose of defining tribal *internality*—for drawing the line between inside and outside and thus defining the kind of population to which *tribes* belong such that they can have institutionalized forms of tradition distinct from other forms of US-recognized law.

The previous choice by Santa Clara Pueblo to limit membership to the children of Santa Clara Pueblo fathers may have functioned for the Pueblo as an act of self-determination in the shaping of their own governance, potentially breaking from a dominant Euro-American model based on bilateral inheritance and the (apparent) separation of lineage from political status. However, from the perspective of the US settler-state, this arrangement still enables citizenship in the Pueblo to be conceptualized as an extension of lineage and domesticity, in ways trying to include non-Indians or to extend jurisdiction over them cannot. My argument, then, is not about whether the United States should allow for tribes to have diverse, and possibly illiberal, membership requirements but about the ways such requirements remain contingent on a racializing imaginary that provides the condition of intelligibility and legitimacy for them from the perspective of US law—whether or not blood quantum is the basis for belonging. Indianness here is not directly coupled with a transmission of racial blood, but the version of tradition for which *Santa Clara Pueblo* makes allowance also remains within the bounds of such racial identification. While this ideological framework acknowledges a version of Native difference, it is interpellated within Euro-American ideologies of enfamilyment rather than appearing as an alternative model of governance at odds with (rather than encompassed within) US sovereignty. Tradition gets (re)coded as an extension of the ultimately private sphere of sexuality (family, parentage, inheritance) that then is given limited political efficacy as tribal sovereignty by Congress.

This translation of Indigenous political orders as modes of racial lineage constructs an ostensibly obvious internality (for the tribe and the nation-state) that is crucial to the jurisdictional geography of the United States. The possibility of Native sovereignty not entirely superintended, regulated, bounded, and ordered around the plenary will of Congress appears impossible in *Santa Clara Pueblo*, despite the decision's apparent endorsement of tribal autonomy. While none of the three decisions from the 1978 session that I've discussed (*Oliphant, U.S. v. Wheeler, Santa Clara Pueblo*) address racial identity per se, all of them rely on *Indianness*. One could argue that Indian is inherently a racial category and that its use enacts modes of racialization regardless of whether "race" explicitly is invoked as such. This claim often works as a way of calling on the Court to refuse to employ racist stereotypes of Native peoples or, instead, to focus on tribes as (semi)sovereign polities rather than as members of a racial group.[63] This line of critique seems to miss the stakes of the settler-state's racialization—or, more to the point, biopolitical interpellation—of Native peoples as a population whose definition is tethered to racial reproduction. The call to choose politics over race—the framing in *Morton v. Mancari*—seems redundant or irrelevant in engaging *Santa Clara Pueblo*. The decision already seems to have divorced race from politics and chosen the latter as its frame.

However, this dichotomy displaces the ways that Indianness functions less as a marker for racial inferiority than as an ideological placeholder for the ultimately non-(geo)political character of tribes that supposedly explains their unique "status." The matrix of Indianness enacts a mode of primitive accumulation in translating Indigenous political orders as collections of equivalently racialized members whose belonging depends on reproductive genealogy. Enfamilyment provides the race-making ideological framework in which Indianness gains coherence as a category that could provide a basis for differentiating and affirming the *tribe* as a separate and unique kind of entity under US law—one whose *traditions* can gain limited legal purchase over other Indians but whose character ultimately must be subordinated to the principles of liberal governance that provide the true basis for, in Morgan's terms, political society.

Families as Culture and Futurity

The Indian Child Welfare Act (ICWA), enacted in 1978, has been hailed as a victory for Native peoples in seeking acknowledgment of their inherent right to self-governance and redress for the ongoing effects of a history of genocidal policies designed to eliminate tribal existence as such.[64] The law's passage was a response to the astronomical rates of states' social service interventions in Native families and of Native children's adoption by non-natives, including a rate of adoption twenty times the national average and the fact that one-quarter to one-third of Native children were taken from their families.[65] In keeping with the overall tenor of the "era of self-determination," as announced by President Nixon in 1970,[66] Congress sought to remedy this most current instantiation of persistent patterns and projects of displacement in which generations of Indigenous youth had been alienated from their peoples in various ways, all justified as supposedly for their betterment and in their best interests. The statute gives tribes exclusive jurisdiction over all child custody proceedings for Indian children domiciled in Indian Country, gives tribes the right of refusal for jurisdiction in such proceedings for Native children outside of Indian Country, puts in place tribal notification requirements and procedures in cases where Indian children are involved, creates greater protections for Indian parents against termination of their parental rights, requires that states use tribally set priorities for foster care and adoptive placement, and provides a set of placement priorities absent the indication of tribal preferences.⁶⁷ While the act has been attacked as adopting an unconstitutionally race-based scheme, its defenders argue that it falls squarely within Congress's authority over Indian affairs and that its application to Indians (pace *Morton v. Mancari*) turns on their political status as members of tribal entities rather than their belonging to a racial group. Both of these claims persistently have been supported by courts at all levels.⁶⁸ However, in linking tribal sovereignty to "family," and offering a narrative of tribal identity as a "cultural" affiliation that follows from genealogical connection, the law ties Indigenous self-determination to Indianness, understood in implicitly reproductive terms. The law's alignment of indigeneity with de facto liberal conceptions of lineage helps further the construction of Native peoplehood as a kind of racialized exception within US law while also reinforcing the necessary role of ideologies of enfamilyment in the scale structure of Indigenous governance—a framing that inadvertently opens toward arguments about various ways Indianness can become generationally attenuated.

The legislation frames itself as an effort to respond to difficulties faced by tribes, particularly seeking to thwart intrusions by others into a vital area of tribal life. In its listing of congressional findings that provides the context for the statute, ICWA states, "Congress, through statutes, treaties, and the general course of dealing with Indian tribes, has assumed the responsibility for the protection and preservation of Indian tribes and their resources" (2.2), and it also indicates that "an alarmingly high percentage of Indian families are broken up by the removal, often unwarranted, of the children from them by nontribal public and private agencies and that an alarmingly high percentage of such children are placed in non-Indian foster and adoption homes and institutions" (2.5). As opposed to trying to eliminate tribes' existence, the official policy of the US government during both the allotment (1887–1934) and termination (1948–1970) periods, Congress has the duty of *protecting* and *preserving* Indian tribes as such. Since "there is no resource that is more vital to the continued existence and integrity of Indian tribes than their children" (2.3), the government must act to undo the "alarming" actions by various agencies that work to dismantle tribes in slow motion through the seizure of their children and placement of them in non-Indian settings. Beyond acknowledging the primary jurisdiction of tribes over such matters in Indian Country (101.a), the law makes clear that in proceedings conducted by states with respect to children domiciled elsewhere that the child's tribe has "a right to intervene at any point in the proceeding" (101.c). Moreover, the field of potential caregivers, and the priorities among them, should conform to "the law or custom of the Indian child's tribe" (4.2; 105.c), and the act expands the definition of those who have standing in a parent-like relation to include the "Indian custodian," meaning "any Indian person who has legal custody of an Indian child under tribal law or custom" (4.6). Cumulatively, these provisions indicate Congress's intention to affirm and extend tribes' ability to operate as self-determining entities with respect to children who are members or are "eligible for membership" (4.4), pegging Indianness to official criteria for citizenship adopted by the Native nation in question, with the caveat that since children have no choice over enrollment the presumption should be in favor of tribal belonging if they are not members at the time of the judicial proceedings but fit the tribe's criteria for membership. ICWA further enables tribes to reclaim jurisdiction that had been transferred to the states via Public Law 280 during the termination era. Passed in 1953, that act gave six states complete civil and criminal jurisdiction over tribes within their boundaries, except for a few named exceptions, and was a vital part of the broader effort to remove federal funding and recognition from Native peoples.[69] ICWA authorizes "any Indian tribe which became subject to State jurisdiction pursuant to the provisions" of Public Law 280, "or pursuant to any other Federal law," to "resume jurisdiction over child custody proceedings" through petitioning the Secretary of the Interior (108.a), and the act also provides criteria for consideration of such petitions (108.b.1.a).

However, if Congress seeks to indicate its commitment to affirming, preserving, protecting, and supporting the *self-determination* of Indigenous peoples on land claimed by the United States, why carve out only this limited exception to the prior transferal of jurisdiction to the states? Why not simply repeal Public Law 280 and similar acts or make their provisions optional for tribes?[70] The focus on Native families enables an implicit account of tribal identity and sovereignty that orients away from the kinds of knotty tensions around jurisdiction, Indigenous territoriality, and political legitimacy (such as those running through *Oliphant*). As noted above, ICWA indicates that it applies only to Indians as members of tribes or as potentially eligible members, rather than as a racial group, and this approach correlates with the logic of the decisions in *Morton* and in *Santa Clara Pueblo*. When speaking of tribal belonging, jurisdiction, and prerogatives in the child custody process, the law often employs language in a different register than that usually used to designate matters of citizenship and the scope and character of political sovereignty. In chastising the states, it notes that their "administrative and judicial bodies" often have "failed to recognize the essential tribal relations of Indian people and the cultural and social standards prevailing in Indian communities and families" (2.5). This phrasing is repeated later in the discussion of how to set priorities for placement, indicating that court decisions should reflect the "prevailing social and cultural standards of the Indian community in which the parent or extended family resides or with which the parent or extended family members maintain social and cultural ties" (105.d). While "tribal relations" might simply refer to relations among members of a tribe and with the tribal government, it seems to bear a different meaning than tribes' acts of governance as political entities. Instead, it comprises "standards" and "ties" of a nature that the law implies usually would be beyond the ken of state courts but that need to be attended to in this instance due to the particular population involved. As with *Oliphant*'s juxtaposition of "social and religious pressure" with "formal judicial processes," or *Santa Clara Pueblo*'s reference to the need to protect "tribal traditions" that hold an "anomalous" place with US law, the use of the phrase "social and cultural" in ICWA marks something other than that which normally enters the field of properly "administrative and judicial" consideration. The acknowledgment of such "relations" is part of an attempt to reckon with and "reflect the unique values of Indian culture" (3). "Culture" and "community" designate a kind of tribal entity that the United States has the duty to *protect* and *preserve*, and the accession to tribal wishes with respect to children is central to doing so.

The designation of tribal jurisdiction and decision-making criteria as *uniquely* Indian resonates with characterizing recognition of Native policy determinations as part of "the special relationship between the United States and the Indian tribes" (2), suggesting that engagement with tribes marks a "special" exception to the usual structure of US law and legal geography. ICWA transposes Native polities' exertion of authority over their citizens and effort to protect them from various modes of settler intervention and invasion into the expression of Indianness, as a set of qualities and inclinations that attaches to particular "communities and families." One might interpret a phrase like "social and cultural" as trying to designate forms of political relation not usually understood as such within US legal discourses, thereby terminologically seeking to encompass and give legal force in state courts to exertions of Indigenous sovereignty that might otherwise be treated as extraneous to judicial determinations. The language of ICWA, then, could be read as indexing a process of translation whereby modes of governance that do not conform to the framework of liberalism get (mis)apprehended as "culture," as opposed to the exercise of political sovereignty.[71]

However, the fact that the act repeatedly characterizes the enacting of Native peoplehood as the retention of "culture" and "community," and then further ties the latter to family formation as the privileged sphere of transmission/realization, casts Indianness in its *social* and *cultural* dimensions as a function of biological reproduction, as emanating from a sphere not itself political but that should be acknowledged due to the "special" connection between the United States and tribes. This depiction of Indigenous peoples as having a "unique" form of sociality that inheres in "families" functions as the flip side to the broader privatizing nuclear conception of family at play in US legal and popular discourses. The specialness of Native communities and culture arises out of an implicit, and implicitly invidious, comparison to the nuclear family form, which serves as the de facto norm. The genealogical relations that supposedly made Native peoples "unique" are rendered as a tribal version of family—an expression of the kind of kinship imaginary discussed in the previous chapter. This depiction reinforces a heteronormative frame of reference in which such relations are tied to biological reproduction, thereby casting them as occupying a social sphere distinct/different from that of politics per se.

Although the (dis)placement of Native children certainly has served as a major vehicle for settler projects of assimilation, dispossession, and detribalization, and the insistence on tribal authority over childcare does seek to redress that (ongoing) history,[72] positioning childcare as the principal means of defining indigeneity aligns and justifies Native jurisdiction as a form of genealogical preservation, instead of presenting control over matters concerning children as merely part and parcel of Native peoples' legitimate exercise of authority as polities. The law makes clear that tribes can set virtually whatever priorities they wish for child placement.[73] However, the statute designates that authority through the phrase "extended family member," which "shall be defined by the law or custom of the Indian child's tribe," but "in the absence of such law or custom" the phrase is taken to mean an adult "who is the Indian child's grandparent, aunt or uncle, brother or sister, brother-in-law or sister-in-law, niece or nephew, first or second cousin, or stepparent" (4.2). The presumptive model is the nuclear family form, with relatives radiating outward from the unit of the marital couple and their children as the axiomatic core. The terms used here seem to treat that pattern as the universally referential basis for defining familial connection, despite the fact that in many forms of Native sociality persons share the same familial title who do not occupy the same position within the Euro-American genealogical grid (where one's "mother" and "mother's sister," or "aunt," are referred to by the same term, for example). In addition, the "family" does not appear to have any political function, despite the historical and in many places continuing role of corporate entities in Native governance and policy-setting (as discussed in chapter 1). In this way, the act implicitly preserves the distinction between the familial and the governmental that is one of the constitutive features of liberal statehood. Whatever *culture* and *community* might entail, then, they seem to be bound to a set of "tribal relations" de facto understood as circulating around the family unit, heteronormatively conceived, as the site for the manifestation and perpetuation of Indian *uniqueness*.

Culture, then, does similar work to race in positioning indigeneity as a set of relations that follows from the procreative transmission of Indianness. This configuration of how to *protect* and *preserve* Indian tribes specifically does not pose a challenge to the continuing insistence of the settler-state on its unquestionable authority over what is cast as its domestic space. In elaborating its aims and their validity, ICWA lists as its first item that "Congress has plenary power over Indian affairs" (2.1).[74] As discussed earlier, this idea is tied in *Oliphant*, *Santa Clara Pueblo*, and earlier court decisions to the self-evidence of national boundaries and the supposedly necessary corollary that the federal government must have "overriding sovereignty" in that space. A dialectic emerges in and around ICWA in which culture and its correlates seek to name something that exceeds the administrative scope of, and differs in content from, US political and legal processes with respect to non-natives. That difference, though, is cast as only realized through family in ways that allow whatever *culture* might name to be presented as commensurate with the self-evidence of congressional superintendence of Indigenous peoples as "dependent communities."[75] "Culture" coordinates with "family," the former gaining its explanatory force from its linkage to the latter. In providing an apparently nonpolitical basis around which to collect and define cultural difference, enfamilyment offers a mode of inherited distinction that does not appear to be about racial identity.[76] Moreover, Indianness-as-cultural-difference can be scaled up from an immanent quality attached to particular individuals to encompass a "tribal entity." As an enfamilied legal fiction, *culture* constellates with *race* as related (and often intertwined) means of articulating Indianness as something reproduced and transmitted generationally in ways that can surrogate for indigeneity—the geopolitics of self-determination as peoples and political orders.

That process of translation can be seen in the House of Representatives report that preceded the passage of the act (often cited in scholarly and judicial discussions of the law), *Mississippi Band of Choctaw Indians v. Holyfield* (1989), and *Adoptive Couple v. Baby Girl* (2013), all of which point toward tendencies present within the act itself.[77] The House report insists, "The wholesale separation of Indian children from their families is perhaps the most tragic and destructive aspect of American Indian life today." However, in articulating the nature of the destruction wrought by that mass alienation, the report observes, "In judging the fitness of a particular family, many social workers, ignorant of Indian cultural values and social norms, make decisions that are wholly inappropriate in the context of Indian family life and so they frequently discover neglect or abandonment where none exists," adding, "Many social workers, untutored in the ways of Indian family life or assuming them to be socially irresponsible, consider leaving the child with persons outside the nuclear family as neglect and thus as grounds for terminating parental rights." The systemic pattern—"wholesale separation"—appears here to be due to social worker ignorance and prejudice. They have a notion of proper childcare modeled on "the nuclear family," described elsewhere in the report as "a white, middle-class standard," and that orientation blinds them to other possibilities for family and household formation. The issue is one of failed "cultural" awareness, an inability to recognize extant "values" and "norms" in particular communities—a specifically *Indian* way of ordering "family life."[78] From this perspective ICWA will force state workers and institutions to acknowledge and respect those patterns.

On what basis, though, will it do so? The report invokes Congress's "plenary power" and its "broad, unique powers with respect to Indian tribes," indicating the federal legislature's right to make rules for tribes based on their *special* relationship to the US government. In articulating this authority, it also cites *U.S. v. Kagama* and *U.S. v. Nice*, Supreme Court decisions from the late nineteenth and early twentieth centuries that cast Native peoples as *dependents* whose need for protection (especially from the states) licenses federal actions and exceptions on their behalf.[79] Furthermore, defending the choice to include children who are eligible to be tribal members under the act, rather than solely those who already are members, the report asserts, "Blood relationship is the very touchstone of a person's right to share in the cultural and property benefits of an Indian tribe." In this way, the "values" and "norms" that the legislation is meant to protect appear as themselves a function of a "blood" relation, which provides the "touchstone" for the "cultural" bond that defines belonging to a tribe. This emphasis on a nexus of culture, family, and blood, though, arises despite the report's documentation of the ways the seizure of Indian children usually occurs "without due process of law" and is lubricated through pressure by welfare agencies on whom Native people rely for "survival."[80] Such tracking of the jurisdictional violence of states' exertion of control over Native citizens and lands and the impoverishing effects of prior and ongoing settler policies of intervention and appropriation does not lead to an analysis of the need for a broad-based engagement with Indigenous sovereignty and self-determination. Rather, it confirms "the special problems and circumstances of Indian families and the legitimate interest of the Indian tribe in preserving and protecting the Indian family," reaffirming the jurisdictional placeholder of specialness and pegging its content to "the Indian family" as the scalar core of tribal existence.[81]

In *Holyfield*, the Supreme Court also displaces the issue of Indigenous self-determination in favor of affirming the importance of engaging with enfamilied Indian cultural inclinations. The case concerns the question of whether the Mississippi Choctaw tribal court has primary jurisdiction over the placement of two children who were born off-reservation to tribal members who reside on the reservation and who specifically arranged before the birth for the children to be adopted by a non-Indian couple. The central issue is what constitutes "domicile" for the purposes of the act. In arguing that the children were domiciled on the reservation (despite never having been physically present there) for the purposes of jurisdiction, thus finding that the Choctaw court did have authority in determining custody, the decision rejects the idea that domicile could be dependent on each state's own precedents. Rather, the Court finds that Congress sought to impose a uniform federal principle specifically in order to shield Indian affairs from the states' interests and invidious intrusions. That intent to protect tribal autonomy extends to Native nations' relation to their own citizens: "Tribal jurisdiction . . . was not meant to be defeated by the actions of individual members of the tribe, for Congress was concerned not solely about the interests of Indian children and families, but also about the impact on the tribes themselves of the large numbers of Indian children adopted by non-Indians."[82] Thus, the opinion articulates what scholars have characterized as a tribe's interest in the welfare of its children as part of its maintenance of itself as a viable collectivity, as well as the attendant need to distinguish "tribal jurisdiction" from that of the states without subjecting the former to the rules, definitions, and qualifications found in the laws of the latter.[83] Further, the decision quotes from the testimony before Congress of Calvin Isaac (tribal chief of the Mississippi Band of Choctaw Indians) in the hearings prior to ICWA's passage, in which he says of the taking of Native children by state agencies, "these practices seriously undercut the tribes' ability to continue as self-governing communities. Probably, in no area is it more important that tribal sovereignty be respected than in an area as socially and culturally determinative as family relationships."[84] His comments frame Native nations' jurisdiction in child welfare as part of the larger project of Indigenous self-governance, justifying it on that basis and condemning state intervention for its attenuation of that broader sovereignty. In citing Chief Isaac's argument, the Court implicitly endorses this understanding of the legitimacy and aims of the law.

At other moments, though, *Holyfield* makes the matter less about Indigenous self-determination than a legislatively mandated process designed to avoid endemic misinterpretations. The opinion approvingly quotes the following from a decision on ICWA by the Supreme Court of Utah: "The protection of this tribal interest is at the core of ICWA, which recognizes that the tribe has an interest in the child which is distinct from but on a parity with the interest of the parents. This relationship between Indian tribes and Indian children domiciled on the reservation finds no parallel in other ethnic cultures found in the United States. It is a relationship that many non-Indians find difficult to understand and that non-Indian courts are slow to recognize." The question of "domicile," and thus of the territoriality of Native sovereignty and the relation between Indigenous governance and land, becomes the expression of an "ethnic culture," exhibiting a uniqueness ("no parallel") that itself needs to be respected. Why, though? This statement implies that non-Indians act in ways that illustrate a lack of comprehension of Indian culture and do damage based on that misunderstanding. *Holyfield* confirms this perspective in finding that "it is clear that Congress' concern over the placement of Indian children in non-Indian homes was based in part on evidence of the detrimental impact on the children themselves of such placements outside their culture."[85] The right of tribes to self-governance found in Chief Isaac's statement, presumably based on their status as Indigenous political orders whose existence precedes and exceeds that of the settler government established around and over them, morphs into the need for children to maintain a continuity of "culture" lest they face the "detrimental" effects of a disorienting shift into non-Indian social life. This formulation stages the law as primarily protecting a kind of enfamilied structure due to the *specialness* of Indians, presenting Indianness as transmitted within the scene of "extended" family relations.

This very sense of Indianness as a quality that inheres in families becomes the guiding logic of *Adoptive Couple v. Baby Girl* in ways that efface entirely the question of Native sovereignty at play in *Holyfield*. The case is about the daughter of a man who is a citizen of the Cherokee Nation; her mother put her up for adoption to a couple from South Carolina. The man had waived his parental rights, but under what he asserted were false pretenses, namely that the baby would be raised by the biological mother. In addition, on documents sent to the Cherokee Nation by the adoptive couple, the biological father's name was misspelled and an incorrect birth date was given, so the Cherokee Nation asserted that he was not a citizen, allowing the adoption to proceed. Rather than commenting on the numerous, grievous procedural errors that occurred in the process of the adoption, or what lower courts had found to be the explicit effort of the adoptive couple's lawyers to obfuscate the issue of Native national citizenship in order to facilitate the adoption,[86] the Supreme Court's majority decision focuses on the racial limits of Cherokeeness and the question of what constitutes familial attachment. In the first sentence of the opinion, Justice Alito notes that the case "is about a little girl ... who is classified as an Indian because she is 1.2% (3/256) Cherokee," at the end describing her relation to Indianness as "a remote one" despite her father's enrollment as a Cherokee citizen.[87] These statements frame the issue of Native identity, or of belonging to the Cherokee people in particular, as about relative amounts of inherited Indian racial substance transmitted through heteronuclear lineage. The percentage clearly is meant to suggest that the girl has too little Indian blood meaningfully to count as Native, an insinuation that effaces not only the specificities of citizenship in the Cherokee Nation of Oklahoma in particular (defined by lineal descent from anyone on the Dawes Rolls), but also the sense of Native nations as distinct political orders rather than as aggregations of racially enfamilied persons.[88] In addition, the decision continually returns to ICWA's stated aim of preventing the "breakup of the Indian family," which serves as the unit for "preserv[ing] the cultural identity and heritage of Indian tribes." The Court claims that since the biological father "*never* had custody of the Indian child," the law's goal "to stem the unwarranted removal of Indian children from intact Indian families" is not relevant in this case.[89] The legal scope and character of

Native peoples' sovereignty fades entirely from view, replaced by a sense of racial Indianness presented as too attenuated to constitute an "Indian family" and, thus, be the bearer of "cultural identity."

When confronting critics' portrayal of ICWA as a constitutionally suspect use of racial criteria, defenders of the law have emphasized its enactment of a mode of political recognition. As I have been suggesting, however, such a reading underexamines the deep ambivalence in the law itself (and in the surrounding supportive legislative and judicial explanations of it) about the status of Native peoples. Specifically, supporters overlook the ways the attempt to manage the jurisdictional and ethical conundrums posed by the geopolitics of the settler-state, and to acknowledge the existence of Native peoples as autonomous political orders, gets displaced onto *family* and *culture* as cross-referencing, not-quite-political vehicles of Indianness. Family serves as the normalized vehicle for transmitting Indianness, understood both as race and culture in ways that are interwoven, and this process of enfamilyment provides a means of transposing indigeneity into the scale structures of liberal governance. Even as policies like ICWA underline the supposed specialness and uniqueness of tribes, they frame Indianness as a congressionally acknowledged kind of difference that attaches to a particular racial lineage, rather than engaging Indigenous peoplehood as preceding and exceeding US jurisdiction and, thus, not reducible to the categories, principles, and superintendence of the settler-state. The figuration of family serves as a vehicle through which to recast Indigenous political orders as an exceptional (distended) private sphere countenanced by the federal government in extraconstitutional ways. This very issue at play in the legislation, as well as contemporary Indian policy writ large, is what enables legal assaults on ICWA like the "existing Indian family exception" and the more recent challenge to it as unconstitutionally "commandeering" the states, which both understand the law as a limited and exceptional grant of federal authority rather than an acknowledgment within US law of the prior and inherent self-determination of Indigenous peoples as distinct political orders.[90]

To be clear, I'm not suggesting that ICWA *really* is racial rather than political, as its detractors suggest, nor am I downplaying the significance of the law given current policy conditions and dynamics—including the continuing existence of rates of Native child seizure that rival those prior to ICWA's passage.[91] If measured in terms of a *race* versus *politics* binary, ICWA would seem to fit firmly in the second category. The law, however, also relies on a dominant understanding of Native identity figured in reproductive terms, even if not in the more evidently racializing ways *Oliphant* does. Instead, "culture" and "community" serve as the gradients for assessing, affirming, and protecting Native distinctness and continuity, and in developing these ways of indexing indigeneity, ICWA foregrounds what might be termed kinship as the matrix through which to determine the boundaries of Nativeness. Representing Native peoples through the prism of enfamilyment, though, does not so much repudiate the principles of *Oliphant* as supplement them. ICWA produces a vision of Indigenous belonging still based on calculating *Indian* descent, segregating the content and determination of such enfamilied genealogical relation from the sphere of politics proper. Although perhaps more capacious, and certainly less dismissive, this approach to Indian policy shares in the kind of heteronormative and racializing orientation guiding *Oliphant*.

Feminist Remappings of Scale and Relation

Oliphant, Santa Clara Pueblo, and ICWA illustrate how the recognition of Native polities by the federal government depends on their figuration through the prism of Indianness. As the site of racial reproduction and the transmission of cultural forms, which are seen as attaching to lineage and as distinct from the dynamics of political institutions, the family serves as the core unit around which notions of *tribal* identity and jurisdiction turn. It provides a form through which Indigenous political orders can be converted into or made semi-compatible with liberal conceptions of political scale. Inasmuch as the tribe consists of a collection of families and those families themselves are figured in ways consistent with privatizing and racializing liberal ideologies, tribal governance can be seen as itself built out of localized exceptions made by the federal government for collectives ultimately defined by their Indianness, rather than conceptualizing Indigenous governance as legitimately enacting processes of self-organization and exercising forms of authority that precede and exceed settler superintendence due to their indigeneity. Native feminist work, though, marks and contests this mode of racializing liberal primitive accumulation (as discussed in the introduction). Such work offers alternative ways of understanding the character, contours, and complex dynamics of Indigenous political orders. More than pointing to the heteropatriarchal investments that orient much of what is taken as politics within dominant frameworks, Native feminists illustrate how the division of the familial from the governmental has functioned and continues to function as a means of effacing Indigenous philosophies and modes of worldmaking. That attention to the absence of a clearly defined private sphere also opens toward an engagement with the everydayness of governance, the ways it immanently emerges through ordinary dynamics that are not cordoned off into specialized institutions marked by their separation from the spaces of quotidian self- and community-making. As opposed to a vision of scale as differentiating and hierarchical, as concentric spheres in which jurisdictional units at the same level are envisioned as isolated from each other, Native feminist work understands scale as a mode of relation, as processes of networked imbrication rather than centralized spheres of ranked authority.

Contemporary federal recognition of tribal governance, and the construction of the legal entity that is the *Indian tribe*, depends on the representation of the heteronuclear family as the extrapolitical unit around which tribal political authority coheres. As in dominant liberal ideologies in the United States, the family appears as prior to and beyond the sphere of politics while also serving as its normative core, as seen in the decisions and statutes discussed earlier in this chapter. That dynamic can be traced back at least to the implementation of the Indian Reorganization Act (IRA). Passed in 1934, that law ended the allotment regime that had dominated Indian policy for the prior half century (since the passage of the General Allotment Act—or Dawes Act—in 1887), in which the goal of federal policy had been to break up Native territories into land privately held by nuclear families, to endow those receiving such allotments with citizenship, and to cease to recognize tribes as collective bodies.[92] In replacing allotment policy, the IRA sought to stem the tide of land loss and to acknowledge Native self-governance, albeit in forms that reflected extant liberal frameworks.[93] In "Powers of Indian Tribes," an opinion issued in the wake of the passage of the IRA that sets out the framework for Native self-governance that is largely still operative to this day, the Solicitor General of the Interior Department actually cites the practice of matrimonial management as exemplary of the nature of Native jurisdiction: "The powers of an Indian tribe in the administration of justice derive from the substantive powers of self-government which are legally recognized to fall within the domain of tribal sovereignty. If an Indian tribe has power to regulate the marriage relationships of its members, it necessarily has power to adjudicate, through tribunals established by itself controversies involving such relationships. So, too, with other fields of local government."[94] "Marriage relationships" appear as both a crucial site and sign of tribal jurisdiction while also taking shape around forms of relation that are envisioned as essentially not governmental in nature. The marriage contract is a form that stands outside of tribal sovereignty as such but on which it can act "to regulate" such relations—presumably so as to ensure the proper performance of enfamilyment.[95]

As against the notion of the marital unit as the basis for family life, itself conceived as existing in an extrapolitical (or prepolitical) private sphere, Native feminists highlight the colonial dynamics at play in imposing heteronormative structures and the ways such ideologies efface (or seek to replace) other constellations of relatedness that serve vital functions within Indigenous political orders. One way that such forms often have been described is as "clans," a characterization that from the nineteenth century onward has cast these social units as precapitalist extensions of a de facto norm of nuclear homemaking. However, when viewed not as a substitute or evolutionary precursor to the liberal family, the kinds of configuration translated in English as clans instead can be seen as modes of governance that do not obey the supposedly foundational distinction between familial and political domains. The Haudenosaunee (or Iroquois) Confederacy offers perhaps the most well-known example of this pattern. Each of the six nations that comprise the Confederacy have a specified number of clan-chosen chiefs, and each of those nations has its own separate internal set of clan-chosen leaders. Clan belonging occurs through matrilineal lines, and clan-mothers, the leaders of the clans, are the ones who choose clan-based leaders for the nation and for the larger Confederacy.[96] This structure of governance is precisely the sort targeted by settler policies, in both the United States and Canada, designed to reorganize Indigenous polities to make them consistent with liberal principles of enfamilyment, including the atomization of Indigenous collective processes into heteropatriarchal households and the attendant reformulation of what constitutes Native governance to make it more amenable to state initiatives. As Theresa McCarthy shows with regard to the Six Nations of the Grand River, not only did the Indian Act (1876) impose patriarchal lineage requirements for band membership, the Canadian government in 1924 forcefully imposed an elective band council system to replace the Confederacy.[97] McCarthy notes that for Haudenosaunee peoples, matrilineal clans link them to "extended family networks that transcend the boundaries of our nations. Our clans are the basic building blocks and the working bodies of this governance structure." She further observes that Haudenosaunee languages are verb-based, rather than noun-based like English, and that the word Haudenosaunee itself translates as "they build a house," which "has less to do with building static physical structures than it does with building dynamic relationships among the people who inhabit the metaphorical Longhouse": "'Extending the rafters' is a related expression, which refers to our ability to elongate this structure; to incorporate and accommodate new relatives, including those of diverse backgrounds and outlooks."[98] While describing the clans as "extended family networks," in ways that seem consistent with the kinds of categorization at play in Lewis Henry Morgan's work, the discussion of how they operate pushes against and undoes the conventional notion of family (and most non-native conceptions of kinship), including as that idea operates in Indian policy.

In addition to their vital role as the central units of intranational and Confederacy governance, clans serve as ways of forging relations, and those relations are the stuff of political process and sovereignty. As opposed to the vision of family as insular, producing self-contained units whose purpose is sustaining members in ways that are disjunct from political institutions, Haudenosaunee clans provide the principles and framework through which connections are made at all scales. As a mode of inhabitance that accommodates numerous groups of what in liberal terms would be described as families, linking them as part of a shared collective, the Longhouse conceptually anchors the political infrastructure of Haudenosaunee nations and the Confederacy while offering a vision of capacious possibility ("extending the rafters") in which "new relatives" of various kinds can be brought into the household, nation, and Confederacy. This scalar imaginary differs greatly from one organized around the heteronuclear reproduction of Indianness as an inborn characteristic, in which the racial transmission enacted through familial lineage generates kinds of persons who could be the subject of tribal authority (itself pegged by the state to immanent Indianness). As McCarthy observes, "Haudenosaunee clan-based knowledge has withstood efforts to reduce our nationhood to the racial constructs perpetuated by settler national-states," and she adds that "in order to turn away from colonial structures, there must be something to turn to."[99] As articulated within modes of state recognition, such as in *Santa Clara Pueblo* and ICWA, Indianness emerges as a function of racial reproduction rather than robustly engaging with Indigenous political orders in which social reproduction does not exist in a separate sphere from the principles and processes that shape—and are—the work of governance. Like the Dakota tiospaye discussed in chapter 1, the Haudenosaunee clan illustrates the limits of a vision of indigeneity explicitly or implicitly grounded in the heteronuclear household—the ostensibly extrapolitical race-making unit of the Indian family.

Native feminist scholars further have traced the ways that articulating Indigenous peoplehood through the liberal matrix of enfamilyment often perpetrates structural violence against Indigenous people. Taking up the frames of colonial recognition can animate and legitimize heteropatriarchal ideologies of personhood and social organization that require the exertion of control over women, the pathologization (and often criminalization) of non-heteronuclear kinds of relationships, and the imposition of rigid gender norms through which all Indigenous persons are subjected to various kinds of discipline. While the circumstances of pre-annexation Hawai'i certainly differ from those of contemporary Native nations in the Lower 48, J. Kēhaulani Kauanui's critique of nineteenth-century Kanaka 'Ōiwi (Native Hawaiian) governance, and of contemporary efforts to celebrate it as a model for independent nationhood, provides useful analytical tools for considering the stakes of discourses of enfamilyment for Indigenous peoples in the present.[100] She argues that "Hawaiian people can refuse recolonization by resisting the allure of state sovereignty models as they are inextricably linked to the ongoing pulverizing of Indigenous worldviews and lifeways," and she notes that under the Hawaiian Kingdom, when it faced escalating imperial pressures from the United States and European powers, legal changes were made in order to make Hawaiian sovereignty intelligible to those imperial forces: "The major reorganization of social forms as a strategy to fight Western racism through independent nationhood necessitated a racist transformation of the Indigenous polity."[101] Those changes involved radical limitation and reorganization of extant Kanaka notions and practices of moʻokūʻauhau (genealogy), including the institution of patriarchal modes of marriage, displacement of women from political processes, attempts to eliminate polygamy and polyandry, privatization of land, and disavowal of same-sex erotic relationships.[102] Kauanui illustrates how these institutionalized alterations in Kanaka socialities were part of an effort to remake Hawai'i "in ways conducive to being acknowledged as civilized within the Family of Nations," thus enabling Hawaiians to be seen "as rightful rulers of themselves."[103] This alteration can be understood as "racist" due to its reliance on extant Euro-American notions of non-Western social forms as "savagery."

These changes work toward constructing a liberal distinction between the self-enclosed family and governance, which is understood as occurring in a space apart. By increasingly naturalizing bourgeois homemaking, such policy aligns personhood with the proper performance of insulated heterodomesticity, positioning those who do not do so as potential threats to the nation—remnants of a savage past that needs to be left behind in the name of achieving Western-acknowledged sovereignty. That dynamic enacts what Kauanui refers to as a "colonial biopolitics": "The pattern that we see time and time again within national liberation struggles is the rejection of same-sex practices and women's power and authority by invoking tradition to say that they are Western colonial imports."[104] Similarly, as Cheryl Suzack observes with regard to the implications of *Santa Clara Pueblo*–like understandings of Indigenous identity, "they reduce Indigenous women's gender identity to a reproductive relationship based on kinship, family, culture, and nation; they reinscribe Indigenous women's rights within a cultural framework superseded by tribal sovereignty; they relegate Indigenous female identity to the mythology of a historical past."[105] The effort to generate forms of Indigenous collectivity, of Native nationhood, that can be viewed as such by various imperial/colonial powers (including the settler-state) reciprocally can produce forms of internal reorganization that normalize ideologies of enfamilyment as the commonsensical background for forms of self-rule, often then further entrenching those patterns by casting them as *tradition*.[106] The resulting conception of sovereignty can be predicated on heteronormalizing liberal infrastructures even when peoples are insisting on their separateness from the jurisdiction of the settler-state and when the state recognizes (a regulated version of) that separateness. The point is not that Native governments are merely an extension of settler policy.[107] Rather, the aim here is to highlight how such colonial entanglements, in Jean Dennison's terms, can influence the institutionalized shape of Indigenous political orders in ways that can work to the detriment of Native people, particularly women and queer and trans people.[108]

That colonial influence on government apparatuses, such as those created under the IRA on US-claimed lands, is one of the reasons why Native feminists turn to the everyday. Instead of solely locating governance within a set of specialized institutions, largely contradistinguished from the private sphere, this work situates governance within quotidian webs of practice and relation. As opposed to existing apart from and above the realm of *family*, governance is immanent within ordinary interactions, and such interactions, of association and intimacy, provide the material basis for the ongoing process of enacting peoplehood at all scales. In other words, the everyday does not simply make possible or support Indigenous political orders but is the stuff of which they are made and, thus, cannot be segmented off from the space of politics, including through racial typologies of personhood (assessing who is heterolineally blooded enough to be Indian or determining what configuration of persons can count as an Indian family). As Laura Harjo observes, Mvskoke social forms involve "a collective power that cares about kin and community and that is used to make one another's lives and community better. This works in opposition to commonly received ideas about power, such as authoritative power." This collective power arises and circulates through informal connections: "Collective practices such as celebrations and more casual community gatherings are ways in which to come to know and build a network of relationality.... Sharing community planning conversations over coffee is, in essence, a means of having control over one's life and community."[109] Community gatherings over coffee are not sites of politics, in the sense of institutional frameworks defined by their depersonalized publicness. To understand such gatherings and quotidian conversation as generating infrastructures of governance means rethinking the meaning of collective process, shifting from liberal notions of a distinct political sphere to a more flexible conception of "ways of convening collectivity."[110] Envisioning power as produced within these interpersonal networks refigures it as less a matter of standing institutionalized procedures, policies, and practices and more as enmeshed within and emerging from sustained intimacies not bounded by the family unit. These connections are not institutionally structured, but the absence of an institutional frame on which to hang them does not make them formless, either. The form of peoplehood and dynamics of collectivity coalesce around such non-scripted and ongoing, if not exactly regularized, engagements—modes of "community knowledge" and open-ended negotiations over how the community will function that run through "daily lived practices."[111] The forms of personhood from which peoplehood continually is (re)constituted emerge immanently within such processes (recalling Audra Simpson's and Leanne Simpson's discussion of the Indigenous body as a political order, discussed in the introduction), rather than as a result of the reproductive transmission of *Indianness*.

This reframing of Indigenous political orders in terms of quotidian dynamics that would not conventionally be considered the stuff of politics also alters the kinds of relations that might be seen as expressive or enactive of governance. If jurisdiction posits the centralized (or centrally distributed) exercise of authority over a determinate territory and population, such as the reservation and Indians present on it or who are members of a given tribe, conceptualizing intimacy as a vector of governance (or, perhaps, a central principle of it) refuses jurisdictional models of self-determination. Instead, the focus shifts to the character of the connections among those who belong to a people, understanding such belonging in terms of embodied webs of interdependence—to other persons, place, and nonhuman entities. Discussing Kanaka modes of self-determination, Jamaica Heolimeleikalani Osorio foregrounds interpersonal pilina (ties or relationships) as the basis for conceptualizing the ordinary relations that comprise the lāhui (nation).[112] She notes, though, that "a close analysis of pilina in our Hawaiian dictionaries reveals that nearly all pilina were translated through the institution of marriage": "It is not just that these specific pilina lack proper English and Western names but that together these pilina (and others) inform a society whose understanding of relationality, responsibility, and aloha reaches far beyond the nuclear household and heteronormativity."[113] Thinking pilina beyond heteropatriarchally-oriented forms of privacy opens up the notion of intimacy from a kind of relation cordoned off from the public sphere to one that actually constitutes political orders. The bonds between persons are the same bonds that link persons to lands and waters—and vice versa. Osorio suggests that aloha āina (love of the land) "results in pilina between Kānaka" who then "recognize the aloha" in each other "and are bound in intimacy together because of our shared intimacy and connection to our land," creating a "diverse and vibrant collection of multibodied relationships between Kānaka Maoli, our ancestors, peers, descendants, and the environment"—a "powerful unifying alignment and attraction."[114] Belonging to a people, then, does not arise from a contractual relation among otherwise privatized units, as in liberal theorizations of political form, but instead emerges from a nexus of cross-hatching intimacies that themselves constitute lived personhood and serve as the animating matrix for a collective sense of emplacement.

While Osorio specifically addresses Kanaka epistemological principles and ontological dynamics, as the other scholars addressed do with regard to their peoples, such a recasting of what intimacy is generates intellectual and political possibilities that clearly differ from the racializing models of Indianness enshrined in US law. This reorientation "is not one that strives to change who governs but one that labors to transform what governance means," thinking "leadership" as itself "a relationship that must be cared for and tended to"—a (set of) pilina(s) among others rather than a structure or domain apart.[115] If ICWA, for example, seeks to protect modes of familial intimacy and relation deemed central to tribal identity and survival, what would it mean to understand all aspects of Indigenous peoplehood as subtended by intimacy—to see sovereignty less as the jurisdictional right to regulate certain family matters than as itself a nexus of embodied relations that need tending and that can be endangered by institutionalized liberal notions of extrapolitical, enfamilied personhood?

Centering such Native feminist formulations not only displaces the "Indian family" as the principal unit around which to build the scale structure of Indigenous governance, doing so alters the meaning and dynamics of scale itself. As discussed in the introduction and chapter 1, liberal scalar imaginaries depend on nested hierarchies of jurisdiction in which the presumptively enfamilied private sphere, as the extrapolitical core, sits within spheres of political authority of an ever-increasing scope until one reaches the federal level. Not only is there a break between each of the levels (different kinds of authority pertain with their own rules and regulations), but the various units at the same level are envisioned as not horizontally integrated, instead triangulating through the level above them. As Laura Harjo suggests, in order to contest settler political geographies and categories, we must "examine the processes that created the geopolitical units," which entails a reformulated conception of scale. In contrast to settler-state mappings of nested yet differentiated authority tied to particular insulated units of space, "The scale of the Mvskoke community is produced through relational processes rather than territorial processes."[116] In *Oliphant, Santa Clara Pueblo*, and ICWA, the central issues all circle around what kinds of subjects (both persons and matters) fall under the jurisdiction of tribal governments, and all of them return in one way or another to the self-evidence of Indianness as racial lineage—as a characteristic borne through enfamilied inheritance—in order to define the terms and contours of such jurisdiction. The vision of scale Harjo articulates does not start from an a priori notion of persons as kinds of isolated units with particular immanent properties that determine the extent to which a specific institutional apparatus can exert particular sorts of power over them. Characterizing scale in terms of "relational processes" defines belonging and the functioning of governance less with respect to inherent characteristics (of the person or the political institutional structure) than the ongoing and shifting ways that various persons and communities within a people engage with each other and the principles of negotiation among them—how cross-cutting commitments and relationships animate decision-making at all levels (for example, as discussed earlier, in terms of Haudenosaunee clans or Kanaka ways of employing genealogy).

Moreover, those *levels*—or the geographic/demographic scope of decision-making—are not understood as disjunct, but as bound together, interpenetrating, and interdependent. Mishuana Goeman, as discussed in chapter 1, has referred to such an understanding of scale as based on "conduits of connection rather than impermeable entities."[117] This way of conceptualizing the stuff and scope of governance militates against conventional commitments to development—the construction of capitalist infrastructures of extraction built atop liberal modes of atomization. Discussing the role of fossil fuels in the political economy of the Navajo Nation, Melanie Yazzie suggests that "contemporary notions of Navajo self-determination, nationalism, and decolonization" institutionalized as national policy continue to figure "sovereignty and national control through aspirations for development" in ways that naturalize "capitalist social relations." Furthermore, while presenting "independence over energy development" as a means to achieve the resources for further projects of self-determination, such conceptions of national autonomy thwart "decolonial aspirations" that "are about challenging the very capitalist notion of development that works in tandem with the structure of settler colonialism to reproduce and secure Diné [Navajo] death."[118] To aspire to *development* involves normalizing conceptions of property that enable the negotiation of contractual relations with oil and gas companies as well as a view of what is being extracted as commodifiable natural resources owned by the nation. In addition, the tribal government secures the operation of the market in such resources, ostensibly acting in the interest of the private citizens of the Navajo Nation who will benefit from the funding made possible by leases for fossil fuel extraction. However, as Yazzie argues, the very structures of relation that make possible such a national economy "reproduce and secure Diné death" through the toxic and environmentally destructive effects of processes of extraction on persons, lands, waters, and other nonhuman entities. Those processes also help foster a privatized understanding of Navajo lifeworlds, in the sense of both individual workers who participate due to the need for wages and the uneven effects of mining on nearby families. In contrast to the scalar imaginary that facilitates these forms of development, Yazzie offers a "politics of relational life," such as the kinds of caretaking enacted by "Indigenous feminist and Diné land defenders" in their embrace of "the responsibility of being a good relative to all of one's relatives, including other-than-human relatives." Doing so "becomes the priority and basis for political organization and action."[119] As opposed to what we might characterize as a liberal jurisdictional framework, in which the institutional apparatus of state has certain delimited forms of authority over particular matters while citizens appear as relatively isolated—yet enfamilied—subjects in whose name that apparatus acts, Yazzie articulates principles of governance rooted in an integrative ethos of care.

While many of these feminist (re)formulations of scale speak to lands recognized as under Indigenous governance within settler law, they also provide means of engaging Native people(s) in what are taken to be non-Indigenous territories, particularly city spaces. As many scholars have noted, Native land often is seen as rural, perhaps even the opposite of urban modernity.[120] From this perspective, Indigenous political orders lie beyond city limits, such that the parameters of federal Indian law discussed earlier do not apply to urban Natives who are often envisioned as deracinated and cut off from their peoples. However, if one moves away from the terms and frames of state acknowledgment, the principles of relation I've been discussing—Indigenous feminist scalar imaginaries—provide ways of addressing existing and potential modes of urban governance.[121] Such remappings address the heteropatriarchal enfamilyments that attach to and help shape the reservation/city dichotomy while also highlighting the ways situated self-determination is continuous with (rather than antithetical to) networked relations to other places.

As part of US Indian policy, the idea of the reservation powerfully has taken shape around conceptions of nuclear straightness in which the insulation of familial domesticity provides an ideological touchstone through which to figure the reified insularity of legally recognized Native space. I've been arguing that federal Indian law in the *era of self-determination* grounds itself in racializing narratives of reproduction and family life. In addition, though, that de facto nexus for defining Indianness helps animate understandings of what constitutes a specifically Native space, as contrasted with other places that aggregations of individual Indian persons might inhabit but that do not count as Native space in the way the reservation does. As Beth Piatote argues, "Indian domesticity [has served] as the site through which the settler state has exerted force to gain control over the tribal-national entity," but, reciprocally, "the domestic is also the locus through which Indian families and nations have expressed resistance."[122] However, the very inhabitation and attempted reversal of settler projects of detribalization invest Indian domesticity with metonymic power to signify the tribal-national. The race-making capacities of Indian reproduction also enact a placemaking dynamic—(re)creating the space of the reservation. To live away from that space, then, is also to be external to the proper geographies of Indian family, implicitly casting such dwelling as deviating from the situated scene of authentic indigeneity. Official geographies of Indianness conjoin with liberal ideologies of privatization to reinforce the sense of the reservation as the insulated and exclusive site of Native governance, itself envisioned as a public and jurisdictional (if racialized and thus not fully political) manifestation of the principles of Indianness contained in the family, which provides the normative core for the tribe. As Goeman suggests, though, "The settler narrative of the rez/off-rez dichotomy is a lie in its very conception," one that dissimulates the truth that "unlike the maps that designate Indian land as existing only in certain places, wherever we went there were Natives and Native space, and if there weren't, we carved them out."[123] If being off the reservation violates the Indianizing scalar logic of tribal identity (as envisioned within federal law and policy), attending to such supposed deviancies can open toward a remapping of peoplehood, sovereignty, and self-determination.

Such deviance provides an alternative way of figuring what kinds of emplacements and relations might serve as the stuff of governance—of political orders. In the late 1940s, federal Indian policy shifted toward the goal of what would come to be called *termination*: the attempt to "emancipate" Indigenous peoples from the reservation and supposedly stifling federal oversight by rescinding federal recognition of tribal governance and extending states' civil and criminal jurisdiction over Indian Country.[124] This effort also was about *freeing* Native lands and their natural resources for non-native possession, exploitation, and extraction. This project involved encouraging Native people to move from rural to urban areas, including the authorization of the Relocation Program, which provided time-limited resources for those who moved to particular target cities. Native people created a wide range of institutions in urban areas, including community centers, arts and social service organizations, and activist groups, and they arose out of complex networks of relation among those recently arrived, those who were second- or third-generation inhabitants, and those whose peoples' traditional territories were close by or comprised the land of the city itself.[125] However, such formal entities need not provide the model for conceptualizing off-reservation Indigenous governance.[126] Rather, trans-household webs of interdependence can be seen as giving rise to and sustaining Native institutions as well as exceeding their parameters and purview. As Chris Andersen suggests, "Unlike on First Nations reserves, where social networks might be comprised largely of extended family, informal urban networks are less likely to contain family and more likely to contain friends," and those networks provide an infrastructure for the kinds of vernacular sovereignties that Harjo addresses, albeit ones not situated within the jurisdictional geographies of tribal nations.[127] These urban communities, then, might themselves be viewed as political orders, ones that often cross the boundaries of tribal identification (containing persons from a range of peoples) and that might include or overlap with non-natives who also live within those areas. The very matrices of care, intimacy, and quotidian engagement that Native feminist scholars locate at the core of peoplehood—and that often are encapsulated as *kinship*—also appear in urban areas and stretch across Native nationalities, in ways that speak to older patterns of shifting, networked relation that precede the kinds of tribal belonging instituted by the United States and Canada over the course of the nineteenth century.[128]

The located genealogies of Indianness privileged in federal policy, then, are at odds with longer and ongoing dynamics of Indigenous migration, periodic and recursive gathering, and trade, of which urban residence provides a contemporary example. While cities and neighborhoods within them are their own situated territories, and are themselves part of the homelands of specific peoples (a fact not always acknowledged in figurations of urban indigeneity and the legacies of relocation policy), they are also sites of mobility and connections across difference. As Renya Ramirez observes, "Indian movement into the cities has increased the possibility for gathering and politically organizing," further underlining that "Native senses of rootedness can be transported."[129] She has characterized such multidimensional ways of making place as the creation of *hubs*. This notion is double-sided: it captures how Natives living in places outside of what they consider to be their people's territories continue to be intimately involved in those grounded relations through ongoing returns and communication with those who still reside there; and it also points toward sustained and sustaining patterns of care, mutual aid, solidarity, and organizing in cities among persons from varied peoples. The process of what Ramirez refers to as "hub-genesis," though, can be seen as less a phenomenon of the last century than as an instantiation of longstanding philosophies and practices of what often has been described as making kin.[130] Building such connections of mutual respect, resource sharing, and collective deliberation with those who previously had been strangers, or who have their own separate webs of affiliation and alliance, involves creating forms and processes of belonging that do not obey the logic of clearly bordered (and enfamilied) tribal units, the scalar imaginary at play in federal Indian law and policy.

Rather, such contemporary relations in the city, and elsewhere, might be said to mobilize principles of community-making—principles for assembling, participating in, and rejuvenating overlapping kinds of disparate political orders—that precede the tribalizing geographies imposed in the nineteenth and early twentieth century and that have been treated as the commonsensical background for state recognition (and Indianized reproduction) up to the present. The possibility for an Indigenous individual or group to be enmeshed in and sustained by a range of hubs, complex and interleaving networks of relation that are not understood as competing with each other, defies the segmenting structure of reservation-based mappings. Such enduring notions of belonging and collectivity as malleable, mobile, layered, and noncontradictory have been articulated through figures of kinship, although in ways that I've suggested can appear as privatizing within a de facto liberal frame. As Ramirez suggests, "Native ideas of belonging are not only about fighting against dominant notions of national [and, one might add, tribal] citizenship, but are also about reimagining communities based on Native philosophies of respect and love," and she later notes that attending to "gathering sites" and kinds of relations often seen as "private" "calls into question masculine notions of citizenship, which focus solely on political rights within the public sphere of the nation-state."[131] Moreover, foregrounding those networks and modes of networking may facilitate a movement beyond citizenship as a frame and toward more capacious models of what governance is and does. If the matrices of transtribal connection on display in urban areas—as well as connections between Indigenous people(s) and other racialized and minoritized groups—are thought of less as a new or isolated phenomenon than as an expression of how Indigenous political orders are (re)made, then the kinscapes of current Indigenous geographies can be seen as enacting scales of governance that not only move beyond reservation boundaries but that are organized otherwise.[132]

* * *

Federal Indian law and policy turns on the distinctness of Indianness. It signifies, as per *Morton v. Mancari*, a political status whose status as *political* comes from its not being *racial*. This contradistinction of the political from the racial has served as a lever within Native studies to pry Indigenous peoplehood away from its internalization as a minority identity within the settler-state. As against this scalar incorporation of indigeneity as an inescapably domestic (set of) issue(s), the argument goes, Indigenous peoples are autonomous polities whose lands, persons, and modes of governance have been colonially subjected to settler jurisdiction, management, intervention, and dispossession. While true, that framing also often takes shape around a differentiation of Indigenous people(s) from other racialized subjects—those consequently, if largely de facto, envisioned as properly subject to state definition/regulation.[133] Such a formulation gains force from its association with the legal parameters of federal policy. However, as I have argued through attention to signal and still efficacious developments in the Indian policy–defining epochal moment of 1978, racialization inhabits state understandings of Native nationhood via the centrality of a reproductive, enfamilied Indianness that grounds the terms and contours of state-recognized indigeneity. Not only does this set of definitional entailments raise questions about strategies (political and intellectual) that seek to segregate race and politics, it suggests the desirability of critically considering the conception of governance—its organization, scope, scale, and geographies—given shape by federal determinations.

While not seeking to challenge the legitimacy of Native national governments, and absolutely rejecting any argument that they are insufficiently expressive of what is taken to be an axiomatically more authentic indigeneity, I have sought to highlight how Indianness as a racial grammar provides a somewhat incoherent structure and limit for the forms of tribal sovereignty legally acknowledged by the United States. The infrastructure of Indian law and policy consistently employs racial genealogy as a way of figuring the ultimately extrapolitical character of Indigenous governance. This policy framework conveys the sense that Native sovereignty depends on the reproductive inheritance of a generically commonsensical Indianness and that it exists only due to the beneficence/sufferance of Congress, which has carved out a not fully political sphere for the enactment of a not-quite-politics that has no independent standing other than as a function of the exceptionality of congressional will in this area. Although notions of Native peoples' "inherent sovereignty" are part of affirmative court decisions and legislation, such as in *Santa Clara Pueblo* and ICWA, that apparent acknowledgment of a self-determination that precedes and exceeds (and, if taken to its logical conclusion, fundamentally puts in question) the authority of the settler-state repeatedly is conjoined with an assertion of the plenary authority of Congress to do whatever it deems fit in *Indian* affairs. The logic of such qualification—or, perhaps, inversion—of Native sovereignty makes the affirmative moments of law and policy little different from the federal demurrals and outright denials of Native jurisdiction, as in *Oliphant*. What cuts across these otherwise seemingly quite differently oriented approaches to Indian policy and Native nations is the positing of an underlying Indianness that supposedly justifies the adoption of such contradictory and aporetic principles. The need to recognize Indigenous peoples arises from the inability to understand the ongoing existence of the United States as anything but a vicious colonial project in the absence of a sense of collective acquiescence by *the Indian tribes* (for example, the gestures toward "tribes' forfeiture of full sovereignty").[134] Reciprocally, to view Indigenous polities as fully sovereign radically would undermine, or raise a cascading series of unanswerable questions about, the legitimacy of US claims to "domestic" space. The racial specificity of Indianness serves as the necessary ideological hinge to manage this double bind. Thus, Indian law and policy recognizes a politics and polities that are conceived of as not really either a politics or polities but, instead, ultimately collections of families that form racial enclaves given special status by Congress.

One option in rejecting this series of colonial mistranslations, evasions, and involutions is, as suggested earlier, to insist on the severing of the (Indigenous) political from the (Indian) racial, but in doing so, what actually constitutes the form, scope, and character of governance? To what extent does the segmentation of the truly political from the invidiously racial reproduce liberal categories and mappings as the de facto frame, further reinforcing the transposition of Indigenous governance into the state's terms in ways that normalize the racializing discourses of enfamilyment? In other words, the political as formulated in Indian law and policy does not exist without the racial Indianness that gives it its shape and character, and, moreover, the notions of family, reproductivity, and privacy that anchor liberal governance (as discussed in chapter 1 and further in the next chapter) attach and give form to the *political* as a distinct category within US legal and administrative formations. To endorse a political vision of indigeneity against the background of federal Indian policy, then, entails pretending to have banished race while it continues to serve as a crucial supplement in delineating the boundaries of what can count as politics and a polity. Race still serves as a supposedly privatized quality of persons that (dis)qualifies them for acknowledgment as (capable of being) a particular kind of political subject. Engaging with the ways racialization works to limit the bounds of what is seen as constituting governance opens up another way of approaching the politics vs. race issue with regard to Native peoples. Instead of choosing one over the other, the very scenes and relations taken as the site of enfamilied genealogical transmission of Indianness can be rethought as sites in which governance, the stuff of the political, is enacted, albeit in ways that liberal ideologies would disavow and often cast as aliberal deviance—in this case as Indian cultural difference (the multicultural flip side of attributions of barbarism).

Native feminist analysis takes up this challenge of recasting the where and how of Indigenous governance, refusing the scalar model of a politics ordered around an ostensibly extrapolitical space of enfamilied privacy. As I have been arguing, that liberal model naturalizes the insularity of nuclear homemaking and attributes disruptive deviancy (along with threats of state force) to social forms and political orders that do not fit that model. In contrast, Indigenous feminist work explores how relations, affects, and projects of placemaking that would be deemed personal within liberal frames function as ways of generating and maintaining networks of collectivity. Insistence on political intelligibility within settler terms appears as allied with a colonial biopolitics in which heteropatriarchy and the family serve as vehicles for remaking, managing, and containing Indigenous peoplehood. Refusing such colonial orientations and visibilities entails turning toward spaces and modes of connection deemed informal from the perspective of state (and state-endorsed) institutional apparatuses. Everyday interactions, intimacy, networks of care, and mobility come to the fore as means through which peoplehood, and a sense of polity, is (re)constituted as well as lived in webs of overlapping relation (as opposed to the singular bordered-ness of conventional conceptions of jurisdiction). Such reformulations of governance also open out beyond the spaces recognized by the state as Indigenous, providing means for thinking and tracing political orders in non-reservation areas (such as urban centers) while also enabling an attention to webs of connection across geographic spaces—the longstanding processes, diplomacies, and mobilities through which Indigenous people(s) have built shifting and flexible networks. Neither setting aside the extant institutional apparatuses of Native national government nor reifying them as the necessary or principal form taken by Indigenous political orders, attending to these feminist remappings of political organization, relation, and scale pluralizes and renders more capacious the potentials for acknowledging social matrices *as governance*. That shift creates possibilities for recasting Indigenous institutional structures while also potentially building connections with other racialized groups, turning toward the ways racialization shapes the terms of what constitutes the "political" rather than disowning the "racial" as a diversion from the real work of sovereignty/self-determination.

THREE

Marriage, Privacy, Sovereignty

THERE IS NOTHING obvious about the nuclear family, either as an atomized unit of social reproduction or as a normative ideal/horizon for political institutions that are differentially distinguished from that private sphere. In addition to the fact that other societies have been and are organized on alternative principles, the "artificial unity," in Michel Foucault's terms, of bourgeois family-making and homemaking emerges in the territory claimed by/as the United States in fraught relation with social configurations that do not obey liberal principles.[1] These other modes of life, though, do not simply defy liberal social forms; they help produce such forms, in the sense that dominant conceptions, practices, and legalities of home and family in many ways take shape in response to these other social configurations, as an effort to assert control over populations and regions otherwise deemed ungovernable by the US state. Or, put another way, the process of constituting, exerting, and legitimizing liberal governance entails recoding such other forms within a racializing matrix of kinship that contains them in the private sphere and casts them as disruptive and/or degraded aberrations from nuclear homemaking. In this way, *family* serves as a principal vehicle for ongoing race-making due to its unique capacity as an ideological and institutional template to naturalize the sociopolitical architecture of liberalism as integral to human reproduction itself and to contain nonliberal formations and modes of life within the scale structure of liberalism as deformations of the private sphere, potentially dangerous but not fundamentally challenging the validity of the political infrastructures of liberal governance.

The emergence of the nuclear family model as the paradigm for life in the United States, then, cannot be divorced from processes of racialization through which it was consolidated and distinguished from savage, degraded, and threatening alternatives. As many scholars have illustrated, the notion of the insular, self-sufficient domesticity of the parents-children unit as the natural form for social life proliferated and achieved its widespread status as cultural common sense over the course of the first half of the nineteenth century.[2] Shifts in the political economy of households and the ways they articulated with markets, forms of labor, modes of production, and forms of political subjectivity—as well as attendant changing notions of homemaking, domesticity, and the sentimental character of familial life—helped give rise to the model of the liberal private sphere that became dominant by mid-century. However, as Lisa Lowe argues, "there is also a colonial division of intimacy, which charts the historically differentiated access to the domains of liberal personhood, from interiority and individual will, to the possession of property and domesticity," and that racializing division is part of "a particular calculus governing the production, distribution, and possession of intimacy" given that the privileged intimacy of bourgeois whiteness "depends on the 'intimacies of four continents,' in other words, the circuits, connections, associations, and mixings of differentially laboring peoples, eclipsed by the operations that universalize the Anglo-American liberal individual."[3] The forms of capitalist development and state regulation of property (including enslaved people), contracts, marriage, inheritance, and legitimate kinship on which the emergence and continuance of the nuclear family relies are themselves dependent on the production of a series of racializing statuses and relations that enabled the making fungible of unfree labor and bodies (particularly through Black enchattelment); the expropriation and seizure of territory (especially Indigenous lands); and the importation of goods, materials, and laborers through imperial networks (particularly with regard to Asia). Inasmuch as *the family* is an artifact of liberal conceptions and geographies of intimacy, it cannot be separated from the matrices and mappings of race that make possible its existence: both by securing the material conditions of governance and production through which family takes shape; and by distinguishing between those who can be subjects of enfamilyment (and, thus, also subjects recognized as citizens by/under the state) and those whose supposed inherent tendencies exclude them from that status/possibility.

If racialization enacts forms of primitive accumulation by translating alternative political orders as tendencies toward failed enfamilyment (as discussed in the introduction), then attending to the legal construction of the legitimate domestic sphere and its differentiation from various modes of threatening deviance draws attention to the intimate relation between race-making and family-making in the (re)production of US jurisdictional imaginaries. Discussions of the shape and internal dynamics of the private/familial/domestic sphere contain within them an elaboration of the possibilities for envisioning what can, will, and should constitute governance, but in ways that are disavowed. That disavowal makes this sphere into a site through which to contain and pathologize nonliberal modes of governance by casting them as forms of racialized incapacity that in their deviation from proper family and, thus, personhood pose a threat to civilized political order. As noted in the introduction, Uday Mehta has illustrated how Euro-American liberalism casts itself as universally available while continuing to insist on a minimum set of "anthropological capacities" that, while "ascribed to all human beings," have "a thicker set of social credentials that constitute the real bases for political inclusion."[4] However, those capacities, such as the ability to form and maintain bourgeois homes and families, operate less as "social credentials" that enable one to be included in the liberal social order than as indices of the existence of a matrix of relations in which liberal political economy already immanently organizes the dynamics of everyday life. To have proper homes and families signifies that one already exists within liberal social forms, even as such enfamilyment is presented, such as in Lewis Henry Morgan's formulations, as the condition of possibility for the emergence of (and/or entry into) such forms.[5] Conversely, the absence of these normative patterns and spaces of private/familial/domestic relation potentially signifies the existence of other background formations of governance, which is what makes them threatening to the geographies and scale structure of liberalism. Addressing such nonliberal deviations as failures of domesticity allows them to be cast as racialized tendencies rather than as alternative formations of sovereignty, marking them as normatively unacceptable in ways that insulate the liberal state and its forms from critique or alternative configurations of governance. Indigenous articulations and theorizations of such dynamics, addressed in chapters 1 and 2, provide a countervailing framework through which to register both the violence of that translation and the consequent erasure of Indigenous (and other) matrices of governance that do not conform to liberal categories and geographies. In this way, by looking for the various modes of racialization that animate the dialectic of liberal privacy and sovereignty, we can trace the presence of practices of collectivity (denied the status of *political society*) against which liberal institutions seek to secure themselves.

From this perspective, we can trace the intertwined roles privacy, family, and personhood play in framing and normalizing articulations of sovereignty by the liberal state. A twofold pattern can be seen at play across the history of US law: the simultaneous citation of the private/domestic/familial sphere as defining the condition of possibility for and the character of state sovereignty while that sphere itself is cast as beyond political contestation; and the characterization of alternative formulations of collective life as racial tendencies, for which the inability to sustain a properly contoured private sphere serves as evidence of ingrained racial incapacity. Since the proper performance of privacy marks the potential for partaking in political life, as well as supposedly providing the normative principles that guide the work of political institutions, populations whose deviancy manifests in their wrong domesticities can be understood as threatening public order such that they need to be directly managed, contained, and/or dispersed by the state. Legal articulations of family and privacy, then, provide sites for tracing dominant formulations of liberal sovereignty and for tracking how various kinds of racialization are crucial to the (re)making of bourgeois domesticity.

If Morgan's *Ancient Society* provides a conceptual allegory for illustrating the work of enfamilyment within liberalism (as discussed in chapter 1), this chapter aims to give greater historical texture to that sketch by turning to three different sets of legal negotiations stretching from the late nineteenth century through the early twenty-first century—three kinds of legal conflict that further illustrate the matrix of privacy, sovereignty, and racialization discussed above. These three controversies are Mormon polygamy prior to Utah statehood, the emergence of the right to privacy in the late 1960s and early 1970s, and the evolving legal status of queer sex and relationships from the 1980s through the 2010s. Centering discussion on relevant Supreme Court cases, I aim to show how US law defines the terms and boundaries of the private sphere in ways that naturalize the jurisdictional architecture of liberal governance, by positioning the principles of enfamilyment as separate from the work of political institutions and presenting countervailing social forms as expressive of racialized aberrance.[6] In this way, the judicial construction and affirmation of the infrastructure of state sovereignty through the positing of an extrapolitical space of home/family/privacy remains punctuated by the presence of other kinds of social formations, which are managed by casting them as racial tendencies. The Mormon cases offer the most direct example of this pattern. More than simply condemning the existence of polygamy, which had been criminalized under federal law for the Territories, those decisions draw a line between the domesticity of the home and that of the nation by understanding polygamy as itself indicative of a broader Mormon challenge to US sovereignty, one apprehended in explicit terms as a loss of whiteness. The right to privacy decisions, which turn on birth control and abortion, figure a normative marital space envisioned as properly free from state intervention, even as the state determinations that produce and contour such a space are occluded. Moreover, the domestic subjectivity formed in that space gains meaning by being differentiated from charges of criminality (increasingly associated with blackness), as further illustrated by the non-applicability of the concept of privacy to contemporaneous welfare regulations and eugenically motivated practices of sterilization—both presented as containing and disciplining pathological forms of racialized sociality that threaten national order. Finally, the cases focused on the (de)criminalization of sodomy and recognition of same-sex marriage return to the question of what constitutes a civilized state and the fundamental role of marriage in sustaining it. They further illustrate how the reconfiguration of the private in the name of equity and inclusion does not itself displace its work in the making of liberal sovereignty, instead often reaffirming and reanimating the modes of racialization through which alternative matrices of governance are disavowed as perverse forms of failure and threat.

Containing Barbarous Contagion

The federal government's legal assault on the Church of Jesus Christ of Latter-day Saints (LDS), commonly known as the Mormons, from the 1860s through the 1880s quite dramatically illustrates how the liberal state limits the potential for nonliberal modes of governance through the ways it delineates the boundaries of the private sphere. For decades, Mormonism featured prominently in governmental and popular discourses as a danger to the nation. The first presidential platform of the Republican Party in 1856 referred to polygamy and slavery as "twin relics of barbarism," presidents from James Buchanan onward repeatedly denounced the

Mormons, anti-polygamy fiction gained significant popularity, and the press routinely decried the excesses and deviancy of Mormon household formation and governance.[7] Any number of alternative communities were organized throughout the nineteenth century (particularly in the 1830s and 1840s, when Mormonism itself emerged from Joseph Smith's visions), many of them involving nonnormative configurations of homemaking, sexual relations, and childcare;[8] yet, they were not subject to anything remotely like the intensity and scale of condemnation and prosecution of the LDS Church. The Mormons were a special case, a particular danger. As Christine Talbot notes, "What middle-class American political culture attempted to keep separate the ideals surrounding the practice of polygamy brought together": "the Mormon community 'publicized' individual families" and "made little distinction between the private family and the broad Mormon community," thereby building "an entire alternative political culture, complete with its own privatized political institutions." This failure to distinguish public and private—or, put another way, the organization of what putatively should be "private" life in ways that legitimized and instantiated a conception of governance characterized at the time as "theocratic"—was seen as less a bounded phenomenon than a potential danger at all levels to the structure of the United States. Talbot observes, "By the mid-1870s, no metaphor was as ubiquitous in anti-Mormon literature as that of contagion."[9] Mormonism came to be understood as a fundamental threat to the normative and administrative infrastructure of liberal political economy.[10] In response, officials articulated a vision of family that was cast as axiomatically grounding the political life of the nation. In its major Mormon cases—*Reynolds v. United States* (1879), *Davis v. Beason* (1890), and *The Late Corporation of the Church of Jesus Christ of the Latter-Day Saints v. United States* (1890)—the US Supreme Court lays out the centrality of the monogamous marital family to the functioning of US policy and civilized social order. These decisions demonstrate how the violation of normative conceptions of home and family indexes the presence of political orders that challenge the sovereignty of the state, forms that are dismissed and contained through their racialization.

A series of laws passed by Congress from 1862 to 1887, justified on the basis of the federal government's plenary authority over the Territories, sought to outlaw all forms of polygamy, to cleanse the political arena of its taint, and to dismantle the politicized church apparatus that licensed it and was sustained by it. Part of the exigency of the extension of authority over the Mormons, though, lay in the fact that their presence in what became Utah preceded not only the official organization of the Territory under federal law but the jurisdiction of the United States over those lands. Prior to the close of the Mexican-American War, the Latter-day Saints moved to the Great Salt Lake in 1847 and founded what they called the state of Deseret without seeking permission from Mexican authorities. As Brent Rogers suggests, they were settling "a place they expected to make *their* country, *their* cradle of liberty."[11] They were fleeing from Nauvoo, Illinois, where they had held a municipal charter authorized by the state legislature that gave the Mormon community local jurisdiction and a militia unit prior to Joseph Smith's declaration of martial law in June 1844 and his subsequent murder later that month by a local mob—the act that prompted their collective migration farther west under the leadership of Brigham Young. Young would publicly announce their commitment to the principle of plural marriage in 1852 and would remain the head of the church until his death in 1877. Before moving to Nauvoo, they had been chased out of Missouri in 1836 and New York a few years earlier.[12] In journeying to what would be Utah, they purposefully left the United States in order to achieve full self-governance and to avoid state jurisdiction, entering Indigenous lands (particularly those of the Utes, for whom the territory and state would be named) while not understanding such inhabitance as making them subject to Native authority. Moreover, once the United States officially laid claim to the area as a result of signing the Treaty of Guadalupe Hidalgo (1848) and organized a territorial government (1850), the Mormon-controlled territorial legislature passed a series of acts incorporating the Mormon Church, granting it full authority over the marriages of all its members, enabling the church to acquire real and personal property without any specified limit, giving effect to all laws passed under the Deseret state (those not in conflict with the US Constitution or the acts of Congress for the Territory), setting up a system of probate courts with jurisdiction over matters that usually would fall under the federal district courts (thereby seeking largely to bypass those courts and their federally appointed judges in favor of church officials appointed to probate positions), and denying the relevance of common law precedent and court decisions from any other state jurisdiction in territorial court proceedings.[13] These maneuvers created numerous conflicts with various federally appointed officials, helping prompt President Buchanan to send 2,500 troops to Utah in 1857—one-fifth of the army at that time. While largely justified on the basis of rumors and reports that the Mormons were violating federal Indian law and seeking to form an independent alliance with Native peoples against the United States, this deployment served as an indication of the assertion of federal power over the territory and was accompanied by the presidential appointment of Alfred Cumming to replace Brigham Young as governor of Utah Territory as well as congressional action to separate the position of governor from that of the superintendent of Indian Affairs in the territory, as those roles had been previously fused in Utah and elsewhere in the West.[14]

Congressional responses to polygamy sought to challenge this pattern of what was understood as defiance of federal authority, but even as the president sent troops to contain and chastise the territorial government, legislation with regard to polygamy and what might otherwise be seen as the Mormon private sphere was mired in controversy prior to the outbreak of the Civil War. The question of whether the federal government could regulate home and family formation remained caught within debates over slavery, itself understood as a form of "domestic relation."[15] In the same year as the deployment of troops to Utah, the Supreme Court's infamous decision in the case of *Dred Scott v. Sanford* limited congressional authority in the Territories by indicating that the effort to outlaw slavery there was an unconstitutional taking of property.[16] Moreover, the Republican Party's depiction of polygamy and slavery as "twin relics of barbarism" principally had to do with an argument against the legitimacy of the concept of "popular sovereignty"—the right of citizens in the Territories to make decisions about their own legal systems, particularly with regard to recognition of chattel slavery—which had enabled a deeply fraught and increasingly precarious détente between proslavery and antislavery legislators over the course of the 1850s. Even as partisans on all sides of this debate condemned polygamy and what was perceived as LDS control over Utah's political system, the issue of precisely how the federal government could intervene remained controversial and hotly debated. For Congress to legislate against polygamy opened the Pandora's box of the potential for similar federal regulation of the peculiar institution, indicating significant disagreements over what properly constituted the private/domestic sphere even as such a domain repeatedly was cast as beyond the scope of politics and as providing the normative principles around which institutions of governance were organized.[17] For example, while arguing strongly in favor of a congressional statute outlawing polygamy in the Territories, a House Judiciary Committee report issued in March 1860 observes, "Variant as the construction of different persons may be as to what is property and what are the rights of property secured by the Constitution, there can be no question that [in the Territories] ... it is competent for Congress to declare any act criminal which is not sanctioned or authorized by the provisions of the Constitution."[18] Notably, actual legislation with regard to polygamy had to wait for passage until after the South's secession and the attendant political shifts in Congress, accompanying other federal efforts to manage the West including the Homestead Act and the Pacific Railroad Act.[19]

Despite this fraught history of struggle with regard to jurisdictional authority, justifications for federal intervention, and the vision of familial and household order instituted through legal action (even as all of those domestic visions were cast as extrapolitically self-evident), the laws passed by Congress offer no sense of such conflicts.[20] The Morrill Act (1862) criminalized legal marriage to more than one person in any "place over which the United States have exclusive jurisdiction," except in cases where the spouse has "been absent for five successive years without being known to such person within that time to be living," and it annulled all acts by the legislature of the Utah Territory "which establish, support, maintain, shield, or countenance polygamy," noting that even in doing so, the law shall not interfere "with the right 'to worship god according to the dictates of conscience.'" As the law makes clear, this kind of congressional enactment with regard to marriage and family relations is possible because it only covers areas directly under federal jurisdiction, given that such questions otherwise would fall under the jurisdiction of the states. The act further prevented any religious or charitable corporation in any of the Territories from possessing real estate valued at more than $50,000.[21] In 1874, Congress passed the Poland Act, which extended federal authority with regard to the judicial system in Utah (in terms of personnel, subject jurisdiction, and jurors) in order to prevent the circumvention of the district courts by the LDS use of the probate court system and the packing of juries with Mormons.[22] The Edmunds Act (1882) replaced the Morrill Act, extending criminal charges beyond those who formally marry more than one person to any man who "cohabits with more than one woman." It also allowed for challenges to any juror who not only "is or has been living in the practice of bigamy, polygamy, or unlawful cohabitation" but who "believes it right for a man to have more than one living and undivorced wife at the same time" or to cohabit with more than one woman. Perhaps most dramatically, the law denied the right to vote or serve in public office to any person engaged in polygamy (Mormon women had possessed the right to vote since 1870), although unlike with respect to jury service it specified that simply having a positive "opinion" with regard to "the subject of bigamy or polygamy" would not disqualify someone from voting and public service.[23] Five years later, Congress passed the Edmunds-Tucker Act, expanding the previous law by defining cohabitation as "adultery" that would result in a three-year prison term; requiring a legal certificate for all marriages; denying inheritance to all illegitimate children (specifically in Utah); disenfranchising all women in Utah; requiring that all prospective voters, officials, and jurors take an oath indicating that they would support the US Constitution, did not and would not take part in polygamy, and "[would] not, directly or indirectly, aid or abet, counsel or advise, any other person to commit any of said crimes"; and dismantling the LDS Church by abolishing it as a legal corporation and providing for the government seizure of all its assets and real estate.[24] As a result of these measures and the resulting prosecutions (nine hundred indictments for unlawful cohabitation in 1886–1888 alone),[25] the LDS Church formally renounced polygamy in 1890, paving the way for Utah statehood in 1896.

More than simply outlawing relationships and households that could be deemed polygamous, these federal statutes indicate that participation in such relationships disqualifies one from serving as a political subject within republican institutions, while also presenting Mormonism as having breached the proper boundaries of liberal political order by exerting undue authority over the rendering of justice, the distribution of resources, and the organization of collective placemaking. The Supreme Court cases ruling on the constitutionality of these federal measures reflect such sentiments and help provide a more expansive sense of why Mormon marital and family forms have such profound political implications. Although the cases are different from each other and turn on a range of legal points, they all confirm the inapplicability of the First Amendment's religious freedom clause to the practice of polygamy as well as the jurisdictional supremacy of the federal government over the Territories.[26] In *Reynolds v. United States*, which decided the constitutionality of the Morrill Act, the Court cites the act authored by Thomas Jefferson to secure religious freedom in Virginia, noting the clause that allows for state interference "when principles break out into overt acts against peace and good order" and adding that in this phrase "is found the true distinction between what properly belongs to the church and what to the State."[27] The decision further observes that "from the earliest history of England polygamy has been treated as an offence against society."[28] In addition to marking a distinction between belief and action, which has been a hallmark of understandings of the limits of First Amendment religious protections, this approach cast polygamy as itself inherently disruptive, as necessarily injurious to public order and a challenge to the well-being of the populace.[29] Given the insulation of households from each other within liberal social geographies, though, how can the relationships at play in one set of private arrangements bear on matters of the public peace, never mind having significant implications for the entirety of "society"?

More than simply characterizing plural marriage as morally depraved or as indicative of individual antisocial tendencies, the Court presents it as exceeding the domestic sphere in its effects on the organization of public life. Further describing the marital home as the "most important feature of social life," the decision in *Reynolds* says of marriage, "Upon it society may be said to be built, and out of its fruits spring social relations and social obligations and duties, with which government is necessarily required to deal. In fact, according as monogamous or polygamous marriages are allowed, do we find the principles on which the government of the people, to a greater or less extent rests."[30] The legislature must deal with the matter of polygamy, because to fail to do so means surrendering control over the character of the polity itself. The form of family life bears within it the "principles" that shape the operation of governance writ large.[31] The nation itself is "built" out of the cumulative array of monogamous marital households. In her analysis of anti-Mormon fiction, Nancy Bentley argues, "The struggle against Mormon plural marriage proved that relatively recent ideas about domesticity had become fundamental, not incidental, to U.S. national symbology," adding that "the way novelists and lawmakers made polygamy a defining limit of national identity" gave "American nationalism the structure of a domestic novel."[32] However, more than a symbol of national identity or analogical prism through which to represent it, monogamous marriage appears as an indispensable building block, as both the base on which the government "rests" and the extrapolitical source from which "spring" the concrete "relations" and "obligations" that contour the law and to which it bears normative witness.[33] As the Court indicates in *Davis v. Beason*, which concerns the administration of an antipolygamy oath as a qualification for voting in Idaho Territory,

> Certainly no legislation can be supposed more wholesome and necessary in the founding of a free, self-governing commonwealth, fit to take rank as one of the coordinate States of the Union, than that which seeks to establish it on the basis of the idea of the family, as consisting

in and springing from the union for life of one man and one woman in the holy estate of matrimony; the sure foundation of all that is stable and noble in our civilization; the best guaranty of that reverent morality which is the source of all beneficent progress in social and political improvement.[34]

The family unit that arises through monogamous union produces the condition of possibility for a "self-governing commonwealth," providing the material impetus for the nation's development.[35] Here we see the reverse of Ella Deloria's depiction of "kinship" as "all-encompassing" (discussed in chapter 1); instead, the liberal home in its isolation models the putatively extralegal principles of liberal political economy writ large. Even as the Court recognizes the need for legislation to secure the boundaries of such sanctified domesticity and to criminalize deviations, this form of liberal privacy seems to precede the governmental structures that then *spring from* it.

Conversely, from this perspective, polygamy endangers the infrastructure of liberal political economy by creating a dangerously deformed private sphere that engenders politically aberrant subjects and that undoes the scale structure of liberal legal geography. In his first address to Congress, President Grover Cleveland asserts, "The strength, the perpetuity, and the destiny of the nation rests upon our homes, established by the law of God. These homes are not the homes of polygamy."[36] Polygamy produces perverse kinds of homes that not only do not obey the principles of republican governance and cannot support them in the nation's political institutions and public life but that produce people ill-prepared to live such principles and to take part in those institutions. The Court's running presentation of polygamy as a threat to public order lies partially in the idea that it inculcates modes of being and social orientations that cannot generate the forms of personhood necessary to sustain the liberal state and that, instead, encourage authoritarian governance. This perspective explains the reasoning behind the Edmunds Act's outlawing of voting and service in office by those practicing plural marriage as well as the Edmunds-Tucker Act's extension of this ban to anyone who endorses such relationships. In this vein, as Talbot notes, "To anti-Mormons, plural marriage by definition lacked any private sphere that might constitute an appropriate home in which an individual citizen and his civic virtue might be fashioned," and thus, polygamy "obliter[ated] any possible self-ownership and equality upon which free and public government in Utah might rest. As such, Mormonism sustained no individuals capable of making the kind of unfettered political choices upon which republicanism depended. A community with no qualified citizenry could not maintain free republican government."[37] Here we see judicial confirmation of the ideological connection between proper enfamilyment and politically viable personhood. The *Reynolds* decision cites Francis Lieber, an immensely popular and influential legal theorist who wrote primarily prior to the Civil War, as articulating the notion that "polygamy leads to the patriarchal principle, and which, when applied to large communities, fetters the people in stationary despotism, while that principle cannot long exist in connection with monogamy."[38] Polygamous households and personal relations instill values that promote "despotism," while also eliding the proper distinctions between the family and the state. If the monogamous union is meant to inspire democratic governance, it does not take part in political processes. However, polygamy is envisioned as depending on and encouraging an erasure of that distinction, creating a "patriarchal" transit in which obedience to the singular father of the plural family takes part in a culture of subservience that infects and comes to organize all of society.[39] That process of transformation, conducted under the cover of religious freedom, threatens to shatter the sovereignty of the state: "to make the professed doctrines of religious belief superior to the law of the land" would be "in effect to permit every citizen to become a law unto himself. Government could exist only in name under such circumstances."[40]

Beyond failing to promote liberal forms of private and public life, Mormon patriarchy produces its own kind of sovereignty that works to displace that of the United States. From the 1850s onward, the LDS Church was condemned by any number of officials, in all branches of government, for its flouting of US law and political institutions: its supposed efforts to set up a "theocratic" quasi-monarchy that challenged the jurisdictional integrity of the nation.[41] Justice James McKean of the Utah Supreme Court famously declared that Utah under Mormon control was an "*imperium in imperio.*"[42] Secretary of War John B. Floyd asserted in 1857, "This people have claimed the right to detach themselves from the binding obligations of the laws which governed the communities where they chanced to live. They have substituted for the laws of the land a theocracy," and he further suggested that they were "prepar[ing] for a successful secession from the authority of the United States and a permanent establishment of their own." As part of his inaugural address in 1881, President James Garfield said of the LDS Church that it could not "be safely permitted to usurp in the smallest degree the functions and powers of the National Government."[43] Summarizing this long history of charges that the existence of the Mormons in their collective form posed a substantial and unacceptable challenge to the sovereignty of the United States, the Court in its decision in *The Late Corporation of the Church of Jesus Christ of Latter-Day Saints v. United States*, which affirms the legitimacy of the Edmunds-Tucker Act, asserts, "It is unnecessary here to refer to the past history of the sect, to their defiance of the government authorities, to their attempt to establish an independent community, to their efforts to drive from the territory all who were not connected to them in communion and sympathy. The tale is one of patience on the part of the American government and people, and of contempt of authority and resistance to law on the part of the Mormons."[44] The statutory and judicial dismantling of the LDS Church over the course of the latter half of the nineteenth century—including the denial to it of all control over legal matters, disincorporation of the church, and seizure of all its properties—appeared as a necessary effort to prevent its ongoing and inappropriate assumption of political functions.[45] In these articulations, Mormonism competes with the public authority of US governance in ways that far exceed the proper boundaries of religious institutions by creating what amounts to a quasi-sovereign entity with pretensions to political autonomy.[46]

The matter of polygamy, though, was central to understanding the peril Mormonism posed to US institutions and authority. There is a temptation to characterize either polygamy or theocracy as the primary concern at play in anti-Mormon discourses, with the other one serving as a metonymic stand-in for the principal issue.[47] However, polygamy signified the dangers of theocracy and gained meaning as an instantiation of antirepublican tendencies. Anti-polygamists saw plural marriage as materializing a set of principles that not only propelled the expansion of the Mormon Church as a prospectively sovereignty-wielding institution but also fundamentally molded the character of the kind of polity bodied forth by the church. More than embodying a dangerous set of philosophical precepts, in their "patriarchal" despotism as well as disregard for the liberal distinctions between both church and state and public and private, polygamous marriages and households were envisioned as providing the underpinning structural support for an apparatus of governance that cannot be encompassed within US political geographies. In *Reynolds*, the Court observes with regard to Mormon influence in Utah's governance, "A colony of polygamists under an exceptional leadership may sometimes exist for a time without appearing to disturb the social condition of the people who surround it," and the decision in *Late Corporation* goes even further in tying the political and legal dangers of the LDS Church to plural marriage, describing Mormonism as "a community for the spread and practice of polygamy," a collective orientation that constitutes "a return to barbarism."[48] What gives the Mormon "colony" its disruptive shape and force is polygamy, in its replacement of nuclear family intimacy with a distended private sphere that also throws into disarray the forms of propertyholding naturalized as the basis of the liberal social order. When *Late Corporation* then refers to the LDS Church as "a contumacious organization" that uses "its resources" and "immense power in the Territory of Utah" to "thwart and subvert . . . the will of the government of the United States," the decision invokes a recalcitrance and malignance that is cast as deriving from the practice of polygamy.[49] As a lived relation that produces improper political subjects, an interlocking set of ideological commitments (including to "patriarchal" modes of tyranny), and an aliberal form of sociality, plural marriage serves as the extrapolitical matrix that arranges and animates Mormon (pretentions to) sovereignty and that, therefore, endangers the sovereignty of the US state. Wrong enfamilyment gives rise to pathological kinds of sovereignty that endanger the body politic.

In their unequivocal condemnation of polygamy, the Mormon cases illustrate the ways the liberal private sphere appears as both naturally extrapolitical and foundational to the organization of political society, which is what makes the collective practice of polygamy so threatening, but the decisions additionally demonstrate the ways the disruptive potential of alternative political formations is managed through processes of racialization. As many scholars have noted, despite the fact that most of the members of the LDS Church otherwise would have been legally classified as white, the Mormons consistently were cast as failing in their whiteness, as degenerating into Asiatic, African, and Indian barbarisms.[50] Nancy Bentley observes, "Mormons were refused the status of white people," and she adds that "even a white population could fail to count as members of the race if they did not have 'white' families" such that "Utah polygamy is described as literally producing a distinct and inferior race."[51] In this way, attributions of non-whiteness to the Mormons did not so much mistake their racial identity, or use race as a metaphor, as indicate the ways race itself operates as a vehicle for constructing populations on the basis of attributed deviancies with regard to homemaking, family formation, and sexual intimacy.[52] The history of the Mormons in the nineteenth century, in Peter Coviello's terms, "is the story... of how whiteness itself came into being in nineteenth-century America, and came into being in part through its elaboration as against the form and arrangement of life called 'Mormonism.'"[53] As Sarah M. S. Pearsall observes, "Asserting a people's 'natural' tendency to polygamy helped to create modern American notions of race."[54]

The articulation of Mormonism as a problem of racial character and destiny appeared as early as the 1850s and served as a running theme in public and political anti-polygamous rhetorics through the 1890s. In his 1855 article in *Putnam's Monthly* from which the Court quotes in *Reynolds*, Francis Lieber describes monogamous marriage as "one of the pre-existing conditions of our existence as civilized white men.... Strike it out, and you destroy our very being; and when we say *our* we mean our race—a race which has its great and broad destiny, a solemn aim in the great career of civilization."[55] At various times, and sometimes in the same account, Mormonism was cast as resembling Asiatic, African, or Indian proclivities, and the very proliferation and indeterminacy of these forms of racial attribution suggests the insecurity driving such characterizations and the desire to discredit Mormon political collectivity through a piling on of invidious comparisons. In addition to being seen as potentially fomenting war between the United States and Native peoples, the Mormons themselves repeatedly were associated with the latter, in terms of both their support for polygamy and the role of Indigenous peoples within Mormon cosmology as the descendants of the Lamanites (themselves a group of descendants of ancient Israel who settled in what is now the United States, chronicled in the *Book of Mormon*).[56] As part of a speech in Congress in 1887, Representative John Randolph Tucker says of anti-Mormon legislation in relation to the passage of the Dawes Act (which instituted allotment policy), "We dissolve tribal relations of the Indians in order to make the Indian a good citizen; so we shatter the fabric of this church organization in order to make each member a free citizen of the Territory of Utah,"[57] linking the legal assault on the LDS Church to forms of intervention with regard to Native sovereignties. Despite the limitations placed on Black LDS church members' access to positions of authority and physical entry into the main temple,[58] Mormons also were associated with blackness due to the supposed prevalence of polygamy in Africa as well as the lingering connections in anti-Mormon discourse between polygamy and enslavement.[59] The linkage of Mormons to Asia arose through long-standing Orientalist representations of Arab and Muslim populations, particularly in the Ottoman Empire, coupled with increased anxieties from the 1870s onward about Chinese immigration.⁶⁰

In addition to offering a narrative of human progress in which normative Euro-American modes of social life appear as the apex of human development, as in Morgan's framework discussed in chapter 1, efforts to tie the outlawing of polygamy to the defense of "civilization" positioned plural marriage as expressive of communal inclinations toward barbarism. Representative Caleb Lyon declares in a speech before Congress in 1856, "Point me to a nation where polygamy is practiced, and I will point you to heathens and barbarians," further indicating that Mormon polygamy "seriously affects the prosperity of States, it retards civilization, it uproots Christianity."⁶¹ To be *civilized* means possessing as well as inculcating capacities for rational, enlightened, republican forms of governance, for which the liberal private sphere simultaneously serves as evidence and crucible, and whiteness functions as the emblem and consequence of such capacities. Commitments to other kinds of familial/household arrangements signal tendencies that angle away from civilized social order, illustrating perverse and ingrained kinds of collective orientation that themselves are the stuff of racial identification. More than simply applying an existing kind of racial categorization to the Mormons, anti-polygamy discourses register the challenge the Mormons pose to the dialectics of liberalism—the "precarious vulnerabilities" of bourgeois political economy, in Ann Laura Stoler's terms.⁶² Plural marriage appears to express an immanent, ingrained set of qualities that manifests in the deformation of proper domesticity.

Framing Mormonism in these racializing terms, though, presents the sovereignty-generating propensities attributed to plural marriage as indicative of savage and criminal forms of deficiency, instead of as an alternative political order. Even as polygamy's detractors describe it as engendering a mode of governance that competes with that of the United States, the depiction of Mormonism as failed whiteness, as a drift toward non-European forms of backwardness, depoliticizes that challenge to state jurisdiction, thereby reinforcing liberal governance as the sole legitimate option. The *Reynolds* decision declares, "Polygamy has always been odious among the northern and western nations of Europe, and, until the establishment of the Mormon Church, was almost exclusively a feature of the life of Asiatic and of African people." In addition, the Court in *Late Corporation* insists, "No doubt the Thugs of India imagined that their belief in the right of assassination was a religious belief; but their thinking so did not make it so.

The practice of suttee by the Hindu widows may have sprung from a supposed religious conviction.... No one, on that account, would hesitate to brand these practices, now, as crimes against society, and obnoxious to condemnation and punishment by the civil authority."[63] These moments illustrate how association with non-European peoples—themselves described not as "nations" but in the continental terms that historically have provided the principal modes of racial attribution in the United States—taints polygamy and the claim that it can be justified on the basis of "religious belief." Or, rather, polygamy appears as an index and instantiation of the very ingrained incapacities that mark such non-white populations' inability to enact civilized governance. Saying that plural marriage illustrates barbarism (a falling away from "civilization") and mirrors the practices of non-white peoples displaces the question of what political institutions and processes might be, what possible forms they might take.[64] Liberal privacy serves as axiomatic for the operation of governance—governance that can be recognized as valid by and within liberal *political society*. Racialization mediates what kinds of collective formations can count as sovereignty by measuring such formations against a biopolitical norm for which the jurisdictional principles and scale structure of bourgeois political economy serve as the necessary background.

Contemporary arguments for the decriminalization and legal recognition of polygamy tend to understand such nineteenth-century racializing dynamics as outmoded forms of white animus toward non-white populations, and for this reason, such arguments lose track of the ways that racialization helps (re)produce, legitimize, and naturalize the liberal private sphere by recasting alternative formations in biopolitical terms as threats to national well-being. In doing so, current pro-polygamy positions largely reaffirm liberal mappings of jurisdiction and domesticity, thereby reinstalling their processes of racializing normalization but in other terms that continue to generate the sense of the private/familial/domestic as an extrapolitical zone. In *Brown v. Buhman* (2013), a Tenth Circuit federal court decision about the constitutionality of Utah's statute outlawing polygamy and cohabitation (in which the plaintiffs were the Brown family, from the reality show *Sister Wives*), the court finds that the cohabitation portion of the law violates the free exercise clause of the First Amendment and the due process clause of the Fourteenth Amendment.[65] As part of reaching this analysis, the decision offers an account of the "crusade" against Mormon polygamy in the nineteenth century and its implications for interpreting the *Reynolds* decision. While finding that

Reynolds remains good law with regard to whether polygamy can count as a "fundamental right" and the interpretation of the scope of First Amendment protections, the court decries that decision for its racial assumptions.[66] Citing Edward Said's *Orientalism*, the decision states that the "social harm" attributed to polygamy had to do with prejudices against "'oriental' races" believed to be "civilizationally inferior." In this vein, the court insists that such reasoning would not pass constitutional muster now due to developments in the latter half of the twentieth century with regard to the rights of minorities and the resulting construction of an "intentionally racially and religiously pluralistic society."[67] Aside from questions one might raise about the accuracy of this characterization, it frames the understanding of what race means in the nineteenth-century Mormon cases and, consequently, what those cases suggest about the role of racialization in mediating the relation between the putatively private sphere and practices of governance. The court finds that polygamous cohabitation, as opposed to legal bigamy, is "an individual's choice" to take part in a kind of relationship that is "highly personal" and that there is no rational state interest at stake in regulating such behavior.[68] While "the state has an important interest in regulating marriage" as a "legal status," cohabitation falls within the "liberty" interest the US Supreme Court has found (particularly in *Lawrence v. Texas* [2003]) that "essentially draws a line around an individual's home and family."[69] What goes missing here, though, is precisely how the racialization of Mormonism worked to delegitimize an alternative kind of sovereignty for which Mormon "home" and "family" provided the infrastructure.

As with the kinship imaginary, discussed in chapter 1, the decision understands the personal and its protection as about a space beyond the sphere of governance, a space whose privatized individuality makes it inherently disjunct and properly insulated from the work of political institutions. Polygamous cohabitation is deemed not a threat because it is *personal*, not governmental, and there supposedly is no valid liberal political interest in intervening in the domestic sphere so long as it takes the shape of home and family in ways modeled on the (extra)legal ideal of marriage. The salience of race appears only as an outmoded attitude toward "nonwhite" populations that intrudes on the liberty interest of personal decisions, rather than as a biopolitical technology for generating and policing the boundaries of the private such that it does not challenge the geographies and scale structure of liberal jurisdiction. Similar kinds of formulations arise in scholarly defenses of polygamy. They describe the matter of choosing a partner or deciding on one's living arrangements as "a deeply personal matter," "the most personal of personal choices," "the most important aspects of people's private lives," "an intensely personal process," and as "inherent in the concept of individual autonomy."[70] The decision in *Brown* and such arguments for the recognition of plural families register and seek to ameliorate the kinds of shame Kim TallBear notes with regard to the supposed failure to enact the ideal of the nuclear family (as discussed in chapter 1), but these pro-polygamy arguments divorce their analysis from a broader critique of the racializing and colonial dynamics that animate processes of enfamilyment and that seek to pathologize and dismiss alternative political orders.

To clarify, I'm not seeking to challenge the arguments for decriminalizing polygamy or legally recognizing polygamous or polyamorous relationships. Rather, I want to draw attention to what such arguments normalize and efface with regard to the history of anti-Mormonism and what that history suggests about state management of the possibilities for envisioning what can constitute governance. These arguments distinguish between "private enclaves" and "alternative political orders" and include caveats about such relationships deserving legal acknowledgment so long as they do not "threaten civil order," and they suggest such relationships should not be subject to "unjustified interference by the state," such that each of us is "capable of choosing the lifestyle we think is best."[71] The commonsensical surround of liberal presumptions and apparatuses of governance protects "marriage-like" relationships, even when they are "not predicated on romantic or sexual intimacy."[72] In these formulations, personhood continues to emerge from an enfamilyment thought to train one in how to have a politics predicated on privatized enclaves, albeit ones whose contours may differ somewhat from each other based on extrapolitical and politically insignificant kinds of "lifestyle." In this vein, the *Brown* decision and these other defenses of polygamy displace the ways that racialization continues to serve as a means of categorizing and regulating the kinds of personhood that should emerge from proper enfamilyment—the difference between the liberty-exercising civil individual and the barbarously inclined criminal.[73] Read in this way, the Mormon decisions provide a means of seeing how the "liberty-interest" developed in the "right to privacy" cases of the late twentieth century turns on the projection of an extrapolitical matrix for producing liberal personhood that itself is animated by a biopolitics that recodes other social formations and political orders as antisocial, racialized nonpersonhood requiring direct state intervention. I now turn to those cases.

The (Racial) Realm of Personal Life

When talking about privacy, we usually default to some version of an individual's right "to be let alone."[74] In their famous article "The Right to Privacy" from 1890, Samuel D. Warren and Louis Brandeis argue for "the right to privacy, as part of the more general right to the immunity of the person,—the right to one's personality," and they characterize that right as necessarily "inviolate."[75] However, if arguing for the rights and liberty of the individual citizen provides the principal way of constitutionally validating legal recognition of something called "privacy," those ideas take shape against a set of background assumptions about the kinds of personhood and modes of relation covered by this concept. Liberal notions of enfamilyment provide the ideological infrastructure in which privacy gains form and meaning. Being a proper subject of personal as well as public life entails both emerging from and tending toward the sphere of bourgeois domesticity. Absent such immersion in the supposedly extrapolitical yet politically foundational norms of the family, a person appears less as a viable citizen-subject than as a bearer of potentially contagious kinds of aberrance, backwardness, and/or criminality that threaten to undo the liberal political order and the jurisdictional structure of the state. The popular depiction of and legal assault on the Mormons offers perhaps the most spectacular example of this pattern. Narratives of legal change over the latter half of the twentieth century, though, tend to cast such racializing visions of proper family and state intervention as a thing of the past, replaced by a commitment to individual dignity, autonomy, liberty, and civil rights largely legally grounded in interpretations of the Bill of Rights and the Fourteenth Amendment.[76] Yet, not only do the foundational decisions recognizing a right to privacy validate it by tying it to the extrapolitical obviousness of bourgeois homemaking, they differentiate such enfamilied subjectivities from those punishable as criminality. In this way, the legal imaginary of privacy helps produce and animate the understanding of other kinds of social formations as racialized zones of deviancy, increasingly characterized less through explicit racial categorization than attributions of ingrained pathology in need of sovereign management by state actors or their surrogates. The sterilization of women of color and the shifting terms of welfare policy help illustrate the dominant equation of personhood with privatized enfamilyment and the ways racialization works in biopolitical ways to present alternative formations as a threat to the health, welfare, and sovereignty of the liberal state.

While articulations of privacy as a legal principle date to at least the late nineteenth century, it emerges as an explicit official frame for constitutional interpretation (and, thus, for popular remobilization) in *Griswold v. Connecticut* (1965). The case concerns a state statute preventing the use of any "drug, medicinal article or instrument for the purpose of preventing conception" and threatens with criminal sanction "any person who assists, abets, counsels, causes, hires or commands another to commit any offense" of that ban with the same punishment "as if he were the principal offender."[77] Estelle T. Griswold, the executive director of the Planned Parenthood League of Connecticut, and C. Lee Buxton, a doctor who volunteered at the Planned Parenthood clinic opened in 1961, were arrested in what they intended to be a case to test the constitutionality of the law. In the Court's majority opinion, Justice William Douglas finds unconstitutional the law's intrusion on married couples' ability to exercise their liberty with regard to matters of reproduction. However, as has been noted and critiqued by many legal scholars since that time, the decision does not so much tie this matter to a particular constitutional provision—such as the Fourteenth Amendment's requirement that no state shall "deprive any person of life, liberty, or property, without due process of law"—as indicate the existence of "penumbras" that stand behind or are "emanations" from the Bill of Rights that index the existence of a foundational "zone of privacy."[78] Douglas implicitly draws from the kind of reasoning at play in Warren and Brandeis's formulation of privacy seventy-five years earlier, positing a set of integrative and more expansive principles that provide the background for and ostensibly justify the more clearly delineated rights and prohibitions in existing precedent. The opinion, though, refashions that earlier articulation of privacy both as a constitutional principle (rather than one focused primarily on tort law) and as one organized around the bourgeois household.

The Court finds that Connecticut's law violates the sanctity of that private space in the ways it inserts the state into the "intimate relation of husband and wife," thereby intruding upon the proper separateness of marital couplehood and homemaking from the sphere of politics and public policy. The decision further describes the former realm as "older than the Bill of Rights—older than our political parties, older than our school system," adding, "Marriage is a coming together for better or for worse, hopefully enduring, and intimate to the degree of being sacred. It is an association that promotes a way of life, not causes; a harmony in living, not political faiths; a bilateral loyalty, not commercial or social projects."[79] As a crucial aspect of national being and becoming, marriage and the privileged realm of intimacy created by it exist before and beyond the apparatuses of the state, making possible the "way of life" those institutions exist to protect and enable and thus lying outside the purview of legislative intervention. That union/zone explicitly is not "political" or the result of specific "social projects." As in *Reynolds* and the other Mormon decisions, marital couplehood and familial nuclearity appears to animate the law itself, as the self-evident unit that does not so much emerge through law and policy as create the conditions that enable (liberal) governance to exist as such. The "right to privacy" formulated in *Griswold* depends on understanding marriage and the sphere of its intimacy as, in Marc Stein's terms, "a pre-constitutional space"—one that makes possible the liberal political order without actually lying within it.[80] In his concurrence, Justice Arthur Goldberg presents "the right of marital privacy" at issue in the case as "fundamental," citing a range of cases that he suggests "have respected the private realm of family which the state cannot enter" and describing "the traditional relation of the family" as being "as old and as fundamental as our entire civilization."[81] While less prominent in the majority opinion, such an invocation of "our . . . civilization" points to the racializing assumptions at play in normative articulations of the private, the ways they take shape by implicit contrast with other modes of sociality and conduct—barbarous and criminal—which are understood as threatening to undo or rupture the enclosed space of family.

In the decision, the apparent obviousness of "the family" relies for its coherence on an unacknowledged and dehistoricized whiteness. As discussed earlier, the dominant conception of the marital couple and their biological children as an affectively enclosed entity that provides the basis for household formation and gendered economic subsistence arose in uneven and contested ways over the course of the nineteenth century, in complex relation to conceptions of enchattelment and its legacies, Indian savagery, and irreducible forms of Asian (particularly Chinese) alienness. Moreover, the particular version of the ideal of enclosed familial self-identity treated as given in the decision depends on taking for granted the distribution of benefits through the GI Bill in the wake of World War II, which made possible extensive nonagricultural homeownership for whites while rampant state-sanctioned redlining and massive government investment in transportation infrastructure made possible the construction of the suburbs that gave material, segregationist shape to the notion of single-family detached insularity on which the decision implicitly draws in figuring the "private" as a self-contained space apart.[82] The narrative offered by the decision also edits out the extensive Progressive-era commitment to eugenic policy, including the state and federally accepted use of sterilization on those understood as impeding national progress, especially people deemed mentally and developmentally disabled or criminally unredeemable (legalized practices related to, although still distinct from, the federally funded sterilizations of women of color in the 1970s and 80s, which I will address shortly).[83] In addition, as Martha Minow illustrates, the cases cited as precedent for the right to family privacy offered in *Griswold* "more accurately reflect struggles between majority and minority religious or ethnic groups. The Court treated those struggles as problems of families, individuals, and the state."[84] Notably, despite the fact that the Connecticut law in question in *Griswold* primarily affected clinics serving impoverished women (including women of color) rather than actions by private physicians, since the latter's advice to patients was markedly less visible, the decision does not address the potential equal protection issues at stake in the law's uneven enforcement, including the racial and class differentials of the criminalization it enacts. Instead, the vision of the marital home as isolated, intimate, and legally inviolable becomes central in ways that not only erase the material circumstances of prosecution and its uneven effects but that reinforce a distinction between privacy and criminality that turns on what is de facto a model of bourgeois whiteness. In this way, the notion of marriage and the family as inherently part of a "zone" of privacy at play in *Griswold* introjects and normalizes the racializing policy architecture of the early- to mid-twentieth-century United States as both self-evident and self-evidently extrapolitical in its founding/authorizing relation to constitutional governance.

One might argue, though, that even if the "right to privacy" as it emerges from *Griswold* derives from an investment in nuclear homemaking, the kinds of individual liberty interests at stake in the concept's application have moved far from such marital/familial doctrinal origins. However, if one looks at cases unrelated to the rights of married people, they extend the scope of privacy by reasoning through analogy to the private realm of family at play in *Griswold*, such that legally recognized and valued kinds of personhood are derived through their relation to liberal enfamilyment. Such cases help illustrate the de facto ideological commitments at play in seeking to extend notions of the private sphere. Most directly, *Eisenstadt v. Baird* (1972) takes the decision in *Griswold* and applies it to unmarried people as well, holding that a Massachusetts statute criminalizing the circulation of contraceptives to single people also violates the Constitution. The decision states, "If under *Griswold* the distribution of contraceptives to married persons cannot be prohibited, a ban on distribution to unmarried persons would be equally impermissible," adding, "If the right of privacy means anything, it is the right of the *individual*, married or single, to be free from unwarranted governmental intrusion into matters so fundamentally affecting a person as the decision whether to bear or beget a child." This language seems to move away from a right that inheres in marriage or the supposed zone of intimacy it creates, instead suggesting a more broadly conceived sense of sexual freedom or personal autonomy. Yet, the Court quite specifically centers its ruling on equal protection principles, the idea that there is not "some ground of difference that rationally explains the different treatment accorded married and unmarried persons" under the Massachusetts statute. The opinion explicitly sidesteps the issue, raised in the decision by the Court of Appeals, of whether "fundamental human rights" are at stake with regard to single persons' use of contraception.[85] In other words, the "individual" who possesses a right to access birth control does so because the dynamics in which the law seeks to intervene approximate those with regard to married people, whose proper insulation from public intrusion appears axiomatic.[86]

To be *like* marital privacy, to engage in conduct *like* that which founds and shapes bourgeois homemaking, is to have similar kinds of rights, absent the government's ability to indicate a substantive policy reason for different treatment.[87] Similarly, in *Roe v. Wade* (1973), the Court finds unconstitutional a Texas law criminalizing abortion (except to save the mother's life) on the basis of its invasion of "a right of personal privacy" that attaches to "certain areas or zones of privacy" that include "activities relating to marriage . . . ; procreation . . . ; contraception . . . ; family relationships . . . ; and child rearing and education." While also finding that the state has a valid interest in the "protection of health, medical standards, and prenatal life" that becomes increasingly relevant after the first trimester, the Court presents what it understands as an individual decision by a woman, whether married or not (the appellant in the case was not), as a function of a (set of) right(s) rooted in a vision of the supposedly sacrosanct, intimate *zone* of marital homemaking. The subjectivity of the person exercising this right takes shape through an ideology of enfamilyment, as a qualified broadening of the principles of liberal privacy.[88] As elaborated in *Planned Parenthood v. Casey* (1992), which reaffirms what it presents as the central holdings of *Roe* while setting aside the trimester framework of the earlier decision and allowing for various increased efforts by states to delay and complicate access to the procedure, abortion appears as part of "a realm of personal liberty" for which the marital privacy of the bourgeois household provides the exemplary instance. The Court cites previous cases' articulation of "constitutional protection [for] personal decisions relating to marriage, procreation, contraception, family relationships, child rearing, and education" (from *Carey v. Population Services* [1977]) and for "the private realm of family life which the state cannot enter" (from *Prince v. Massachusetts* [1944]) as outlining the "realm" of privacy in which abortion lies.[89] For a choice or matter to count as "personal" for the purpose of constitutional protection, it must conceptually remain in the orbit of the classic liberal private sphere of the nuclear household and its ostensibly internal concerns. In characterizing the nature of the decision to have an abortion and the implications of carrying a child to term, the Court repeatedly employs the terms "intimate" and "personal" as a kind of mantra meant to signal a commonsensical set of assumptions about how to understand pregnancy in relation to the public sphere and the realm of political debate.[90]

This sense of pregnancy as fundamentally belonging to an extrapolitical space of privacy defined in terms of heteronormative homemaking dominates these decisions despite moments when they gesture toward concerns and contexts that trouble this framing. For example, *Roe* elliptically invokes issues of "population growth, pollution, poverty, and [the] racial overtones" that "complicate" the matter of abortion and reproduction more broadly, alluding to environmental and economic policy as well as widespread practices of state-sanctioned sterilization on eugenicist and racist grounds. In striking down the parts of the Pennsylvania statute at issue in the case that mandates spousal notification and documentation of such before an abortion can be performed, the decision in *Casey* spends almost ten pages outlining findings with regard to domestic violence that militated against such notification, while also noting that such a requirement "embodies a view of marriage consonant with the [earlier] common-law status of married women but repugnant to our present understanding of marriage and of the nature of the rights secured by the Constitution," in which marriage does not annul a woman's separate liberty interests.[91] As opposed to an affirmation of the enduring and inherent character of the zone of personal life, these moments suggest that it has been and continues to be defined and shaped, in differentially raced and classed ways, by public policy decisions and legal interpretation and that it continues to function as a site of heteropatriarchal violence, in ways that are presented as entrenched rather than exceptional. The conception of (sexed) personhood affirmed in these decisions is one for which "the private realm of family life," organized paradigmatically around the self-enclosed marital household, provides the putatively extrapolitical grid of intelligibility despite acknowledgment (albeit limited) of the historicity of this ideal, the limits of its application in public policy, and its significant failures to secure the health and well-being of "family" members.

Rather than highlighting debates and decisions around birth control and abortion per se, I want to draw attention to how privacy takes shape as an institutionalized norm in ways that naturalize the nuclear family form and envision the existence of a personal zone (modeled on bourgeois homemaking) that exists apart from matters of governance. Reciprocally, practices that otherwise would be prosecutable cannot be understood as such when viewed as an extension of family life. We need to remember that what's at stake in *Griswold*, *Eisenstadt*, and *Roe* is not solely access to particular methods for preventing pregnancy or ending it but the discursive and institutional processes by which the line is drawn between legal respectability and criminality. To partake in practices, forms of subjectivity, and modes of relation not analogically comparable to the internal workings of the nuclear household is potentially to be made criminal, positioned as a threat to public order and national welfare (as in the case of Mormon polygamy). We should remember that privacy emerged as a constitutional principle at the same time that the Supreme Court was constricting Fourth Amendment rights of protection from search and seizure only to spaces, in the words of *Katz v. United States* (1967), where there is a "reasonable expectation of privacy,"[92] suggesting a dialectical relation between delineating zones of privacy and criminality. The putative distinctness and insulation of a zone of personal life also means that the rights that attach to the privacy of that space cease to exist, or at least are readily curtailed and bracketed, when it can be understood as having become public via the provision of governmental funds. The foundational ideological distinction between the public and private that enables the construction and legitimation of such ever-expanding zones of rightlessness also animates racializing attributions of wrong enfamilyment that license actions to curtail the social menace such supposedly dysfunctional formations represent. Beyond the family lies the potentially criminal, a threat manifested in the failure to be properly private. Framed slightly differently, if the notion of the private sphere recasts the everyday materialization of liberal legal geography as an extrapolitical realm outside or beyond the law, the failure to enact that ideal potentially challenges liberal jurisdictional imaginaries by suggesting the possibility of differently configured kinds of social forms, ones not organized around privatized propertyholding. Casting bodies living such potential political orders as racialized, deviant, and criminally threatening weaponizes privacy as a biopolitical norm.

With regard to the government's legal authority to intervene in what otherwise would be considered (following the logic of *Griswold*) to be private matters, race does not appear as an explicit means of validating such action by the state, but processes of racialization shape what get to count as rights-bearing forms of home and family. A racialized ideal of the private serves as the political basis for delineating the supposedly extrapolitical zone of privacy that the state presents itself as merely recognizing in the attribution of rights to that zone. Unlike in the Mormon cases, (re)-definitions of the right to privacy do not directly cite the threat of non-white social forms taking root in US space in ways that disrupt the nation's sovereignty. Instead, discourses of familial autonomy, or the lack thereof, become ways of figuring encroachments upon the public sphere, equating dependence on government funds with deviancy such that persons and groups appear as pathological and de facto criminal in their failure to remain within the bounded realm of the private. Race animates such distinctions, even in the absence of conventional modes of racial classification, through the understanding of the violation of norms of bourgeois privacy as expressive of ingrained collective tendencies in need of disciplinary management—either directly by the state or in ways sanctioned by it.[93]

This pattern can be seen through attention to two important Supreme Court precedents regarding the ability of states and the federal government to limit the provision of federal funds: *Dandridge v. Williams* (1970) and *Harris v. McRae* (1980). In *Dandridge*, the Court finds family caps—the limitation of welfare benefits to cover only a certain number of children in a given family—to be constitutional. Justifying this restriction, the decision affirms "the principle that the Fourteenth Amendment gives the federal courts no power to impose upon the States their views of what constitutes wise economic or social policy," and the opinion earlier indicates that "here we deal with state regulation in the social and economic field, not affecting freedoms guaranteed by the Bill of Rights." A state, in this case Maryland, supposedly has an interest "in encouraging gainful employment" and "in providing incentives for family planning" that trumps any potential liberty interest on the part of such families with regard to their internal composition.[94] If privacy outlines a constitutionally protected zone, the provision of welfare is imagined as constitutively piercing that boundary such that matters that otherwise would be considered "personal" and "intimate" become subject to the political regulation of *economic and social policy*, of which "family planning" apparently is a part. The *Harris* case concerns what has become known as the Hyde Amendment, limiting (and largely preventing) the use of federal funds for abortion. The opinion distinguishes between "direct state interference with a protected activity," in this case seeking an abortion, and "state encouragement of an alternative activity consonant with legislative policy," finding that the state (whether individual states or the federal government) has the "power to encourage actions deemed to be in the public interest."[95] While a right theoretically exists, one validated in its association with elements of life understood as belonging to a properly insulated and extrapolitical "realm of family life," not only does the government have no responsibility in facilitating the exercise of this right, but it actively can endorse and financially incentivize countervailing options that it deems "to be in the public interest." As Khiara M. Bridges argues with respect to various forms of governmental intervention into poor women's lives, "poor mothers actually *do not* possess privacy rights"; she suggests that "wealth is a condition for privacy rights and that, lacking wealth, poor mothers do not have any privacy rights," as "their socioeconomic status has already precluded their possession of any privacy rights that the state is obliged to respect."[96] In both *Dandridge* and *Harris*, the private sphere appears as a phantom ideal against which poor people can be found wanting and, thus, subjected to various kinds of state discipline (whether explicitly cast as such or not) for failing to fulfill a legislatively endorsed vision of family and reproduction that itself supposedly merely acknowledges an extralegal, natural norm. Building on Bridges's analysis, one can understand privacy less as a kind of right poor people do not have than as a way of envisioning how the sphere of rights enables and in many ways actively promotes the production of zones of rightless and potentially criminal abjection. If citizenship in the eighteenth and nineteenth centuries attached to notions of masculine autonomy, largely illustrated through heteropatriarchal control over women, children, and other dependents, conformity to a particular model of family life—nuclear, middle-class, and putatively self-sustaining—provides the new criteria for autonomy, now called "privacy," that licenses one to be legally regarded as a full citizen.[97]

Although the determinations at play in these cases do not appear on their face to be about race, the designation of those receiving state aid as pointedly subject to the regulatory social policy of the state should be understood as underwritten by processes of racialization. The de facto pathologization of particular ways of performing home and family not only disproportionately targets people of color and presents them as paradigmatic of the failure to be proper national subjects (offering something like the narrative of contagion employed with regard to the Mormons), but the association of alternative formations with non-white deviance allows for them to be cast as distensions and deformations of the private in need of state intervention. In his dissents in both *Dandridge* and *Harris*, Justice Thurgood Marshall lays out the limits of looking to explicit racial classifications in understanding the role of the law in producing forms of racial(ized) distinction. He presents extant principles of due process and equal protection review as working in formalistic ways to evade addressing who actually is impacted by given laws and policies as well as such laws' violent effects on those people's lives. As against the process of deciding whether a "fundamental right" is at stake and, if not, then only applying "rational basis" review unless a "suspect class" (such as African Americans) is directly referenced in the legislation, Marshall argues for the importance of attending holistically to "the character of the classification in question, the relative importance to individuals in the class discriminated against of the governmental benefits [withheld] . . . , and the asserted state interests in support of the classification." He notes that absent such analysis, part of what goes missing in rhetorics of privacy and its limitation is the relative impact of withheld benefits or circumscribed rights on people of color, such as the "substantial portion" of women de facto denied access to abortion by the Hyde Amendment who "are members of minority races."[98] Yet, in seeking to indicate the existence and legal significance of forms of disparate racial impact, Marshall is struggling against the portrayal of home and family as having been cleansed of state-produced racial differentiation. In the wake of *Loving v. Virginia* (1967), which found bans on interracial marriage unconstitutional due to their promotion of "White Supremacy," the private zone created by marriage and the legal realm of personal liberty derived from it appear to be free from racist state interference.[99] If the state cannot explicitly regulate access to privacy rights on the basis of direct racial classification, though, that fact does not mean that race ceases to operate as a vital part of how the boundaries of privacy are drawn.

The idea of a constitutional right to privacy arose amid the increasing demonization and disciplinary regulation of welfare recipients and the vast increase in state-supported sterilization of women of color receiving various kinds of state funding.[100] Presumptions of criminality and a proclivity toward violence serve as the flip side to the extension of privacy rights: citizen-subjects deemed worthy, partially as a function of their performance of bourgeois enfamilyment, are the bearers of rights; whereas those groups that illustrate what are taken to be pathological patterns of enfamilyment are, by virtue of that putative failing, understood as immanently disruptive and dangerous, as having implicitly forfeited the right to have rights.[101] Although largely identified with people of color starting in the late 1960s, particularly African Americans, the system of federal provision of benefits for impoverished children that came to be known as welfare began in the 1930s as part of an effort to address the effects of the Depression and was directed away from offering resources to non-whites.[102] Created as a way of providing funds to single-parent households, largely envisioned as those led by widows, the Aid for Dependent Children (ADC) Program was administered by states in ways that restricted access to women who had been married to their children's father, who were not currently in a romantic relationship, and who were not otherwise working, while routing funds away from people of color, especially African Americans. As with the design of Social Security benefits such that domestic service and agricultural labor did not count toward eligibility, thereby excluding most workers of color (both men and women), states defined and managed eligibility criteria for ADC in ways that almost entirely excluded non-whites. One of the less discussed struggles during the Civil Rights Era is Black inclusion within government benefit programs, including ADC, which officially was reconfigured in 1962 as Aid to Families with Dependent Children (AFDC) in ways that facilitated far greater access to the program for African Americans. The Personal Responsibility and Work Opportunity Reconciliation Act (PRWORA) passed in 1996 under Bill Clinton (who, in 1992, vowed to "end welfare as we know it") replaced federal grants-in-aid to states based on numbers of people eligible for welfare benefits with fixed block grants—Temporary Assistance for Needy Families (TANF)—while limiting total time on welfare (to five years), incorporating far more extensive work requirements, and including provisions with regard to promoting marital respectability (including beginning with the "findings" that "marriage is the foundation of a successful society" and "marriage is an essential institution of a successful society which promotes the interests of children").[103] This legislative change took place against the background of increasingly punitive discourses regarding African American family and household formation and the charge that federal resources were encouraging modes of Black deviance.

Such narratives of aberrance and the perversity of dependence on state aid transpose matters of governance and political economy into the register of a collective inability or unwillingness to be properly private.[104] Deindustrialization and urban restructuring in the 1960s and 1970s, combined with ongoing patterns of white flight underwritten by government-supported redlining, racialized cities as sites of decay and social disorganization.[105] Widespread forms of non-nuclear family and household formation came to be understood as causing urban patterns of pathology. Habiba Ibrahim argues, "the city had to gain its character of deviance from a naturalized affinity with black people. . . . If the ghetto was a place for sequestering, criminalizing, and regulating blackness, the new national goal tautologically suggested that blackness transformed the city into a dangerous, dysfunctional ghetto."[106] Political and economic policies that produce and sustain racialized impoverishment ideologically are converted into the spectacle of a collective inability or unwillingness to perform liberal privacy, perhaps most infamously in the Moynihan Report's diagnosis of Black female-headed households as the reason for the absence of Black progress and the prevalence of what were presented as antisocial tendencies.[107] As a legal and popular ideal, privacy gains meaning through contrast with increasingly prominent narratives of people of color's failure to perform normative enfamilyment, circulating perhaps most prominently with regard to welfare.

Reciprocally, within dominant discourses, attending to modes of explicit racial reference and their absence can defer an analysis of the ways law and policy differentially produce populations through managing access to the material conditions needed to sustain nuclear family life. As Dána-Ain Davis observes, "Welfare reform's singular reference to 'self-sufficiency' . . . brushes over the complexities of how communities are marked by the disappearance of jobs and the restructuring of labor markets, which exacerbate hierarchies, particularly racial ones."[108] My point is not that the nuclear family form is inherently desirable but that it is posited as an extrapolitical norm in ways that efface the structural processes that distribute in a massively uneven way the resources necessary to sustain that form while also presenting the effects of that inequity as due to ingrained inclinations toward antisocial behavior supposedly inculcated by wrong ways of enacting home and family.[109] Discourses around welfare, including the figure of the "welfare queen," "blamed single Black mothers for many of the upheavals of the 1960s [and afterwards], including poverty, riots, protests," casting children raised in such wrong enfamilyment as "likely participants in civil disorder."[110] Within the ideological matrix of privacy, viable personhood and political subjectivity depend on emergence from the realm of nuclear family life, and modes of collective opposition and experiments with other social configurations appear as sovereignty-disrupting expressions of pathological intimate life (or life lived without an appropriately self-regulated and insulated realm of privacy).

The supposed failure to be discretely private is demonized not simply because it is (imagined as) correlated to actions by non-white persons but because such failure is understood as expressive of non-whiteness, an ingrained inclination toward deviancy that bespeaks the backwardness and menace of a given population—such as with the Mormons. In addition to conceiving of people of color as deviant and portraying practices as deviant because they are associated with persons of color, there is the coding of practices, relations, and social formations as racially deviant in their distinction from liberal enfamilyment, which also helps drive the first two dynamics.[111] This pattern can be seen at play in the ways welfare came to be seen as a racialized phenomenon despite the fact that there were more white people on it than people of color.[112] These dynamics fuse in the depiction of people of color as bearing within them tendencies toward unmanageable modes of sociality and personhood. As Dorothy Roberts notes, "It is believed that Black mothers transfer a deviant lifestyle to their children that dooms each succeeding generation to a life of poverty, delinquency, and despair. A persistent objective of American social policy has been to monitor and restrain this corrupting tendency of Black motherhood." She later adds, "Many Americans believe not only that Black mothers are likely to corrupt their children, but that Black children are predisposed to corruption."[113] Discourses demonizing state dependence biopolitically convert matters of governance into qualities of bodies—pathological inclinations that symptomatically manifest as wrong home and family.[114] Sterilization, then, appears as a solution to such racialized failures of privacy.

While forced sterilization had been legal in various states starting in the early twentieth century, the scope for such government-sanctioned eugenic projects expanded greatly in the age of the "right to privacy," often being justified on the basis that the women involved receive state funding of one kind or another. The notion of "eugenics" emerged in the writings of an English scientist named Sir Francis Galton at the end of the nineteenth century, but although he largely framed it in terms of proliferating "the more suitable races," the idea of engineering a better national population through reproductive interventions took hold in the United

States in the form of efforts to prevent procreation by what were deemed undesirable populations. Indiana was the first state to pass such a law in 1907, targeting criminals and "imbeciles" for involuntary sterilization; by the 1930s, twenty states had passed similar legislation.[115] In *Buck v. Bell* (1927), the Supreme Court found such practices to be constitutional. The majority opinion says of the Virginia statute in question that, by sterilizing those deemed mentally unfit, it prevents defective persons "[from] becom[ing] a menace" while also preventing the birth of "socially inadequate offspring" who would further "sap the strength of the State" in ways that would leave it "swamped with incompetence" by "those who are manifestly unfit." The decision closes with Justice Oliver Wendell Holmes's infamous declaration: "Three generations of imbeciles are enough."[116]

While these laws came under increasing criticism in the wake of World War II and the understanding of the Shoah as a state-sponsored eugenics program, mass involuntary sterilization gained increasing popularity as de facto public policy in the early 1970s, targeting women of color—particularly Black, Native, and Puerto Rican women.[117] In the case of *Jessin v. County of Shasta* (1969), a California appeals court "ruled that 'voluntary sterilization is legal when informed consent has been given, that sterilization is an acceptable method of family planning, and that sterilization may be a fundamental right requiring constitutional protection.' Prior to this case, many physicians had assumed that sterilization as a birth control method was illegal."[118] The previous year, President Lyndon B. Johnson had partnered with Nelson Rockefeller (whose father had created the Population Council in 1952 to address the supposed scourge of excess fertility among poor populations, particularly in the Third World) to create the Committee on Population and Family Planning to provide poor people with access to forms of birth control. In 1970, President Richard Nixon created the Commission on Public Growth and the American Future to explore possibilities for addressing what was understood as the problem of population growth. That same year, Congress passed the Family Planning Act, which provided up to 90 percent reimbursement to doctors for the cost of sterilization for those receiving government-covered healthcare, and the budget of the Department of Housing, Education, and Welfare (HEW) for family planning increased from $51 million to $250 million a year.[119] As Megan Devlin O'Sullivan observes, "The government made sterilization inexpensive and available for Americans on public assistance in an era overwhelmingly marked by reductions in healthcare services. From 1970 to 1977, federally-funded sterilizations increased nearly 300%

from 192,000 to 548,000 each year."[120] In Native communities served by the Indian Health Service, estimates for the percentage of women of childbearing-age sterilized during the 1970s range anywhere from 25 to 50 percent.[121] The push for sterilization also helps explain what may seem like the contradictions of federal policy in simultaneously supporting family caps for benefits and denying funding for abortion. Absent women having resources to raise a child or to terminate a pregnancy should it accidentally occur, sterilization appears as the only state-subsidized family planning and support option for poor women of color.[122]

In the midst of the articulation and expansion of the constitutional "right to privacy," the federal government actively facilitated the targeting of women of color for involuntary sterilization by enthusiastically funding and promoting such procedures. While these surgeries were not conducted under a law enabling sterilization of people without their consent, as were those conducted under earlier forms of eugenic legislation by various states, the matter of informed consent—and, often, any form of authorization by the patient—routinely was bypassed for women of color on Medicaid and Native women receiving treatment from the Indian Health Service. This flagrant pattern of disregarding the matter of women's consent occurred despite federal court requirements that such consent be secured and federal regulations laying out the process for doing so, both of which also forbade threatening the loss of benefits should a woman refuse sterilization—a threat made frequently.[123] Various studies conducted over the course of the 1970s, independently and by the Government Accountability Office, found rampant and clear disregard for patients' wishes alongside explicit declarations by doctors of the importance of using sterilization to curb what they understood as abuses of the welfare system and to promote the good of the country by diminishing social disorder. A study conducted by the Health Research Group in 1973 registered white male physicians' belief "that they were helping society" by "enabling the government to cut funding for Medicaid and welfare programs while lessening their own personal tax burden": "Some of them did not believe that American Indian and other minority women had the intelligence to use other methods of birth control effectively and that there were already too many individuals causing problems in the nation, including the Black Panthers and the American Indian Movement."[124] The wrong enfamilyment illustrated by dependence on government aid produces subjects who engage in the disruptive and deviant publicness of radical movements. Or, read in reverse, the countersovereignties and political orders staged in such movements are understood in racialized terms as expressive of failed homemaking—as the result of an inability to be private that justifies putting an end to dysfunction-generating procreation by pathologically ill-adjusted persons and families.

If the bodies of Indigenous and racially marginalized people can be understood as bearing political orders, as discussed in the introduction and chapter 1, involuntary sterilization offers perhaps the most egregious example of efforts to strangulate such orders through their translation as a dangerous deformation/distension of the liberal private sphere. The violence of welfare reform and state-sanctioned coercive sterilization cannot be remediated simply through the expansion of what constitutes legitimate or legally recognized forms of domesticity. Building on scholarship and activist intellectual work developed through reproductive justice frameworks, I want to suggest not only that racialized and racializing determinations about what constitutes privacy invidiously limit possibilities for autonomous decision-making with regard to procreation, mothering, and other elements of social reproduction, but that the right to privacy itself depends on producing other persons, spaces, and relations as inappropriately public in ways understood as endangering liberal geographies of property and political authority.[125] As with the contemporary attempt to normalize polygamy discussed in the previous section, delineating the contours of appropriate homemaking, whatever those contours might be, preserves the sense of a private sphere that can be differentiated from public matters. The work of liberal ideologies in naturalizing the jurisdictional grids that sustain private propertyholding and capital as merely the extrapolitical stuff of home and family—as well as the racialization of anything that undermines or exceeds such distinctions—can continue to proceed (shifting slightly, in Uday Mehta's terms, the "anthropological minimum" of inclusion within liberal universalism, but still retaining it). Roberts argues, "I am not so sure that the precise ground used to justify punishing Black women for having babies matters—whether Black children's intrinsic problems are traced to genetics, or to crack, or to a cycle of welfare dependency, or to ghetto culture": "Whether it is Justice Holmes pronouncing 'three generations of imbeciles are enough' or Justice Broadman [in a case in the 1980s in California] declaring 'three generations of welfare recipients are enough,' the degrading effect is the same."[126] That effect of engendering not-quite personhood—including the variability of the biopolitical metrics used for casting collectivities as deviant populations—inheres in the ongoing (re)production of liberal privacy as an extrapolitical sphere. As Ann Laura Stoler suggests with regard to colonial policy in Southeast Asia, "finer scales measuring cultural competency and 'suitability' often replaced explicit racial criteria."[127] From this perspective, collective organizing for change and the staging of alternative political orders appear as symptoms of such unsuitability—as regressive tendencies toward criminality, dependence, and savagery that can be seen in the failure to be properly (privately) enfamilied.

From Criminality to Conjugality

From 1986 to 2015, the Supreme Court had a somewhat remarkable turnaround on issues related to same-sex eroticism and relationships, moving from upholding laws criminalizing sodomy (in *Bowers v. Hardwick*) to affirming a constitutional right for same-sex couples to marry (*Obergefell v. Hodges*). While often characterized as a progressive expansion of understandings of liberty, equal protection, and civil rights, including in the narratives offered by the decisions themselves, this shift also has been understood as enfolding queerness into liberal political economy and whiteness.[128] Katherine Franke has characterized "the same-sex marriage movement" as "racialized," both in the tendency to "equat[e] homosexuality with whiteness" and the ways "claims to rights for same-sex couples and families are based on appeals to their inherent dignity and decency, thereby distinguishing them from other undeserving, dysfunctional, or immoral sexual or kin formations that are almost always understood in racial terms."[129] This argument resonates with Jasbir Puar's discussion of "the ascendancy of whiteness, which is not a conservative, racist formation bent on extermination, but rather an insidious liberal one proffering an innocuous inclusion into life," a dynamic "bound to heteronormativity" that differentiates "between queer subjects who are being folded (back) into life" and "racialized queernesses" that mark populations as threatening and/or disposable.[130] In this way, racialization inhabits and organizes the legal recuperation of same-sex relationships for privacy and family, naturalizing liberal governance and pathologizing alternative formations. Attending to such processes helps clarify the stakes of seeking to expand a legally recognized *zone of privacy* or *realm of personal liberty*,[131] including how such efforts can themselves limit the potential for envisioning what governance might entail by continuing to take the nuclear family form and liberal legal geographies as the de facto background for social (justice) imagination. Reading for the "implicit racial grammar," in Stoler's terms, that emerges across and helps shape the Court's cases focused on same-sex desire and marriage foregrounds how sociopolitical formations not organized around liberal privacy come to appear as deviant and destructive.[132] Rather than addressing the status of people of color as such within the decisions, I want to focus on how these cases tie personhood to liberal enfamilyment, juxtapose the liberty interests of such subjects against forms of criminality and excessive publicness (implicitly associated with non-whiteness), and figure marriage in ways that deracialize its history and resituate inclusion of homosexuality within a progressive narrative de facto organized around whiteness. That narrative not only presumes the superiority of Anglo-American "civilization" but, in doing so, renders commonsensical the shape of state sovereignty.

The right to engage in consensual sexual activity with another adult and to have a state-recognized marriage are not equivalent and, in many ways, point in different directions with regard to understanding legal personhood. The one is about forms of bodily autonomy and being potentially subjected to prosecution for particular kinds of acts with another person, and the other entails a change in legal status, largely unrelated to criminal law, that bundles together a host of federal and state rights and obligations and that bind two persons into what functions for many purposes as a single unit.[133] The decriminalization of erotic acts between persons of the same sex, and of nonreproductive sexual relations more broadly, need not inherently bear on or be conceptualized in terms of legally recognized forms of kinship and household formation. For almost the entirety of the twentieth century, though, homosexuality—defined principally in terms of sexual object-choice, although also powerfully involving discourses of gender inversion—was viewed in popular and official terms as antithetical to family life and, thus, beyond the realm created by heteroconjugal pairings.[134] As a kind of subject, the homosexual gained public meaning in contradistinction to marriage and childrearing, viewed and represented not just as exterior to these social dynamics but as a threat to them (including through the linkage of same-sex eroticism with pedophilia). The history of marriage rights and the right to privacy both can be interpreted as taking shape around repudiations of nonnormative sexual activity, particularly homoeroticism.[135] The question of the legal status of homoerotic expressions of desire and of the definition of marriage (and the realm of privacy it engenders and paradigmatically anchors) remained ideologically entangled in ways that tended to loop the discussion of one into an engagement with and commentary on the other. While marriage also prominently has been distinguished from other modes of life and groups characterized as deviant, such as the flagrant and predatory singleness of the (presumptively Black) "welfare queen,"[136] homosexuality enters public discourse as something of a foil for marriage as such, as that which lies beyond the latter's historical, conceptual, and moral boundaries and that operates as a kind of contagion endangering the stability and primacy of marriage within national life.

Across the decisions focused on same-sex eroticism and marriage, the issue of (sexual) personhood continually is staged against the background of the institution of marriage, such that the former appears as necessarily a function of its relation to the zone established by and defined through the latter. In *Bowers v. Hardwick* (1986), which concerns prosecution of two men for the violation of a Georgia statute that made illegal all oral contact with the genitals or anus of another person (regardless of the sex of the persons involved), the Court argues that there can be no "constitutional right of homosexuals to engage in acts of sodomy" because "no connection between family, marriage, or procreation on the one hand and homosexual activity on the other has been demonstrated." The right to "private and intimate association," which the Court of Appeals for the Eleventh Circuit articulated based on prior cases (including *Griswold*, *Eisenstadt*, and *Roe*), could not extend to "homosexual" acts due to the ways they remain outside the bounds of liberal norms of domesticity. In his much-cited dissent, Justice Blackmun observes that the "privacy interest" at play in prior cases involves "certain *decisions* that are proper for the individual to make" and references "certain *places*" that have a protected status, insisting that this case "implicates both the decisional and spatial aspects of the right to privacy." He derives a right to sexual privacy from the fact that decisions with regard to such activity "form so central a part of an individual's life," reciprocally suggesting that "we protect the family because it contributes so powerfully to the happiness of individuals."[137] Family (and, implicitly, marriage) arises out of individual choices and contributes to individuals' well-being, and in this way, Blackmun picks up certain strands of *Eisenstadt* and *Roe*. The figure of the decision-making individual serves as the pivot that ties "homosexual activity" to family, marriage, and procreation, so as to access the rights articulated with regard to enfamilyment (as discussed in the previous section).

Yet rather than opening up conceptual space between the rights-bearing "individual" and the scene of marital domesticity, later decisions intensify this tie, increasingly construing the personhood recognized by the law as necessarily enmeshed in and derived from the extrapolitical sphere of conjugal privacy—the zone of enfamilyment. In *Lawrence v. Texas* (2003), the Court struck down a Texas anti-sodomy law as unconstitutional, reversing the decision in *Bowers* and further indicating that the ruling had been wrong at the time it was made. Defining the liberty interest at stake in the case, the decision notes, "To say that the issue in *Bowers* was simply the right to engage in certain sexual conduct demeans the claim the individual put forward, just as it would demean a married couple were it to be said marriage is simply about the right to have sexual intercourse," adding that this case "touch[es] upon the most private human conduct, sexual behavior, and in the most private of places, the home." The opinion also invokes the decision in *Planned Parenthood v. Casey* that "our laws and tradition afford constitutional protection to personal decisions relating to marriage, procreation, contraception, family relationships, child rearing, and education."[138] Despite the fact that the two persons at the center of *Lawrence* (John Geddes Lawrence and Tyron Garner) were not in a long-term relationship (they basically had a one-night stand), the decision speaks as if the sexual conduct for which they were prosecuted was necessarily synecdochic for a marriage-like connection.[139] The right at issue in the case is presented as one associated with *couplehood*, further suggesting that legal recognition of that connection would prevent the otherwise presumably *demeaning* narration of sexual conduct as the principal matter at hand. Or, put another way, the possibility of legally acknowledging an individual right to such conduct appears contingent on routing it through bourgeois domesticity—the realm delineated in the list from *Casey* of kinds of protected "personal decisions." The attendant vision of personhood takes shape through association with marriage and privatized homemaking, such that they serve as the background through which to imagine what constitutes the individual as a rights-bearing entity.

This rendering of the liberal private sphere, shaped around monogamous marital homemaking, as *the* extrapolitical frame through which to understand normative and legal personhood, becomes central in *Obergefell v. Hodges* (2015). This case finds that states' failure to recognize same-sex marriages is an unconstitutional violation of the due process and equal protection clauses of the Fourteenth Amendment, building on the finding two years earlier in *United States v. Windsor* that the Defense of Marriage Act's (DOMA) prevention of federal recognition for same-sex marriages authorized by states violates the Fifth Amendment's due process guarantees. The majority opinion in *Obergefell* observes, "The Constitution promises liberty to all within its reach, a liberty that includes certain specific rights that allow persons, within a lawful realm, to define and express their identity. The petitioners in these cases seek to find that liberty by marrying someone of the same sex." Over the course of the decision, though, personal identity and liberty increasingly appear indissoluble from marriage. It asserts, "Its dynamic allows two people to find a life that could not be found alone, for a marriage becomes greater than just the two persons. Rising from the most basic human needs, marriage is essential to our most profound hopes and aspirations," underlining "the centrality of marriage to the human condition," and the decision later adds that denying recognition for same-sex marriage would "disparage their choices and diminish their personhood," since marriage "embodies the highest ideals of love, fidelity, devotion, sacrifice, and family. In forming a marital union, two people become something greater than once they were."[140] While the focus on marriage is understandable given that it is at the center of the case, these ways of talking about it present it as not simply an expression of personal liberty but as the paradigmatic way of conceptualizing what personhood is. Marriage is depicted less as a kind of social institution whose contours, dynamics, and social functions are historically and legally contingent than as a basic feature of humanness, without which interpersonal connections become impoverished. To be an individual sans marriage de facto appears as itself a kind of diminished personhood, as one having failed to satisfy the conditions for achieving "our most profound hopes and aspirations."

While portrayed in terms of an affectively saturated space of mutual care, this vision of maritally centered personhood remains animated by the notion of an extrapolitical and even prepolitical realm. That realm operates in self-contained and self-sufficient isolation, exists beyond the sphere of political debate and action, and is imagined as itself serving as the legitimizing and normative core for liberal governance. If the ways of figuring such autonomy shifted over the course of the first half of the nineteenth century from wealth in private property to heteropatriarchal whiteness,[141] by the mid to late twentieth century it had morphed into a vision of healthful relations of emotional and sexual companionate support within the bourgeois household—what Elizabeth Povinelli characterizes as the "intimate event" of liberal ideology and policy.[142] As Julian Carter has illustrated, notions of the sexual and marital "normal" came to be narrated as such in the first few decades of the twentieth century. He argues, "Normality discourse drew on and extended several earlier conceptual vocabularies, especially those of civilization and evolution, in a way which made it possible to talk about whiteness indirectly, in terms of the affectionate, reproductive heterosexuality of 'normal' married couples," and he adds that "normality discourse appeared to be politically neutral in large part because it so often framed its racially loaded dreams for the reproduction of white civilization in the language of romantic and familial love" while "at the same time and through the same gestures, that civilization's core racial value was redefined in terms of love."[143] The explicit attribution of civilizational unfitness and perverse aberrance to non-whites at play, for example, in the work of Lewis Henry Morgan, or the popular and official representations of Mormon polygamy, largely shifted over the course of the twentieth century into discourses of familial abnormality, as in the depiction of welfare discussed in the previous section. When racial destiny is transposed into the biopolitics of marital privacy, conjugal expressions of homoeroticism can be incorporated into a universalizing vision of white familialism. The unmarking of whiteness—its "race-evasive" and "power-evasive" recasting "as love"—valorizes and extends liberal political economy as merely an acknowledgment of the immanent promise of maritally oriented personhood.[144] Such apparent recognition normalizes the principles of liberal governance as basic to "the human condition" rather than a racialized field in which other configurations of care, desire, and intimacy come to be characterized as expressive of dangerous inclinations in need of policing and state discipline (including the denial of resources and punitive relation toward those deemed dependent). The Court's fusion of marriage and personhood reanimates the racial politics of liberal homemaking but does so in ways that do not appear to attach to persons of color; race appears irrelevant with regard to access to personal identity and rights understood in terms of conjugal unity and privacy, a dynamic magnified by the ways *Loving v. Virginia* is cited by many as an analogy through which to think same-sex marriage rights.[145]

The Court's account of marital insularity articulates lawful (homo)sexuality as occurring within the household (a clearly delineated, privatized space apart), and this conception of autonomous privacy depends on a series of racializing assumptions through which other visions of sociality—other political orders—appear not as their own ways of collectively enacting personhood but as expressions of antisocial tendencies toward backward and criminal forms of excessive publicness. As with *Griswold*, *Eisenstadt*, and *Roe*, the decisions in *Bowers* and *Lawrence* concern the question of whether state governments should have the power to criminalize particular actions—using birth control, getting an abortion, or having anal/oral sex. At issue in these decisions, though, is not simply the matter of prosecutable conduct but also the extent to which certain persons can or should be deemed criminal for partaking in these actions, whether they can or should be understood as a type of deviant subject in contrast to upstanding citizens.[146] Part of the work these decisions perform, then, is in defining relations between sorts of acts, kinds of persons, and forms of political subjectivity. The majority opinion in *Bowers* declares that "otherwise illegal conduct is not always immunized whenever it occurs in the home," but Justice Blackmun in his dissent insists, "the right of an individual to conduct intimate relationships in the intimacy of his or her own home seems to me to be the heart of the Constitution's protection of privacy." The zone of privacy that is one's "own home" transmutes what might otherwise be criminal into an expression of intimacy. Blackmun adds, "the mere fact that intimate behavior may be punished when it takes place in public cannot dictate how States can regulate intimate behavior when that occurs in intimate places," and the attempt to do so involves "invading the houses, hearts, and minds of citizens who choose to live their lives differently."[147] The repeated multiplication of the terms "intimate" and "intimacy" suggests a territorialization of the behavior: it is intimate by virtue of belonging to spaces deemed intimate, namely the possessive and privatized enclosure of the home. Yet, the household indicates more than a space that is both discreet and discrete: it stands for the "hearts" and "minds" of citizens in their separateness from institutions of governance, the extrapolitical individual personhood that liberal institutions putatively exist to protect.

To be criminalized for *intimate* behavior practiced in private places is to be made a criminal kind of subject in ways that violate liberal norms of propertyholding and personal identity (as well as the understanding of personal identity as a form of property, as self-possession).[148] The majority opinion in *Lawrence* builds on this view, arguing, "Liberty protects the person from unwarranted government intrusions into a dwelling or other private places. In our tradition the State is not omnipresent in the home." The supposed non-appearance of law and policy in the *home*—itself de facto figured as a conjugally oriented space in ways discussed earlier—delineates the contours of independent *personhood*. The decision further indicates, "The petitioners are entitled to respect for their private lives. The State cannot demean their existence or control their destiny by making their private sexual conduct a crime," quoting the idea from *Carey v. Population Services* (1977) that the Constitution recognizes "a realm of personal liberty which the government may not enter." To criminalize their "private" actions would be to "demean" them as people, as a class of people. In this vein, the opinion addresses how the criminalization of same-sex eroticism "imposes" a "stigma" that affects "the dignity of the persons charged" but also those who could be deemed criminal within the terms of statute.[149] The transition away from the *stigma* of criminality to full political subjectivity, as signified by state "respect" for one's "private" choices, is summarized in the declaration in *Obergefell* that "outlaw to outcast may be a step forward, but it does not achieve the full promise of liberty," which apparently comes with full inclusion into liberal nuclear enfamilyment.[150] The dignity accorded by the state, though, depends on the behavior and relations in question remaining within the "realm" whose boundaries are drawn around the single-family household. To be insufficiently *private* and *intimate* is to tarry with the criminal. The public is the space of potential punishment, or as the decision in *Lawrence* reassures, the liberty of which it speaks "does not involve public conduct."[151]

The potential for criminality attaches to publicness, in the sense of performing properly private acts in a nonprivate place, failing to contain oneself within the bounds of the private sphere, and/or appearing as part of a collective that exceeds the intimate event of nuclear couplehood.[152] Such excessiveness violates the terms of normative personhood: what should remain confined and concealed within the household—the space of liberal enfamilyment—spills out into the streets in disruptive and dangerous ways. The sense of such performances of public collectivity as a threat redeploys evolutionary and eugenic articulations of the difference between white civilizational development and the messy backwardness of non-white populations while transposing such racializing narratives into a different ideological register.[153] With regard to the policing of neighborhoods historically seen as gay enclaves, such as Greenwich Village in New York City, Martin Manalansan notes, "various styles of occupying everyday public spaces have been radically altered [and] . . . can easily be couched as 'loitering,' 'vagrancy,' or a suspicious congregation of people. Thus these public spaces are subject to intense monitoring." The policies designed to prevent such publicness are "about fencing off unwanted colored bodies, yet . . . [they] are rhetorically rendered as positive outcomes and developments for all queers."[154] The legal recognition of realms of privacy for same-sex couples actually can intensify forms of criminalization that largely target people of color by casting publicness as itself expressive of a disordering deviance.[155] In addition to targeting persons and communities of color, the criminalization of collective publicness enacts a racializing distinction between those capable of understanding and performing liberal intimacy/autonomy and those who are not—a division that parallels the one between self-sufficiency and dependent aberrance in the debates over welfare and sterilization discussed earlier. In the sodomy and same-sex marriage cases, the implicit differentiation between subjects of intimate dignity and of public criminality replays earlier accounts of civilizational progress—such as Morgan's division between civilized and barbarous peoples (those who remain unable to separate the descriptive family from the confused morass of classificatory kinship). The inability to appreciate and perform liberal privacy marks one as potentially criminal, as bearing a perverse orientation toward publicness that illustrates an ingrained incapacity to respect and enact "the highest ideals of love, fidelity, devotion, sacrifice, and family."[156] The personhood affirmed in these cases with regard to same-sex eroticism and marriage takes shape against the background of ongoing processes of racialization through which liberal enfamilyment is cast as a set of natural tendencies whose absence indicates a kind of inherent and unruly deficiency requiring state intervention.[157]

In addition, the formulation of rights in the same-sex marriage decisions involves recasting racial identity and institutionalized racism as matters that already have been resolved and that have no direct bearing on the issues at stake in the decisions or the persons affected by them. In this way, whiteness serves as the de facto framework for the legal principles in the decisions. Those arguing for and against the majority opinions invoke the history of white supremacy, but in order to suggest its irrelevance for the issues at hand. In this way, racial power surrounds the decisions and their reasoning, shaping them around its apparent absence. In his dissent in *Windsor*, Justice John Roberts says with regard to the majority's characterization of the homophobic intent at play in the passage of DOMA, "Bear in mind that the object of this condemnation is not the legislature of some once-Confederate Southern state..., but our respected coordinate branches, the Congress and the Presidency of the United States." Soon thereafter, he adds, "it is harder to maintain the illusion of the Act's supporters as unhinged members of a wild-eyed lynch mob when one first describes their views as they see them."[158] Alluding to the Civil War and the circumstances of the passage of the Fourteenth Amendment serves as a way of indirectly suggesting that the principles of due process cited by the majority (in terms of the Fifth Amendment but largely arising out of interpretive precedents with regard to the Fourteenth) are not appropriately employed with regard to gays and lesbians. They, presumably, do not inherit protections that arise out of the history of slavery, either directly as themselves descendants of those freed or by analogy. Furthermore, Roberts implies, those who support legislation against same-sex couples are not like the "wild-eyed lynch mob" whose irrational commitment to racist violence merits state intervention to protect their victims (despite the absence until 2022 of any actual federal legislation to prevent or punish lynching). Enslavement and antiblack terror function as the negative instances through which to argue for the inappropriateness of constitutional claims for same-sex couples.

Moreover, Roberts implicitly portrays racism as spectacular (invoking secessionists and an armed mob) and as belonging to a superseded past (the apparent ludicrousness of perceiving contemporary legislators in these outmoded ways). This way of thinking about race helps explain the decisions that same session in *Shelby County v. Holder* and *Adoptive Couple v. Baby Girl* (discussed in chapter 2) in which the Court, respectively, voided the provisions of the Voting Rights Act (1965) that enabled federal oversight of changes in election procedures in named states and counties and recast the Indian Child Welfare Act (1978) as about Native parents' relative racially transmitted traditionalism rather than Native nations' ability to protect their own (prospective) citizens from being alienated (largely by white parents).[159] Discussion of the role of race and racism in ordinary policy and everyday life appears anachronistic and inappropriate, as a bygone phenomenon and/or a category mistake. Roberts's dissent in *Windsor* helps illustrate how this bracketing of race and racialization frames the stakes of legal engagements with same-sex marriage. In his dissent, he implies that only direct acts of racial violence count as the basis for the Court to intervene with regard to defining and defending "due process." Decisions with regard to same-sex marriage are not about race, and therefore, they do not merit federal judicial action. The debate around the legitimacy of such marriages, then, appears to take place on the discursive terrain of presumptive whiteness, severed from principles that pertain to matters of racial discrimination and subjugation.

While differently figuring the terms and stakes of "due process" with regard to DOMA and state bans on same-sex marriage, the majority opinions in *Windsor* and *Obergefell* largely reproduce Roberts's deracialization of marriage. Not only do the decisions avoid engaging the history of the use of marriage in the United States to regulate officially recognized forms of racial identity and familial relation, including who could count as lawful kin and inheritors of property, they also offer a narrative of progress in which the law increasingly recognizes mutuality, love, and personal dignity within and through conjugal couplehood.[160] In doing so, the decisions approach marriage in terms of the kinds of affective relations and capacities that, as discussed earlier, came over the course of the twentieth century to encompass the meanings previously associated with explicit invocations of the evolutionary triumphs and destiny of whiteness. The race-evasive account of marriage in these opinions combines a Euro-American account of marriage's importance to civilization with a story of expansion of equality within and through the private sphere. Both decisions address marriage in civilizational terms, such as the declaration in *Windsor* that "marriage between a man and a woman no doubt had been thought of by most people as essential to the definition of that term and to its role and function throughout the history of civilization," or in the slightly more capacious formulation in *Obergefell* that "the centrality of marriage to the human condition makes it unsurprising that the institution has existed for millennia and across civilizations."[161] While invoking a similar kind of narrative structure as in *Reynolds* and the other Mormon cases in terms of the centrality of marriage to the United States as part of its participation among the community of civilized nations, these opinions also suggest that marriage has changed in ways that promote greater reciprocity and liberty. As *Windsor* proclaims, "The limitation of lawful marriage to heterosexual couples, which for centuries had been deemed both necessary and fundamental, came to be seen in New York and certain other States as an unjust exclusion."[162] Since that case's focus was on the right of states legally to define marriage in ways that the federal government could not contravene (thereby striking down DOMA), it emphasized changes in understandings of marriage at the level of state legislatures.

However, *Obergefell* makes the broader argument for the liberty-interest and due process rights of same-sex couples across the United States regardless of states' policies, and in doing so, it offers a much more sweeping discussion of changes in the ways marriage has been perceived and its social function. The opinion observes, "marriage was once viewed as an arrangement by the couple's parents based on political, religious, and financial concerns; but by the time of the Nation's founding it was understood to be a voluntary contract between a man and a woman," adding, "As the role and status of women changed, the institution further evolved. Under the centuries-old doctrine of coverture, a married man and woman were treated by the Statute as a single, male-dominated legal entity." The Court paralleled these transformations to changed understandings of homosexuality: "many persons did not deem homosexuals to have dignity in their own distinct identity," but "in more recent years ... psychiatrists and others [have] recognized that sexual orientation is both a normal expression of human sexuality and immutable."[163] Such changes are part of a process of evolution in conceptions of liberty "as we learn its meaning" and as distinctions and discriminations that "may have long seemed natural and just" appear as now irrational and invidious.[164] Moreover, such transformations are part of an immanent national process of becoming, one presented as perhaps uniquely American. The Court declares, "changed understandings of marriage are characteristic of a Nation where new dimensions of freedom become apparent to new generations."[165] The expansion of freedom, though, occurs through recognitions of new "dimensions" of the zone of personal life ordered around the paradigmatically conjugal household, as well as within the commonsensical geography of the nation and its jurisdictional structure.

The decisions in *Windsor* and *Obergefell* do not address the role of processes of racialization in the history of what marriage is and what it does, as well as the criminalization of those whose arrangements of care, decision-making, resource distribution, and placemaking do not fit this model and are deemed catastrophically *public*. Moreover, when the decisions do indirectly allude to the history of marriage's role in processes of racialization through invocations of *Loving v. Virginia*, that case is converted into one about interpersonal affection, rather than institutionalized enactments of white power.[166] The story told about marriage in these two cases does not include the prohibition on marriages among enslaved people as well as the nonrecognition of any legal kinship ties between masters and those slaves with whom they had sexual relations or the children that resulted from those inherently coercive interactions. Moreover, there is no discussion of the enforcement of marriage on freed people during the Civil War and Reconstruction; the imposition of US legal marriage on Native peoples in ways that sought to privatize territory and fracture Indigenous sociopolitical systems; the denial of immigration for Asian women on the basis of their presumed sexual immorality or the later restriction of immigration to "family reunion"; the revocation of women's citizenship for marrying foreigners, particularly those ineligible for naturalization (itself involving explicitly racialized criteria into the mid-twentieth century); and the passage of the very anti-miscegenation statutes that *Loving* rendered unconstitutional.[167] In this way, the workings of marriage in US history, its changing contours and aims, and the supposed liberty-enhancing trajectory of its transformation all de facto appear as if they occurred within whiteness. Or, put another way, the story of growing freedom that occurs within and for bourgeois privacy depends on almost entirely bracketing struggles over the racial status of various populations, the nature and scope of both private property and US jurisdiction, the management of racialized groups through the direct regulation of family- and household-formation, and the relationship between forms of collective belonging (chosen or imposed) and US citizenship. This deracialization, then, seems consistent with the understanding of the legal reconfiguration of what constitutes family and kinship as the acknowledgment of an extrapolitical sphere whose scope and workings reproduce existing liberal grids of governance, rather than highlighting the active political process of constructing the private and the ways the framing of a zone of personal life as beyond governance naturalizes liberal geographies of jurisdiction and the sovereignty of the state.

In this vein, *Windsor* and *Obergefell*'s rewriting of *Loving* seems particularly notable. In *Windsor*, the earlier case is cited in passing as indicative of the ways state marriage laws "must respect the constitutional rights of persons," with no mention of the matter of race as such.[168] Although *Obergefell* offers a far more robust engagement with *Loving* (it notes the latter ruling struck down laws that banned "interracial unions"), it repeatedly reroutes the earlier decision toward an affirmation of the centrality of marriage rather than seeing it as marking and repudiating white power. The decision invokes *Loving* as a precedent for the principle that the "Court has long held the right to marry is protected by the Constitution" and that "the right to marry is fundamental under the Due Process Clause." However, it goes on to claim, "This abiding connection between marriage and liberty is why *Loving* invalidated interracial marriage bans under the Due Process Clause," and the opinion later adds, "The reasons why marriage is a fundamental right became more clear and compelling from a full awareness and understanding of the hurt that resulted from laws barring interracial unions."[169] In this telling, the principal issues at play in *Loving* had to do with the intimate character of marriage as an expression of individual liberty and affective connection; conversely, the problem with anti-miscegenation laws was that they blocked the expression and consummation of such essential personal impulses.

However, while the Court's decision in *Loving* certainly cites marriage as a fundamental right, that discussion comes after a lengthy investigation of the ways the Virginia statute in question was "designed to maintain White

Supremacy" and could not be justified except by reference to "the racial discrimination which it was the object of the Fourteenth Amendment to eliminate."[170] What makes anti-miscegenation statutes unconstitutional, in the terms of the opinion in *Loving*, is that such laws actively seek to use marriage as a means of shaping the contours of legal recognition for home and family in ways that promote and secure white supremacy. As Dorothy Roberts observes, "By 1940, thirty states had passed statutes barring interracial marriage. Antimiscegenation laws were a eugenic measure."[171] In recasting the *Loving* decision as chiefly about love within conjugal couplehood and the "hurt" of nonrecognition based on race, *Obergefell* edits out the relation between state-backed processes of racialization and the regulation of what constitutes the private sphere—or, put another way, the relation between the legal construction of the private sphere and the biopolitics of racialization through which alternative formations (what we might describe as political orders) are cast as threatening and criminal. Although the decision in *Loving* might be understood as predicating "the legitimacy of interracial marriage" on "its thorough heterosexualization,"[172] the case's emphasis on the state production of whiteness points toward connections between legal processes of defining marriage/family/domesticity and of racially differentiating populations from each other. These connections are effaced in *Obergefell*'s story of progressive acknowledgment of the extragovernmental dignity of marriage-worthy love.

The decisions focused on gay and lesbian rights (or, more specifically, on sodomy and same-sex marriage) operate within and redeploy a set of racializing framings that shape the contours and character of the space of sexual-marital privacy in which personal liberty can be enacted. While the rights at issue in these cases may tend most to advantage those who already have the most advantages,[173] I less want to foreground relative privilege among queers than the ways seeking to expand rights to state-recognized enfamilyment can reinvest in the (re)production of categories of racialized deviance not attached to same-sex desire as such. Building on Puar's discussion of the distinction between those queers who can be folded into life and other queered persons and populations marked for discipline/death, I'm arguing that the decisions discussed in this section point to the ways modes of collectivity that do not fit liberal mappings of social life can appear as nonpersonhood, criminality, and anachronism. The incorporation of same-sex desire within a historical and legal narrative implicitly organized around whiteness helps point, by contrast, to dynamics of racialization with respect to sexuality, family, and homemaking that exceed object-choice within erotic couplehood. As Marlon Ross has argued, the concept of homosexuality emerged as a way of addressing difference among the civilizationally advanced, as distinct from populations that were understood as having failed to achieve the gendered distinctions or family forms that would enable them to register the perversity of homoeroticism. He suggests that within nineteenth-century sexology the "homosexual subject" appeared "as racially retarded," given that "the perceived racial difference of an African or Asian male could be used to explain any putatively observed sexual deviance." These differential histories of sexuality produced, in Ross's terms, "alternative sexual modernities," such that the deviance that is homosexuality appears as such from within whiteness in contrast to the general sexual-gendered household disorder attributed to populations of color—or through which populations of color are defined as such.[174]

From this perspective, the inclusion of same-sex desire and couplehood within bourgeois domesticity marks more than a homonormative investment in dominant social forms by some queer subjects.[175] That inclusion suggests changes within the ideological matrix of whiteness, including reinscribing and possibly intensifying the distinction between the realm of enfamilied personhood (which de facto credentials proper political subjects as such) and pathologized zones of deviant, dangerous, and criminal publicity. The racializing attribution of wrong forms of home and family that historically has served as the flip side to visions of marital normativity—including in attacks on the Mormons in the nineteenth century and the campaigns for welfare reform and sterilization in the twentieth century—serves as the unacknowledged background against which legal determinations about sodomy and same-sex marriage come into focus. The representation of sexual activity in terms of conjugally oriented personhood and the framing of marriage itself as a (national sovereignty-affirming) private sphere of love and dignity help produce a rearticulation in which homosexuals implicitly are figured as rights-bearing subjects to the extent that they can be resituated within the whiteness from which they categorically were cleaved (or at least segmented) in the late nineteenth century.

* * *

Law and policy decisions with regard to privacy, welfare, sterilization, sodomy, and same-sex marriage do not seem like they have much to do with the sovereignty of the liberal state. These issues certainly are pertinent with regard to thinking about state-sanctioned or state-promoted forms of social reproduction, and they bear directly on consideration of the biopolitical frameworks through which rights and legal personhood are conceptualized, regulated, and distributed. However, these issues and determinations do not appear related to the scope and character of the state's jurisdiction as such, unlike in the case of the *imperium in imperio* represented by the Mormon Church. The spectacle of Mormon collectivity and self-governance, along with the federal assault on the Church's proto-sovereignty via the outlawing and prosecution of polygamy, provides a means of thinking about the stakes of discourses of marriage/privacy/domesticity with regard to what constitutes governance. In dismantling Mormons' political formations, the federal government cast those formations as expressions of racialized deviance, enabling liberal political economy—organized around privatized nuclear units—to appear as the self-evident form for healthful, moral governance, itself also understood as a function of whiteness. As illustrated in the example of the Mormons, charges of wrong home and family reframe debates over political organization, jurisdiction, and subjectivity as relative conformity to an inherently extrapolitical set of principles that provide the practical and normative basis for social order as such. To the extent that determinations with regard to things like privacy, welfare, sterilization, sodomy, and same-sex marriage seem like they have little connection to the form of state sovereignty, they implicitly have been situated within the racializing matrix of enfamilyment in ways that treat the marital/private/domestic sphere as axiomatic rather than as a means of managing (including criminalizing) forms of collectivity that challenge the legal geographies and legitimacy of the liberal state.

Seen in this way, the project of expanding or reconfiguring modes of legal recognition for that sphere and its internal relationships does not undo the racializing work of the private sphere. Extending rights to marry variously defined kinds or numbers of persons, for example, does not prevent those not so enfamilied from being cast as aberrant and potentially dangerous in their nonunion. Moreover, and more importantly for my argument here, the orientation of political and intellectual work toward redrawing the bounds of the protected zone of personal life can impoverish possibilities for envisioning collective governance that are not routed through the state and its forms while also indirectly accepting the racialized representation of such forms of collectivity as dangerous and disruptive kinds of publicness in need of state intervention, since in terms of scope or aims these collectivities fail to remain enclosed within the boundaries of that private/privatized zone. What's at issue, then, is how the articulation of concerns as "about" privacy or privatized space de facto normalizes the character and legitimacy of liberal governance in ways that can have devastating effects for those whose processes of networked relations, in Leanne Simpson's terms, are deemed inappropriate due to their failure properly to perform privacy.[176] As illustrated by the privacy cases, attempts to expand this right to cover various other forms of decision-making involve enfolding the new issue or relation within a conception of extralegal personhood modeled on the marital household and the aspects of life (family, reproduction, childrearing) it supposedly embodies and encloses. That dynamic positions those who do not fit this image of privatized autonomy as legitimately subject to state-sanctioned violence while reciprocally facilitating the portrayal of non-privatized modes of sociality (where personhood is not predicated on enfamilyment) as chaotic incursions into the property rights of others.

My point, though, is less about the relative tactical value of such efforts to expand or shift the topoi of liberal lawmaking (who exactly is included or benefited by such maneuvers) than about the ways those efforts can orient away from and possibly decrease the potential for acknowledging, building, and investing in other-than-liberal models of governance—alternative political orders. The issue on which I seek to focus is not that certain strategies for change depend on valorizing those understood as deserving or who are the most privileged among a given oppressed group, although such dynamics are important as part of social justice work.[177] Rather, I aim to illustrate how political claims made through the prism of enfamilyment reinforce the terms and networks of liberal jurisdiction in ways that can facilitate the ongoing targeting for government discipline of forms of collectivity deemed criminal, excessive, perverse, and/or disruptive. Such limitations on the potential for alternative modes of governance might be understood as the racializing reverb generated by, even ostensibly progressive, attempts legally to inhabit the sphere of *kinship*. The question of sovereignty, therefore, inhabits discussions of household and family formation in at least two ways: state legal geographies form the background grid against which social formations come to appear as proper home and family; and, conversely, other collective processes of decision-making, forming place, and distributing resources that are targeted as dangerous in their publicness can be understood, instead, as enactments of governance.

Nonheteropatriarchal modes and matrices of relation might themselves be (re)conceptualized as networks of governance, as, in Charlene Carruthers's terms discussed in the previous chapter, shaping spaces for "the project of collective liberation."[178] The liberal private sphere appears as both beyond politics and as the normative background for political decision-making, and thus discussions of *home* and *family* implicitly reinvest in the legal geographies and jurisdictional scale structure on which those categories depend and that they normalize. Approaching modes of collective organization and movement as governance or political orders, whether self-described in this way or not, helps distinguish them from expansions or reconfigurations of liberal privacy, thereby further acknowledging and tapping into their transformative potential rather than implicitly isolating them within an exceptionalized zone. Peter Coviello suggests that we might understand the Mormons' repudiation of polygamy in the 1890s and subsequent investment in the narration of themselves as hypernormative as a crucial part of the genealogy of homonationalism.[179] Following this logic, we might see the issues of contending conceptions of governance so clearly at play in the legal assault on the Mormons as also at play in other state formulations and negotiations around home, family, and sexuality. In addition, we might read for the ways the racial imaginary of liberalism on display in the case of the Mormons—the presentation of alternative sociopolitical formations as expressions of racial deviance— also organizes discussions and debates with regard to the (re)construction of the private sphere. In this way, the regulation of what constitutes home and family might serve as a prism through which to view the history of racialization in the United States, and reciprocally, those sites treated as evidence of wrong enfamilyment—the failure to be properly private—might serve as loci for tracing and further envisioning alternative political orders and possibilities for governance beyond liberal paradigms.

FOUR

Blackness, Criminality, Governance

IN HER FIELD-CHANGING essay "Black Nationalism and Black Common Sense," Wahneema Lubiano argues that "black nationalism" has functioned as "black American common sense," suggesting that "its circulation has acted both as a bulwark against racism and as disciplinary activity within the group." Given that Black people in the United States, in "their 'being-as-a-group,'" have not controlled the means of production or a clear territorial space, and did not until the 1960s engage in "meaningful participation in formal public politics," Lubiano indicates that "culture has been our terrain of struggle." However, the cultural work of Black nationalism, she suggests, has not operated outside the terms of the state but in complex dialectical relation with them: "Even as it functions as resistance to the state on one hand, it reinscribes the state in particular places within its own narratives of resistance. That reinscription most often occurs within black nationalist narratives of the black family."[1] Lubiano critiques such nationalist framings for the ways they normalize heterogendered and privatizing notions of *family*, themselves largely imposed by the state (as elaborated in the previous chapter), as the infrastructural basis for what presents itself as an oppositional imaginary. Even as Black nationalism marks and contests the racialized and racializing character of US political economy, the distinctions, in Lewis Henry Morgan's terms (discussed in chapter 1), between "domestic institutions" and "political society" persist. In this way, such nationalism remains in the orbit of the very state forms it would seek to contest, raising questions about the potential for conceptions of *governance* to incubate or speak to alternative social forms. We might understand this Black feminist line of critique as providing much of the animating force for more recent articulations within Black studies of the need to eschew notions of politics and political belonging in order to pursue possibilities less tethered to conceptions of property, privatization, and the ideological and jurisdictional parameters of the liberal state.

To what extent, though, can the state, and modes of nationalism understood as entwined with state discourses and projects, be taken as the de facto referent for governance or a notion of political orders? We might address this question by placing it alongside the issue of whether collective modes of emplacement necessarily can be understood as *property*. In a recent article that addresses the pattern within some scholarship (particularly Afropessimist work) of characterizing Indigenous landedness as an extension of dominant logics of ownership, the authors note that the "understanding of land remains ontologically attached to settler colonial understandings of land as property," and in a similar vein, Mishuana Goeman argues that "a consequence of colonialism" has been the "translation or too easy collapsing of *land* to *property*," in ways that efface "land as a storied site of human interaction" and "as a meaning-making process rather than a claimed object."[2] The equation of collective emplacement with property is paralleled by and intertwined with another equation, namely that of governance with the nation-state or state-like institutional apparatuses, ideologies, and jurisdictional geographies.

From this perspective, governance necessarily means some version of nationalism modeled on or indissolubly intertwined with the state. One of the anonymous reviewers for this project (to whom I am deeply grateful for their careful attention and insights) noted that "there is no operative concept of 'political order' outside of the history of liberalism." However, as Cheryl Harris notes, "While we typically associate aspirations for sovereignty with Indigenous peoples, and the quest for citizenship with Blacks, history suggests a more complicated reality in which Blacks sought something more than citizenship."[3] How might the notion of *political orders* help speak to the contours and character of that "something more than" in ways that exceed "the history of liberalism"?[4] Discussing the "common-sense black nationalism that currently solidifies black belonging," Kara Keeling argues that such nationalism "explains and secures the group's cohesion as black, giving the notion of 'belonging' to that group a political force that is antagonistic to those forms of racist domination and exploitation that assist in the consolidation of white bourgeois hegemony in the United States."[5] Building off the kind of analysis offered by Lubiano, Keeling suggests that this common sense effaces what she terms "the black femme function," which she uses to refer to forms of self-understanding, modes of interpersonal relation, and kinds of social dynamics that do not fit into stagings (particularly cinematic ones) of what constitutes political blackness. Drawing on Angela Davis's discussion of the life-preserving labor of Black women, Keeling observes, "While common-sense black nationalism valorizes death, presenting 'dying for the people' as a more noble form of resistance than surviving enslavement and violence, it devalues the tactics used by those who forged ways of sustaining life and communities in the face of violence, exploitation, and oppression," highlighting the "invisible, affective labor" that makes such survival possible and that remains "out-of-field"—not signifiable as part of the *political* scene within a nationalist imaginary.[6] What happens, though, if that very labor, those "ways of sustaining life and communities," could be understood not as a personal or domestic scene (often referred to as *kinship*) disjunct from the political but as the very site for the workings of governance? What if the labor of social reproduction were also the labor of forging and sustaining alternative political orders?[7] I want to suggest that within a certain intellectual common sense such "network[s] of relationality" and "daily lived practices" (drawing on Laura I Iarjo's terms, discussed in chapter 2) cannot count as governance, as part of the workings of political orders.[8]

What if the dynamics that remain out-of-field in understandings of what counts as the political were themselves vital parts of the "something more than" that repeatedly has been sought in the wake of emancipation? In chapter 2, I address the ways that understandings of Native sovereignty that seek to cleave the racial from the political can miss the ways that contemporary settler governance in the United States works through the positing of the racial—in the form of the Indian family and blood genealogy—as the contouring limits and implicit legal infrastructure for such sovereignty. In a reciprocal vein, this chapter aims to explore how certain current intellectual approaches also cleave blackness from the political, but in this case to understand governance as necessarily a function of antiblackness. The purpose of my analysis is to increase possibilities for attending to how the violence of racialization is enacted through ongoing processes of primitive accumulation (as discussed in the introduction) that recast Black political orders—collective processes of self-governance—as signs of criminogenic deviance, as the constitutive inability to be properly enfamilied. Tracing such patterns is itself in the interest of highlighting and further capacitating modes of situated Black collective self-determination that are neither necessarily statist in character nor predicated on the familial as a privatized sphere.

While such a reading may not exactly reflect the self-description of those formations by participants, this *redescription* opens toward a thinking of, in Jodi Byrd's terms, "grounded relationalities" among Black, Indigenous, and other racialized people(s) that neither ignores differences between and among them nor redeploys intellectual equations that foreclose Indigenous peoplehood and self-determination. Byrd points to "the value that the place-based epistemologies that have been the bedrock of Indigenous thought" can bring "when placed alongside other fields as a turn against the old enmities that serve settler colonial capitalism," including the denial of place and belonging and the making fungible that is central to antiblackness.[9] In a piece Byrd co-authored with Alyosha Goldstein, Jodi Melamed, and Chandan Reddy, the authors ask, "How might building capacities for relationality outside the logics of propriation [of propertyholding] make it possible to handle incommensurate demands for justice?"[10] Attending to situated Black political orders beyond the state form is an effort to help build such capacities. Not only does doing so aim to open further potentials for marking and engaging Black projects of collective self-organization and self-determination, I want to suggest that it generates greater resources for alliance by further moving away from what can be an exceptionalizing discourse of indigeneity that defines it in contrast to racialized national minorities that are understood, in contrast to Native nations, as seeking inclusion in the state. I might characterize the approach I'm pursuing here as rereading through an Indigenous studies-oriented frame, in which what often gets called kinship speaks less of an expanded/distended familial sphere than modes of emplaced governance. That rereading seeks to see what possibilities might come into view—to think the "out-of-field," in Keeling's terms, beyond certain forms of extant critical common sense.

Historically, discourses of Black criminality are bound to depictions of Black people as unable to form and maintain proper families. As suggested by the rhetoric of welfare "dependency" and justifications for the sterilization of Black women discussed in the previous chapter, as well as the continuing invocation of crime as the obverse of the liberal sphere of privacy, the deviation from normative patterns of domesticity signals both the failure to embody the principles that make possible the liberal state (upon which it ostensibly is erected and toward which it is oriented) and the production of kinds of persons who will be unable to live lawful lives and contribute appropriately to society. The threatened disorder supposedly generated by such patterns is what constitutes the basis of charges of ingrained/incipient tendencies toward crime. As a number of scholars have shown, Black people may be seen as *heterosexual* while still falling outside the boundaries of the *heteronormative*.[11] Regardless of the matter of object-choice, African Americans' formations of desire, care, association, procreation, childcare, and residency have been cast as aberrant, degraded, and menacing. Such patterns are treated as illustrating ingrained, if not inherent, predispositions toward unruly behavior that need to be monitored, contained, and managed by the state. In many ways, blackness in the wake of emancipation comes to be defined in dominant terms as the failure to enact liberal domesticity, thereby illustrating a pathological set of tendencies that lead to disruptions in matrices of intimacy, maturation, and political-subject formation as well as in geographies of jurisdiction and propertyholding. Perversity begets criminality, and criminality expresses a perversity within blackness that manifests first as wrong home and family. Such incipient criminality provides the supposed explanation for the need for state intervention to ensure productive Black labor (such as in the policies of the Freedmen's Bureau) and for the lack of real estate value and capital investment in majority-Black areas (particularly in cities) that supposedly justifies cycles of white flight and gentrification in the twentieth and twenty-first centuries.

However, what if those patterns taken to be deviant and dysfunctional, such as the movement of persons and resources within networks that exceed the nuclear household, were instead understood as expressive of modes of governance? Turning back to Leanne Simpson's analysis of Indigenous bodies as political orders, addressed in the introduction and chapter 1, Black bodies generatively are enmeshed in grounded matrices of connection within and among households that sustain not merely individual persons or discrete families but flexibly bounded and overlapping collectivities. Those relations can be thought of as the workings of systems of governance that do not rest upon a particular institutional architecture. In this way, what often gets described as *kinship* within Black social formations alternately might be characterized as already operating as a politics, at odds with and in implicit dissent from liberal political economies and modes of personhood.[12]

This chapter explores how the attribution of specific kinds of wrong home and family to Black people operates as a way of formulating and legitimizing antiblack policies that enable white extraction while also condemning, assaulting, and seeking to dismantle Black sociopolitical formations that pose a challenge to the liberal geographies that undergird and organize US political economy. The very failures of bourgeois domesticity that are taken as marking endemic Black perversity and the resulting need for state discipline/containment instead can be seen as pointing toward what Erica Edwards has described as "raucous collectivity from below" and "the heterogeneity of the movements toward black self-determination."[13] From Reconstruction onward, one can trace clear patterns of portraying Black deviance as an immanent tendency toward wrong home and family while criminalizing Black people on that basis. Reciprocally, those very tendencies can be understood as the sites of Black worldmaking that proffer possibilities for governance otherwise—for alternative political orders. In order to suggest the possibilities of such an analysis, including the value of engaging Indigenous studies frames in addressing the "something more than" of Black freedom dreams,[14] I engage three historical periods: the first years of Reconstruction, the last half of the 1960s, and the 2010s. My aim is to return to perhaps somewhat familiar ground, like the policies of the Freedmen's Bureau and the Moynihan moment of the early to mid-1960s, in order to consider what happens if we shift the prism a bit by looking for governance where (failed) kinship has been seen before.

Ungovernability and the Politics to Come

Before turning to the historical arc that comprises the majority of this chapter, I want to spend a bit more time teasing out what seems to me to be a certain tension in approaches to the political within Black studies. Returning to the comments of the anonymous reviewer noted earlier, the idea of "ungovernability" speaks to the association of governance with a forcible, normativizing construction of social order that works through racialized and racializing liberal conceptions of personhood. From this perspective, seeking to be *ungoverned* refuses the notions of the human implemented through state institutional apparatuses and the political economies of racial capitalism. Figures of flight, disorganization, and desirable and inherently unpayable debt serve as indicators of kinds of sociality beyond property and beyond the desire to produce normalizing forms of order.[15] Such articulations, though, not only can create difficulties when engaging

Indigenous conceptions of sovereignty, peoplehood, and collective landedness (implicitly and sometimes explicitly presenting them as merely extensions of dominant frameworks of ownership), but can also overlook the (often gendered) work of creating and sustaining community infrastructures for Black flourishing—what Keeling describes as the "out-of-field" in nationalist imaginaries. The effort to raise questions about the representational potential of Black politics, in terms of both what and whose issues are featured, also can take a more ambivalent turn. Such accounts mark the limits of extant formulations of *the political* while holding on to the potential for a kind or version of politics that might better speak to the needs, self-understandings, and aspirations of a wider range of Black people, beyond an assimilatory elite or efforts at inclusion predicated on enacting classed and heteropatriarchal forms of respectability.[16] The relation between forms of organizing targeted at transforming existing institutionalized structures (such as law and policy) and other modes of Black sociality not mobilized toward such goals, though, remains somewhat unresolved, including the extent to which the latter should be understood as a politics at all. The notion of political orders can speak to this tension by providing a means of talking about collective social forms in ways that are not pegged to liberal institutional structures (and their grids of intelligibility) or notions of (pathological) culture but that highlight self-organized forms of regularity, care, (re)distribution, and placemaking that exceed—and arguably contest—ideologies of enfamilyment.

Work in Black studies has offered sustained analysis of the production of dominant accounts of personhood and the ways they are constituted through the abjection of blackness. Following Sylvia Wynter, one might characterize dominant Euro-American notions of the human as organized around a set of racializing distinctions that "secur[es] the well-being of our present ethnoclass (i.e., Western bourgeois) conception of the human, Man, which overrepresents itself as if it were the human itself." In doing so, non-white peoples/populations are defined as subhuman through reference to supposedly natural/evolutionary "degrees of rational perfection/imperfection."[17] Building on Wynter's work, as well as Hortense Spillers's theorization of blackness as *flesh* (rather than body),[18] Alexander Weheliye notes that the ideology of "Man" "tends to recognize the humanity of racialized subjects only in the restricted idiom of personhood-as-ownership." He further suggests that "the benefits accrued through the juridical acknowledgment of racialized subjects as fully human often exacts a steep entry price, because inclusion hinges on accepting the codification of personhood as property, which is, in turn, based on the comparative distinction between groups."[19] To assert the humanity of Black subjects as self-possessed beings would be to reinforce the very systems of property through which those subjects categorized as Black historically have been made to signify as subhuman, as malleable and fungible flesh in the service of white interests and worldings.[20] Moreover, such a project would also involve the heteronormalizing ideologies through which liberal personhood is structured. As Weheliye indicates, the "anchoring of racial difference in physiology and the banning of black subjects from the domain of the human occur in and through gender and sexuality."[21] As opposed to the pursuit of inclusion/recognition, he "advocates the radical reconstruction and decolonization of what it means to be human," which he suggests, following Wynter, entails exploring other "genres of the human": "what different modalities of the human come to light if we do not take the liberal humanist figure of Man as the master-subject but focus on how humanity has been imagined and lived by those subjects excluded from this domain?"[22] Such modalities allow for non-propertied notions of personhood, which also entails rethinking the privatizing model of social reproduction that helps naturalize the scale structure of liberal governance. However, once one turns to attend to alternative forms of worlding and kinds of social infrastructures, how should those forms of collective self-organization be conceptualized?

In engaging these questions, many scholars in Black studies have contested notions of political sovereignty and related articulations of distinct peoplehood, suggesting that they do not so much offer an alternative to dominant conceptions of personhood and social order as reduplicate the terms of those frameworks.[23] Many of the arguments against versions of sovereignty have to do with critiques of regimes of propertyholding and the operation of state structures, both domestically and internationally. For example, Weheliye argues, "Given that peoplehood represents the foremost mode of imagining, (re)producing, and legislating community, and thus managing inequality in the intertwined histories of capitalism and the nation-state, peoplehood sneaks in as the de facto actualization of diasporas in the national context."[24] The form of peoplehood as imagined here is necessarily entwined with "capitalism and the nation-state," thereby inherently reproducing their racializing dynamics. Similarly, in her discussion of the complex politics of belonging that arise as a result of the African diaspora, the transatlantic slave trade, and European colonialism in Africa, Saidiya Hartman traces the limits of investment in membership in the nations formed out of either the profits of that trade or postcolonial independence. She suggests that the project of freedom is the search for a "commons created by fugitives and rebels," which is "a dream of autonomy rather than nationhood."[25] The "commons" appears to be defined against the notion of a regularized polity, one whose ordering might be characterized as governance, since the organization of such an entity reproduces the dynamics of exclusion and subordination through which systems of enslavement and empire have operated. In this vein, Stefano Harney and Fred Moten conceptualize the "undercommons" as a "fugitive public" made out of a "form of feeling [that] was not collective, not given to decision, not adhering or reattaching to settlement, nation, state, territory or historical story; nor was it repossessed by the group, which could not now feel as one, reunified in time and space," instead defying the inherently "correctional" dynamics of "politics" and the modes of "self-management" that are part of projects of "governance."[26]

These figurations of governance, though, bear little resemblance to the relational, nonprivatizing networks—and attendant visions of interdependent and nonpropertied personhood—at play in many Indigenous accounts of political orders. We might understand this disjunction as being a result of differently configured problem-spaces. As noted in the introduction, David Scott defines a problem-space as "an ensemble of questions and answers around which a horizon of identifiable stakes (conceptual as well as ideological-political stakes) hangs," further suggesting that distinctions among problem-spaces include their "tropes, modes, and rhetoric" and the "horizon in relation to which [they are] constructed."[27] A problem-space organized around tracking and contesting the dynamics of racialized personhood within (liberal) regimes of propertyholding is not easily reframed as one shaped by concerns about collective (landed) self-governance.[28] Yet, if racialization works to maintain normative models of personhood that secure a capitalist mode of production and that naturalize the scale structure of existing institutions of liberal governance, contesting the terms of racialization seems to point toward consideration of what alternative forms of social order—of decision-making, placemaking, belonging, resource distribution, etc.—would be desirable, including those already developed or incipient among the very people who have been racialized in ways that target them for state management, discipline, containment, and assault. Why must one assume that all modes of peoplehood, of collective self-organization, automatically conform to the terms of racial capitalism and statist structures? Implicitly, the notion of a political order seems to be equated with existing dominant systems of governance, both the liberal state and the global emphasis on the nation-state form.[29] Yet, the idea of political orders can be useful in marking the existence of the kinds of nonliberal forms of collective self-determination toward which Weheliye and others implicitly gesture as alternatives to dominant institutionalized conceptions of the human. From this perspective, Ruha Benjamin's insistence that "cultivating kinfullness is cultivating life" can be understood less as a matter of something like extended-family networks than as attending to, facilitating, and amplifying the networks of relation and principles of everyday communal self-organization that Black people have generated and continue to generate in the face of antiblack terror, dispossession, captivity, and extraction.[30] Further, conceptualizing those forms as political orders can help in tracking the character and force of antiblackness in suppressing such alternative modes of social life.

Understanding such formations *as governance* also brings to the fore elements of Black radical analysis that often can be overshadowed in the critique of racializing ideologies of personhood. If the racialization of bodies as Black recasts structural dynamics of subordination, segregation, expropriation, and sanctioned violence as the commonsensical effects arising from the immanent qualities of those bodies and the distinct population they represent, analysis of the dynamics of racialization and how to dismantle them would seem immanently to turn toward addressing the kinds of reparative and resurgent social networks in which such bodies already are enmeshed, as well as what kinds of networks of worldmaking and care would better capacitate conditions of flourishing for them collectively. Katherine McKittrick argues "that space and place give black lives meaning in a world that has, for the most part, incorrectly deemed black populations and their attendant geographies as 'ungeographic,'" and she later notes that "often . . . the only recognized geographic relevancy permitted to black subjects in the diaspora is that of dispossession and social segregation." In this way, McKittrick suggests, "local-contextual black geographies hold in them the ability to destabilize places—and times—outside the historically dispossessed body."[31] The dominant understanding and representation of Black bodies as aberrant and errant functions as a way of not only denying the existence of Black collective geographies and modes of placemaking but of seeking to dislodge and dismantle them in asserting (white) control over those spaces.[32] Characterizing those formations as political orders can work as a way of refusing the de facto legitimacy of state framings while also drawing attention to the enactment of (explicit or implicit) modes of self-determination by those cast as part of racialized populations, modes that are not dependent on state frames and that are alternative "genres of the human"—suggesting other "horizons" of collective life.

Without being held to the scale structure of the nation-state, such visions and accounts, already present within Black critical intellectual work, start to sound a lot like the kinds of political orders addressed by Indigenous intellectuals. For example, when rejecting nationhood as an aspirational horizon, Hartman draws on the example of Gwolu, a town in northwest Ghana originally founded by those fleeing enslavement. She suggests of them, "It didn't matter that they weren't kin . . . because genealogy didn't matter . . . building a community did": "'We' was the collectivity they built from the ground up, not one they inherited, not one that others had imposed." She suggests the town illustrates "the fugitive's legacy," which inhered in "shared dreams" that "fueled flight and the yearning for freedom."[33] The story of Gwolu told slightly differently, though, is less a repudiation of collective governance (nationhood) than a vision of a kind of governance, a political order, not structured around institutionalized narratives of normative genealogies but, instead, the forging of a flexible "we" through networks of relation that refuse the terms of the identities and modes of domination that had been imposed on them. Similarly, might one refigure Harney and Moten's "undercommons" as a form or forms of collectivity, producing kinds of "we"-ness not dependent on liberal personhood, privatized social reproduction, and attendant racializing narratives of the supposed pathological failure to conform to that model? The idea of alternative political orders might be understood as a prism through which to mark, trace, and affirm the ways forms of "we"-ness coalesce in efforts to realize projects of worldmaking that do not obey the templates and principles of liberal governance. As Charlene Carruthers argues, "Governing is the process of making decisions that impact groups of people. How are we governing in our organizations and communities?" She further suggests, "Making collective decisions about how our lives are lived is governance. It's in that space that we can live out the project of collective liberation."[34] Such experiments in liberation do not have to take a statist form, fit into liberal scalar imaginaries, or reiterate privatizing and racializing accounts of social reproduction. In materializing other modes of collectivity, these experiments can be understood as envisioning and enacting governance otherwise. Moreover, attending to these formations *as political orders* moves away from the necessary association of such governance with indigeneity, which also opens up the potential for thinking about, in Leanne Simpson's terms, "practices of sharing space" among "nations and communities" in which there are "political mechanisms to respect each other's governance" without positing, as Joanne Barker puts it, an "aboriginality," envisioned as preconquest and unchanging, as the basis for such mutual recognition and respect.[35]

This approach, though, still raises the question of how to think about the relation between such governance and the institutions of the state, especially to the extent that such institutions continue to be seen by many as the horizon of what can be termed *political* activity. In "Deviance as Resistance," Cathy Cohen highlights "the potential for politics in the everyday decisions and actions of [those] individuals and groups" that have been deemed perverse from within liberal ideologies of enfamilyment. Such sites and practices, she argues, bear the "potential for the production of counter normative behaviors and oppositional politics." While not necessarily intending to be "subversive," instead expressing "the struggle of those most marginal to maintain or regain some agency in their lives," the collective forms of Black worldmaking that get labeled as deviant might serve as a staging ground for a reimagined vision of political ideals, goals, and movements for change: "It just might be that after devoting so much of our energy to the unfulfilled promise of access through respectability, a politics of deviance, with a focus on the transformative potential found in deviant practice, might be a more viable strategy for radically improving the lives and possibilities of those must vulnerable in Black communities."[36] Such transformation for Cohen, though, involves an explicit politicization that entails shifting from an implicit enactment of alternative norms to an organized effort to alter existing institutional structures and power arrangements. As Cohen observes, "While there may be political possibilities in the deviant or defiant acts of marginally positioned people, that potential has to be mobilized in a conscious fashion to be labeled resistance," and she argues that such practices and networks "can be used as a point of entry into a mobilized political movement."[37]

Yet, might we see such matrices of interdependence, placemaking, and collective belonging as less the potential for a politics than the enactment of one? Cohen indicates the need to look beyond "those clearly defined political spaces like churches, civil rights organizations, and unions."[38] The spaces and dynamics that conventionally would be understood as part of the private sphere, as outside the domain of politics, offer models of networked relationality that could be seen as the infrastructure for alternative modes of governance—whether or not such modes explicitly are enacted and narrated by participants as in oppositional relation to extant structures of law and policy.[39] Erica Edwards gestures in this direction in her critique of notions of masculine and masculinist *charisma* as necessary for conceptualizing Black movements for change. Edwards foregrounds the ways individual masculine leadership gets understood as the animating force of Black politics, "a set of assumptions about authority and identity that works to structure how political mobilization is conceived and enacted" and in which such leadership appears as the "motor of black history." What comes into view when one brackets this patriarchal vision of the political, though, is "the arduous, undocumented efforts of ordinary women, men, and children to remake their social reality." Edwards later refers to such efforts as expressive of the "silent subaltern collectivity" that serves "as the epicenter of radical black resistance."[40]

If the site of the political can shift away from scenes of direct engagement with the state and toward other visions and processes of collectivity, then projects of governance can be envisioned in ways not beholden either to heteropatriarchal social ideals or extant modes of law and policy. Instead, the work of the political—specifically of shaping alternative political orders—might lie within subaltern matrices that do not obey the public/private distinction that underlies forms of charismatic leadership. However, at times Edwards suggests less another kind of politics than a flight from politics as such. Discussing the ways post-Civil Rights literature imagines possibilities beyond male-led oppositional mass spectacle, she highlights the potential for "a radical withdrawal, an anarchic exit, a refusal to consent to the terms of order," in which "the scene of black radicalism" comprises "fugitivity, an erasure, an escape from the scriptural order of racialized capital" in which, citing the work of Cedric Robinson, "radicalism [is] retreat." At other moments, though, Edwards suggests more of a spectrum of organizational efforts, social infrastructures, and projects of communal self-fashioning, critiquing accounts that posit "the black freedom struggle as a liberal rights struggle produced by gifted leadership rather than as a series of collective attempts to remake the world that ranged from the liberal rights struggle to the radical attempts to preserve an alternative mode of being."[41] If such struggle often entails turning away from liberal institutions and frameworks, why must those processes of remaking the world (or generating alternatives to racializing state grids of intelligibility) necessarily be understood as *flight*, especially when the modes of collectivity in question enact forms of placemaking? As Edwards refuses the equation of Black freedom dreams with masculinist scenarios and political imaginaries, why cede the notion of governance to the state or liberal ideologies of what can constitute *political society*? Understanding the construction and sustaining of collective forms as governance underlines the worldmaking potentials of such practices as distinct from the state as well as highlighting how such efforts get recoded as *deviance* in ways that legitimize state abandonment, intervention, and dispossession.

If the idea of being *ungoverned* speaks to a refusal of systems of racializing rule organized around white claims to property, we might see that formulation as running parallel with a refusal of "the human," in the sense that concept, as Wynter argues, emerges from and continues to rely on racialized hierarchies of being. The Eurocentric singularity of the human, though, can be displaced in favor, in Wynter's terms, of *genres of the human*. In this vein, what might come from thinking genres of governance—the presence of political orders beyond the state? If we rethink those matrices of collective worldmaking as governance—if we use governance as, in Charlene Carruthers's terms, a "lens" through which to redescribe such processes—then the racialization of those social formations as evidence of ingrained, destabilizing tendencies toward deviance comes to look more like an effort to crush a competing political order so as to legitimize liberal economies, mappings, and modes of state violence.[42] As with Wynterian analyses of the category of the human, how might the supposed singularity of governance projected within liberal ideologies depend on the erasure, subjugation, pathologization, and attempted dismantling of such other genres (which can be seen as the modes of collectivity through which other genres of the human are lived)? That process is what I have characterized as the operation of race as primitive accumulation. The representation of blackness in the wake of emancipation as failed enfamilyment and as immanently bearing criminogenic deviance, as I will argue, does precisely that work.

Emancipation Carceration and Emergent Black Political Orders

In the wake of the Civil War, enslavement was both ended and transformed into incarceration by the Thirteenth Amendment.[43] There could no longer be "involuntary servitude" except as a "punishment for crime," a caveat that enabled the recuperation of much of the social and economic architecture of slavery by other means. While blackness had been associated with criminality prior to the war and emancipation, that linkage became a principal vehicle for resubjugating African Americans to coercive patterns of exploitation, extraction, and containment. Addressing patterns of criminalization in the late nineteenth century, Sarah Haley argues that Black women consistently were cast as "queer" in the Jim Crow South in ways that constituted possibilities for (white) normative femininity: "As under slavery, reproduction continued to enable forced labor; in this instance through the notion that the black female body reproduced criminality and, by extension, a class of subjects that could be made captive and worked mercilessly," and in this way, "Gender regulation was necessary for the development of racial regimes of carceral capitalist development."[44] Building on this work, I want to suggest that dominant visions of Black deviance worked expansively in the Reconstruction period as a way of undermining and seeking to dismantle alternative socialities and modes of governance not pinned to the nuclear family model. Accounts of Black tendencies toward crime in the period gained ideological force and cohesion by being projected through the prism of family—the supposed ignorance and failure of Black people to conform to bourgeois conceptions of marriage, household formation, and childrearing. While *vagrancy* was the principal criminal accusation leveled against African Americans, that term gained meaning through its distinction from proper enfamilyment, constellated as vagrancy was with charges of licentiousness, adultery, fornication, and the abandonment of children to destitution. The insistence on measuring Black life against the liberal, nuclear ideal gave greater moral power to narratives of Black criminality (presented as a violation of natural law) and licensed assaults against emergent assemblages of Black governance that encompassed localities, transected individual households, generated alternative economies, and produced and sustained networks of association (institutionalized and not) that worked to enact forms of Black communal self-determination.[45] Seeking to break up such matrices into nuclear units while criminalizing the exceeding of those *family* units enabled the installation of extractive labor regimes and worked to delegitimize and dismantle expansive modes of Black collective worldmaking.

While those emergent assemblages often have been characterized as kinship, that framing diminishes the political character and generativity of these forms by casting them as informal, incipient, and awaiting true realization in a more recognizably political shape rather than as themselves expressions of nonliberal governance in action, albeit under extreme duress amid circumstances of ongoing mass violence. A vast proliferation of kinds of institutions and associations emerged out of Black communities in the South in the early years of Reconstruction and continued through the end of the nineteenth century, including churches, Union Leagues, mutual aid and benevolent societies, and schools.[46] In scholarly accounts of the period, though, Black networks that were not codified in an institutionalized form repeatedly are depicted in ways that cast them as prepolitical, as *in the process* of becoming meaningful forms of collectivity. For example, Eric Foner suggests that in this period "institutions like the church, fraternal orders, and the political party became increasingly important elements of cohesion within the black community," and foregrounding the emergence of forms of Black "associational life," Steven Hahn notes that Reconstruction "gave tremendous stimulus" that "extend[ed] the already dense civic sphere found in the cities and larger towns into the countryside," giving a kind of coherence to the "weakly elaborated" ties that previously had extended across "scattered plantations and farms" and creating a "rural political infrastructure" in the process.[47] The relations that preceded the construction of those institutions and associations, by contrast, often are described as "informal" and "casual."[48] Such accounts implicitly frame quotidian Black rural life as on the way toward something else or as gaining meaning primarily through the construction of forms intelligible as governance to the liberal state, which provide, in Erica Edwards's terms, the *scenario* for what counts as (a) political order.[49]

While rural Black socialities illustrated immense capacities to produce organizations for channeling community life and resources toward a range of purposes, the emergence of such institutional entities often is narrated as if that institutionalization were the substance of self-governance and "civic" life, rather than the means of further directing, crystalizing, and increasing in scale processes of collective organization, modes of relation, and patterns of responsibility and accountability already present within emplaced Black networks. Discussing the proliferation of such organizations and movements in postwar Atlanta, Tera Hunter observes that the development of such "a major infrastructure for weaving together individuals and families" can be seen as a "testimony to the fact that they embodied and drew on preexisting values that stretched back over many generations."[50] One might add that more than drawing on long-standing shared "values," this institutionally visible infrastructure depended on the geographies and webs of interdependence and care that have been characterized as kinship. Hahn indicates that "as in most rural societies in the preindustrial world, kinship relations composed the social and political foundation of the slaves' world."[51] This formulation broadly reproduces Lewis Henry Morgan's evolutionary distinction of the *gens*, of whatever size and function, from the civilizational lineaments of *political society* (as discussed in chapter 1). Yet, many of the institutions and associations presented as developmentally surpassing kinship in creating cohesion and infrastructure for Black collectivity are themselves also described as emerging from and coalescing around kinship networks.[52] As Laura Harjo says of "kinship-based sovereignty" among Mvskoke people, "Through this relationality, social relations between blood and nonblood kin are forged, which creates the conditions for energy and relationality to construct futurity at the most fundamental level. Then, energy and kinship are operationalized to act and do not require permission from normative governance structures."[53] While Harjo suggests the ways that networks of connection and mutual reliance serve as the basis for forms of governance that do not fit dominant notions of (what a) political order (is), the notion of kinship within discussions of Reconstruction-era Black socialities continues de facto to be constellated with the personal in ways that contradistinguish it from matters of political life and governance. Kinship repeatedly is linked with the idea of "family," which is positioned as providing a framework for what is sometimes characterized as "the idiom of kinship" or "fictive" extensions beyond a presumptive nuclear/genealogical base.[54]

Thinking back to the discussion in chapter 1, though, to what exactly does kinship refer? In the Reconstruction period, the webs of relation that continue to be designated as kinship extended beyond the nuclear family—and, really, any genealogical principle—and cannot be encompassed within any coherent definition of the *domestic*. Such patterns include a wide range of relations of care and sharing of space. Shared responsibilities for gardens and raising animals regularly extended beyond the nuclear family and even those who resided in the same household. Often there was a common area understood as shared by a collection of neighboring households, which could be used for hunting, fishing, and other forms of subsistence. Nearby households and households in which those deemed relatives lived were seen as affectively linked in mutual responsibility and concern, and persons routinely moved among such linked households, whether or not such residence was viewed as their official dwelling (by white landowners or in state records). The question of relatedness was itself somewhat diffuse given that conventional familial terms—such as "mother," "father," "brother," "sister," "aunt," "uncle"—were used to refer to persons with whom one had no blood relation, in ways that marked emotional connection and mutual accountability but not necessarily any mirroring of Anglo-American genealogical frameworks. Households themselves were organized in a wide range of ways, sometimes with a married couple at the center with other persons who were not their blood relatives and sometimes unmarried persons who may or may not have a sexual relationship. Childcare and domestic labor also were often distributed among various households. A wide range of goods and resources were exchanged among nearby households and with other households in which *relatives* lived, and resources often were pooled in order to support or sustain persons and households considered to be part of the local network. Although modes of residency and the configurations of labor differed among regions, these social patterns were widely present among African Americans across the rural South.[55] Nancy Bercaw draws on the notion of *neighborhood* to think about this sort of emplaced collectivity and the shared trans-household principles that organize it. She argues, "Their households did not stand apart from one another, but were intimately interwoven into the social fabric of friends and neighbors," such that "no one could stand alone, and no family lived detached from the neighborhood," and she adds, "They did not perceive their households as discrete, isolated social units, but as integrally enmeshed in the neighborhood's social fabric."[56]

While the relations characterized as kinship certainly capacitated the construction of Black institutions (such as churches, Republican party groups, churches, and schools), what's at stake in viewing those institutions as the developmental horizon of an otherwise prepolitical kinship and seeing matters of (self-)governance as arising only upon the emergence of such civic projects and associational units?[57] From this perspective, kinship relations appear as something of a backward formation, or one whose value ultimately lies in its necessary evolution into something else.[58] Instead, Black social formations during Reconstruction might be described as "cartographic kinscapes," as emplaced expressions of an alternative political order that was nonstatist and noninstitutionalized and that generated practices of freedom through the enactment of shared principles of decision-making, resource allocation, land use, and collective responsibility.[59] Governance emerges immanently out of these ongoing practices of relation and the communally held philosophies of mutual responsibility and care that shape them. As Charlene Carruthers observes, "communities should commit to creating a culture of care," and she later adds that "people and their relationships are—and must be—at the core of long-term transformative change." When she says governance is the creation of "space [where] we can live out the project of collective liberation," that process need not involve an institutionalized apparatus through which such decision-making, construction of non-privatized place, and imagination of expansive freedom can occur and be materialized.[60]

Prior to and surrounding the construction of institutions and associations, local networks among otherwise seemingly discrete Black households and families (themselves quite often constituted along other-than-nuclear lines) already were enacting a politics that offered a capacious vision for Black life, as against the carceral conception of blackness as aberrance in need of state management. While not characterizing these dynamics as the work of something like Black political orders, scholars have suggested a range of ways that enslaved and recently emancipated people engaged in processes of collective deliberation and self-governance. Councils likely were present among enslaved people on larger plantations, constituted by representatives from kinship groups (however configured), and such social forms would have extended into emancipation, providing a basis for communal organization and adjudication of intracommunal conflicts absent white intervention. Those residing on former plantations in areas where Black people had claimed abandoned property organized committees to coordinate among them (particularly to resist efforts to restore the lands to their former owners). Many Black communities created "squads" through which to share and distribute agricultural work and the resulting resources, and those networks also played a role in negotiating with whites over the terms of labor in the area, conversations in which women were active participants.[61] In all these instances, complex overlapping matrices of what has been characterized as kinship served as the basis for generating collective processes of consideration, decision-making, and mediation of relations with those considered outsiders.[62]

Moreover, reports by agents of the Freedmen's Bureau, who had been tasked with restoring commodity production through the administration of a contract system, register the existence of Black collective entities and processes, although agents characterized such formations as disruptive and antisocial. Stating that "all acts of lawlessness or violence by any body of freedmen will be suppressed by force," an agent in Mississippi linked such lawlessness to the presence of "organization[s] among the freedmen for the resistance to law." While intimating the perceived threat posed by armed Black men, this moment also speaks to the presence of modes of collective self-organization among the emancipated, understood as thwarting the grids of labor and enfamilyment that the bureau sought to impose as the basis for lawful order. That opposition was presented as indicative of "idleness" and "vagrancy" and as a response to the government's refusal to recognize Black placemaking ("No lands or property of any kind will be divided among them").[63] Bureau agents also complained of integrated efforts to refuse to work for or contract with whites and collective plans to move elsewhere to create "colonies," drawing on the possibilities of homesteading to settle multiple contiguous sites that would operate in cohesive ways.[64] These references in Freedmen's Bureau records index, albeit in negating and counterinsurgent ways,[65] dynamics of Black collective self-fashioning that suggest how the social matrices collated as kinship generate processes of governance.

Seeking to incapacitate such networks by casting them as deviant and expressive of criminal tendencies was a chief part of securing the political economy of whiteness, which then appeared as merely the neutral recognition of the natural principles of enfamilyment and proper household formation. Representing African Americans as unable to maintain familial commitments legitimized the passage and enforcement of a series of laws, including with regard to "vagrancy" and "fornication," that worked to limit the reach and potential modes of grounded relation within and among Black communities, seeking to break them up into smaller and ostensibly more easily controlled family units.[66] The idea of contract and the practices surrounding its implementation, particularly by the Freedmen's Bureau, provided the most prominent way through which family and criminality were mutually and differentially defined in ways that sought to rupture Black political orders. Created on March 3, 1865, the Freedmen's Bureau was to serve as the primary governmental body overseeing the needs of those recently freed, their legal and economic relation to white southerners, and the implementation in everyday life of federal policy with regard to reconstructing the states of the former Confederacy.[67] Formally part of the Union army, its official name was the Bureau of Refugees, Freedmen, and Abandoned Lands, during the span of its existence from 1865–1872. Among the first issues of concern for bureau agents was the employment status of those who had been freed.

While committed to challenging former slaveowners' efforts to continue practices of extracting unremunerated labor from Black people, the Freedmen's Bureau also was dedicated to ensuring that recently emancipated persons were engaged in systems of commodified labor that would prevent the need for government provision of rations and would make possible the resumption of the Southern agricultural economy.[68] In his autobiography, Commissioner of the Freedmen's Bureau O. O. Howard expresses concern that, in the wake of the war, "millions had left their places of work and abode and had become indeed nomadic, wandering wherever want drove or untutored inclination enticed them," later characterizing formerly enslaved people in search of land as "drifting hordes of negroes."[69] He suggests that the way to prevent such barbarous wandering by undifferentiated masses is the creation and enforcement of a system by which newly freed people could be tied to particular properties as workers.[70] To this end, the bureau developed a system of contracts between Black workers and their (nuclear) families and white landowners that would be overseen by bureau agents, in which formerly enslaved people swore to remain for an entire year in exchange for pay at the end of the growing and harvesting cycle. In implementing this system of "free" labor, Howard observes, "Wholesome compulsion eventuated in larger independence."[71]

The securing of such contracts, though, was cross-referenced with the need for former slaves to participate in that other central liberal institution of contract—marriage. As Amy Dru Stanley observes, "Bureau agents were as exacting about marriage as about labor contracts. Requiring former slaves to marry by law, they performed weddings, formulated rules for legitimating slave unions, and adjudicated the complex claims arising from the forced separation of slave couples."[72] In *Plain Counsels for Freedmen*, an advice manual for the recently emancipated, Clinton B. Fisk, who oversaw Tennessee and Kentucky as an assistant commissioner for the Freedmen's Bureau, begins his explanation in the chapter on "Contracts" by noting, "A contract is something which binds two or more parties. For example, John and Mary agree together to get married. John promises Mary, and Mary accepts John," adding, "Contracts are very numerous; numerous as the leaves on the trees almost; and, in fact, the world could not get on at all without them." He later observes, "If you wish your children to spend their lives in jails or workhouses, or to end their days in the prison or on the gallows, bring them up in idleness. Whenever you allow your children to loiter about, with nothing to do, you advertise them for the devil."[73] As a paradigm for what a contract is and entails, marriage highlights consent, mutual promise, and the coming together of free agents in the making of a relation whose legal force is assured by the contract but in which the contract gives durable shape to a set of moral principles and modes of social order that remain irreducible to the form of the contract *per se*. To fail to understand and obey contracts plunges one into a life of crime, and such tendencies arise through the failure to sustain—or, perhaps, acquire—proper forms of familial organization, discipline, and management.

Bureau discourse and policy consistently tied the familial relations generated through marriage to the patterns of labor that were to be secured through contracts with white landowners, often African Americans' former masters. As Tera Hunter suggests, "Marriage was treated as the infrastructure that would build self-sufficient labor units among the newly freed to perform the agricultural work so important to these new enterprises."[74] The enforcement of the nuclear family model allowed white landowners to negotiate contracts with Black men for the labor of their wives and children as well, a policy backed by the bureau.[75] This arrangement normalized a hierarchy of dependencies organized around heteropatriarchal leadership and envisioned "the family," so construed, as an integrated unit of labor, thereby seeking to cut off the need for employers to provide for other residents in Black households as well as to break up lateral connections among Black households. As Nancy Bercaw observes of the Mississippi Delta, "nonnuclear households dominated the cities and the countryside until 1866. Then, suddenly, they vanished on the plantations. By 1870, nuclear families comprised 89 percent of all African-American households remaining on the land."[76] While inhabitants in Black households that were not encompassed within the nuclear family might add to subsistence and available resources through (increasingly limited) forms of gardening, employers would no longer provide for their basic provisions, making those additional residents into a net drain on nuclear family units who then needed to provide for them. More than simply reducing the number of laborers for whom they provided nominal support, white landowners, backed by the Freedmen's Bureau, were seeking to break apart Black social networks, to create stability for commodity production and white political rule by severing matrices of Black mutual support and patterns of resource distribution, decision-making, and collective placemaking into more fungible nuclear units.

The bureau enacted what it envisioned as instruction in contractual relations, teaching former slaves to understand themselves as free subjects and to understand what freedom means as the adoption of forms of subjectivity organized around proper enfamilyment centered on the conjugal household. The use of coercion to enforce regimes of labor was cast as benevolent tutelage in the relations of responsibility necessary for a "free" society, and that labor itself was treated as expressive of the apolitical principles of family life that shape the national polity, in which Black people also had to be instructed. In the 1863 report of the American Freedmen's Inquiry Commission, which had been charged by the secretary of war with reviewing the status of former slaves who had been covered under Lincoln's Emancipation Proclamation, the commissioners indicate that the freedpeople have no "notions of the sacredness of property" and "no just conception of what the family relation was," including "the relation between man and wife." The report further asserts that "free compensated labor" and "legal marriage" could instruct the freedman in his "obligation to support his family."[77] While formerly enslaved people certainly had traditions of family and household formation that had developed amid and against the authority of masters and the demands of enchattelment,[78] such patterns of relation were understood by officials as expressions of deviance that illustrated the limits of Black capacities for self-determination absent white intervention. For example, in an 1865 address to Black citizens of South Carolina, the Freedmen's Bureau agent observes, "In slavery the domestic relations of man and wife were generally disregarded. Virtue, purity, and honor among men and women were not required or expected. All this must change now that you are free. The domestic altar must be held sacred.... Colored men and women, prove by your future lives that you can be virtuous and pure."[79] The denial under slavery of enslaved people's ability to have state-recognized kinship via marriage and parenting is portrayed as freedpeople's lack of moral integrity, in which they must be coached via training in the workings of conjugal, nuclear domesticity.

Not only did bureau agents consistently make mention of marriage relations in close proximity to discussion of the process of securing contracts, agents presented the latter as fundamentally in the service of sustaining the former—as providing a basis for future family life. In a circular to freedpeople issued in July 1865, the agent for North Carolina insists, "Some of you have families; it is your duty to support them.... It is your duty, in common with all men, to obey the laws of the land," adding, "Your freedom gives you new privileges. You can now live in families. The marriage tie is as sacred among you as among your neighbors. As soon as you acquire the means you can have your own homes, and continue to improve them in comfort and beauty."[80] The agent from South Carolina asserts, "Your first duty is to go to work at whatever honest labor your hands can find to do, and provide food, clothing, and shelter for your families"; he also issued a series of "Marriage rules," perhaps the most extensive from the bureau, which closes with the reminder, "The sacred institution of marriage lies at the very foundation of all civil society. It should be carefully guarded by all the agents of this bureau."[81] These formulations stage legally sanctioned marriage as the necessary precursor to the formation of proper families and as the means of achieving independent households.[82] Further, conjugal homemaking provides the foundation for "all civil society." Commitment to one's family, as signified by marriage, entails participation in "honest labor" that can secure provisions and subsistence for them. Laboring for commodity production, mediated by bureau-overseen contracts, then, *means* supporting one's family, such that to fail to adhere to the one signifies perverse inclinations away from the other—the persistence of the prevalent forms of Black aberrance inculcated through slavery.

Conversely, vagrancy and criminal activity more broadly were portrayed as resulting from an aggregate Black inability to perform the moral norms and commitments of the liberal private sphere. The absence of an orientation toward contract labor was cast as expressing a more profound lack of the moral sensibilities and commitments to intimate others represented by the maritally organized family. Vagrancy charges were depicted as part of a social pedagogy, as a means of inculcating a respect for the integrity of and responsibilities entailed by the domestic sphere of family and property.[83] Idleness represented afamilial forms of criminogenic errancy, signifying a dangerous unfixedness that seemed to spring from a habituated disregard for the proper units and relations of personal life.[84] An 1867 report from an agent in North Carolina observes, "About one third of the State Docket of each County Court in this Sub. Div. is taken up with indictments against Freedmen for Larceny and Bastardy. The first of these crimes seems natural and irradicable, the second together with Fornication its necessary antecedent, is I regret to say, largely on the increase."[85] The absence of proper marital relations is offered as the cause of criminal activities and what makes them of particular concern. Furthermore, charges of fornication and adultery against African Americans were quite common.[86] The dialectic of nuclear family homemaking and criminality—in which the failure to adhere to the former is portrayed as indicative of tendencies toward (or directly as acts of) the latter—works to foreclose nonliberal configurations of Black worldmaking. In articulating a need to instantiate Black familial order, the bureau's discourse codes other-than-nuclear intimacies, affections, residency configurations, and matrices of care as deviant and as the wellspring for patterns whose putatively antisocial character makes them criminal.[87] The outlawing of these alternative formations secures a political economy conducive to commodity production by white property holders while seeking to rupture modes of Black sociality that generate other potentials for collective life and governance.

Narratives of Black familial deviance and attendant inclinations toward criminality ideologically legitimized the effort to foreclose geographies of Black community formation. Across the South, but particularly in the Mississippi Delta as well as in the area of what was called "Sherman's Reservation," African Americans took control over lands that had been abandoned by white property holders or had been seized by order of the Union army. In 1863, General Ulysses S. Grant captured much of the Mississippi Delta, and while a number of the large plantations were leased to Northerners, with former slaves serving as agricultural laborers, some tracts of land, most notably Davis Bend, were leased to freedpeople. By 1864, Davis Bend alone had thousands of African Americans working an area of about 5,000 acres.[88] Even more well-known and extensive were the lands set aside by General William Tecumseh Sherman, who after his march to the sea through Georgia issued his Special Field Order No. 15 on January 16, 1865, setting aside the Sea Islands, part of the lowcountry rice fields near Charleston, and the lands extending 30 miles inland for exclusive Black settlement, which was to be divided into forty acres per family.[89] At the war's close, the Freedmen's Bureau was in control of almost 900,000 acres, since it had been tasked with managing seized Confederate property. The bureau's authorizing legislation indicated this land was to be divided into forty acre plots for Black families in ways that paralleled Sherman's order.[90] Despite the actions of Union generals and the congressional charge to the Freedmen's Bureau, President Andrew Johnson issued a proclamation in May 1865 providing amnesty for most Confederates and indicating that they would be able to reclaim their abandoned property.[91] In order to restore territory that had already been claimed, the bureau had to remove tens of thousands of Black residents, many of whom tried to defend their lands against this campaign of dispossession.[92]

This particularly spectacular seizure of Black-held lands, themselves governed through processes not recognized by white officials as politics, was continuous with the broader policy of denying Black people property rights to the territory they inhabited.[93] However, characterizing such collective occupancies as *property* can translate those modes of placemaking as a version of Euro-American ideologies of ownership under liberal governance rather than understanding the role of land within Black freedom dreams as an extension of the operation of Black political orders. In distinguishing the sense of property held by enslaved and then recently emancipated people from that legalized by the plantation order and enforced by the Freedmen's Bureau, Dylan Penningroth argues that for the former "property was enmeshed in several overlapping, sometimes competing, social relationships that made ownership possible for slaves and that turned possessions into property."[94] While those networks of relation involved questions of access to particular spaces (households, gardens, etc.), control over items within households, and the distribution of agricultural resources, characterizing them as property claims focuses attention on the legitimacy of an individual's ownership rather than the character of the dense web in and through which that legitimacy emerges.

As I've been arguing, the mesh of relationships that crisscrossed households, provided the basis for shaping and inhabiting place, and gave rise to forms of communal deliberation and conflict resolution among what conventionally are referred to as *kinship* groups constitutes a political order, especially inasmuch as the federal and state governments sought to break up these networks in order to enable privatized white control over the territory in question and the extraction of Black labor through the contract system and its imposition of ideologies of conjugal domesticity. A bureau agent in Georgia insists in December of 1865 that "freed people who have sufficient property, or are so situated that they can support themselves and families, without making contracts for their labor, have the right to refuse to make contracts . . . ; but in all other cases, . . . it is absolutely necessary that they make contracts to insure a supply of food."[95] We can see a tautology at play here. *Property* conjoins with *contracts* as a means of reinforcing the supposed unsustainability of Black processes of self-provision, as they undercut the legitimacy of white ownership and the fracturing of Black communities into a series of individual nuclear families. African Americans' capacity for self-support (and, thus, right to refuse contracts) is evaluated in terms of their ability to generate subsistence (largely imagined in terms of access to cash and the production of saleable commodities) as isolated *family*-units, not simply refusing to acknowledge collective dynamics of farming and resource-sharing but de facto categorizing those dynamics as themselves deviant and criminal violations of white property rights. An agent from Mississippi notes in July of 1865, "All the colored people are entitled to wages for work done. It must be clearly understood that belonging to a place and lying about without work does not entitle any one to wages, nor even to food," and another message from the Mississippi agent in January of 1866 makes the point even more directly, "Your houses and lands belong to the white people, and you cannot expect that they will allow you to live on them in idleness. It would be wrong for them to do so, and no officer of the government will protect you in it. If you stay on the plantations where you are, you must agree to work for the owners of them."[96] While recognizing some version of sustained Black "belonging" to the place of the "plantations," that inhabitance is rendered prospectively criminal in the face of white property rights. To live on those lands without "work," meaning contracted labor by nuclearized families for white property owners, is inherently to be *idle* and, thus, to be rightfully subject to state discipline.[97]

This vehement insistence on white propertyholding, however, seems articulated against what appears to be a widespread sense not simply of an entitlement to the lands they had worked as enslaved people but the legitimacy of forms of communal Black dwelling that do not involve "work" (again, extracted labor for whites) and that themselves contest white assertions of ownership (that these lands "belong" to whites). The implicit assertion that the existence of such collective networks of self-provision and organization are morally offensive ("would be wrong") resonates with and alludes to the attribution of criminogenic deviance to (failed) Black enfamilyment in bureau discourse discussed earlier. The endorsement of white property claims and efforts to nuclearize Black sociality in ways that facilitated contracts was consistent with the bureau's backing of state laws that criminalized the kinds of land use that provided for Black communities, including prosecuting for trespass as a result of hunting, fishing, or grazing animals on land legally recognized as belonging to another person.[98]

Even when formally purchasing land, African Americans in the rural South illustrated extended networks of relation that exceed the terms of liberal ideologies of propertyholding. Funds often were gathered from among a collection of relatives (itself a very flexible concept, in ways discussed earlier), and the lands bought would be understood as belonging to that more expansive group, rather than as an extension of the nuclear household. Such purchases also usually would be clustered together, creating unofficial towns—sometimes called "colonies"—that at times moved forward to formal incorporation.[99] Municipalization and official recognition as a jurisdictional unit of governance, though, need not be considered the ultimate trajectory of patterns of emplaced collectivity, as the proper developmental horizon for such collectivity to achieve meaningful existence. Instead, we might reverse the orientation of that view and see Black towns as a particular administratively legible form taken by situated relational networks, which enact a politics of self-determination—operate as political orders—prior to and outside of state recognition in terms that often do not register as "politics."[100]

Black desires and demands for land, then, were less about an investment in private propertyholding and the right to take up the kinds of legally recognized practices of possession from which they had been excluded as enslaved people than about the potential for materializing forms of communal self-organization. Theorizing the aims of Black agricultural cooperatives from Reconstruction to today, Monica M. White describes them as creating "a space and place to practice freedom," offering an opportunity to "build alternatives to existing political and economic relationships," and Clyde Woods suggests, "African Americans wanted to abolish and dismantle the plantation regime, to establish self-governing communities, and to become landowners, both individually and collectively."[101] Black articulations of landedness express modes of collectivity that arise out of grounded networks of relation—everyday regularities of engagement and interdependence. Without seeking to diminish the scope of white supremacist violence to which newly freed people were subjected in the decades after emancipation,[102] Black processes for giving meaning to freedom took shape through immanent patterns of communal place-making and governance—call them Black political orders—at odds with liberal geographies of family and household formation. State-sanctioned discourses of blackness as criminality drew on and took shape around attributions of deviance that emphasized African Americans' supposedly ingrained inability to enact proper modes of enfamilyment. Not only did claims of populational perversity legitimize the coercive nuclearization of Black households in ways that facilitated subjugation to a regime of "free" labor that served the interests of white property holders, such charges of deviance enabled webs of emplaced Black sociality to be presented as expressions of antisocial aberrance in need of white intervention. The coordinated effort to fracture Black networks of governance, then, appears as if it were liberal tutelage in healthful and civilized home and family. While not legally acknowledged and, in fact, pathologized and targeted for legal assault due to the challenge they posed to the state-backed geographies of white propertyholding and liberal privatization, Black formations of living and working together organized around what get described as *kinship* relations provided the infrastructure for processes of collective decision-making, accountability, protection, pooling and redistribution of resources, and visioning for the future.[103]

Moynihan and the Police

In his now infamous 1965 report, *The Negro Family: The Case for National Action*, Daniel Patrick Moynihan includes a summarizing quote from African American sociologist E. Franklin Frazier: "Family disorganization has been partially responsible for a large amount of juvenile delinquency and adult crime among Negroes." For Moynihan, though, "family structure" is the "fundamental problem" facing urban African Americans, one that explains Black participation in patterns of antisocial disorder.[104] We might describe this logic as the Moynihan matrix, in which Black exceptionality inheres in socially destructive modes of wrong enfamilyment. As the Frazier citation suggests, the horizon through which Moynihan understands the meaning and effects of Black familial deviance is the commission of crime. While this report was immensely influential in the period and for decades afterwards, its articulation of criminality as an ingrained tendency arising out of Black people's failure to be properly enfamilied was already (at least) a century old at the time the report was issued. To characterize the problems facing densely populated, primarily Black urban neighborhoods as "crime" conceptualizes the issues at stake as the violation of liberal notions of property and its privatizing geographies rather than the systemic processes by which Black life is made unlivable through state-endorsed segregationist policies. The invocation of failed family works to correlate the presumptive valuelessness of the *ghetto*, its status as monstrous lack, with its inhabitants' lack of values—the enduring moral disarray and interpersonal disorganization that is their blackness. In this way, accounts of Black pathology not only normalize the scalar dynamics of residential segregation but actively produce them, in ways that also facilitate further white extraction.[105] Conversely, as in the Reconstruction era, the very collective strategies developed by Black people to enact self-governance amid their subjection to structural dynamics of coercion, segregation, and hyperexploitation are cast as expressive of deviant tendencies that themselves produce patterns of criminality.

In her groundbreaking study *All Our Kin*, Carol Stack describes the focus of her research, conducted in the late 1960s, as "the social-cultural network of the urban black family," and she offers an account that challenges public narratives of Black poverty as indicative of "family disorganization, group disintegration, personal disorganization, resignation, and fatalism." In contesting this vision, though, Stack relies on the figure of "family" in ways that do not quite capture the expansive scope and trans-household character of the webs of relation, responsibility, and interdependence she traces. At one point, she suggests that the "network of kinsmen" in which her subjects are enmeshed "proved to number more than one hundred," yet she characterizes it as "domestic cooperation of close adult females."[106] That size dwarfs anything that in conventional liberal terms could be described as family or a domestic unit, especially as a lived set of dynamic, crosscutting connections of care and support (as opposed to, say, a genealogical tabulation of people in the present who are related by "blood" but who do not share meaningful regular engagements with each other). Moreover, persons who can be incorporated into such networks of interdependence include those who would be understood as "family" within a liberal frame (to whom one would be seen as being "related"), friends, others with whom one has mutual responsibilities and accountability, and the additional array of such persons for anyone with whom you share such a network.[107] Although Stack speaks in terms of "domestic networks," she also indicates that these webs of connection, obligation, reciprocity, shifting inhabitance, and shared resources extend beyond individual households while linking them to each other: "Participants in domestic networks in The Flats [the pseudonym Stack uses for the area about which she's writing] move quite often and hold loyalties to more than one household grouping at a time. The members of the households to which individuals hold loyalties share mutually conceived domestic responsibilities." Thus, while concepts like domestic and family may name the fact that these complex, overlapping webs of everyday care coalesce around spaces and kinds of relations deemed private within liberal ideologies, such terms cannot really encompass how those webs generate kinds of collectivity whose magnitude and shared principles of conduct come to function like patterns of governance—albeit of a nonliberal sort.[108]

Calling these relations *kinship* marks their distinction from the terms of official political life, but that very naming can orient away from an understanding of such *systems* and *networks* as an alternative mode of self-governance, one that arises amid and responds to the oppressive force of antiblack deprivations and extractions while remaining irreducible to them. To cast those networks as kinship does not so much displace the

Moynihan matrix as reinflect it, holding on to the sense of exceptionality via distended domesticity. Those nonprivatized webs of relation and the social dynamics they capacitate can be seen as the target of ongoing processes of primitive accumulation through which Black people and spaces are cast as in need of state management and rehabilitation. That institutionalized ideological transposition is a crucial part of continuing projects of capitalist extraction. From this perspective, refusing the Moynihan matrix involves seeing the sites of *kinship* as themselves manifestations of a politics that contests the political economy of racial capitalism.

Moynihan's report registers the circumstances of ongoing deprivation and discrimination faced by African Americans while conceptualizing such dynamics through the prism of the nuclear family's role in generating socially productive subjects. He argues that "the deterioration of the fabric of Negro society" is due to "the deterioration of the Negro family," warning that "unless this damage is repaired, all the effort to end discrimination and poverty and injustice will come to little." Conceding that "three centuries of sometimes unimaginable mistreatment have taken their toll on the Negro people," he also proclaims that, in the wake of the *Brown v. Board of Education* decision (1954) and the Civil Rights Act of 1964, "the demand of Negro Americans for full recognition of their civil rights was finally met."[109] In this way, the history of discrimination lives on, but as maladaptive forms of household and family formation that threaten to derail and undo the potential gains from the (white) granting of civil rights. Once again, blackness marks the failed, perverse, squandered freedom endowed by whites, to whom African Americans remain indebted.[110] Given the report's suggestion that legalized racism has been eliminated, supposedly ending three centuries of subjugation, Moynihan turns to Black domesticity as the site for understanding the reproduction of equality endangering aberrance. He insists that "the family is the basic unit of American life" due to its role in "socializing" children. He notoriously refers to the state of the Black private sphere in the city as a "tangle of pathology" that results in "a disastrous delinquency and crime rate." The apparent prevalence of Black crime, especially among youth, testifies to the failures of the home environment that produces "most of the aberrant, inadequate, and antisocial behavior" witnessed in urban areas. The degeneration evidenced by rates of "divorce[,] . . . female family head[s], children in broken homes, and illegitimacy" illustrate how *disorganized* Black family structures create a self-perpetuating set of disabilities "without assistance from the white world."[111] The increasing absence of nuclear households in and of itself can explain the modes of excessive and disruptive publicness that manifest as criminal acts.[112]

That understanding, though, takes shape within an existing policy discourse on juvenile delinquency that positions Black youth, and Black people generally, as a problem in need of management by the state. In 1961, four years prior to Moynihan's report, Congress passed the Juvenile Delinquency and Youth Offenses Control Act, which framed increasing poverty within urban areas as a matter of controlling antisocial inclinations among young people. That same year, by executive order, President Kennedy created a Committee on Juvenile Delinquency and Youth Crimes to coordinate related activities among various cabinet departments, and the committee's report published a year later portrays the growing crisis that led to the legislation and the committee's formation as a dangerous wave rising from the slums.[113] The report observes, "In one of our major cities, it has been shown that nearly 15 percent of all the children of the city were destined to come to court on delinquency charges before reaching their 18th birthday," and it further notes that the rate "for Negro boys" was 40 percent and that "in some neighborhoods" as many as 59 percent of the children had "been to court on delinquency charges by the age of 18," suggesting such rates are common across the country's "large and expanding urban centers." Stemming this tide involves moving beyond the idea of the "personal delinquency of the individual" lawbreakers, instead attending to "the underlying social conditions which would continue to generate new acts of deviance."[114] The notion of "deviance" here does double work: marking instances of deviation from the modes of behavior enshrined in the law; and casting such aggregated acts as expressive of a more expansive, collective kind of aberrance. The invocation of "social conditions" alludes to dynamics of economic deprivation and political marginalization for those living in "urban centers." This liberal gesture toward oppression in need of redress, though, tips quite readily into an attribution of pathology to the Black neighborhoods about which such statistics are amassed.

This use of crime and crime prevention as the administrative frame through which to approach urban policy and social change became more entrenched within federal policy over the course of the 1960s, and that trend reinforced existing frameworks within state and municipal policy in ways that registered the intensifying forms and effects of residential segregation but cast those dynamics in terms of narratives of Black pathology—particularly that of failing families.[115] In the same month as Moynihan originally circulated his report within the Labor Department,

President Lyndon Johnson sent the Law Enforcement Assistance Act to Congress, which he would sign five months later in the wake of the uprising in Watts, the neighborhood in southern Los Angeles into which Johnson had sent the army to restore order. The previous year, in the wake of uprisings in Harlem and Philadelphia, Johnson asserted that his administration "will not permit any part of America to become a jungle."[116] In 1966, he said in a speech to state law enforcement planners, "If we wish to rid this country of crime . . . we must cut its roots and drain its swampy breeding ground, the slum," and he went on to sign the Safe Streets and Crime Control Act in 1967 based largely on the report of the Crime Commission he had appointed earlier that year.[117] The Crime Commission report consistently depicts Black urban neighborhoods as negative space, as constituted through deficit in ways that make impossible the "norms and values of legitimate society": "the slums are producing the highest rates of crime, vice, and financial dependence." Perhaps most importantly/damningly, the "home" is not a place of family but "a set of rooms shared by a shifting group" of persons, and since "the family is the first and most basic institution in our society," its absence has profound criminogenic effects, giving rise to a pathological "environment" from which Black youth must be "rescued."[118] As these statements and policy developments suggest, the understanding of the city as a space of crime and crime as a problem attached to the cities—or, more specifically, the "jungle" of *the slums*—treats the circumstances of urban life as bearing within themselves the dynamics of a self-fulfilling cycle of rotting reproduction. When viewed against the background of preventing "crime," these spaces appear as a "breeding" ground, with blackness as a perverse contagion. Moynihan's specific account of Black familial pathology emerged out of and contributed to this larger trajectory of federal and state policy, in which the discourse of crime normalizes both the pervasive effects of residential segregation and the use of police as a force for sustaining urban apartheid.

The story of Black households and families as expressive of perverse and antisocial tendencies helps create and legitimize segregationist assemblages, which are accompanied and enforced by modes of police occupation. Two aspects of the Moynihan report help illustrate this dynamic. He repeatedly refers to "the Negro family" as "crumbling" and "disintegrated."[119] These are architectural metaphors that would apply quite readily to the older, inadequately maintained buildings in which most African Americans were forced to live, such that the state of Black dwellings metaphorically seems to emanate from or reflect the degraded state of the familial relations of those housed within them. Also, Moynihan characterizes city spaces as "the urban frontier," casting entry into the city as a quasi-western with predominantly Black-occupied neighborhoods as versions of Indian reservations. This analogy was not unusual in the period. In their account of urban underdevelopment, James and Grace Lee Boggs argue that "the nation's major cities are becoming police states" such that the United States either would resort to the "wholesale extermination of the black population" or a version of reservation policy "as with the Indians," and in the early 1970s, the Presidential Task Force on Urban Renewal observes, "There is perhaps no greater danger to the future of our democracy than the possibility" that "the central cities [will be] converted into reservations for the black and poor."[120] Although tending to present Indigenous peoples as disappeared, past victims of genocidal violence rather than contemporary polities engaged in their own movements for sovereignty and self-determination, these moments implicitly point toward the ghetto as a space of racialized containment.[121] Even as Moynihan invokes a sense of savagery and danger through the allusion to Black neighborhoods as the "frontier," his formulation, like the architectural resonances of his figuration of Black familial disarray, implicitly points toward the processes of state engineering through which such geographies are imposed and the work various kinds of racialization do in normalizing and justifying those mappings.

The conditions of deterioration in African American neighborhoods that often were cited in official and popular accounts in the 1960s and afterwards as evidence of pervasive Black deviance and tendencies toward crime and violence were the direct result of federal policies that failed to challenge, normalized, and at times outright required residential segregation, the attribution of valuelessness to Black-occupied spaces, and the simultaneous hyperextraction of value from those spaces.[122] The simultaneous mass destruction of Black neighborhoods for "development" and ubiquity of discrimination in home loans led to astronomical rates of overcrowding.[123] By 1954, the Federal Housing Administration (FHA) was estimating that African Americans lived in overcrowded residences at a rate four times that of whites.[124] The immense demand for housing, combined with institutional blocks to moving elsewhere, incentivized landlord negligence as well as vastly exorbitant rents, since failure to maintain buildings or charging insanely high rent would not result in vacancies.[125] These dynamics also meant that Black homeowners often could not afford routine maintenance and had to take in boarders and subdivide rooms.[126] These policies institutionalized the ideological equation of supposed Black familial deviance (and, thus, criminal propensities) with the value-destroying powers of blackness in ways that materialized economies of diminished value for African American-occupied spaces, which then were and still are treated as simply empirical evidence of the perverse and contaminating threat of blackness's spread.

Public policy in the 1960s helps generate, animate, and materialize narratives of blackness as an immanently perverse and pathological force that ruptures and/or disintegrates the geographies of liberal political economy, and officials at all levels consistently characterize that force as *crime* in ways that further license expansive state intervention and violence. However, that space-making, race-making, and fundamentally segregationist story—call it the Moynihan matrix—depends on an account of African American collectivity and placemaking as *disorganized* that has little relation to the extensive processes of governance at work in Black spaces. As an alternative to ongoing histories of depicting Black neighborhoods through deficit, as lacking this or that which would qualify them as worthy (of resources, public concern, political capital, etc.), they can be rethought as "chocolate cities." This "interpretive template" foregrounds interconnected Black modes of collective flourishing in sites across the United States in which "strategies of resistance and Black power have taken shape and taken hold"—building rich Black lifeworlds amid conditions of intensifying antiblack pressure and punishment.[127] Mindy Thompson Fullilove suggests that the dynamics within and among Black spaces, their "dispersal-in-segregation," constitutes an archipelagic "state, a many-island nation," within the United States.[128] Earlier, I invoked the figuration of the ghetto-as-reservation during the 1960s and afterwards as a way of underlining the racializing construction of urban areas as an imprisoning space apart for African Americans, but this linkage also can be read in another way, following the logic of non-statist Indigenous political orders that I've addressed (particularly in chapters 1 and 2). We might approach the space of the "slum" as transected by networks of relational interdependence and processes of political self-organization that do not appear as either political or organized from the perspective of liberal institutions. The webs of relation understood as indicative of criminogenic, value-destroying deviance—as signs of failed enfamilyment—can be reconceptualized as modes of collective self-rule that carry forward long remembered and deferred freedom dreams and that coalesce within conditions of escalating oppression while remaining irreducible to them.

African Americans living in urban neighborhoods enacted processes of collective self-organization that had regularities of practice and principle, aimed to create and sustain conditions of livability at a scale that encompassed yet exceeded the household, were flexible and shifting without being arbitrary, and were responsive to changing conditions without being mechanically determined by them. The very dynamics in Black neighborhoods that are taken as indications of failure and criminogenic tendencies instead mark expansive and flexible matrices of interconnection that create lived forms of community infrastructure, which can be understood as expressions of and experiments with governance. The porousness of familial and household boundaries and relationships indicates webs of care, mutually sustaining processes of resource redistribution, and shared normative frameworks that do not fit the terms of bourgeois domesticity.[129]

The communal character of what might otherwise be cast as purely personal relations can be seen in the revisioning of motherhood that occurs within Black urban neighborhoods. Public housing projects, for example, developed what sometimes were called "mothers' clubs," or in at least one instance "Mama's Mafia."[130] These mostly informal groups would provide support for the women who participated while also often extending beyond those particular persons to others who lived in the vicinity (e.g., adjacent floors, adjacent buildings), offering services such as caretaking for children, watching over communal spaces in the buildings, providing emergency loans, sharing food, and providing sanctuary in cases of domestic violence. In her study of women who became workers in community action programs during the Johnson administration's War on Poverty, based on interviews with mostly African Americans who lived in the neighborhoods on which the programs focused, Nancy A. Naples develops the notion of "activist mothering." She seeks to capture how kinds of commitments to and projects of collective well-being that might be presented as political in character were seen, instead, as extensions of "mothering and community caretaking [for] those who are not part of one's defined household or family."[131] While engaging in what might be viewed as activism, these women neither understood such activities as radically distinct from those that were part of everyday mothering nor positioned themselves as engaged in kinds of work fundamentally differentiated from those of other women who were not part of community organizations.

Regularly engaging in unpaid work "maintaining the social fabric of neighborhoods, communities, and social institutions" both before and during their time officially working for community programs, these working-class, largely African American women did not view what they were doing as *political* in character, since they associated that term with particular governmental institutions, the persons who occupied them, and those institutions' failure to engage issues of concern to poor people, people of color, and the neighborhoods in which they live.[132] However, conceptualizing mothering as exceeding the boundaries of home and family, Naples argues, "serves to counter traditional constructions of politics as limited to electoral politics or membership in social movement organizations as well as constructions of motherwork and reproductive labor that neglect women's political activism on behalf of their families and communities."[133] Casting these modes of collective labor as enactments of governance draws on the implicit refusal by those undertaking such work to understand the often gendered responsibilities of care and community building as either properly contained within a personal zone of privacy or as merely an aggregation of private(/ized) acts. While framed within what might be described as a familial idiom, this vision and praxis of mothering, whether undertaken by those who have children or not, can be seen as disowning ideologies of enfamilyment, including the sealing off of the realm of *kinship* from that of *political society* (as in Lewis Henry Morgan's formulation discussed in chapter 1). As I have suggested, to the extent that networks of relation categorized as kinship exceed the boundaries of the nuclear household, they become subject to racializing narratives of such formations as distended, deformed, excessive, and dangerous. Here, though, terms and identities associated with the liberal private sphere become the vehicle for describing extra-domestic (or perhaps trans-domestic) modes of social provision, redistributive networks, shared normative frameworks, and processes of decision-making that usually would be narrated as the stuff of political life.[134]

The work of governance at play in the areas dismissed as "ghettos" and "slums" also included the organization of alternative economies and the communal construction of shared modes of accountability. Residents of Black urban areas routinely engaged in extensive patterns of in-kind trade, forming what might be characterized as an "exchange system."[135] Often such activity took the form of "swapping," the circulation of material items of various sorts among friends, relatives, and neighbors and creating networks of sharing through these transfers that were less about a transaction of one thing for another than about building ongoing relations of support.[136] While any given instance of such gifting might be seen as the mark of a particular connection among persons, a private kind of aid, the aggregation of such practices across overlapping networks of persons and households creates what can be described as an economy, a collective though not centralized pattern of subsistence guided by commonly held (if debated) principles for what constitutes fair dealing and durable modes of interdependence. The transfer of resources via such "networks, alliances, and informal collectives" constitutes an extralegal system of exchange. In his study of Chicago's Robert Taylor Homes, a public housing complex, Sudhir Alladi Venkatesh says of such relations, "There is no better word than 'hustle' to capture the informal and clandestine processes of exchange, sharing, and support in Robert Taylor and other ghettos at the dusk of the Civil Rights era. The hustle was only partly an act of necessity. It was also an expression of determinism and self-efficacy, writ at the level of everyday community life." He adds, "Hustling, then, was more than a blind adaptation to poverty; it was also a cultural practice through which individuals developed a sense of who they were in relation to their local community and to the wider world."[137] Given the scope of this matrix and mode of connection and its centrality for sustaining those in and around public housing, might it not be understood less as a "cultural" phenomenon than a form of political economy? In suggesting so, I do not mean to present these networks as altogether desirable or as free from the ongoing pressures, including segregationist assemblages, that shaped and constrained Black neighborhoods. Rather, I mean to point toward self-organized regularities that might productively be conceived of as governance—as opposed to pathology, deviance, and crime.

Those regularities included processes for making decisions and for sanctioning behavior. Even in the absence of centralized representative bodies, neighborhoods had widely shared normative frames of reference for what constituted acceptable activity and how extra-household dynamics should function. As Venkatesh suggests, "Just like any other system of exchange, hustling required at least a minimal set of rules, codes of conduct, and mutual consensus among those involved for it to operate in a predictable manner and not completely threaten social order."[138] Similarly, the organization of childcare often did not follow "the publicly sanctioned laws of the state," and residents would actively attempt to thwart efforts by outside agencies to intervene in matters of "residence, guardianship, or behavior of children."[139] Refusal to follow such collective norms could lead to being denied access to interhousehold networks of exchange, the goods and services of alternative economies, and vital sustaining interpersonal connections. While there is not an official apparatus of discipline, patterns of nonengagement as a response to the violation of the principles of appropriate conduct could leave one without the ability to draw on necessary resources, which could be devastating.

Moreover, in public housing, there were more formal apparatuses of leadership and representation, although operating in ways quite different than housing authorities had planned. Starting in 1941, the manual for the United States Housing Authority encouraged the creation of councils within buildings in order to promote community activities and to decrease the likelihood of antisocial behavior.[140] However, Black residents in public housing across the country organized resident councils and systems of formal leadership that could advocate for them with municipal and state housing authorities and that could manage conflicts among residents, including helping define and police acceptable conduct, particularly in public spaces within the housing complex.[141] The existence of such leaders (whether by floor or building, depending on the city and housing complex) often was supported by housing administrations, since they could serve as a bulwark against tenant complaints, and the process of formal representation could allow tenants to feel involved in ways that might generate less direct antagonism. However, the work performed by such figures far more often ran counter to the role imagined for them by municipal and state officials. In addition to consistently voicing and channeling mounting tenant complaints about the failure properly to maintain buildings and to keep up with the repairs, building leaders managed much of the alternative economy as it took place within housing complexes. Such oversight involved looking the other way with regard to extralegal and officially unauthorized commercial activities that were not understood as posing a threat to community safety (in contrast to, say, selling drugs in public spaces) while collecting moneys from those activities that then regularly were used as a fund for tenants having difficulties (with rent, bail, food, etc.).[142]

These regular—though not routinized or bureaucratized—activities, modes of interpersonal and interhousehold connection, normative frames, and forms of accountability and oversight can be seen as generating a kind of governance. It is reminiscent of Leanne Simpson's articulation of Indigenous sovereignty as "the place where we live and work together," suggesting that it "is at its core about relationships": "we use it to mean authentic power coming from a generated consensus and a respect for dissent rather than sovereignty coming from authoritarian power or power-over style of governance."[143] It emerges through everyday networks of relation rather than as a set of centralized principles implemented through an institutional apparatus that itself is understood as definitionally distinct from the realm of enfamilyment. In their conceptualization of Black urban spaces as chocolate cities, Marcus Anthony Hunter and Zandria F. Robinson draw on the notion of "the village" as a way of understanding dynamics of self-organization and community formation that occur amid geographies of systemic antiblackness: "the village is the fundamental unit or nucleus for chocolate cities and Black geographies; it is also a metaphor and evidence for the enduring practice and importance of place making for marginalized and oppressed citizens. In short, it first takes a village to make a chocolate city." They add that such a perspective "is not, as political scientist Adolph Reed Jr. has called it, 'romancing Jim Crow,'" but rather "a political imagining and reimagining of the village as a site of past, present, and future resistance. Strong villages became the bricks for chocolate cities, expanding chocolate maps and cementing together the fortunes of Black places."[144] Without celebrating the segregationist assemblages that produce structures of urban containment, the very relations among persons, families, and households that are taken to be the evidence of criminogenic deviance and in need of strict state supervision and intervention, instead, can be redescribed as the ongoing (re)making of the village—as the formulation and enactment of political orders.

Such projects and formations access collective possibilities within conditions of intensifying state assault and extractive abandonment. As with efforts to engage in forms of landed Black worldmaking during Reconstruction, the efforts to enact modes of self-governance in Black neighborhoods in the city, distinct from the apparatus of city administration, took shape amid a dispossessive policy regime that continually worked to diminish Black places and resources. As a result of the Great Migration, many of the people taking part in these projects of urban community (re)formation in the 1960s and early 1970s were only a generation or two away from the freedom dreams of creating emplaced networks of Black self-determination in the South, which persisted long past Reconstruction despite increasing campaigns of state-backed subjugation and white racial terror.[145] However, millions of African Americans were pushed out of the rural South from the 1940s through the 1970s due to federal backing for land monopolization by white elites and corporations, the technologization of production (especially of cotton), retribution for Black participation in Civil Rights activities (which themselves often had to do with farming and land policy), and severely racially restrictive access to FHA and USDA funding.¹⁴⁶ That displacement helped create the circumstances of overcrowding in cities that was then bemoaned as "blight." Federally funded policies of urban redevelopment then ruptured neighborhood networks and patterns of situated self-governance developed over the first half of the twentieth century, with devastating effects for residents dislocated from those systems of support and from each other.¹⁴⁷ In the public housing projects that supposedly were meant to compensate for those losses, the poor architectural planning and vastly inadequate government funding for maintenance created exponentially unlivable conditions that put ever more pressure on residents' capacities to work within and around these structural failures on the part of the state.¹⁴⁸ While struggling with these basic problems of habitation amid the psychological and material costs of what for many were multiple dislocations within only a couple generations, African Americans in urban areas further were subject to hyperextraction (exorbitant prices for everything and rerouting of tax revenue to services and resources elsewhere), abandonment (failure to enforce building and safety codes, provide reasonable police protection, and maintain consistent public services), and invasive and assaultive police presence (to discipline the Black population rather than aid them).

While recognizing the modes of structural violence in which those collective efforts of self-organization emerged, the possibility of engaging with local patterns of collective activity as political formations offers an alternative to seeing them either as a version of kinship (potentially reaffirming the model of liberal enfamilyment against which blackness is cast as distending deviance) or as merely a precursor to the development of organizations/parties/institutions more attuned to ostensibly larger structural conditions and concerns. In this period, the federal government fleetingly did attempt to recognize modes of Black self-governance through the Community Action Program of the War on Poverty, albeit in limited and somewhat self-interested ways that eventually were reconverted into a discourse of crime prevention and a policy of police saturation in Black neighborhoods. In 1964, in the wake of uprisings that summer in Harlem and Philadelphia, Congress passed the Economic Opportunity Act (EOA), the central piece of the Johnson administration's recently announced War on Poverty. Part of the legislation provided direct federal funding to local organizations—community action programs (CAPs)—that were directed to operate with the "maximum feasible participation" of those to be served by such entities. As many have noted, this vision of enhanced service provision, ostensibly more responsive to local concerns and voices than existing city and state agencies, did not involve significant challenges or changes to the basic distribution of public resources, the operation of municipal governance and other jurisdictions, the segregationist assemblage that produced Black population densities in particular areas, or the operation of private enterprise.[149] With regard to the CAPs, Alyosha Goldstein suggests that they were fundamentally shaped by liberalism as "a political logic animated by varying notions of self-help and self-determination, premised on the pluralist extension of formal political power as a strategy of containment."[150] However, the EOA provided funding that, at least initially, could bypass state municipal authorities, enabling resources to be channeled to a range of kinds of groups with variously configured profiles and agendas whose aims were not simply reinforcing liberal geographies and ideologies by inserting poor people into them.[151] Not only did such funding provide jobs for tens, if not hundreds, of thousands of people in poor neighborhoods, "many workers hired by the antipoverty programs were often chosen because of their previous community work."[152] In this way, the CAPs helped provide wider legitimacy for some activities that already were taking place, offered a platform through which to help coalesce and expand that work, and provided a vehicle through which to understand everyday activities of care and engagement as potentially political in character.

For all its problems, the EOA opened possibilities for conceptualizing activities, relationships, and networks that already had existed in poor neighborhoods as the stuff of governance. Naples suggests that "CAPs increased the organizational sites through which community activist women forged a sense of connection with others facing similar problems in their neighborhoods and, consequently, the programs served as a key location in which definitions of community were constructed and sustained," and Rhonda Williams observes with regard to African American women in Baltimore in the 1960s, "These CAA [Community Action Agency, part of the same program as the CAPs] jobs further validated poor black women's concerns and empowered them to speak; after all, they believed they had the federal government behind them," adding that many women living in public housing "used the CAA to start tenant councils and to mount consumer campaigns and also used HUD to fight for citywide representation and voice."[153] The *Workbook* released in March 1965 by the Office of Economic Opportunity (which oversaw the EOA) to explain how federally funded community action programs should work illustrates this effort to understand poor neighborhoods as having their own systems of self-organization with which the government should engage. The goal of community action "is the full mobilization of the resources of the community," including making "specific efforts to enlist the social, educational, spiritual, governmental, civic, and economic leaders and organizations." The *Workbook* later articulates this aim as "the goal that poor people organize themselves for actions which they believe will lead to changes of major significance for them." These moments suggest an awareness that people in these targeted areas, largely Black, had their own internal forms of leadership and extant networks of decision-making and that they had the capacity to draw on those extant processes and modes of relation in generating positive change—at one point citing tenant groups in public housing as a prominent example.[154] While other moments certainly point toward a far more paternalistic and limited vision of such capacities, in terms of both the creation of organizations that would be "competent to exert political influence on behalf of their own self-interest" and the need for extensive forms of oversight and training by educated professionals for anyone hired into funded organizations, the *Workbook* offers a sense of people in poor neighborhoods as possessing valuable knowledge about their conditions and as potential "representatives" of their communities due to their connection to "an organized constituency" and their immersion within "a wide range of acquaintance with members of the community" through which they gathered collective "respect."[155]

The EOA's uneven conceptualization of the politics of neighborhood life as exceeding the grid of existing governmental agencies and service institutions, I want to suggest, opens a policy window onto another way of approaching Black neighborhoods, one that was publicly available in the 1960s and that potentially treats everyday relations as part of the work of governance in their difference from the ideologies and procedures of existing political institutions. Such a perspective can be contrasted, for example, with that of Moynihan's critique of the CAPs as a failed means of "resolv[ing] the private difficulties of young persons."[156] He also suggests, "It may be that the poor are never 'ready' to assume power in an advanced society: the exercise of power in an effective manner is an ability acquired through apprenticeship and seasoning. Thrust on an individual or a group, the results are often painful to observe, and when what in fact is conveyed is not power, but a kind of playacting at power, the results can be absurd."[157] This suspicion toward the possibility of self-governance by those in poor neighborhoods, particularly African Americans who are the usual unstated referent for "the poor" in public policy discourses with regard to cities, is consistent with Moynihan's demonization of supposed Black familial pathology in his infamous 1965 report, further suggesting the ways his linkage of deviance with crime functioned as a way of abjecting Black political orders. As Naples suggests, in the creation and funding of CAPs, "the Economic Opportunity Act inadvertently broke down the false separation between paid employment and unpaid nurturing activities traditionally performed by women in poor communities."[158] These sites themselves, though, were folded back into a discourse and set of policy formulations organized around criminogenic deviance, including the installation of police stations in public housing projects where community action programs had been and the transfer of funds to community-based crime control programs that provided services on the basis of designating youth as likely to be delinquent (what later would become known as "at risk").[159] However, the CAPs might be seen as opening a window onto, or as bearing the traces of, dynamics of Black self-governance that preceded and continued beyond the War on Poverty and that illustrated the very kinds of supposedly excessive failures of enfamilyment cast as pathological and in need of state intervention within public policy discourses in the period.

The Matter of Mattering

Narratives of criminogenic Black familial deviance, of Black people's supposed lack of values, normalize ongoing dialectics of disinvestment and extraction by displacing discussion of the integrated, amplifying effects of antiblack public policy decisions at all scales. Institutionalized ideologies of Black deviance since the 1980s continually present failed enfamilyment and excessive publicness as key to addressing what are cast as the toxic social ecologies of *the underclass*.[160] As Alicia Garza observes with regard to white perspectives on Black people across the political spectrum, "All believed that there was something inherently wrong with us," and in her research on young Black women living in a shelter in Detroit, Aimee Meredith Cox notes, "They understand that being at risk is a characterization that cannot be easily erased by their efforts and good intentions"; in the words of one of the shelter's residents, Janice, terms like "at-risk" and "high-risk" were "other ways for people to say that Black people are messed up."[161] Such narratives of Black pathology help organize, legitimize, and materialize compounding modes of segregation that have only intensified since the 1960s (despite the illegality of de jure segregation as such).[162] The ideology of Black deviance justifies the exponential expansion of police, prisons, and other disciplinary apparatuses that absorb vast resources directly at the expense of the lives of Black people (who are murdered, imprisoned, and abandoned to destitution).[163] In this context, organizing against the police and the maldistribution of social resources to criminal justice institutions is about more than reforming those state practices. Such organizing offers alternative visions for what will constitute the basis for governance, developing a holistic framework of care, well-being, and resource redistribution that refuses the privatizing logic of enfamilyment and that draws on earlier and ongoing projects of Black self-governance and self-determination. To insist that Black lives matter is to repudiate institutionalized narratives of Black valuelessness, the charges of deviancy on which such narratives rely, and the extractive carceral networks built and maintained through those narratives' recirculation.[164] How might such mattering extend to valuing the quotidian networks labeled as deviant as themselves enactments of Black self-determination? How does the mattering of blackness alter the matters that constitute a political order?

The program of disinvestment in African American neighborhoods operative at all governmental levels from the 1970s onward actively reinforces the prior explicitly segregationist policy infrastructure, artificially creating crises due to the absence of resources and then presenting such crises as if they are immutable effects of the ingrained deviance of the population that occupies those spaces while creating further cycles of extraction through increased policing. Even as legal protections for rights like voting and access to public programs increased, Black people gained employment in more sectors (especially the civil service), and Black middle-class families became more popularly visible, government resource provision for Black-majority areas significantly decreased, concentration of poverty increased, and incarceration exponentially expanded and intensified.[165] The cuts in state funding and the targeting of those cuts in majority-Black areas served (and serves) as part of a political project of both forcibly reducing Black residence and seeking to increase cities' attractiveness to potential creditors and wealthier residents through the system of spatial extraction often referred to as gentrification.[166] The prominence of the frontier trope in contemporary accounts of urban redevelopment in Black areas and the attendant Indianizing of African Americans reflects the understanding of the latter as pathological in their ingrained collective failure to adopt civilized norms (exemplified by liberal nuclear homemaking) while also, on that basis, casting them as valueless with regard to capitalist production—in contrast to the undeveloped land they occupy, the improvement of which requires their removal.[167]

The assemblage of legislative and administrative decisions at play in creating those policy formations depend on an ideological commitment to understanding blackness as having value only inasmuch as it licenses the direction of resources toward capture, containment, and dispersal. Todd Clear refers to this process as the transformation of economic value into "penal capital."[168] The redirection of public resources toward criminal justice networks positions criminalized communities as ongoing sources of what might be termed carceral value—as sources from which value is extracted in legitimizing the direction of state resources to police and prisons.[169] Currently, the United States has the highest rate of incarceration in the world: 440 persons per 100,000. The rate for African Americans is three times that figure.[170] If one also includes all of those who have been arrested in a given year and who currently are in criminal justice databases, the numbers of affected people skyrocket, especially African Americans, given that they often are arrested at rates ten times higher than for non-Black people.[171] Alongside this massive increase in rates of imprisonment, there has been a parallel growth in allocation of funds to police departments, especially in cities. Since 1995, police spending per capita has increased 46 percent nationally, and in inflation-adjusted terms, such spending rose by 29 percent between 2000 and 2017.[172] In light of the well-documented failure of such policies substantively to affect patterns of crime, we need to ask what function they serve.[173] Perhaps the most evident connection between criminal justice and the economy is the role of the former in managing masses of unemployed Black and brown people.[174] State and private funds that were spent on prison construction could have been employed otherwise. In this vein, Simon Balto argues, "it is an unforgivable absurdity for a city like Chicago . . . to complain that it can't afford to provide basic human necessities for its citizens while at the same time spending $1.5 billion every year to surveil and police those same citizens."[175] The presence of such alternative possibilities for social investment alongside the absence of a significant correlation between imprisonment/arrest rates and crime further underlines the political character of the reorientation of state policy and funds toward criminal justice institutions. State support for maintaining such institutions produces jobs for those they employ, whose livelihoods depend on continuing state commitments to keeping criminal justice spending at least at the same level, which itself requires that there be consistent or expanding levels of arrest and incarceration.[176] Those funds come at the expense of directing resources away from communities, which then are targeted for policing and incarceration in patterns that are themselves extractive.[177] Furthermore, as spectacularly underlined by federal examination of the city of Ferguson's use of criminal justice mechanisms to finance much of the city's budget, conducted in the wake of the police murder of Michael Brown in 2014, many municipalities rely on such funding schemes, further stripping assets from the most vulnerable.[178]

Within this extractive matrix, urban police function as "the armed wing of the real estate state," enforcing "what planners and policy makers enact" in ways that lead to the implementation of what has been characterized as "broken windows" policing.[179] Based on an article published in 1982 by James Q. Wilson and George L. Kelling, this strategy involves targeting neighborhoods seen as at-risk for descent into profound disorder, addressing small infractions before they compound into what is cast as irretrievable chaos. Such policies have been used in cities across the United States since the 1990s,[180] and they continue to be employed, despite significant evidence that the perceived blackness of a neighborhood is the principal predictor of assumptions about the prevalence of crime there.[181] If one looks back to Wilson's writing on crime, one can see that the original formulation of "broken windows" theory is predicated on precisely an understanding of Black persons and families as vectors of disorder, characterizing their supposed failure to embody middle-class norms as the problem to which policing is the solution.[182] Describing a study in Washington, DC in which more police were put on foot patrol, Wilson notes that the study indicated that crime itself had not gone down but that residents felt more safe. He observes, "We tend to overlook another source of fear—the fear of being bothered by disorderly people. Not violent people, nor, necessarily, criminals, but disreputable or obstreperous or unpredictable people."[183] "Crime" and (perceptions of) "disorder," then, do not bear an inherent relation to each other (the one may go up while the other goes down), but the latter is more important to a sense of public safety due to its role in managing the "disreputable," which Wilson understands to be the primary goal of neighborhood policing.[184] He later asserts, absent any proof, that "at the community level, disorder and crime are usually inextricably linked, in a kind of developmental sequence," and in a matter of months, "a stable neighborhood" can become "an inhospitable and frightening jungle."[185] The "jungle," with all of its virulently antiblack associations, then, seems to lie within community residents, just below the surface, awaiting the failure of proper external oversight.[186] Elsewhere in his writings, Wilson provides further indications of what such community order entails. He indicates that "the creation of middle-class community requires that middle-class values dominate, and this applies with equal force, perhaps with special force, to blacks."[187] Blackness proves particularly recalcitrant with regard to bourgeois enfamilyment, and that persistent and pernicious set of failures—the seemingly intractable inability of Black people *en masse* to enact "middle-class values"—lies at the heart of the disorder that police supposedly must contain, manage, and punish.[188] Projections of a presumptive Black failure to enact the heteronormative scripts (of family, gender identity/difference, and privatized occupancy) that organize liberal conceptions of social order justifies the use of police as agents of civilizing discipline, with "crime" as the template for legitimizing such systemic state violence.[189]

The Black Lives Matter movement, broadly construed, fundamentally contests this institutionalized attribution of worthlessness and criminogenic deviance to Black spaces while insisting on an expansive vision of the kinds of Black self-governance that are possible when communities are freed from criminalizing assault, extractive immiseration, and tokenized recognition.[190] As a distinct phrase/concept, Black Lives Matter first was created as a hashtag in July 2013 in response to the acquittal of George Zimmerman for the murder of Trayvon Martin in Sanford, Florida, in February 2012. Alicia Garza, Patrisse Cullors, and Opal Tometi worked together in developing and popularizing the hashtag, generating an online presence for the emergent organization and creating what would become the Black Lives Matter Global Network. In one of their first statements after coming together, they posted, "#Blacklivesmatter is an affirmation and embracing of the resistance and resilience of Black people. It is a reminder and a demand that our lives be cherished, respected and [that we be] able to access our full dignity and determination."[191] The BLM Network further describes itself as "affirm[ing] the lives of Black queer and trans folks, disabled folks, undocumented folks, folks with records, women, and all Black lives along the gender spectrum. Our network centers those who have been marginalized within Black liberation movements."[192] As against a hierarchy or standard of normality, ordered around conformity to racialized liberal notions of heterogendered and privatized personhood, these articulations of acceptance and advocacy foreground the necessity of refusing dominant conceptions of deviance in envisioning pathways to collective dignity and self-determination, insisting on the value of Black sociality regardless of its relation to extant systems of legality and productivity. Similarly, the organization BYP100 describes itself as working "through a Black queer feminist lens," and Charlene Carruthers, the group's founding national director, suggests that the use of "queer" in this way highlights how Black people historically have been cast as outside normative gender and sexuality, such that "in more ways than one, blackness is inherently queer."[193] These commitments illustrate more broadly how the activist and organizing work operating within the Black Lives Matter movement takes "Black feminist politics" as its frame in ways that differ from previous forms of "Black-led mass struggle."[194]

In rejecting what they characterize as "respectability politics," these organizations seek to differentiate themselves from previous strategies of Black political organizing and governance that have relied on forms of brokerage within existing institutional structures and hierarchies.[195] Keeanga-Yamahtta Taylor suggests that Black elected officials often circulate a rhetoric of "imagined racial solidarity" while "ignoring their role as arbiters of political power who willingly operate in a political terrain designed to exploit and oppress African Americans and other working-class people."[196] African American leaders and organizations that play this role, positioning themselves as mediators between the institutions of the state and Black communities, often employ notions of proper, enfamilied personhood tied to "middle-class/dominant constructions of moral, normative, patriarchal citizenship" as the basis for how they channel resources and advocacy.[197] In doing so, they redeploy existing discourses of Black deviance, although seeking to contain its contagion within the most nonnormative and, therefore, presumptively disordered and disordering segments of the Black population.[198] As Alicia Garza observes, "The narrative of personal responsibility for systemic failures has often been used by Black leaders to secure their seat at the table while making no tangible changes in the lives of Black communities."[199] The critique and jettisoning of such a "respectability" based framework enables groups like BLM and BYP100 to develop a movement for change that breaks from not only that paradigm of liberal homemaking but from, in Erica Edwards's terms, the attendant *scenario* in which the work of politics is defined as implicitly separate from the privatized space of the family while also treating that naturalized space as normatively orienting political institutions and struggles.

These activist articulations reject pathologizing narratives of Black communities and challenge the legitimacy of attendant modes of state criminalization, disinvestment, and extraction; yet, in their accounts of the work of organizing for change, they at times reiterate dominant scalar narratives in which the state is the horizon of political imagination in ways that can limit possibilities for conceptualizing the shapes, locations, and textures of Black self-determination in which the dynamics of everyday life might themselves be understood as constituting matrices and modes of governance. In *The Purpose of Power*, Garza defines organizing as "the process of coming together with other people who share your concerns and values to work toward a change in some kind of policy, usually of the government." She later adds that it is "about building relationships and using those relationships to accomplish together what we cannot accomplish on our own," specifically "build[ing] power" since "without power, we are unable to change conditions in our communities that hurt us." In order to affect conditions in substantive ways, policy must be altered, which itself requires developing forms of power through the construction of mass movements. She argues, "when it comes to politics, when it comes to governing, when it comes to building power, being small is something we cannot afford."[200] Organizations that work to mobilize large bodies of people, to transform popular understandings, and to connect and coordinate with each other at ever-larger scales of engagement, then, are crucial in the effort to develop and implement modes of governance that can create conditions for Black flourishing. When Garza declares that "we must be involved in our governance" and that "governance is power," she indicates the importance of "a whole web of institutions" that speak to the needs, desires, and interests of Black communities and for processes of movement-work that can produce such (state) institutions and hold them accountable.[201]

From this perspective, part of why activist organizations and a coordinated movement are necessary is that they incubate and inculcate modes of relation that do not take dominant heteropatriarchal and racialized norms of hierarchy, respectability, and worthiness as their commonsense background. In this way, organizing is not just a coalescence of popular will but a process of transforming existing consciousness so as to materialize alternative matrices of social relation. Garza suggests that activist organizations, and the processes of organizing that they implement, engage in "political education" that "helps individuals and groups analyze the social and economic trends, the policies and ideologies influencing our lives—and use this information to develop strategies to change the rules and transform power."[202] She further argues that the idea that "Black communities come into the world fully conscious of the systemic challenges we face and ready to dismantle them" is a kind of naive and "shallow" political fantasy that incapacities the development of "tools" through which people can address "the impact of generations of exclusion, gaslighting, extraction, disenfranchisement, exploitation, domination, and oppression of Black communities."[203] Similarly, Charlene Carruthers observes that "activists, organizers, and intellectuals living under capitalism, colonialism, anti-Black racism, and patriarchy require years of unlearning or decolonization," since "the ongoing project of colonialism lives in each of us and manifests itself in our movement."[204] In response, she suggests, "Our movements must and can work toward a decision-making culture that produces different terrains in which we live our lives," enacting forms of "community organizing that [work] to dismantle systems of oppression and replace them with systems designed to allow collective dignity and power."[205] Organizations whose aim is to produce and sustain movements to alter public policy—to craft and work toward implementing a vision for more just institutions and social relations that do not perpetuate extant oppressive patterns (at all scales, from the interpersonal to the broadly systemic)—serve as the crucible for generating and disseminating new modes of consciousness that lie at the center of the effort to reorder extant systems of domination. Such organizations, therefore, are positioned as the engines for conceptualizing and realizing possibilities for Black governance and for people to achieve power over the conditions of their lives.

Yet, the emphasis on the need for the activist work of organizing and for modes of political education also implicitly can suggest a current state of disorganization in which Black subjects do not have a politics and/or are mired in forms of false consciousness. Such a de facto orientation may inadvertently give further momentum to deviance-based narratives of deficit even as they contest the propositional content of such narratives. The effort to foreground organizing as distinct from everyday formations and the modes of relation and understanding that shape them can cast such ordinary forms of Black sociality, geography, and collectivity as themselves lacking. Moreover, the emphasis on the need to scale-up organizing to engage national law and policy also can normalize liberal scalar imaginaries as the commonsensical background for conceptualizing what governance *is*. While certainly structural change is needed to redress ongoing forms of state-perpetrated and state-perpetuated anti-black violence and extraction, the emphasis on structural transformation and the importance of generating kinds of consciousness that can support such movement work can seem to position current quotidian beliefs and practices as failed or, worse, as an active drag on the potential for more organized, policy-oriented mass coalescence.[206] In their analysis of chocolate cities, Hunter and Robinson present such ordinary webs of relation as "lifeworlds," "social, economic, and political places of dynamism and great consequence," or as part of ordinary modes of collective placemaking and networks of relation that they, along with Mary Pattillo and Keeanga-Yamahtta Taylor, have described as "the matter of black lives."[207] How does such "matter" come to matter as more than evidence of the pervasive presence of antiblackness within the insistence that Black lives matter? How might everyday lifeworlds be important in conceptualizing and addressing the mattering of Black lives, and how might that mattering entail recognizing non-statist modes of collectivity as political orders (including seeing them as targeted by state modes of primitive accumulation)?

While turning to the state serves as a powerful horizon for envisioning and enacting change, as well as for demanding accountability,[208] it can also efface the importance of existing quotidian webs of connection and matrices of relation as sources of political imagination. Doing so can leave intact the scalar ideologies of liberal governance through which Black people are cast as inadequate citizen-subjects due to the racializing portrayal of their supposedly failed domesticity. As Cox suggests of the young women she studies, "Black girls are not the problem. Their lives do not need sanitizing, normalizing, or translating so they can be deemed worthy of care and serious consideration," and she further notes that "tropes of marginalization, isolation, victimization, and absence are so pervasive that they conceal Black girls' centrality in the spaces they inhabit as well as how girls nurture connections, relationships, and community in these spaces."[209] As with the networks of placemaking, decision-making, and resource distribution at play in the Reconstruction South and the mid-twentieth-century urban North, discussed in the previous sections, attention to the matrix of connections and relationships Cox indexes can provide alternative ways of thinking about governance that neither displace such formations from the political (as *kinship*, for example) nor implicitly cast them as merely parochial (possibly pathological) forms that need to be transcended in the adoption of a properly scaled sense of political society. To see such ordinary formations as themselves sources and sites of governance may open possibilities for acknowledging and amplifying ongoing experiments with Black collective self-determination, particularly highlighting potentials not tied to liberal notions of enfamilied citizenship and social order. This potential, as Cox implies, also involves shifting away from privileging an idiom of resistance, which tends to recenter the state and its organizing frameworks, instead foregrounding the construction of ethical and material alternatives within ordinary Black life. How can the state be held accountable for the conditions it creates without taking that process as the orienting frame through which to understand and enact Black worldmaking?

Within accounts of activist organizing, though, there are gestures toward such dynamics that point away from the state and back toward everyday processes as sites of alternative political form(ul)ations and that open up possibilities for redescribing ordinary Black lifeworlds as themselves already sites of governance.[210] As discussed in chapter 1, Carruthers insists on the need to think about governance in expansive terms, both as "not synonymous with becoming part of the governments we live under" and as occurring "inside and outside of official government institutions." While then looking to "our movements" as the spaces for creating "different terrains in which we live our lives," her emphasis on the importance of a capacious conception of governance also implicitly turns toward other webs of relation than those generated through organizations. If, as noted earlier, "people and their relationships are—and must be—at the core of long-term transformative change," then that core set of principles and those modes of relationality largely arise outside of specifically articulated movements and projects of policy transformation.[211] Part of the work of making possible activist organizations and campaigns lies in seeing and valuing social networks and processes of community self-direction that are not the stuff of extant institutional life—what, in Laura Harjo's terms, might be described as *vernacular* spaces and experiences.[212] Viewing such dynamics through the lens of governance reimagines them as already expressive of Black self-determination and, thus, as incubating further radical possibilities. Carruthers addresses the importance of refiguring the "Black radical tradition" through "a Black queer feminist lens," which offers "a more holistic telling" of that tradition. What if that telling foregrounded everyday forms of collectivity—of decision-making, resource distribution, and placemaking—that do not present themselves and usually are not narrated as political formations?[213] What if they were understood as implicit or incipient political orders, ones in their own ways strangulated by the state but not less ethically and philosophically rich or less meaningful within lived Black networks for that fact?[214] Garza similarly underlines the importance of "human connection and building relationships" as part of making possible alternatives to extant antiblack institutional systems; although she locates such relationships *within* processes of organizing, this emphasis is not merely instrumental, as a means for coalescing connections within activist organizations. Rather, such modes of relation appear as a normative principle informing the character of the vision for change. Not only do they provide "infrastructure" for explicitly political work, they are part of "the complex web of ideas, values, and beliefs" that offer an alternative to "the status quo."[215]

Garza at times characterizes this domain outside of governmental institutions as "culture."[216] As noted in the introduction and chapters 1 and 2, the language of culture can serve as a way of implicitly denying sites of governance their role as such, instead normalizing the state and its apparatuses as the principal site of political formation while also participating in extant discourses of racialization (culture, like race, being envisioned as passed along genealogical lines, with the two categories often surrogating for each other). Read in reverse, we might see Garza's gesture toward the cultural sphere as suggestive of Black political orders that do not count as such within and for liberal institutions. Turning to the "Vision for Black Lives" platform created by the Movement for Black Lives, many of its recommendations for political and economic transformation involve calls for increased community control, especially with respect to "elevating the experiences and leadership of the most marginalized Black people."[217] In this vein, the document often references the importance of investment in "community-based resources," support for "cooperative social and economic networks," and the use of restorative justice and participatory budgeting frameworks that foreground community-based values and needs assessment.[218] While realizing these principles does involve constructing institutional infrastructure and processes, including organizing in order to do so, such demands emphasize building off of existing knowledges, practices, and matrices of relation—tapping into, affirming, and extending existing vernacular frameworks. Conceptualizing such frameworks as governance underlines their formative power, understanding them as a politics even when not principally oriented by or to the state.

Both Garza and Carruthers indicate the importance of the stories that we tell for what kinds of political imagination seem possible.[219] Telling a different kind of story about the character of Black governance need not romanticize existing conditions or cast the institutions and networks of the state as extraneous to potentials for worldmaking. Instead, telling a story of everyday Black political orders seeks to value the ordinary as a space in which ongoing projects of collective self-determination germinate and are given form, even when they are not acknowledged as such. As Cohen indicates in her research on Black youth, they often "internalize and reiterate" a "certain set of norms and values" that then serve as the basis for critiquing the actions of other Black people, and she adds that "in the absence of honest discussion about the truly representative forms of sexuality, intimacy, and family structure in black communities," a particular "heteronormative family model" remains the ideal against which to measure and judge as deviant and failed Black people and communities that do not fit that model.[220] Telling a different kind of story about what governance is and how Black people have enacted it under conditions of extreme oppression, abandonment, and extraction provides the possibility of seeing in those more demographically *representative forms* a matrix of relation—a lifeworld, a political order. Refusing to narrate that matrix as simply a function of deprivation also challenges the ideology of liberal enfamilyment that has legitimized extractive, criminalizing narratives of Black valuelessness.

* * *

In *The Purpose of Power*, Garza suggests that "Black communities are woefully unorganized," in the sense that there is not "an agreed-upon agenda or set of goals" toward which they are working in a concerted fashion.[221] Although she is talking about the possibility of mass mobilization for significant policy change, this characterization seems reminiscent of discussions of the Reconstruction era that focus on the extent to which recently emancipated communities had formed associations that facilitated or advocated for participation in the political system. As I argued earlier, this emphasis can overlook the ways African Americans organized themselves into trans-household landed collectivities with their own ways of managing communal affairs. Not only were such networks not recognized by the state, their conditions of possibility actively were criminalized in order to create isolated nuclear families that were the desirable units for labor on land declared to be white property. Despite such state interventions (in the name of creating social order and inculcating liberal conceptions of decency and privatized personhood), Black communities continued to forge emplaced political orders as a vital part of defining for themselves what freedom would mean. To characterize these struggles to assert self-determination as kinship relations that capacitate the real work of politics seems to do a profound disservice to the power of those formations and their role in Black freedom dreams. In this way, the narration of Black communities as "unorganized" also resonates with Moynihan's assessment of such spaces as *disorganized*. Even if the former denounces the charges of deviance that drive the latter, both position everyday formations as a problem to be remedied through proper political intervention, rather than as themselves enacting a politics whose orienting principles do not align with those of the liberal state and that can help (re)shape the terms of engagement with governmental institutions.

The conventional understanding of those relations and networks labeled as kinship as (properly) outside the public/governmental sphere not only limits the possibilities for thinking the character of Black political imagination, but also can leave intact processes of racialization through which the performance of wrong privacy serves as the sign and substance of Black criminogenic perversion. As Danielle Purifoy argues, "countergovernance is itself an old tradition in black communities, which have scarcely been able to rely on dominant white governing bodies to protect their interests," and she adds that "in the long tradition of black communities, turning inward for alternative strategies untethered to traditional politics and governance offers some limited promise for black communities attempting to direct the development of their communities."[222] In episodically moving from the Reconstruction era to the present, this chapter has sought to explore the possibilities for tracing and understanding such countergovernance in ways that can acknowledge modes of, in Leanne Simpson's terms, "networked relationship" through which "governance was[/is] made every day,"[223] in which such governance may look like distensions of the private sphere when viewed from the perspective of liberal domesticity. Centering those alternatives, ones that do not look like politics from within a liberal framework, enables a valuing of the communal labor involved in creating and sustaining those networks while also refusing the deviance-making perspective in which they appear merely as racially ingrained transgressions of the terms of healthful, lawful order managed by state institutions.

Such formations are neither utopic nor themselves beyond critique, but serve as sites of collective experimentation with the matter of political order, with how to construct worlds whose livability is not predicated on the isolation and insulation of nuclear households, thereby troubling (if not de facto refusing) the notion of a privatized sphere around which the public and governmental is meant to pivot. Addressing these relations in varied historical periods—the Reconstruction era, the 1960s, and the past decade—illustrates both the continuing presence of vernacular Black political assemblages and the ways the castigation of such assemblages as expressions of profligacy, ungovernability, and incipient criminal tendencies insistently has helped shape and animate institutionalized accounts of blackness while also enacting extraction-enabling modes of primitive accumulation. The story that I seek to tell about the longue durée of Black self-governance aims to highlight the self-sufficiency of Black worldmaking, not in the neoliberal sense of being privatized agents responsible for their own systemic deprivation and abandonment by "the market" but in the sense of collectively not needing to conform to structurally impossible state metrics of proper enfamilied personhood (in order to qualify as redeemable subjects of value). The historical sketches I have offered, then, are in the interest of amplifying a refusal to cede the terms of collective life and governance to the state in order to open possibilities for acknowledging modes of emplaced Black self-determination.

Coda

Inside/Outside State Forms

I'M WRITING THIS in the summer of 2022, in the wake of the disastrous and devastating wave of US Supreme Court decisions issued in the last two months. These decisions include opening abortion to outlawing by the states, limiting the EPA's ability to promulgate regulations in response to climate change, gutting Miranda rights, hobbling states' and municipalities' ability to regulate guns (amid a record number of mass shootings), and enabling states to exert criminal jurisdiction over non-Indians on reservation. This latest wave of reactionary backlash/entrenchment further illustrates the power of the state and, perhaps even more so, the power of the central government. If we did not already learn this lesson from the actions of the Trump administration, control over the state matters. Its authority, institutional and infrastructural reach, and the resources it commands are vital for creating and sustaining conditions for livable lives in the present. Or, at least, the state and its multiform apparatuses cannot be left to look after themselves or treated as somehow extraneous to the conditions of the everyday. That awareness also drives home the matter of scale—the role of government at all levels in affecting quotidian being and becoming and the importance of generating constituencies in struggle large enough to shape the direction of public policy. With all of that being said, the emphasis I've placed on refusing liberal scalar imaginaries and on attending to the existence of political orders that do not fit those frames (and that are disciplined as racialized disorder/

deviance as a result) is, I believe, more important than ever. If the actually existing state cannot be ignored, due to its concentration of power and potential (largely to harm), it also cannot be the horizon for envisioning governance or for understanding how governance can be, and has been, lived by racialized people(s).

In this vein, I would like to take up the Supreme Court's decision in *Oklahoma v. Castro-Huerta* as a way of illustrating and teasing out the conceptual and political torsions that animate the argument of *The Politics of Kinship*. The opinion speaks to the dialectical intertwining of race and scale in the reproduction of US jurisdictional mappings as well as both the importance and insufficiency of state recognition in the making of alternative political orders. The case concerns Oklahoma's prosecution of a non-Indian man, Victor Manuel Castro-Huerta, for the neglect and abuse of his stepdaughter, who is Cherokee, on land that is part of the reservation of the Muscogee (Creek) Nation and that, therefore, is part of Indian Country.[1] The issue at stake is whether or not the state of Oklahoma has the authority to exert criminal jurisdiction over non-Indians in federally recognized Native territory. In a 5–4 decision, the Court finds that Oklahoma, and other states, do in fact have such criminal jurisdiction. The ruling repeatedly characterizes federally recognized Native lands as being *inside* the boundaries of states and thus subject to states' authority. The opinion describes the matter in the case as "the status of that part of Oklahoma as Indian country," later noting that "Oklahoma's territory includes Indian country" and that "Indian country is part of the State, not separate," such that "a State has jurisdiction over all of its territory including Indian country"—with the exception that Congress has the authority to limit such jurisdiction with regard to Native lands, persons, and matters, including in order to protect the coherence of tribal governance.[2] The logic here depends on the assertion that Native lands simply lie within the regular jurisdiction of states and that the federal government carves out limited exceptions within the sovereignty of the states for tribes in Indian Country.

Before going further, I should note that this decision, and its central claim, is legally incoherent and historically inaccurate. It overlooks a great deal of federal precedent that Native nations are distinct from states, not subject to their jurisdiction except in limited circumstances, and that tribal jurisdiction is not an endowment from the federal government but is, instead, an exertion of "inherent sovereignty."[3] Moreover, it mobilizes the same kind of nonsensical claim made in *Oliphant v. Suquamish* (discussed in chapter 2) that at some point Native peoples stopped being recognized by the United States as distinct nations and became subject to US jurisdiction.[4] What is notable here is less the Court's dissociation from history, precedent, and logic *per se* than what this rhetorical assemblage suggests about how state discourses (re)construct relations among race, space, scale, and legal geography.

One way of reading the decision is seeing it as even greater evidence of the importance of federal recognition in ways that specifically understand Native peoples as political entities rather than as members of a racial group—as *Indians*. While referencing the existence of tribal governance and its import, the opinion in *Castro-Huerta* largely understands Native peoples as aggregations of Indian persons. When speaking of Castro-Huerta's stepdaughter, the decision refers to her as "a Cherokee Indian," rather than referencing her citizenship in the Cherokee Nation.[5] Further, its jurisdictional logic, like *Oliphant*'s, turns on the distinction between "Indian" and "non-Indian." In doing so, the decision understands jurisdiction in terms of kinds of bodies—a biopolitics of persons rather than a geopolitics of Indigenous territoriality. Particular forms of law and jurisdiction attach to racially defined persons instead of applying across a delimited area, as commonly is the case in Anglo-American legal logics. The notion of *non-Indians* as immanently bearing another jurisdiction understands "Indian" not as designating a sovereign space of governance but as an extension of the bio-genealogical transmission of a kind of identity that provides the basis for limited tribal exceptions from the background political society of the United States. The effect of this racialization of indigeneity is that Indigenous jurisdiction is pervaded and perforated by another set of laws, geographies, and policy frames wherever *non-Indian* bodies move, denying the potential for coherent Native jurisdictional space (like *Oliphant* does, but in a greatly intensified way). Such an introjection also threatens to play havoc with Native legal systems as they operate in practice. If there long has been a call for a congressional *Oliphant*-fix that would extend Native nations' criminal jurisdiction to nonnatives living on tribal lands, *Castro-Huerta* suggests the need for an even more expansive fix that would divorce the notion of Indigenous governance from a racial imaginary of the kinds of bodies to which it might apply, including inasmuch as other jurisdictions are thought immanently to attach to persons deemed non-Indian. The damage wrought to federally recognized tribal governments in the absence of such congressional intervention may be incalculable.

While acknowledging the potentially devasting effects of this decision on tribal governance, including the role of the Court's racializing frame in making possible the opinion's precedent-defying conclusions, one also might see in the case an example of both the fickleness of state recognition and the racial-scalar assumptions that remain in play even in ostensibly *good* decisions within federal Indian law and policy. The decision itself is a response to the opinion in *McGirt v. Oklahoma* (2020), in which the Court found that the Creek reservation had never been disestablished by Congress and, thus, continues to exist despite over a century of federal and state policy operating *as if* the reservation had been dissolved as such. After the Court in the previous case found that the boundaries established by the treaty with the Creek Nation in 1866 had never been eliminated by Congress, such that the reservation boundaries delineated in that treaty remained intact, not three years later the Court in *Castro-Huerta* declares that "those treaties [the ones negotiated with the Five Tribes in the wake of the Civil War, including the one with the Creek Nation at issue in *McGirt*] have been supplanted . . . no later than the 1906 Act enabling Oklahoma's statehood."[6] The conceptual and jurisprudential whiplash of the movement between these decisions might give anyone pause with respect to the idea of turning to the federal government as a vehicle for defining the contours and character of Indigenous peoplehood, territoriality, governance, and self-determination. The likely implications of *Castro-Huerta* for the operation of Native national governments, as well as the uncertainty it generates in everyday life on reservation as to which legal regime is operative among persons at any given moment, underline the significance of state practices and the need to argue against the decision and for better law and policy. However, simultaneously, the capriciousness and inconstancy of such policy underlines the need to conceptualize and enact Indigenous political orders in ways disconnected from the colonial vicissitudes of settler governmental frames.[7] Moreover, even a positive decision, like *McGirt*, does not itself upset the bioreproductive notions of Indianness that implicitly provide the ideological infrastructure for much of the contemporary architecture of federal Indian law (as discussed in chapter 2). Racialized enfamilyment still proves central to the scalar structures of US jurisdiction, just with a particular *plenary* exception (or perhaps distension) for the racial-cultural genealogical formation that is *Indianness*. In its failings and incoherencies, *Castro-Huerta* also implicitly draws attention to the problematic presumptions at play even when the institutions of the settler-state affirm Native sovereignty. In this way, it suggests the expediencies, affordances, colonial mistranslations, and blockages created by state-recognized modes of governance, as Indigenous peoples are folded into the terms of *political society*—and, concomitantly, the racialized field of enfamilyment.

Raising questions about the capacities of legally acknowledged kinds of governance opens up possibilities for emphasizing the importance of, in Laura Harjo's terms, the *vernacular sovereignties* enacted by Indigenous peoples in everyday ways, and doing so also points toward the potentials for foregrounding the political orders of non-Indigenous racialized communities, potentials that themselves usually are effaced in Indian policy discourse. We can see the ways such issues haunt *Castro-Huerta* in how it discusses the location of the crime at the heart of the decision and the import of jurisdiction over that space. Castro-Huerta resided in Tulsa, which had not officially been considered part of Indian Country until the *McGirt* decision. The fact that Tulsa was now under the jurisdiction of the Creek Nation makes a significant difference for the Court's ways of envisioning the proper scope and scale of Native governance. The decision observes, "the eastern part of Oklahoma including Tulsa is now recognized as Indian country. About two million people live there, and the vast majority are not Indians."[8] While seeming to turn on the presence of *non-Indians* in Indian Country, the opinion clearly registers what it takes as something of a crisis in the extension of jurisdiction of Native nations over white people. The language here underlines the size of the nonnative population and of the change made by *McGirt* in what are often described as the settled expectations of whites when confronted with the possibility of legally recognizing Indigenous sovereignty over spaces claimed to have become part of the regular jurisdiction of the settler-state.[9] Although the question of whether states could exert criminal jurisdiction over non-Indians in Indian Country may have been an issue previously, it "did not previously matter all that much and did not warrant this Court's review"; it "was relatively insignificant in the real world." Now, though, post-*McGirt*, the issue "has suddenly assumed immense importance."[10] What exactly is this "importance"? The key to that question lies in the word "suddenly." Although the point of the *McGirt* decision is that the Creek reservation had never actually been disestablished, and that acting as if it had been (regardless of the intervening period in which that fiction had been taken and implemented as fact) was in violation of US law, the federal acknowledgment of the rightful jurisdiction of the Five Tribes over "43% of Oklahoma" appears as if it were a sudden rupture in white jurisdictional and property mappings.[11] The decision implicitly correlates "real world" significance to white geographies and their commonsensicality, signaling a kind of hysteria when what it treats as the usually "insignificant" presence and politics of Native peoples seemingly bursts into the kinds of racialized cartographies that the opinion takes as the frame for *the real.*

Notably, that vertiginous disorientation, and accompanying sense of pressing exigency in restoring "public safety,"[12] occurs with respect to Tulsa. The decision might foreground the fact that the crime was committed in Tulsa in order to underline the scale of the Creek Nation's "new" jurisdiction, since the city is the second largest in Oklahoma and has a population of almost half a million people. In this way, though, the Court folds Tulsa into its de facto white panic narrative of mass absorption of persons and places within what it casts as an anachronistic Indianness. The distinction between "Indian" and "non-Indian," though, cannot capture the complex histories of residence, collectivity, jurisdiction, and governance in Tulsa. The city is an iconic site of both Black placemaking and antiblack, white supremacist mass violence. Known in the early twentieth century as "Black Wall Street," the Greenwood District of Tulsa was a thriving area of Black inhabitance, homeownership, entrepreneurship, and semiautonomous governance.[13] In May 1921, putatively in response to an allegation that a Black man had sexually assaulted a white woman in an elevator, white mobs destroyed over 1,000 Black homes and businesses, burned down 30 square blocks, displaced 1,250 Black families, and murdered from 100 to 300 African Americans, seeking to cleanse the city of its Black presence in what has come to be known as the Tulsa Race Massacre.[14] While the most famous of the Black enclaves in Indian Territory, the Greenwood District certainly was not the only one. Fifty towns predominantly inhabited by African Americans, colloquially known as "Black towns," were founded in what is now Oklahoma, 13 of which remain to this day.[15] Some of them were created by Creek Freedmen in the wake of the end of slavery among the Five Tribes brought by the treaties of 1866.[16] Many of the others were also in the territory of the Creek Nation and took shape around allotments that had been sold by Black Creeks to African Americans who had emigrated from the South. There was mass migration during Reconstruction and afterwards by Black people seeking the kinds of situated networks of landed relation that those recently emancipated sought to build in the South but that were repudiated, criminalized, and dispersed in the interests of white propertyholding (as discussed in chapter 4).[17] Jovan Scott Lewis describes those recently emancipated migrants as searching for a "geography of freedom" in Indian Territory, arguing that what they sought was "the power of a sovereign relationship to place"—

one that Black people continue to seek.[18] Tulsa serves as something of a historical and popular metonym for the kinds of Black collectivity, placemaking, and self-governance that proliferated in Indian Territory prior to Oklahoma statehood and that were subject to intensive white assault and dispossession in its wake.[19] The citation of Tulsa as a figure for the necessity of "non-Indian" (read white) jurisdiction, then, is bitterly ironic, especially given the ongoing role of state intervention and policing targeted at Black people in North Tulsa.[20]

However, those Black political orders, the freedom dreams from which they emerge, and the continuity of collective desires for emplaced self-determination to which they speak also are not captured in the staging of a dichotomy between state and tribal jurisdiction. While highlighting efforts to reduce state-recognized Native sovereignty, attention to the Court's efforts to limit tribal governance can miss the Black geographies that dwell within yet are effaced by the decision's conception of Tulsa as properly a "non-Indian" space. Attending to those geographies—including, for example, the continuing projects of self-determination in North Tulsa as well as the remaining Black towns elsewhere in Oklahoma—points toward both the multiplicity of political orders that have existed and that continue to exist on the lands claimed by the United States and the ways foregrounding state jurisdictional frames can limit the potentials for engaging the presence and significance of that multiplicity.[21]

Positing alternative political orders in noninstitutionalized dynamics and spaces, as I have done, however, also flirts with a dangerous and potentially exploitative romanticism. As Elizabeth Povinelli has argued, when groups develop "alternative social projects" as means of enduring and surviving in conditions of structural immiseration and the wasting absence of resources, that labor can create possibilities for critiquing dominant political economy, but having to live in zones of abjection and exhaustion "create[s] such reduced conditions of life that the political desire for them to spawn or foster alternative worlds can seem naïve at best and sadistic at worst."[22] The story of kinship's racializing translations—of a kind of primitive accumulation that converts nonliberal political forms into racial types—threatens to invest in abjection in the ways about which Povinelli warns. Similarly, in his analysis of the kinds of *idealizations* that often animate queer studies, Kadji Amin defines that process "as a *purification* of one's object that relies on the *repudiation* of its relationship to normative social forms." This drive toward social forms ostensibly unimplicated in systems of domination pushes intellectual work toward "focusing on ever more marginalized populations with fewer resources for collective and self reinvention" that are simultaneously seen as "actualiz[ing] real-life alternatives to existing relations of oppression."[23] My discussion of racialization as primitive accumulation might be seen as enacting this dynamic, treating contingent formations of collectivity whose contours and character are deeply affected by ongoing patterns of racism, dispossession, and capitalist extraction as if they somehow existed outside of those very oppressive dynamics.

Rather than dismissing this intellectual risk, I would like to spell out a bit more explicitly why I believe it is worth taking. The book's reframing of racialization can be seen as part of a reparative effort, less to renounce the state and its forms entirely than to increase intellectual and political capacities for thinking in ways not bound to liberal institutionalities, subjectivities, and scalar logics—either by automatically affirming or negating them. Put another way, how do we think a politics that does not so much axiomatically repudiate the state or state-like institutional apparatuses as refuse to naturalize them as the commonsensical mode for envisioning and living governance? The notion of other political orders provides conceptual and affective leverage in attending to the ways, in situated circumstances and struggles, the structures of the liberal state are sometimes enabling, sometimes not, and often a complicated mesh of both.

In this way, the project of this book might be thought of as posing a series of reorienting hypotheticals: What if Indigenous conceptions of political orders were used to think non-Indigenous social formations as well? What if formations conventionally described as family/kinship were redescribed as political orders? What if racialization were viewed as a means of (mis)translating and managing such political orders, whose coordinates do not match the terms, mappings, and scales of liberal political economy? What possibilities for thought and action might these conceptual or perceptual shifts open? The aim here is less to expose liberal ideologies and associated state structures than to reformulate the description of them so as to turn attention toward other potentials for thinking the self-organization of collective life by racialized, minoritized, and marginalized people(s).[24] If the point is not that reveal, that exposure, then the social matrices I characterize as political orders also need not be understood as idealized *alternative worlds* whose value for thought and life lies in the extent to which they can be seen as utterly separate from—a complete negation of—the violence enacted by liberal political forms.

The strong version of what I've been arguing would place emphasis on the inherent normative value of alternative political orders: they are innately better than the liberal forms that seek to contain, regulate, and eliminate them and, therefore, must remain uncontaminated by the state. From this perspective, state forms, particularly liberal modes of governance, necessarily produce racializing translations in which privacy/family/kinship serves as a container for recoding alternative political orders as deviance, disorder, and dysfunction that needs to be managed by the state, often through violence. The corollary, then, is that such state forms can only ever enact such dynamics and, on that basis, must be utterly repudiated. Since they can only ever produce the same results, any effort to engage, negotiate, or appropriate state forms not only must be doomed to failure but must result in a fundamental degradation/cooptation of the persons, communities, movements, and collectivities that attempt to do so. Moreover, an attempt to draw on or appeal to state forms cannot be strategic or tactical but marks an identification with them that indicates a subjectivity futilely oriented toward those forms.[25] To invest in socialities other than state forms is to open up the possibility of an outside that is unimplicated in such forms' racializing violence. While my discussion of primitive accumulation seeks to redescribe racialization in the United States as a transposition of modes of governance into ideologies of enfamilyment, I'm less interested in casting those modes as themselves free of all violence than in drawing attention to the question of what might count as governance and how that issue gets displaced through the interdependent figurations of race and family. I want to tell a different story about what *the political* might be, one that allows for leveraging certain concepts and frames normalized within liberal governance as well as for mobilizing Indigenous analytics in order to provide a *redescription* of the work of race in the United States. A non-idealizing conception of political orders opens up the potential for a perhaps more capacious set of relations to dominant systems, including state apparatuses.

One might think about this intellectual and political aim, or the aim of this reframing of the political, as increasing options for enabling and tracing patterns of disidentification—multiplying the sites from which it is launched, the range of projects and imaginaries it contains, and developing even further the shift from *against* to *beside*.[26] In José Esteban Muñoz's terms, disidentification marks "a failed interpellation within the dominant public sphere" in which racialized minoritarian subjects draw on majoritarian tropes and frames but do so "working on and against" them in ways that "[labor] to enact permanent structural change while at the same time valuing the importance of local or everyday struggles of resistance."[27] The relation of nonwhite publics and networks of governance to the state, then, might be understood in such terms: the state seeks to interpellate those forms into the grids of liberal intelligibility even as minoritarian collectivities may refuse that process while seeking to refunction aspects of extant law and policy so as to redirect resources and create more room for minoritarian worldmaking. *The Politics of Kinship* marks the force of liberal mappings, scalar logics, and ideologies of personhood and the damage they have wrought and continue to wreak against alternative political orders while I also want to hold on to the ways that engagements with the state and its forms might be tactically important in negotiating extant circumstances. For example, as discussed earlier, we can see how the *Castro-Huerta* decision illustrates the value of federal recognition of Indigenous sovereignty not permeated by states' jurisdictions *as well as* showing the ways legal conceptions of Native jurisdiction in Indian Country remain bound to notions of Indian enfamilyment and resistant to engaging other political orders. How might attending to vernacular sovereignties of various sorts provide ways of stepping *to the side* of the sovereignty of Native national governments, opening up other normative and organizational possibilities while also acknowledging those governments' confrontation/negotiation with the settler-state and the everyday importance of that process in the present?[28]

This *beside* also extends to thinking about the dense relations among varied racialized groups and their modes of belonging, governance, and placemaking. Turning back to the histories of Black collectivity and self-determination in what, as of 1907, was Oklahoma (a ghosted story within the *Castro-Huerta* opinion), we can see a refractive set of inhabitances, displacements, and contingent alignments.[29] The Creek Nation was removed from their territory in the US Southeast in the 1830s, moved onto lands from which the Osage had been removed, and part of the Creek population held people of African descent as slaves. In the wake of the treaty of 1866, those enslaved persons were emancipated and made citizens of the Creek Nation, formed their own towns (the largest in the nation) that were represented as part of the Creek legislature in the House of Kings and the House of Warriors, played a very significant role in Creek national politics throughout the pre-allotment period and in resisting the imposition of allotment in the wake of the Curtis Act of 1898, and were given allotments when that policy was enforced on the Creek Nation, even as Black Creeks also were officially listed on the Freedmen Roll by the Dawes Commission (regardless of their actual genealogical relation to non-Black Creek people, including parents). During the late nineteenth and early twentieth century, as noted earlier, many African Americans moved to Indian Territory, particularly the lands of the Creek Nation, in order to seek their own possibilities for modes of freedom denied in the South. There was significant mutual suspicion and hostility between those Black people who had immigrated to Indian Territory and Creek Freedmen (as they were known), who all understood the significant differences between those who were citizens of Native nations and those who were US citizens.[30] Those who created Black towns out of land purchased from Black Creek people specifically sought these allotments because all of the government restrictions on them had been removed (unlike the complex calculus for the allotments of those officially recognized as having *Indian blood*). These interpenetrating layers of exploitation, extraction, and dispossession as well as tactical and strategic maneuvering within their cross-currents suggest how worldmaking for dominated people(s) often does not fit well with stories of political innocence.[31] Instead, what appears are difficult choices within efforts to negotiate the conditions created by white supremacy and the US state.

What I want to argue for is not a notion of political orders that are utterly unimplicated in the dynamics of US political economy or that can be narrated as utterly free from extant forms of power and privilege. In particular, I don't want to lose track of the ways heteropatriarchy also can manifest within alternative social formations, including conscripting women into particular care and domestic roles, effacing questions of gendered violence, and demonizing and exiling queer and trans people from such networks of relation.[32] Instead, my goal is help open up possibilities for understanding what constitutes a political order so as to better engage the variety of projects for emplaced collective self-governance at play, historically and currently, on the lands claimed by the United States. In this vein, my understanding of primitive accumulation is not the (ongoing) loss of a utopian commons, of an unsullied before/outside, but the process by which race works—via discourses of enfamilyment—to recode nonliberal social formations as failed, perverse, backward, and criminal in ways that license state intervention, management, and violence. My focus, then, is on the racializing work kinship performs in shaping what gets counted as governance and on how various political orders may exist beside each other, with complex and shifting relations among them and with the state. Without in any way exonerating the liberal state, I want to leave open the question of how Indigenous peoples and non-Indigenous racialized communities tactically and strategically have engaged and might engage the state's existing authority, resources, and scalar structures in order to capacitate their own survivance amid domination and extraction.

Conversely, approaching modes of emplaced collectivity *as political orders* enables reading across forms of racialized difference in ways that highlight the copresence of nondominant modes of worldmaking and struggles for self-determination (even if they may, at times, be in tension). In a recent published exchange of letters, Robyn Maynard and Leanne Simpson discuss the possibilities and urgencies for Black and Indigenous relation in ways that speak to the potentials I hope this book will facilitate. Maynard expresses her desire to "think together about what it means for us to build livable lives together in the wreckage," and she further indicates, "We are, already, living and organizing on entirely different terms than those laid out by the monsters." She asks, "What does it mean to try to build worlds that affirm, rather than destroy, life?" Simpson similarly insists that "we are linked in our distinctive world-building relationalities," asking, "What worlds do Indigenous and Black land-based politics give breath to, and how do we connect these to anti-colonial movements outside of North America and beyond?" Simpson observes, "There is no justice in Land Back if it is not in concert with the destruction of racial capitalism, and if Black people remain landless. There is no justice in Land Back if we are silent with regard to the radical imaginings of Black futures and Black struggles for freedom, just as there is no justice if Black liberation is framed through the ongoing dispossession of Indigenous peoples."[33] Drawing on the notion of political orders to think about forms of non-Indigenous collectivity as well aims toward the goal of highlighting the "different terms" through which world-building is and has been occurring. By doing so, I have sought to emphasize how the landed self-governance of Indigenous peoples can be thought of as a frame through which to conceptualize emplaced ("land-based") projects of Black liberation, historically and in the present. Reciprocally, thinking such relationalities opens toward a conceptualization of race as (at least in part) a multidimensional matrix through which modes of governance are translated as ingrained, genealogized pathology, thereby speaking to the copresent violences of racial capitalism and settlement without necessarily collapsing them into each other nor needing to route land-based nonnative formations through discourses of (self-)indigenization that efface the continuing presence of Indigenous peoples.[34]

Moreover, the significance of such political orders does not lie in their capacity to be scaled up. Given the importance of the state in the distribution of resources, regulation of life-chances, and claimed monopoly over legitimate violence (including murder by the police and incarceration), the state can help generate a romance/tragedy of scale in which the only way to alter existing circumstances seems to be to create mass mobilizations that can influence state institutions or in which the absence of such mobilization means the unchanging continuance of an exhausting, immiserating, and wounding status quo. Such mobilization can make a difference in lived circumstances and possibilities, and the state does serve as an unavoidable terrain of struggle in the present. Yet, such an investment in or identification with scale can overlook, or underemphasize, the socialities in which other ways of living are incubated, sustained, and proliferated. Those projects of collective worldmaking—call them political orders—may not be scalable. Further, desire for that scalability may replicate the infrastructural imaginary of the state. Alternative political orders exist alongside the state, even as the latter racializes, assaults, and seeks to contain/dismantle them. That *besidesness* challenges the obviousness and legitimacy of state frames without seeking to become the (new) state and without those other modes of governance necessarily articulating themselves as in an antagonistic relation to the state, even as their forms contest the assumptions at play in liberal ideologies. To see them *as governance*, though, refuses the ways they have been privatized as racial deviance—as expressions of wrong home and family that testify to the existence of a backward, criminal, degenerate population that needs to be managed and from whom the general public (of properly enfamilied citizen-subjects) needs protection. Looking for the presence of such political orders widens the capacity to envision governance otherwise while also suspending the scalar imperatives that continue to make the liberal state seem like the only option around.

NOTES

Introduction: Enfamilyment, Political Orders, and the Racializing Work of Scale

1 National Conference of State Legislatures (NCSL), "Disproportionality and Race Equity in Child Welfare," January 26, 2021, https://www.ncsl.org/research/human-services/disproportionality-and-race-equity-in-child-welfare.aspx; Southern Poverty Law Center (SPLC), "Family Separation under the Trump Administration—a Timeline," June 17, 2020, https://www.splcenter.org/news/2020/06/17/family-separation-under-trump-administration-timeline; US Department of Health and Human Services, Administration for Children and Families, *The AFCARS Report*, 2021, https://www.acf.hhs.gov/sites/default/files/documents/cb/afcarsreport27.pdf. See also Beardall and Edwards, "Abolition, Settler Colonialism"; Beltrán, *Cruelty as Citizenship*; Brady, *Scales of Captivity*; Briggs, *Taking Children*; Jacobs, *A Generation Removed*; Pierce, "In Good Relations"; Roberts, *Shattered Bonds*; Speed, *Incarcerated Stories*; and Threadcraft, *Intimate Justice*.
2 See Povinelli, *Economies of Abandonment*.
3 On the politics of scale, see Biolsi, "Imagined Geographies"; Brady, *Scales of Captivity*; Goeman, "Ongoing Storms and Struggles"; Massey, *Space, Place, and Gender*; and McKittrick, *Demonic Grounds*. On genealogies of efforts to define liberalism, see Bell, "What Is Liberalism?"
4 See Simpson, "The State Is a Man." On the imposition of patriarchal forms for defining "Indian" identity and governance in Canada through the Indian Act, see Cannon, *Men, Masculinity*; Lawrence, *"Real" Indians and Others*; Million, *Therapeutic Nations*.
5 Simpson, *As We Have Always Done*, 41, 112.
6 On Indigenous modes of life as an alternative to the liberal state and capitalist political economy, see Coulthard, *Red Skin, White Masks*; Estes, *Our History Is Our Future*; Pasternak, *Grounded Authority*; and Yazzie, "Decolonizing Development."
7 On this dynamic, see Barker, *Native Acts*; Byrd, *The Transit of Empire*; Rifkin, *When Did Indians Become Straight?*; and Simpson, *Mohawk Interruptus*.
8 Scott, *Conscripts of Modernity*, 4, 19.
9 See Latour, *Reassembling the Social*; Massey, *Space, Place, and Gender*.

10   Dillon, *The Gender of Freedom*, 24, 35, 127. For discussion of the import of unwaged work for sustaining such supposed privacy, as well as for the scale structure of capitalist political economy, see Federici, *Patriarchy of the Wage*.

11   Perry, *Vexy Thing*, 21, 24. See also Lowe, *The Intimacies of Four Continents*.

12   Here I build on, but differ from, Amy Kaplan's conception of "manifest domesticity," in that I am interested less in how domesticity serves as a vehicle for conceptualizing and validating forms of imperial intervention than in how ideologies of domesticity translate political orders as (failed/perverse/dangerous) enactments of bourgeois privacy. See Kaplan, *The Anarchy of Empire*.

13   See Weheliye, *Habeas Viscus*. In addition to drawing on Perry and Weheliye's arguments, this analysis builds on feminist and queer studies work on the relation between family and racialization. In addition to the scholarly sources in note 1, see Cohen, "Punks, Bulldaggers, and Welfare Queens"; Eng, *The Feeling of Kinship*; Ferguson, *Aberrations in Black*; Franke, *Wedlocked*; Holland, *The Erotic Life*; Macharia, *Frottage*; Stevens, *Reproducing the State*; and Weinbaum, *Wayward Reproduction*. However, where I differ from much of this work is in its understanding of the connection between racialization and "kinship" as indicating that the relations indicated by kinship (meaning privatized modes of social reproduction pinned to the nuclear family) need to be displaced. Instead, my argument is that "kinship" often functions as a way of (mis)translating formations of collective praxis and governance *as* racialized reproduction in ways that insert them into a privatizing liberal frame, rather than acknowledging them as alternative modes of sociality—ones that contest the terms and scalar structure of liberal political economy.

14   Foucault's work has been critiqued for not attending to ongoing dynamics of direct state domination, particularly within colonialism and against racialized persons/groups (inside and outside state boundaries). In addition to Stoler, *Race and the Education of Desire*, see also Mbembe, "Necropolitics"; Weheliye, *Habeas Viscus*.

15   Stoler, *Race and the Education of Desire*, 97, 98, 99, 133, 176, 12.

16   On the historical complexities of Asianness and Latinness as racial categories in the United States, especially in their shifting relation to whiteness, see Day, *Alien Capital*; Guidotti-Hernández, *Unspeakable Violence*; Haney López, *White by Law*; Martinez, "Mexican Americans and Whiteness"; Rifkin, *Manifesting America*; Saldaña-Portillo, *The Revolutionary Imagination*; and Wong, *Racial Reconstruction*.

17   Foucault, "Society Must Be Defended," 255, 256.

18   As David Kazanjian suggests in his analysis of racial governmentality in the early US republic, "U.S. citizenship does not demand the assimilation of difference to a homogenous national norm, but rather depends on the active production of a particular kind of difference—the calculable racial

difference of a population" (*The Colonizing Trick*, 123). Additionally, Michelle Murphy argues that "race is the grammar and ghost of population," and, as she further explains, "to materialize people as the managerial noun of population is to expose them to designations of being living forms of waste available for destruction" (*The Economization of Life*, 135).

19 Within the dynamics of governmentality, Foucault suggests, the family is "no longer a model [of the state in miniature] but a segment. Nevertheless, it remains a privileged segment, because whenever information is required concerning the population (sexual behavior, demography, consumption, and so on), it must be obtained through the family. But the family becomes an instrument rather than a model—the privileged instrument for the government of the population and not the chimerical model of good government" ("Governmentality," 216). The norms and forms of normalization that are central to governmentality cluster around notions of proper family formation, or what I have been describing as *enfamilyment*.

20 On racialized "flesh," see Spillers, "Mama's Baby, Papa's Maybe"; Weheliye, *Habeas Viscus*.

21 In this formulation of the relation between biopolitics, racialization, and settlement, I draw on, while differing from, Scott Morgensen's analysis of how "Western law attains universality by containing and eliminating differences in the functional extension of settler colonialism as liberal governmentality" ("The Biopolitics of Settler Colonialism," 58).

22 Hyde, *Empires, Nations, and Families*, 5, 29.

23 Hyde, *Empires, Nations, and Families*, 30, 484.

24 Hyde indicates, "Residents of the West seemed quite ambivalent about nationality, easily claiming new citizenship when it served personal or business needs. During a time when no one knew which nation or empire would finally impose control, effective trade was the sole source of power." But soon thereafter, she notes, "Having kinship ties to many different Indian nations became a business advantage" (*Empires, Nations, and Families*, 30, 39).

25 Hyde, *Empires, Nations, and Families*, 226.

26 My discussion here in many ways takes inspiration from Lauren Berlant's analysis of "intimate publics." See Berlant, *The Female Complaint*. In that case, persons engage with public discourses of personal life as a way of understanding themselves as in a similar, privatized situation as that of others—a shared public mode of fantasy and identification that depends on a sense of mutual privatized seriality.

27 Johnson, *Wicked Flesh*, 3. A similar dynamic can be seen in Jennifer Morgan's recent efforts to trace how persons were made into countable, calculable objects in the early centuries of the African slave trade. She offers wonderful analyses of how enslaved persons, particularly enslaved women, came to understand and negotiate that system of calculation, but in doing so, she often juxtaposes the dehumanizing effects of such

quantification to the affective fullness of family/kinship, in terms that resonate with nineteenth-century conceptions of the private. See Morgan, *Reckoning with Slavery*.

28 Johnson, *Wicked Flesh*, 143.
29 Simpson, "The State Is a Man."
30 Simpson, *As We Have Always Done*, 104.
31 Lara, *Queer Freedom*, 12.
32 Simpson, *Mohawk Interruptus*, 138.
33 Simpson, *Mohawk Interruptus*, 109, 175, 189.
34 Harjo, *Spiral to the Stars*, 12, 39.
35 Harjo, *Spiral to the Stars*, 42.
36 Although using different conceptual coordinates, this understanding of political orders resonates with Kris Sealey's theorization of creolization "as a process that is both resistive and creative" and that "allows . . . communities to invent mechanisms through which their discursive (and sometimes material) liberation becomes possible at the level of the everyday." Sealey explains that "the alternative spatiotemporal orderings of community life and alternative modes of living with difference that emerge in creolization are not simply about generating new lifeworlds; rather, they are about the grounding of that newness in an oppositional, everyday politics that survives alongside and despite those master codes of violence" (*Creolizing the Nation*, 46, 72).
37 For discussion of such dynamics, see Brooks, *Our Beloved Kin*; Deloria, *Speaking of Indians*; DeMallie, "Kinship and Biology in Sioux Culture"; Harmon, *The Power of Promises*; Kauanui, *Hawaiian Blood*; McCarthy, *In Divided Unity*; and Perdue, *Cherokee Women*.
38 See Carroll, *Roots of Our Renewal*; Deer and Richland, *Introduction to Tribal Legal Studies*; Dennison, *Colonial Entanglement*; Doerfler, *Those Who Belong*; Lyons, *X-marks*; Pasternak, *Grounded Authority*; Richotte, *Claiming Turtle Mountain's Constitution*; and Turner, *This Is Not a Peace Pipe*.
39 As Elizabeth Povinelli illustrates, Anglo settler regimes often are willing to recognize forms of Indigenous collectivity, but only on the condition that they are not "repugnant" in some way—that they do not violate liberal conceptions of proper social order, subjectivity, and domesticity. See Povinelli, *The Cunning of Recognition*.
40 Mehta, *Liberalism and Empire*, 48–49, 52.
41 Rawls, *Political Liberalism*, 43, 68, 137, 258. For an intellectual history of Rawlsian thought, see Forrester, *In the Shadow of Justice*.
42 Notably, Rawls also indicates that "legally recognized rules of property" are, along with "the nature of the family," part of the basic structure, and we might understand these two points as informing each other. As Jonathan Quong observes, "Private property rights . . . are perfectly consistent with the idea of fair cooperation amongst free and equal people;

indeed it seems unlikely that this moral ideal could be realized without property rights" (*Liberalism without Perfection*, 308). Rawls's theory of justice is fundamentally distributive, about how goods and resources might be dispersed in equitable ways not dependent on accrued forms of social advantage or accidents of birth, and Iris Marion Young notes of the distributive paradigm that it "implicitly assumes a social atomism, inasmuch as there is no internal relation among persons in society relevant to considerations of justice": "In such a possessive model the nature of the possessing subject is prior to and independent of the goods possessed; the self underlies and is unchanged by alternative distributions" (*Justice and the Politics of Difference*, 16–17).

43 See Federici, *Patriarchy of the Wage*.
44 Rawls, *Political Liberalism*, 60–61.
45 As Jonathan Quong indicates, "Unreasonable doctrines are thus doctrines whose beliefs directly contradict the fundamental political values of a liberal democratic regime": "Views that are unreasonable are not simply non-public doctrines: they have an inescapably political element because they reject the central political values of liberal democracy" (*Liberalism without Perfection*, 291, 303).
46 Benhabib suggests a deliberative framework "encourages discourse about the lines separating the public from the private," "is much more oriented to the ways in which political processes and the 'background culture' interact," and foregrounds "processes of opinion formation in an unrestricted public sphere" (*The Claims of Culture*, 109). In turning to Benhabib, I am building off of the critique Glen Coulthard offers with regard to the implications of this conception of deliberative democracy for Indigenous sovereignties. See Coulthard, *Red Skin, White Masks*, 79–103.
47 Benhabib, *The Claims of Culture*, 47.
48 Benhabib, *The Claims of Culture*, 53, 141. On the understanding of Indigenous peoplehood in "cultural" terms by settler-states, see Barker, *Native Acts*; Coulthard, *Red Skin, White Masks*; Engle, *Elusive Promise of Indigenous Development*; Moreton-Robinson, *The White Possessive*; Povinelli, *The Cunning of Recognition*; Simpson, *Mohawk Interruptus*; and Yazzie, "US Imperialism." On the problems of "culture" as an appropriative and depoliticizing rubric for other racialized groups in the United States, see Ferguson, *The Reorder of Things*; Hong, *Death beyond Disavowal*; Lee, *Urban Triage*; and Melamed, *Represent and Destroy*.
49 A similar dynamic can be seen even when "multicultural" minorities are presented as having (limited) rights to governance. See Kymlicka, *Multicultural Odysseys*.
50 On the interdependence of "race" and "culture" as categories, see Baker, *Anthropology and the Racial Politics of Culture*; Balibar, "Is There a 'Neo-Racism'?"; Barker, *Native Acts*; Chow, *The Protestant Ethnic*; Visweswaran, *Un/common Cultures*; and Weheliye, *Habeas Viscus*. Liberal

theory often understands race as an accident of birth for which remedial redistributive mechanisms are appropriate. Perhaps the most expansive version of this argument can be found in the work of Charles Mills. See Mills, *Black Rights/White Wrongs*. Mills continues to endorse a liberal framework, which largely leaves intact the dynamics of racializing enfamilyment I discuss.

51 Simpson, *As We Have Always Done*, 41.
52 Byrd, *The Transit of Empire*, xxiii, xxiv; Nichols, "Contract and Usurpation," 103, 110.
53 Byrd, *The Transit of Empire*, 125.
54 See Trask, *From a Native Daughter*, 25–40.
55 See Rifkin, *Settler Common Sense*; Rifkin, *When Did Indians Become Straight?*
56 I am implicitly building on a large body of work that addresses the relation between Indigenous people and other racialized groups, including the complex overlaps among them. On Black-Indigenous relations, see Arvin, *Possessing Polynesians*; Byrd, *The Transit of Empire*; Chang, *The Color of the Land*; Klopotek, *Recognition Odysseys*; Miles and Holland, *Crossing Waters, Crossing World*; Prud'homme-Cranford et al., *Louisiana Creole Peoplehood*; Rifkin, *Fictions of Land and Flesh*; Sharma, *Hawai'i Is My Haven*; Sturm, *Blood Politics*; and Sturm, "Rethinking Blackness and Indigeneity." On Asian American–Indigenous relations, see Day, *Alien Capital*; Kim, *Settler Garrison*; Le, *Unsettled Solidarities*; Pegues, *Space-Time Colonialism*; and Saranillo, *Unsustainable Empire*. On Latinx-Indigenous relations, see Blackwell et al., "Introduction: Critical Latinx Indigeneities"; Guidotti-Hernández, *Unspeakable Violence*; Saldaña-Portillo, *The Revolutionary Imagination*; Speed, *Incarcerated Stories*; and Trujillo, *Land Uprising*.
57 Coulthard, *Red Skin, White Masks*, 7, 10, 12.
58 Nichols, *Theft Is Property!*, 30–31, 80. As Aileen Moreton-Robinson argues, "Indigenous communal property rights are never accorded equal value because ontologically white possession requires that Indigenous people are not perceived as being out of a state of nature. White possession can only recognize Indigenous people as being out of nature through private property rights via the prism of citizenship. Indigenous people can own property in this sense, but not a different epistemological and ontological embodiment of possession that is outside the logic of capital" (*The White Possessive*, 121–22).
59 See Povinelli, "The Governance of the Prior."
60 On the potential of centering dispossession as a way of putting the struggles of Indigenous peoples and other racialized groups into a shared frame, see also Bruyneel, *Settler Memory*; Byrd et al., "Predatory Value"; Goldstein, "Finance and Foreclosure"; and Mays, *City of Dispossessions*. On the emergence of peoples post-contact and the problem of locking Native peoples into the past, see Andersen, *"Métis"*; Anderson, *The Indian*

Southwest; Barker, *Native Acts*; Lowery, *Lumbee Indians*; O'Brien, *Firsting and Lasting*; Prud'homme-Cranford et al., *Louisiana Creole Peoplehood*; and Shepherd, *We Are an Indian Nation*.

61 On the issues at play in notions of "internal colonialism," see Byrd, *The Transit of Empire*; Higashida, *Black Internationalist Feminism*; and Young, *Soul Power*.

62 Lewis, *Violent Utopia*, 192, 196, 208.

63 See Byrd et al., "Predatory Value."

64 Melamed, "Racial Capitalism," 77, 79, 80. On racial capitalism, see also Jenkins and Leroy, *Histories of Racial Capitalism*; Robinson, *Black Marxism*.

65 For feminist and queer critiques of such nationalisms, see also Anzaldúa, *Borderlands/La Frontera*; Ferguson, *Aberrations in Black*; Keeling, *The Witch's Flight*; Lorde, *Sister Outsider*; Lowe, *Immigrant Acts*; Lubiano, "Black Nationalism and Black Common Sense"; Moraga, *Loving in the War Years*; and Rodríguez, *Next of Kin*.

66 Hong, *Death beyond Disavowal*, 77. For a reading of Lorde as advocating forms of nationalism for racialized groups in the United States, in the context of an international vision of movements for self-determination globally, see Higashida, *Black Internationalist Feminism*, 134–57.

67 Hong, *Death beyond Disavowal*, 19–20; Ferguson, *Aberrations in Black*, 113, 140.

68 Hong, *Death beyond Disavowal*, 4.

69 Reddy, *Freedom with Violence*, 160. See also Beltrán, *Cruelty as Citizenship*; Das Gupta, *Unruly Immigrants*; Luibhéid, *Entry Denied*; Nguyen, *The Gift of Freedom*; and Speed, *Incarcerated Stories*. On the history of immigration policy in the United States, see also Hernández, *City of Inmates*; Kim, *Ends of Empire*; Lew-Williams, *The Chinese Must Go*; Molina, *How Race Is Made in America*; and Ngai, *Impossible Subjects*. On the relation between migration from Latin America and indigeneity, including the ways Indigenous people get classed as Latinx in ways that efface their indigeneity, see Blackwell et al., "Introduction: Critical Latinx Indigeneities"; Speed, *Incarcerated Stories*; and Trujillo, *Land Uprising*.

70 Gopinath, *Unruly Visions*, 15, 61. On queer diaspora, see also Eng, *The Feeling of Kinship*; Gopinath, *Impossible Desires*; and Puar, *Terrorist Assemblages*. On Black feminist diasporic imaginaries, see Ellis, *Territories of the Soul*; Hartman, *Lose Your Mother*; Pinto, *Difficult Diasporas*; and Stephens, *Black Empire*.

71 Eng and Puar, "Introduction: Left of Queer," 18.

72 Scott, *The Art of Not Being Governed*, 7, 30, 132, 326.

73 Scott, *The Art of Not Being Governed*, 323.

74 Scott, *The Art of Not Being Governed*, 324.

75 Hong, *Death beyond Disavowal*, 16.

76 Ferguson, *One-Dimensional Queer*, 82–83. In this vein, Gopinath also gestures toward "the ways in which viable modes of dwelling and rootedness

are created in the wake of dispossession and displacement," a dynamic that she refers to as "diasporic rootedness" (*Unruly Visions*, 88, 99).

77 Here I am also thinking about the ways that the specificity of any given place arises through its complex relations with other places. See Goeman, "Ongoing Storms and Struggles"; and Massey, *Space, Place, and Gender*.

78 Spillers, "Mama's Baby, Papa's Maybe," 228–29.

79 Here I am refiguring Sylvia Wynter's conception of "genres of the human." See McKittrick, *Sylvia Wynter*; Weheliye, *Habeas Viscus*; and Wynter, "Unsettling the Coloniality."

One. Kinship's Past, Queer Interventions, and Indigenous Futures

Parts of chapter 1 previously were published as "Beyond Family: Kinship's Past, Queer Worldmaking, and the Question of Governance," in *Queer Kinship: Race, Sex, Belonging, Form*, edited by Elizabeth Freeman and Teagan Bradway.

1 Ahmed, *Queer Phenomenology*, 77, 81.
2 Rodríguez, *Sexual Futures*, 37, 47.
3 Foucault, *The History of Sexuality*, 154.
4 Sahlins, *What Kinship Is*, ix, 44.
5 Clarke, "Introducing *Making Kin Not Population*," 2, 33.
6 Schneider, *Critique of the Study of Kinship*, 6, 108, 62. See also Franklin, *Biological Relatives*; Franklin and McKinnon, "Introduction"; Yanagisako and Collier, "Toward a Unified Analysis"; and Yanagisako and Delany, "Naturalizing Power." Richard Feinberg somewhat unreflexively demonstrates this point when he seeks to critique Schneider by suggesting, "Every English-speaking American I know is familiar with such terms as 'kin,' 'kinship,' 'kinsmen,' 'kinfolk,' 'relatives,' and 'family,' and everyone has a fairly clear idea of what those terms mean" ("Introduction," 12). Some scholars have suggested that kinship provides a culturally specific way of tracing how various peoples/societies themselves mark the distinction "between what is given and what is made" (Carsten, *After Kinship*, 189). However, this claim seems to fall back into the same problem of how we come to know a particular relation/formation is "kinship," and the potential distinction between the "given" and "made" extends far beyond those relations/formations that have been placed under the rubric of "kinship." Similarly, Sahlins argues that "relations of procreation are patterned by the kinship order in which they are embedded," such that "human birth is a semiotic function of a kinship order, rather than kinship as a biological sequitur of birth." Though if "kinship" is, in Sahlin's terms, "mutual relations of being" and "participation in one another's existence," why would "kinship" be centered on birth or provide

a principal form for situating "relations of procreation" (*What Kinship Is*, 76, 87, 18)? The nuclear family continues to serve as the referential field for kinship even as it expands/shifts and is understood as not determined by "biological" facts.

7   On Morgan's influence across multiple kinds of discourses and institutions, see Ben-Zvi, "Where Did Red Go?"; Carsten, *After Kinship*; Fortes, *Kinship and the Social Order*; McKinnon, "The Economies in Kinship"; Simpson, *Mohawk Interruptus*; and Trautmann, *Lewis Henry Morgan*.

8   For recent anthropological approaches to the ways "kinship" and "state" are understood in relation to each other, see Thelan and Alber, "Reconnecting State and Kinship."

9   See Deloria, *Playing Indian*, 71–94; Michaelsen, *The Limits of Multiculturalism*, 84–106; Simpson, *Mohawk Interruptus*, 67–94; and Trautmann, *Lewis Henry Morgan*, 36–57.

10 Morgan, *Ancient Society*, vii, 121.

11 Anne McClintock quite forcefully captures the intellectual maneuvers at play in this colonial reduction of contemporary peoples to roles in a teleology of Euro-American becoming in her notions of "anachronistic space" and "panoptic time" (*Imperial Leather*). See also Chakrabarty, *Provincializing Europe*; Deloria, *Indians in Unexpected Places*; Fabian, *Time and the Other*; O'Brien, *Firsting and Lasting*; and Rifkin, *Beyond Settler Time*.

12 On the role of "conjectural history" in Morgan's thinking, see Trautmann, *Lewis Henry Morgan*. On the ideological ascension of the nuclear family form in the period, see Coontz, *The Social Origins of Private Life*; Cott, *Public Vows*; Merish, *Sentimental Materialism*; and Stanley, *From Bondage to Contract*.

13 Morgan, *Ancient Society*, 512.

14 Ahmed, *Queer Phenomenology*, 38.

15 Morgan, *Ancient Society*, 5, 9–12.

16 On the historical relation between conceptions of family and procedures for knowing in Euro-American ideologies and practices, see Strathern, *Kinship, Law, and the Unexpected*.

17 In particular, see Morgan, *Ancient Society*, 393–94. As Ann Marie Plane indicates in her study of British interventions in Native social forms in colonial New England, "Given the differences, one must consider the implications of applying the word *marriage* to conjugal relations in the native communities of precontact southeastern New England. Much scholarship has suggested that 'marriage' is not a universally applicable analytic concept. It is more helpful (and less Eurocentric) to think instead about a continuum of male-female relationships in this or in any society, some of which may approximate the particularly Western concept of marriage," and she later adds, "marriage itself became a metaphor; it spoke not about 'Indian practices' alone but about the entire relationship

between the land, the colonizers, and the colonized" (*Colonial Intimacies*, 6, 29).
18 On the operation of a similar dynamic with regard to IVF and new formations of "biological relations," see Franklin, *Biological Relatives*.
19 Morgan, *Ancient Society*, 403–4.
20 Morgan, *Ancient Society*, 404–5, 407.
21 While I focus on *Ancient Society*, the distinction between descriptive and classificatory kinship emerges most clearly in Morgan's *Systems of Consanguinity and Affinity of the Human Family* (1871), and in an earlier draft of that book, Morgan used "natural" and "artificial" to designate this difference, later substituting "descriptive" and "classificatory." See Trautmann, *Lewis Henry Morgan*, 115–47.
22 Schneider, *Critique of the Study of Kinship*, 99, 119, 156.
23 Morgan, *Ancient Society*, 90, 404, 28, 401.
24 Morgan, *Ancient Society*, 4–5, 466.
25 Morgan, *Ancient Society*, 35, 62, 64, 35, 118, 338, 85.
26 Morgan, *Ancient Society*, 62, 66.
27 Morgan, *Ancient Society*, 6, 61, 122.
28 One might describe twentieth-century theorizations of kinship (particularly in British social anthropology) as abandoning this distinction between "kinship" and the "political," and instead separating kinship from the domestic in assessing non-Western societies. As Janet Carsten argues, "From early on, the comparative study of kinship was explicitly defined as *not* being about intimate domestic arrangements and the behavior and emotions associated with them," and she adds that "these anthropologists viewed the primary importance of kinship as providing a stable *political* structure in societies without state or governmental institutions" (*After Kinship*, 11, 35). For an example, see Fortes, *Kinship and the Social Order*; and for discussion of this broader dynamic, see Kuper, *The Reinvention of Primitive Society*. However, as I have suggested, "kinship" lacks referential meaning or conceptual bounding absent its implicit indexing to the nuclear family form, and the elasticity of that referentiality in categorizing nonliberal governance as not really governance is precisely what enables, as Carsten notes, "the boundaries between the West and the rest" in which "kinship was something 'they' have" while "'we' have families" (*After Kinship*, 15).
29 See Dillon, *The Gender of Freedom*.
30 Morgan, *Ancient Society*, 103, 114, 104.
31 Morgan, *Ancient Society*, 512, 6.
32 See McKinnon, "The Economies in Kinship."
33 Morgan, *Ancient Society*, 355.
34 See McKinnon, "The Economies in Kinship."
35 Morgan, *Ancient Society*, 462, 469, 475.
36 Morgan, *Ancient Society*, 464, 484, 482.

37   For such an attempted reformulation, see Fortes, *Kinship and the Social Order*.
38   Povinelli, *The Empire of Love*, 4, 199, 225–26.
39   The liberal individual offers, in Janet Carsten's terms (used with regard to the process of finding a "birth parent"), "a notion of personhood where kinship is not simply added to bounded individuality, but one where kin relations are perceived as intrinsic to the self" (*After Kinship*, 107), and the ideological shape of that intrinsicality is what I am calling enfamilyment.
40   For examples, see Cacho, *Social Death*; Chamberlin, "Akinship"; Luibhéid, *Entry Denied*; Muhammad, *The Condemnation of Blackness*; and Shah, *Stranger Intimacy*. As Brackette Williams suggests, "The same precepts that make possible the creation of kinship also make possible the creation of races within the nation, and represent the embodied historicity of the system of classification within which additional interdicts take place" ("Classification Systems Revisited," 229).
41   Eng, *The Feeling of Kinship*, 47.
42   On the conversion in the early twentieth century of what had been explicitly white-coded models of gender and family life to models of "normal" family and maturation, see Carter, *The Heart of Whiteness*.
43   See Duggan, *The Twilight of Equality?*; Eng, *The Feeling of Kinship*; Ferguson, *One-Dimensional Queer*; Manalansan, "Race, Violence, and Neoliberal Spatial Politics"; Puar, *Terrorist Assemblages*; and Reddy, *Freedom with Violence*.
44   For a recent effort to grapple with the role of kinship in queer studies and imaginings, see Bradway and Freeman, *Queer Kinship*.
45   While not claiming that the texts I engage can stand as representative of work in queer studies, I do think that these examples point to more broadly applicable patterns. I have chosen these texts based on a combination of factors, including the extent of their citation and the complexity of how they engage questions of enfamilyment and "kinship."
46   Berlant and Warner, "Sex in Public," 547, 553.
47   See Povinelli, *The Empire of Love*.
48   Berlant and Warner, "Sex in Public," 554, 558.
49   Rodríguez, *Sexual Futures*, 14; Stallings, *Funk the Erotic*, 167. In addition, claims to queer space in urban areas can take part in broader patterns of gentrification and calls for gay and lesbian "safety" that have further worked to criminalize and displace people of color, including queer people of color. See Ellison, "Black Femme Praxis"; Ferguson, *One-Dimensional Queer*, 81–113; Hanhardt, *Safe Space*; and Manalansan, "Race, Violence, and Neoliberal Spatial Politics."
50   Rodríguez, *Sexual Futures*, 47.
51   Ahmed, *Queer Phenomenology*, 70, 87.
52   Ahmed, *Queer Phenomenology*, 92, 107, 104.

53 On the relation between minoritizing and universalizing formulations with regard to sexuality, see Sedgwick, *Epistemology of the Closet*.
54 Muñoz, *Cruising Utopia*, 65, 72, 35. On such ephemerality and the work of performance for creating spaces for queer of color worldings, see Chambers-Letson, *After the Party*.
55 Muñoz, *Cruising Utopia*, 49.
56 On the significance of "gesture" as a way of addressing political/cultural/ethical desires, movements, and ways of being, see Rodríguez, *Sexual Futures*.
57 Stallings, *Funk the Erotic*, 122.
58 On this point, see also Cohen, "Punks, Bulldaggers, and Welfare Queens"; Ferguson, *Aberrations in Black*; Franke, *Wedlocked*; Hartman, *Wayward Lives, Beautiful Experiments*; Macharia, *Frottage*; Ross, "Beyond the Closet"; and Thomas, *The Sexual Demon*.
59 Stallings, *Funk the Erotic*, 141.
60 On the political trope of marronage, see Bonilla, *Non-Sovereign Futures*; Roberts, *Freedom as Marronage*; and Thompson, *Flight to Freedom*. For other figurations of race, queerness, and fugitivity, see Bey, *Them Goon Rules*; Chambers-Letson, *After the Party*; and Dillon, *Fugitive Life*.
61 On the ways the practices and social forms of communities of "unrelated" adults (particularly in the orbit of queer sexualities) are understood as lacking legitimacy because they cannot claim the generational durability of genealogy/kinship, see Povinelli, *The Empire of Love*.
62 Rodríguez, *Sexual Futures*, 9, 37; Eng, *The Feeling of Kinship*, 25. For similar arguments, see Duggan, *The Twilight of Equality?*; Franke, *Wedlocked*; and Warner, *The Trouble with Normal*. However, as Laura Briggs illustrates, much of the impetus for marriage equality cases came not from the urban areas and lawyers often considered to be at the center of large-scale, national LGBT movement initiatives (who also, Briggs argues, resisted such efforts), but from queer parents in the rural South, largely people of color. See Briggs, *How All Politics*, 149–87.
63 Puar, *Terrorist Assemblages*, 31. As Katherine Franke has observed, "claims to rights for same-sex couples and families are based on appeals to their inherent dignity and decency, thereby distinguishing them from other undeserving, dysfunctional, or immoral sexual or kin formations that are almost always understood in racial terms": "the implicit whiteness of normative homosexuality has delivered a racial endowment to the same-sex marriage movement that has most certainly helped the cause of marriage equality, but sometimes at the expense of the rights and interests of both normative and non-normative families of color" (*Wedlocked*, 13). See also DeFilippis, "Introduction"; Ferguson, *One-Dimensional Queer*; and Reddy, *Freedom with Violence*.
64 Ahmed, *The Cultural Politics of Emotion*, 152, 155. See also Bradway and Freeman, "Introduction: Kincoherence/Kin-aesthetics/Kinematics";

Butler, *Antigone's Claim*; Freeman, *The Wedding Complex*; Jakobsen, "Queer Is? Queer Does?"; Rodríguez, *Next of Kin*; and Weston, *Families We Choose*.

65 Rodríguez, *Sexual Futures*, 36–37. Eng also suggests that "refocusing progressive efforts on household diversity, rather than organizing solely for same-sex marriage, could generate a broad vision of social justice that resonates on many fronts" (*The Feeling of Kinship*, 57).

66 Rodríguez, *Sexual Futures*, 50; Eng, *The Feeling of Kinship*, 91, 196.

67 In her reading of the story of Antigone as an allegory of the relation between kinship and the state, Judith Butler observes, "Antigone represents not kinship in its ideal form but its deformation and displacement, one that puts the reigning regimes of representation into crisis and raises the question of what the conditions of intelligibility could have been that would have made her life possible, indeed, what sustaining web of relations makes our lives possible, those of us who confound kinship in the rearticulation of its terms?" She later argues that "in acting, as one who has no right to act, she upsets the vocabulary of kinship that is a precondition of the human, implicitly raising the question for us of what those preconditions really must be." She further suggests, "If kinship is the precondition of the human, then Antigone is the occasion for a new field of the human, achieved through political catachresis, the one that happens when the less than human speaks as human, when gender is displaced, and kinship founders on its own founding laws" (*Antigone's Claim*, 24, 82). However, I am suggesting that understanding certain relations as "kinship" can work to limit what it means to restage them and their conditions of possibility—or, rather, that their condition of possibility as "kinship" may be the continued existence of liberal ideologies and political economy.

68 The statement is reproduced in its entirety in Boggis et al., "The *Beyond Same-Sex Marriage* Statement," which also contains interviews with many of the original signatories a decade later.

69 Boggis et al., "The *Beyond Same-Sex Marriage* Statement," 119, 120.

70 Boggis et al., "The *Beyond Same-Sex Marriage* Statement," 121, 123.

71 Boggis et al., "The *Beyond Same-Sex Marriage* Statement," 129, 122, 120.

72 Carruthers, *Unapologetic*, 108, 109, 110.

73 I should note that I'm suggesting a taking up of Indigenous analytics rather than the appropriation of indigeneity for non-native oppositional movements. On such dynamics, see Jackson, *Creole Indigeneity*; Morgensen, *Spaces between Us*; Rifkin, *Settler Common Sense*; and Towle and Morgan, "Romancing the Transgender Native."

74 On kinship and/as scale, see Thelan and Alber, "Reconnecting State and Kinship."

75 Simpson, *Mohawk Interruptus*, 101–2, 22. See also Barker, *Native Acts*; Coulthard, *Red Skin, White Masks*; Million, *Therapeutic Nations*; and Povinelli, *The Cunning of Recognition*.

76   Povinelli, *The Empire of Love*, 140.
77   TallBear, "Making Love and Relations," 151, 148, 152, 147.
78   On kinship and tribalization as co-constitutive concepts within colonial governmentality, see Tapper, "Blood/Kinship, Governmentality, and Cultures."
79   TallBear, "Making Love and Relations," 148, 150. On the tiospaye as a sociopolitical formation, see also Biolsi, *Organizing the Lakota*; DeMallie, "Kinship and Biology in Sioux Culture"; Deloria, *Speaking of Indians*; Pexa, *Translated Nation*; and Rifkin, *When Did Indians Become Straight?* On histories of other Indigenous sociopolitical formations that could be characterized as "kinship" on lands claimed by the United States and Canada, see Barr, *Peace Came*; Brooks, *Our Beloved Kin*; Chang, *The World*; Denetdale, "Return"; Denial, *Making Marriage*; Innes, *Elder Brother*; Perdue, *Cherokee Women*; Sleeper-Smith, *Indian Women and French Men*; Stremlau, *Sustaining the Cherokee Family*; and Wilson-Hokowhitu, *The Past before Us*.
80   TallBear, "Making Love and Relations," 152, 149.
81   TallBear, "Making Love and Relations," 157, 161.
82   Rodríguez, *Sexual Futures*, 2; Ferguson, *Aberrations in Black*, 41; Cohen, "Punks, Bulldaggers, and Welfare Queens," 447–48, 453.
83   Stallings, *Funk the Erotic*, 122.
84   Cohen, *Democracy Remixed*, 52, 89.
85   As with my earlier uses of the term, "infrastructural" here refers not to the built environment but to an organizing framework that provides the contours and support for an institution or set of institutions, a system, or an integrated process. See Murphy, *The Economization of Life*.
86   Goeman, "Ongoing Storms and Struggles," 101.
87   On Deloria, see Cotera, *Native Speakers*; Gardner, "Speaking of Ella Deloria"; Pexa, *Translated Nation*; and Rifkin, *When Did Indians Become Straight?*
88   Deloria, *Speaking of Indians*, 24. On settler intervention in the late nineteenth century, see Adams, *Education for Extinction*; Denetdale, *Reclaiming Diné History*; Hoxie, *A Final Promise*; Piatote, *Domestic Subjects*; Rand, *Kiowa Humanity*; Rifkin, *When Did Indians Become Straight?*; and Stremlau, *Sustaining the Cherokee Family*.
89   Justice, "'Go Away, Water!,'" 150. See also Pierce, "In Good Relations."
90   See also Million, *Therapeutic Nations*.
91   Deloria, *Speaking of Indians*, 31, 32.
92   I've been referring to Indigenous "social" relations and formations, but as I will address more explicitly, such connections extend beyond humans to include a range of other beings.
93   Simpson, *As We Have Always Done*, 112, 192. This idea of Indigenous bodies as themselves bearing political orders draws on Audra Simpson's "The State Is a Man."

94 Simpson, *As We Have Always Done*, 23.

95 Goeman, "Ongoing Storms and Struggles," 101.

96 In this vein, Goeman argues for the importance of "think[ing] through land as a meaning-making process rather than a claimed object" (Aikau et al., "Indigenous Feminisms Roundtable," 98). See also Goeman, "Land as Life."

97 For other regional examples, see Anderson, *The Indian Southwest*; Brooks, *Captives and Cousins*; Brooks, *Our Beloved Kin*; Harmon, *Indians in the Making*; and Witgen, *An Infinity of Nations*.

98 Deloria, *Speaking of Indians*, 48. The allotment policy entailed the effort to break up Native lands into privately held units, after which the tribe itself was to be dissolved. The most famous piece of legislation associated with this political project is the General Allotment Act (or Dawes Act, after its sponsor Senator Henry Dawes) passed in 1887. On allotment policy, see Genetin-Pilawa, *Crooked Paths to Allotment*; Hoxie, *A Final Promise*; McDonnel, *Dispossession of the American Indian*; Piatote, *Domestic Subjects*; Ruppel, *Unearthing Indian Land*; and Stremlau, *Sustaining the Cherokee Family*.

99 Deloria, *Speaking of Indians*, 27, 40, 41.

100 Deloria, *Speaking of Indians*, 32.

101 See Briggs, *How All Politics*.

102 Deloria, *Speaking of Indians*, 146; Pexa, *Translated Nation*, 103.

103 See also Barker, *Native Acts*; Carroll, *Roots of Our Renewal*; Cattelino, *High Stakes*; Deer and Richland, *Introduction to Tribal Legal Studies*; Duarte, *Network Sovereignty*; Duthu, *Shadow Nations*; McCarthy, *In Divided Unity*; and Turner, *This Is Not a Peace Pipe*.

104 Pasternak, *Grounded Authority*, 6, 25. Unless otherwise noted, all emphasis in quotations is from the original sources.

105 Kauanui, *Paradoxes of Hawaiian Sovereignty*, 21, 35. Similarly, Theresa McCarthy highlights the importance of "find[ing] a framework for establishing anti- or un-colonial ways to coexist with Indigenous peoples across time" (*In Divided Unity*, 278).

106 Rodríguez characterizes *gesture* as "signal[ing] both those defined movements that we make with our bodies and to which we assign meaning, and an action that extends beyond itself, that reaches, suggests, motions," further indicating that the concept marks "interventions that push, jam, open, block, and twist social forces in the material world" (*Sexual Futures*, 2, 4); and Carruthers argues that "a lens is a good metaphor since in its literal sense changing it changes the way its viewer sees the world" (*Unapologetic*, 8).

107 As Leanne Simpson argues, "Indigenous peoples require a land base and therefore require a central and hard critique of the forces that propel dispossession," adding, "I'm interested in unapologetic place-based nationhoods" (*As We Have Always Done*, 50).

108 TallBear, "Making Love and Relations," 152.

109 Yazzie, "US Imperialism," 111.
110 Justice, *Why Indigenous Literatures Matter*, 48, 78.
111 Justice, *Why Indigenous Literatures Matter*, 86.
112 Justice, *Why Indigenous Literatures Matter*, 74–75, 197. Justice further observes, "The dominant colonial stories about kinship are designed to destroy Indigenous peoples' ties to our homelands, to one another, and to our other-than-human relatives, and ultimately serve to transform those lands into exploitable resources and diverse peoples into memories" (*Why Indigenous Literatures Matter*, 84).
113 Justice, *Why Indigenous Literatures Matter*, 75, 89. As Leanne Simpson suggests of Nishnaabeg nationhood, "It is a web of connections to each other, to the plant nations, the animal nations, the rivers and lakes, the cosmos, and our neighboring Indigenous nations" (*As We Have Always Done*, 8).
114 Benjamin, "Black AfterLives Matter," 65. See also Goddard, "Appropriate Kinship, Legitimate Nationhood."
115 Murphy, "Against Population, Towards Alterlife," 109, 110, 121.
116 Simpson, *As We Have Always Done*, 19.

Two. Indian Domesticity, Settler Regulation, and the Limits of the Race/Politics Distinction

Parts of chapter 2 previously were published as "Making Peoples into Populations: The Racial Limits of Tribal Sovereignty," in *Theorizing Native Studies*, edited by Audra Simpson and Andrea Smith; and "Around 1978: Family, Culture, and Race in the Federal Production of Indianness," in *Critically Sovereign: Indigenous Gender, Sexuality, and Feminist Studies*, edited by Joanne Barker.

1 See Brian Bennett, "House Narrows Scope of Anti-Violence Bill," *Los Angeles Times*, May 17, 2012, 8; Laurie Kellman, "GOP Revises Anti-Violence Bill, Draws White House Veto Threat," *Washington Post*, May 16, 2012, 19; Robert Pear, "House Sets Up Battle on Domestic Violence Bill," *New York Times*, May 17, 2012, 19; and Jonathan Weisman, "Senate Votes to Reauthorize Domestic Violence Act," *New York Times*, April 27, 2012, 13. See also Deer, "Native People and Violent Crime"; and Schaeffer, "Answering Constitutional Challenges." The law originally was adopted in 1994 and last had been reauthorized in 2005, and in its various iterations, it has, among other things, created categories for interstate domestic violence, dating violence, and stalking in federal law and provided funding (for which periodic reauthorization is needed) for the prevention and prosecution of violent crimes against women. The act was allowed to expire in December 2018, but finally was reauthorized in March 2022.

2   In the US code, Indian Country is defined as follows: "(a) all land within the limits of any Indian reservation under the jurisdiction of the United States Government, notwithstanding the issuance of any patent, and, including rights-of-way running through the reservation, (b) all dependent Indian communities within the borders of the United States whether within the original or subsequently acquired territory thereof, and whether within or without the limits of a state, and (c) all Indian allotments, the Indian titles to which have not been extinguished, including rights-of-way running through the same." "18 US Code § 1151—Indian Country Defined," Legal Information Institute, Cornell Law School, https://www.law.cornell.edu/uscode/text/18/1151.

3   This claim is, on the face of it, absurd. As noted in *Oliphant v. Suquamish*, the case that established the principle that tribes do not have criminal jurisdiction over "non-Indians," "Of the 127 reservation court systems that currently exercise criminal jurisdiction in the United States, 33 purport to extend that jurisdiction to non-Indians" (435 U.S. 191 [1978], 196), meaning that at least dozens of tribes were exercising such jurisdiction as of 35 years ago. Moreover, given the fact that for at least the first century of the United States' existence, federal and state governments had little meaningful jurisdiction over many if not most Native peoples within the "domestic" boundaries of the nation, it seems absurd to claim axiomatically that Native peoples did not exert authority over non-Indians engaged in activity that violated the laws and social standards of the particular peoples with whom they resided. To do so is to imagine the boundaries of the United States as static (which they most certainly were not), to treat circumstances in Indian policy at the end of the nineteenth century as if they defined the status quo from the Revolution onward (denying the actual history of the treaty system as well as the fact of ongoing wars with Native peoples, largely over settler incursions), and to take the US government's claims about the extent of its own jurisdiction as actually descriptive of what was occurring in Indian Country.

4   158 Cong. Rec. S2761, 2772, 2786 (2012).

5   Notably, the controversies about adding provisions to protect women in same-sex relationships as part of the VAWA reauthorization and over-extending Native nations' criminal jurisdiction to non-natives were not connected in legislative, popular, or academic discussion of the bill, such that violence against Native women comes to appear as de facto a straight issue and Native lesbians become somewhat invisible. Thanks to J. Kēhaulani Kauanui for highlighting this dynamic.

6   Public Law 113–4, Section 204 (2013). For the Senate's version, see Section 904, S1925, 112th Cong., 2nd Sess. (2012).

7   In Section 204.a.4, the statute indicates that it applies to "an Indian tribe that elects to exercise special domestic violence criminal jurisdiction over the Indian country of that Indian tribe," and in Section 204.b.3.B.I-II, it

indicates that it applies to any victim who is "a member of the participating tribe" or "an Indian who resides in the Indian country of the participating tribe." Indianness, therefore, cannot be defined exclusively by membership in the tribe. On the problems of treating tribal membership as the limit of indigeneity within the United States, see Berger, *Tribal Constitutionalism*, 10–65.

8   On the *reprosexual*, see Luciano, *Arranging Grief*.

9   On the ways distinguishing Indigenous sovereignty from race can aid in supporting forms of antiblackness, see Cordis, "Settler Unfreedoms." On the ways modes of US government recognition of Indigenous peoplehood can rely on antiblackness, see Den Ouden and O'Brien, *Recognition, Sovereignty Struggles, and Indigenous Rights*; Klopotek, *Recognition Odysseys*; Lowery, *Lumbee Indians*; and Miller, *Forgotten Tribes*.

10 For additional background, see *Oliphant v. Schlie*, 544 F.2d 1007 (9th Cir. 1976), the appellate court decision in the case.

11 The decision was endorsed by six justices, with two dissenting in an opinion authored by Thurgood Marshall; one justice did not participate in the decision at all. At this point, I will cease to put *Indian*, *non-Indian*, and *tribe* in scare quotes, but readers should continue to bear in mind the political semiotics of the seemingly straightforward references implied by these terms.

12 Frickey, "A Common Law," 28; Duthu, *American Indians and the Law*, 21.

13 See Duthu, *American Indians and the Law*, 19–24; Russell, "Making Peace," 64–66; Wilkins, *American Indian Sovereignty*, 187–213; and Williams, *Like a Loaded Weapon*, 98–113.

14 *Oliphant v. Suquamish*, 209.

15 I should be clear that here I am referring to the decision's narrative of US authority rather than a description of how such authority/jurisdiction/diplomacy actually operated historically.

16 *Oliphant v. Suquamish*, 211. Steve Russell observes, "If Indian nations were not separate sovereigns in the sense of criminal law then it is unclear how they could have the sovereignty" to cede land to the United States via the treaty system ("Making Peace," 62). On the history of producing legal subjectivities for Native peoples that indicate their putative consent to US legal mappings, see Rifkin, *Manifesting America*.

17 In this way, though, the Supreme Court decision does not go as far as the dissent at the appellate level in *Oliphant v. Schlie*, even though Justice Rehnquist borrows language from it. Written by Anthony Kennedy, who would be appointed to the Supreme Court a decade later, the dissent suggests that the notion of inherent tribal sovereignty is nothing but dicta from the case of *Worcester v. Georgia* (1832) and that "the term 'sovereignty,' then, is merely a veil used where the issue is, in fact, one of federal preemption [of states] in the field of Indian affairs" (*Oliphant v. Schlie*, 1014–1015), meaning that Native peoples have no autonomous sovereignty but only delegated authority from the federal government.

18   Frickey suggests, "The place of federal Indian law in American public law can be understood by imagining layers of law, with American constitutionalism built on top of American colonialism," and he adds, "We have every right to be confused about what we should make of our origins, our evolution, our sense of nationhood, and our creation of a constitutional democracy through colonialism" ("[Native] American Exceptionalism," 467, 489). See also Bruyneel, *The Third Space*; Byrd, *The Transit of Empire*; Cheyfitz, "The (Post)Colonial Construction"; Duthu, *American Indians and the Law*; and Rifkin, "Indigenizing Agamben."

19   *Oliphant v. Suquamish*, 208. The appellate court decision actually uses this phrase as part of its argument that tribes "retain the powers of autonomous states," except under very specific circumstances (*Oliphant v. Schlie*, 1009). The Supreme Court decision demurs from the prior judicial convention of viewing Native nations as autonomous entities save for the explicit limitations placed on their sovereignty by specific treaty provisions and acts of Congress. On the growing displacement of that canon of construction in the latter decades of the twentieth century, see Frickey, "A Common Law."

20   *Oliphant v. Suquamish*, 197. The opinion also quotes an 1834 report from the House of Representatives, noting, "This principle would have been obvious a century ago when most Indian tribes were characterized by 'a want of fixed laws [and] of competent tribunals of justice'" (210).

21   Williams, *Like a Loaded Weapon*, 101.

22   On *Ex parte Crow Dog*, see Harring, *Crow Dog's Case*, 100–141; Russell, "Making Peace."

23   *Oliphant v. Suquamish*, 210–11. The ellipses and interpolations are reproduced here as they appear in the *Oliphant* opinion. On the ways Rehnquist uses ellipses in this decision to edit out the most severely racist expressions of his source material, thereby making nineteenth-century legal conclusions more presentable to a 1970s audience, see Williams, *Like a Loaded Weapon*, 109–10.

24   See *Morton v. Mancari*, 417 U.S. 535 (1974); *U.S. v. Antelope*, 430 U.S. 641 (1977). Both *Morton* and *Antelope* were unanimous decisions, and virtually all of the justices who took part in *Oliphant* also participated in the prior two cases.

25   *Morton v. Mancari*, 554.

26   A corollary raised by the decision is that determinations not directly tied to tribal membership may be constitutionally suspect, disallowing "Indian" status for a variety of purposes. On this possible implication of *Morton*, see Lewis, "Do You Know"; Oakley, "Defining Indian Status"; Villazor, "Blood Quantum."

27   *U.S. v. Antelope*, 645.

28   *Morton v. Mancari*, 551. The indication of a guardian-ward relation refers to the decision in *Cherokee Nation v. Georgia*, and the finding that Congress

has "plenary power" in Indian affairs can be traced substantively to *U.S. v. Kagama*.

29 *Morton v. Mancari*, 554; *U.S. v. Antelope*, 646.
30 *U.S. v. Antelope*, 645; *Morton v. Mancari*, 554.
31 Lewis, "Do You Know What You Are?," 252. Lewis addresses how determining Indianness for prosecution under the Major Crimes Act has never depended exclusively on formal tribal membership, arguing that it should not. For a counterargument that doing so would clarify currently conflicting ways of determining Indianness for prosecutorial purposes, see Oakley, "Defining Indian Status."
32 On the fallacy of the claim that (non-Indian) noncitizens cannot be expected to be subjected to a judicial system by a (Native) government in which they cannot directly take part, see Schaeffer, "Answering Constitutional Challenges."
33 *Oliphant v. Suquamish*, 209–10.
34 Duthu, *American Indians and the Law*, 22.
35 *Oliphant v. Suquamish*, 212. This formulation also presents the prosecution of non-Indian defendants in Native courts as if it were a captivity narrative. On the legacy of the captivity narrative, see Strong, *Captive Selves, Captivating Others*.
36 *Oliphant v. Suquamish*, 194.
37 While *Oliphant* argues for such insulation solely for the purposes of criminal prosecution, the principle of non-Indian immunity has been extended into a series of civil and regulatory matters by later decisions. See Duthu, *American Indians and the Law*, 36–51; Frickey, "A Common Law," 43–45.
38 *Oliphant v. Suquamish*, 206. On the paucity of precedent in the decision, see Quasius, "Native American Rape Victims," 1915, 1935–37; Wilkins, *American Indian Sovereignty*, 204; and Williams, *Like a Loaded Weapon*, 107–11.
39 On the presence of such an understanding in the nineteenth century, see Cheyfitz, "The (Post)Colonial Construction"; Konkle, *Writing Indian Nations*; Rifkin, *When Did Indians Become Straight?*; and Spruhan, "A Legal History." In particular, in *U.S. v. Rogers* (1846), about a murder committed by a white man who belonged to the Cherokee Nation and who sought immunity from federal prosecution as an "Indian," the Supreme Court finds that Indianness and tribal belonging are not equivalent, understanding the former as an inborn racial quality. See Berger, "'Power over This Unfortunate Race'"; Rifkin, "Making Peoples into Populations"; and Wilkins, *American Indian Sovereignty*, 38–51.
40 Ahmed, *Queer Phenomenology*, 121, 122.
41 Ahmed, *Queer Phenomenology*, 128.
42 This statute was changed in 2012 to allow for the children of Pueblo mothers and non-Pueblo fathers also to be citizens.
43 For the text of the law, see Prucha, *Documents of United States Indian Policy*, 250–53. On the case, see Barker, *Native Acts*, 98–145; Berger,

"Indian Policy"; Curry, "A Closer Look"; Milczarek-Desai, "(Re)Locating Other/Third World Women"; and Suzack, *Indigenous Women's Writing*, 17–48.

44 *Santa Clara Pueblo v. Martinez*, 436 U.S. 49 (1978), 54.
45 For a reading of the decision as testifying to Native sovereignty in exercising control over tribal membership, see Riley, "(Tribal) Sovereignty and Illiberalism."
46 *Santa Clara Pueblo v. Martinez*, 55, 62–63, 72.
47 *Santa Clara Pueblo v. Martinez*, 58, 60.
48 *Santa Clara Pueblo v. Martinez*, 56.
49 A decision earlier in that same session, *U.S. v. Wheeler*, underlines this dynamic even more forcefully. Finding that the prosecution of an Indian at the tribal level for a lesser offense emanating from a single action does not preclude federal prosecution under the double jeopardy clause, a conclusion based on the idea that tribes' sovereignty does not derive from the federal government, the majority opinion declares that Native peoples retain "attributes of sovereignty . . . only at the sufferance of Congress" (435 U.S. 313 [1978], 323), later adding that the "problem [posed by the case] would, of course, be solved if Congress, in the exercise of its plenary power over the tribes, chose to deprive them of criminal jurisdiction altogether" (331).
50 *Santa Clara Pueblo v. Martinez*, 72.
51 *Santa Clara Pueblo v. Martinez*, 56, 71. On this trope, see also Rifkin, "Indigenizing Agamben."
52 *Santa Clara Pueblo v. Martinez*, 55.
53 *U.S. v. Wheeler*, 331; *Santa Clara Pueblo v. Martinez*, 72.
54 For discussion of Native peoples as extraconstitutional polities, such that the exertion of US plenary authority over them is logically incoherent, see Frickey, "(Native) American Exceptionalism"; Riley, "(Tribal) Sovereignty and Illiberalism"; and Wilkins and Lomawaima, *Uneven Ground*.
55 *Santa Clara Pueblo v. Martinez*, 63–64.
56 *Santa Clara Pueblo v. Martinez*, 72.
57 Because "tradition" and "culture" can provide a crucial supplement for efforts to cast tribes as a different/lesser/not quite fully governmental entity, and thus justify US superintendence, I am wary of appeals to "culture" as a means of bolstering assertions of Native sovereignty and self-determination. For such a strategy, see Berger, *Tribal Constitutionalism*; Coffey and Tsosie, "Rethinking the Tribal Sovereignty Doctrine." For discussion of the perils of this approach in an international framework, see Engle, *The Elusive Promise*; Yazzie, "US Imperialism."
58 See Barker, *Native Acts*, 98–145; Curry, "A Closer Look"; Milczarek-Desa, "(Re)Locating Other/Third World Women"; and Riley, "(Tribal) Sovereignty and Illiberalism."
59 *Santa Clara Pueblo v. Martinez*, 56.

60 Gunter, "The Technology of Tribalism," 108.

61 Prucha, *Documents of United States Indian Policy*, 290. On the process of federal recognition, see also Barker, *Native Acts*; Field, "Unacknowledged Tribes, Dangerous Knowledge"; Gover, "Genealogy as Continuity"; Klopotek, *Recognition Odysseys*; McCulloch and Wilkins, "'Constructing' Nations within States"; Miller, *Forgotten Tribes*; and Slagle, "Unfinished Justice."

62 Curry, "A Closer Look," 200.

63 For a pronounced version of this argument, see Williams, *Like a Loaded Weapon*.

64 See Beardall and Edwards, "Abolition, Settler Colonialism"; Cross and Miller, "The Indian Child Welfare Act"; Graham, "Reparations"; Jacobs, *A Generation Removed*; Pierce, "In Good Relations"; and Strong, "What Is an Indian Family?"

65 Strong, "What Is an Indian Family?," 205.

66 See Castile, *To Show Heart*.

67 The original text of the law can be found in the *United States Statutes at Large* as Public Law 95-608, 92 Stat. 3069. Quotations from the law will be cited parenthetically by section and clause numbers.

68 See Berger, "In the Name of the Child"; Mall, "Keeping It in the Family"; *Mississippi Band of Choctaws v. Holyfield*, 490 U.S. 30 (1989); and Strong, "What Is an Indian Family?"

69 On policy during the termination period, including the passage of Public Law 280, see Fixico, *Termination and Relocation*; Philp, *Termination Revisited*. On the legacy of that law and changes in its sphere of application due largely to court decisions, see Goldberg-Ambrose, *Planting Tail Feathers*.

70 The Indian Civil Rights Act (1968) made any future extension of civil and criminal jurisdiction by states over tribes dependent on the latter's consent, and it also enabled states that previously had been given or had chosen such jurisdiction to retrocede it in part or in its entirety by petitioning the federal government, which many states have done. See Cross and Miller, "The Indian Child Welfare Act," 17–18; Pacheco, "Broken Traditions," 33; and Pisarello, "Lawless by Design," 1516. However, no mechanism exists for tribes placed under state jurisdiction by federal action prior to 1968 to choose to have it returned to them, and since 1968, no tribe voluntarily has chosen to have state jurisdiction extended over it.

71 See Engle, *The Elusive Promise of Indigenous Development*; Povinelli, *The Cunning of Recognition*; and Simpson, *Mohawk Interruptus*.

72 On the relation between ICWA and customary international law with respect to children's right to remain with their peoples, see Graham, "Reparations."

73 Such authority, though, does need to meet several conditions: it needs to be "in the least restrictive setting which most approximates a family"

(105.b); "Where appropriate, the preference of the Indian child or parent shall be considered" (105.c); and it may be altered when "the continued custody of the child by the parent or Indian custodian is likely to result in serious emotional or physical damage to the child" (102.e).

74　In doing so, it cites the part of the commerce clause in the Constitution that gives Congress power to "regulate Commerce with foreign Nations, and among the several States, and with the Indian Tribes." On ICWA and the commerce clause, see Fletcher, "ICWA and the Commerce Clause."

75　See *U.S. v. Kagama*, 118 U.S. 375 (1886).

76　On the role of racial descent as a means of figuring a continuity in Indianness for various federal purposes, most of which present themselves as not about race, see Berger, *Tribal Constitutionalism*; Brownwell, "Who Is an Indian?"; Goldberg, "Members Only?"; Gover, "Genealogy as Continuity"; and TallBear, *Native American DNA*.

77　See "Establishing Standards for the Placement of Indian Children in Foster or Adoptive Homes, To Prevent the Breakup of Indian Families, and For Other Purposes," H.R. Rpt. 1386, 95th Cong., 2nd Sess. (1978); *Mississippi Band of Choctaw Indians v. Holyfield*; and *Adoptive Couple v. Baby Girl*.

78　"Establishing Standards," 9, 10, 24.

79　"Establishing Standards," 13–14. On *Nice*, see Wilkins, *American Indian Sovereignty*, 119–36.

80　"Establishing Standards," 20, 11.

81　"Establishing Standards," 19.

82　*Mississippi Band of Choctaw Indians v. Holyfield*, 47, 49.

83　Lorinda Mall observes that ICWA "sets out the basic premise that the best interest of an Indian child runs parallel to the best interests of the tribe" ("Keeping It in the Family," 167).

84　*Mississippi Band of Choctaw Indians v. Holyfield*, 34.

85　*Mississippi Band of Choctaw Indians v. Holyfield*, 52, 49–50.

86　See Joanne Barker, "*Adoptive Couple v. Baby Girl*: On the Disarticulation of Native Self-Determination" (presentation at the Native American and Indigenous Studies Association, May 2014); Berger, "In the Name of the Child."

87　*Adoptive Couple v. Baby Girl*, 2556, 2565. On the origin of this claim and its multilayered inaccuracies, see Berger, "In the Name of the Child."

88　On the history and politics of Cherokee citizenship determinations, see Sturm, *Blood Politics*.

89　*Adoptive Couple v. Baby Girl*, 2557, 2565, 2560–61. On the ways this part of the decision is an extension of a larger pattern of dismissal of birth parents' rights, particularly those of unwed mothers, see Berger, "In the Name of the Child." I will return to this topic in the discussion of welfare policy and state-endorsed sterilization in chapter 3 and of representations of Black families in chapter 4.

90 The "existing Indian family exception" has been carved out by some state courts, in which children of parents who are deemed not to have a substantive relation with a particular tribe (even if they themselves are enrolled) do not fall under the purview of the law. The decision by the Fourth California Court of Appeals in *In re Bridget* (1996) is perhaps the most cited example. On this exception, including discussion of *In re Bridget*, see Jaffke, "The 'Existing Indian Family' Exception"; Organick, "Holding Back the Tide"; Strong, "What Is an Indian Family?," 215–18; and Waszak, "Contemporary Hurdles." In 2016, the Bureau of Indian Affairs finally adopted a set of binding regulations for state implementation of ICWA, having refused to do so when the law initially was passed, and this relatively new federal policy framework may prevent some of the actions by state courts to diminish ICWA's scope and effectiveness. See Ogle, "Why Try to Change Me Now?" On the charge that the law commandeers state courts, unconstitutionally forcing them to do the work of federal administration, see Gale and McClure, "Commandeering Confrontation."

91 On these current patterns, see Beardall and Edwards, "Abolition, Settler Colonialism."

92 On allotment policy, see Genetin-Pilawa, *Crooked Paths to Allotment*; Hoxie, *A Final Promise*; McDonnel, *Dispossession of the American Indian*; Piatote, *Domestic Subjects*; Ruppel, *Unearthing Indian Land*; and Stremlau, *Sustaining the Cherokee Family*.

93 On reorganization policy, see Biolsi, *Organizing the Lakota*; Deloria and Lytle, *The Nations Within*; Kelly, *The Assault on Assimilation*; Pfister, *Individuality Incorporated*; Richotte, *Claiming Turtle Mountain's Constitution*; Rusco, *A Fateful Time*; Taylor, *The New Deal*; and Wilkins, *On the Drafting*.

94 *Opinions of the Solicitor of the Department of the Interior Relating to Indian Affairs 1917–1974*, 471.

95 For further discussion of the ways such ideas embed allotment-era principles in the administration of the IRA and state-recognized Indigenous governance, see Rifkin, *When Did Indians Become Straight?*, 181–232.

96 On the complexity of Haudenosaunee histories and the Confederacy, see also Doxtator, "What Happened to the Iroquois Clans?"; Hauptman, *Conspiracy of Interests*; Hill, *The Clay We Are Made Of*; and Simpson, *Mohawk Interruptus*.

97 McCarthy, *In Divided Unity*, 22, 189–91.

98 McCarthy, *In Divided Unity*, 192, 205.

99 McCarthy, *In Divided Unity*, 220, 222.

100 Unlike American Indian tribes and Native Alaskan villages, Kānaka 'Ōiwi are not recognized as self-governing entities under US law. There have been a number of recent efforts to generate such federal recognition that have been resisted by Kānaka. See also Arvin, *Possessing Polynesians*; Kauanui, *Hawaiian Blood*; and Saranillio, *Unsustainable Empire*.

101   Kauanui, *Paradoxes of Hawaiian Sovereignty*, 195, 74.
102   On Kanaka genealogical principles and practices, see also Chang, *The World*; Kameʻeleihiwa, *Native Land and Foreign Desires*; Kauanui, *Hawaiian Blood*; and Wilson-Hokowhitu, *The Past before Us*.
103   Kauanui, *Paradoxes of Hawaiian Sovereignty*, 10.
104   Kauanui, *Paradoxes of Hawaiian Sovereignty*, 19.
105   Suzack, *Indigenous Women's Writing*, 29.
106   See also Barker, *Native Acts*; Denetdale, "Chairmen, Presidents, and Princesses"; Justice, "Notes toward a Theory"; Lawrence, *"Real" Indians and Others*; McCarthy, *In Divided Unity*; and Simpson, *As We Have Always Done*.
107   On the situated complexities of such governments, see also Berger, *Tribal Constitutionalism*; Carroll, *Roots of Our Renewal*; Deer and Richland, *Introduction to Tribal Legal Studies*; Dennison, *Colonial Entanglement*; Doerfler, *Those Who Belong*; Pasternak, *Grounded Authority*; and Riley, "Good (Native) Governance."
108   See Dennison, *Colonial Entanglement*.
109   Harjo, *Spiral to the Stars*, 37, 12.
110   Harjo, *Spiral to the Stars*, 14.
111   Harjo, *Spiral to the Stars*, 40.
112   I provide very loose and gestural translations of the Hawaiian terms. Osorio argues against such (mis)translation, though.
113   Osorio, *Remembering Our Intimacies*, 71, 89.
114   Osorio, *Remembering Our Intimacies*, 13.
115   Osorio, *Remembering Our Intimacies*, 120, 168.
116   Harjo, *Spiral to the Stars*, 42.
117   Goeman, "Ongoing Storms and Struggles," 101.
118   Yazzie, "Decolonizing Development," 28, 31. On Navajo energy politics, see also Powell, *Landscapes of Power*.
119   Yazzie, "Decolonizing Development," 35, 34–35.
120   See Furlan, *Indigenous Cities*; Goeman, *Mark My Words*; Lawrence, *"Real" Indians and Others*; Peters and Andersen, *Indigenous in the City*; Ramirez, *Native Hubs*; and Razack, *Dying from Improvement*.
121   On Native urban life, see also Danzinger, *Survival and Regeneration*; Fixico, *The Urban Indian Experience*; Jackson, *Our Elders Lived It*; Lobo, "Urban Clan Mothers"; Mays, *City of Dispossessions*; Miller, *Indians on the Move*; and Thrush, *Native Seattle*.
122   Piatote, *Domestic Subjects*, 9.
123   Goeman, *Mark My Words*, 104, 5.
124   On termination policy and its legacies, including the use of rhetorics historically associated with slavery and its abolition, see Fixico, *Termination and Relocation*; Goldberg-Ambrose, *Planting Tail Feathers*; Miller, *Indians on the Move*; and Philp, *Termination Revisited*.
125   On the latter, see Mays, *City of Dispossessions*; Ramirez, *Native Hubs*; and Thrush, *Native Seattle*.

126 On the problems of treating such institutions as vehicles of settler recognition in the Canadian context, see Dhillon, *Prairie Rising*.
127 Andersen, "Urban Aboriginality," 59. On sovereignty as arising out of "vernacular" practices, see Harjo, *Spiral to the Stars*, 39.
128 For examples, see Harmon, *The Power of Promises*; Innes, *Elder Brother*; Mandell, *Tribe, Race, History*; Ostler, *The Plains Sioux*; and Smoak, *Ghost Dances and Identity*.
129 Ramirez, *Native Hubs*, 2, 13.
130 Ramirez, *Native Hubs*, 25.
131 Ramirez, *Native Hubs*, 25, 140.
132 On kinscapes, see Justice, *Why Indigenous Literatures Matter*.
133 An example of this dynamic can be seen in Joanne Barker's "Confluence." In seeking to argue for the importance of taking water as an analytic through which one can trace grounded connections and the persistence of complex flows and histories, Barker argues that theories of intersectionality and assemblage often enfold Indigenous peoples, when addressed at all, into "a racial difference that is ultimately the same as others racialized," one that effaces questions of relations to lands and waters, and she calls for "a disaggregation of indigeneity from race and ethnicity" (11, 13). Yet, the thrust of the article is toward "find[ing] a way to affirm one another's concerns and move our liberation struggles forward" (29–30). The argument that indigeneity must be separated from race, then, can displace how, like Indigenous peoples, other racialized groups are denied status as political orders or inserted into liberal modes of governance *through their racialization*. Attending to the work of race in relation to indigeneity can open up the very kinds of linkages and attention to complex patterns of collective placemaking toward which Barker wants to move.
134 *Oliphant v. Suquamish*, 211.

Three. Marriage, Privacy, Sovereignty

1 Foucault, *The History of Sexuality*, 154.
2 See Blumin, *Emergence of the Middle Class*; Boydston, *Home and Work*; Coontz, *Social Origins of Private Life*; Cott, *Public Vows*; D'Emilio and Freedman, *Intimate Matters*; Freeman, *The Wedding Complex*; Grossberg, *Governing the Hearth*; Nelson, *National Manhood*; Sellers, *The Market Revolution*; and Shammas, *A History of Household Government*.
3 Lowe, *Intimacies of Four Continents*, 18, 21.
4 Mehta, *Liberalism and Empire*, 47, 48–49.
5 As Stephanie Coontz argues, "the entire notion of the state undermining some primordial family privacy is a myth, because the nuclear family has never existed as an autonomous, private unit except where it was the

synthetic creation of outside forces. The strong nuclear family is in large measure a creation of the strong state" (*The Way We Never Were*, 190).

6   I should clarify that I'm not positioning Supreme Court cases as be-all, end-all statements of US law or as synecdochic expressions of the perspective of "the state." Given the relationships among branches of the government, the federalist division of powers, the complex relation between states and municipal governments, and the existence of tensions and disagreements within and among these various institutional entities and processes, there is no such thing as a singular "state" perspective that can characterize all of US law and policy. Moreover, court decisions are themselves the result of processes of negotiation and are riven with tensions and even outright contradictions. Rather, my aim is to offer Supreme Court decisions as an institutionally important and ideologically influential snapshot of particular ways of understanding, configuring, and normativizing the private sphere that can help offer a more historically robust sense of the conceptual frameworks at play in liberal governance.

7   See Bentley, "Marriage as Treason"; Ertman, "Race Treason"; Gordon, *The Mormon Question*; Iversen, *The Antipolygamy Controversy*; Mohrman, *Exceptionally Queer*; Rogers, *Unpopular Sovereignty*; and Talbot, *A Foreign Kingdom*.

8   See Delano, *Brook Farm*; Guarneri, *The Utopian Alternative*; Rosenblum, "Democratic Sex"; Spurlock, *Free Love*.

9   Talbot, *A Foreign Kingdom*, 35, 141.

10 Sarah M. S. Pearsall refers to what she terms "the infrastructure of monogamy" (*Polygamy*, 10), which makes polygamy seem unthinkable, but the defense of monogamy, I argue, operates as part of delineating the practical insularity and normative foundationalism of a private sphere that is imagined to provide the basis for the infrastructure of liberal governance.

11 Rogers, *Unpopular Sovereignty*, 9.

12 On these forced movements, see Hyde, *Empires, Nations, and Families*, 359–69; Mohrman, *Exceptionally Queer*, 23–85; and Rogers, *Unpopular Sovereignty*, 26–40. On the theology of Mormon plural marriage, see Coviello, *Make Yourselves Gods*.

13 See Gordon, *The Mormon Question*; Phipps, "Marriage and Redemption"; Rogers, *Unpopular Sovereignty*; and Talbot, *A Foreign Kingdom*.

14 See Rogers, *Unpopular Sovereignty*, 160–63.

15 Cott, *Public Vows*, 6–7; Gordon, *The Mormon Question*, 57.

16 See *Dred Scott v. Sandford*, 60 U.S. 393 (1857).

17 See Rogers, *Unpopular Sovereignty*. On the complex relation between notions of family, domesticity, and slavery in the antebellum period, and debates over how intellectually and legally to formulate those relations,

see Bercaw, *Gendered Freedoms*; Hahn, *Nation under Our Feet*; Hartman, *Scenes of Subjection*; and Stanley, *From Bondage to Contract*.

18 "Polygamy in the Territories of the United States," H.R. Rept. 83, 36th Cong., 1st Sess. (1860), 3.

19 On the relation between radical Republicanism and the passage of the Morrill Act, as well as broader connections between anti-polygamy legislation and Republican accounts of slavery, see Phipps, "Marriage and Redemption."

20 On the anti-Mormon laws passed by Congress in this period, see Gordon, *The Mormon Question*; Phipps, "Marriage and Redemption"; and Talbot, *A Foreign Kingdom*.

21 Morrill Act, U.S. 12 Stat. 501 (1862).

22 Poland Act, U.S. 18 Stat. 253 (1874).

23 Edmunds Act, U.S. 12 Stat. 30 (1882).

24 Edmunds-Tucker Act, U.S. 24 Stat. 635 (1887). On the similarity between the anti-polygamy and anti-Mormon legislation in the 1880s and the requirements imposed on the South in the wake of the Civil War, see Oman, "Natural Law"; Phipps, "Marriage and Redemption."

25 Gordon, *The Mormon Question*, 157–58.

26 Given their shared ideological frames and investments and the principles that cut across them, they productively can be thought of together, and I will move among them, rather than discussing them individually.

27 *Reynolds v. United States*, (98 U.S. 145 [1878]), 163. *Reynolds* involved the prosecution of George Reynolds, Brigham Young's personal secretary, and the case itself was orchestrated between Mormon leaders and federal prosecutors in order to test the legality of the Morrill Act. See Oman, "Natural Law," 669; Phipps, "Marriage and Redemption," 476.

28 *Reynolds v. United States*, 164. The decision in *Davis v. Beason* similarly asserted, "It was never intended or supposed that the [first] amendment could be invoked as a protection against legislation for the punishment of acts inimical to the peace, good order and morals of society" (133 U.S. 333 [1890], 342).

29 On the ways the defense in the *Reynolds* case crafted a theory of the First Amendment's religious freedom protections, see Oman, "Natural Law."

30 *Reynolds v. United States*, 165–66.

31 This argument, although very differently configured, is not all that substantively different than John Rawls's, as discussed in the introduction.

32 Bentley, "Marriage as Treason," 342, 343.

33 In their 1860 report, which pushed forward what eventually would become the Morrill Act, the House Judiciary Committee insists, "Marriage is the foundation of civil society," adding, "Upon it depends the preservation of our social system, and the dearest ties that bind us to earth. Connected with it are some of the most important rights of property"

("Polygamy in the Territories of the United States," Judiciary Committee, H.R. 83, 36th Cong., 1st Sess. [1860], 2).

34 *Davis v. Beason*, 344–45.
35 The decision suggests that "monogamy determines the very nature of the state" (Bentley, "Marriage as Treason," 360).
36 Bentley, "Marriage as Treason," 355.
37 Talbot, *A Foreign Kingdom*, 98, 127. While the Court does not comment on the question of plural wives' consent to such marriage, the decisions' gestures toward the construction of proper political subjectivity implicitly speak to the ways anti-Mormon discourses repeatedly question the potential for Mormon women actually to have consented, given the kinds of domestic arrangements said to make meaningful consent possible. See Bentley, "Marriage as Treason"; Iversen, *The Antipolygamy Controversy*; and Talbot, *A Foreign Kingdom*. On the emergence of Mormon proto-feminisms in the nineteenth century, see Iversen, *The Antipolygamy Controversy*. Notably, women in Utah were enfranchised as of 1870 and also had easy access to divorce, unlike in most other Territories and states. See Gordon, *The Mormon Question*, 97; Iversen, *The Antipolygamy Controversy*, 59.
38 *Reynolds v. United States*, 166. In the piece that the Court cited, published in *Putnam's Monthly* in 1855, Lieber argued, "Monogamy does not only go with the western Caucasian race, the Europeans and their descendants, beyond Christianity, it goes beyond Common Law. It is one of the primordial elements out of which all law proceeds, or which the law steps in to recognize and to protect. Wedlock ... stands in this respect on a level with property.... Wedlock, or monogamic marriage, is one of the 'categories' of our social thoughts and conceptions, and therefore, of our social existence" (Cott, *Public Vows*, 114).
39 On the ways discussion of polygamy in the Atlantic world served as a way of talking about forms of social hierarchy and their relation to modes of governance in the eighteenth and early to mid-nineteenth century, see Pearsall, *Polygamy*.
40 *Reynolds v. United States*, 167.
41 In a speech before Congress in February 1857, Representative Justin Morrill, who later sponsored what became the Morrill Act, "insisted that the people of Utah Territory were hostile to republicanism and no longer recognized federal law, but obeyed only Brigham Young, who 'desired a kingly government, in order to make their patriarchal institutions more homogenous'" (Rogers, *Unpopular Sovereignty*, 146).
42 Talbot, *A Foreign Kingdom*, 54.
43 Rogers, *Unpopular Sovereignty*, 151–52; Ertman, "Race Treason," 303.
44 *The Late Corporation of the Church of Jesus Christ of Latter-Day Saints v. United States*, 136 U.S. 1 (1890), 49.
45 Such charges, though, were not entirely unmerited. As Peter Coviello observes, "Mormons *did* eagerly prophesy the destruction of the United

States, *did* seek to employ Native peoples in the West as against invading armies, *did* seek to override federal authority, and *did* understand Gentile America as fallen, imperialist, doomed" (*Make Yourselves Gods*, 174).

46 With regard to the scope of religious institutions, the 1860 report from the House Judiciary Committee cited the concept of "mortmain," or the limitation of landholdings by religious institutions, as part of the argument for limiting Mormon authority, charging the LDS Church with "establishing a hierarchy obnoxious to the spirit of our institutions, and conferring privileges and prerogatives unknown to any other ecclesiastical denomination. Such monstrous powers and arrogant assumptions are at war with the genius of our government, and should meet prompt and without hesitation the indignant reprobation of Congress" (H.R. 83, 36th Cong., 1st Sess. [1860], 5). On the significance of mortmain in the centuries-long struggle between European monarchies and the Catholic Church, including the effort to remake marriage as a civil union, see Goody, *The Development of the Family*.

47 For example, Martha M. Ertman suggests that "the federal government, and most Americans, were more concerned with the political and racial implications of Mormon polygamy than with the practice of polygamy *per se*" ("Race Treason," 293), adding that "the underlying controversy was more concerned with politics than sexual improprieties" (297). Nancy Rosenblum offers a similar argument, pointing to the legal recognition offered for other religiously organized communities (like the Oneida Perfectionists) that had no pretensions to political authority, and Kelly Elizabeth Phipps argues that prior to the 1880s Congress was far more concerned with the matter of federal jurisdiction than polygamy per se, focusing on the latter largely due to related concerns about Chinese immigration. See Rosenblum, "Democratic Sex"; Phipps, "Marriage and Redemption."

48 *Reynolds v. United States*, 166; *Late Corporation*, 49.

49 *Late Corporation*, 63–64. The OED defines *contumacious* as "a. Condemning and obstinately resisting authority; stubbornly perverse, insubordinate, rebellious. (Of persons and their actions.)" and "b. Of diseases: Not readily yielding to treatment, stubborn."

50 On non-white Mormons in the nineteenth century, see Aikau, *A Chosen People*; Mueller, *Race and the Making*.

51 Bentley, "Marriage as Treason," 357. See also Denike, "Racialization"; Mohrman, *Exceptionally Queer*, 47–84.

52 See Fielder, *Relative Races*; Stoler, *Race and the Education of Desire*; and Tawil, *The Making of Racial Sentiment*.

53 Coviello, *Make Yourselves Gods*, 166.

54 Pearsall, *Polygamy*, 120.

55 Cott, *Public Vows*, 115.

56 On Native peoples as Lamanites, see Aikau, *A Chosen People*; Coviello, *Make Yourselves Gods*; and Hickman, "The Book of Mormon." On Mormon

57 Gordon, *The Mormon Question*, 204.
58 Aikau, *A Chosen People*, 34–35; Mueller, *Race and the Making*, 9–10. On the change in this policy in the late twentieth century, see Mohrman, *Exceptionally Queer*, 233–70.
59 On representations of African polygamy, see Pearsall, *Polygamy*, 115–49. On Mormonism in relation to blackness and enslavement, see Aikau, *A Chosen People*; Bentley, "Marriage as Treason"; Ertman, "Race Treason"; Gordon, *The Mormon Question*; Mueller, *Race and the Making*; Phipps, "Marriage and Redemption"; Rogers, *Unpopular Sovereignty*; and Weber, *Latter-Day Scenes*.
60 See Berman, *American Arabesque*; Ertman, "Race Treason"; Oman, "Natural Law"; Phipps, "Marriage and Redemption"; and Wong, *Racial Reconstruction*.
61 Rogers, *Unpopular Sovereignty*, 88.
62 Stoler, *Race and the Education of Desire*, 97.
63 *Reynolds v. United States*, 164; *Late Corporation*, 49–50. The Court in *Reynolds* asked, "If a wife believed it was her duty to burn herself upon the funeral pile of her dead husband, would it be beyond the power of the civil government to prevent her carrying her belief into practice?" (166). On the citation of British imperial examples in official and popular accounts of Mormonism in the nineteenth century, particularly with regard to sati, see Oman, "Natural Law."
64 The US Supreme Court reiterated these racializing terms in *Cleveland v. United States* (1945), which found that transportation of plural wives across state lines constitutes a violation of the Mann Act (329 U.S. 14, 18–19).
65 *Brown v. Buhman*, 947 F.2d 1170 (10th Cir. 2013). For readings of the decision, see Faucon, "Polygamy after *Windsor*"; Mohrman, *Exceptionally Queer*, 271–302. This decision later was vacated by the Tenth Circuit Appellate Court on the grounds that the Browns could not serve as plaintiffs because the danger of prosecution no longer applied, since they had moved to Nevada. However, the reasoning of the district court in the *Brown* case indicates important questions with regard to how polygamy, and the anti-Mormon campaign in the nineteenth century, is being understood within contemporary legal discourse.
66 On the continuing implications of *Reynolds* in various areas, including immigration, religious exercise, and marriage, see Denike, "Racialization"; Den Otter, *In Defense of Plural Marriage*; and Rogozen, "Prioritizing Diversity."
67 *Brown v. Buhman*, 1183, 1186–87, 1188.
68 *Brown v. Buhman*, 1218, 1224. Legal bigamy involves actually seeking to achieve or claiming legal recognition for more than one spouse, whereas cohabitation may involve referring to someone to whom you are not legally

married as your spouse without ever claiming to have received legal recognition for that relationship.

69 *Brown v. Buhman*, 1218, 1199, 1224. In his dissent in the case of *Obergefell v. Hodges* (2015), which recognized a constitutional right to marriage for same-sex couples, Justice John Roberts cited *Brown v. Buhman* in arguing that the majority decision recognizing same-sex marriage could just as easily be extended to polygamous unions. See *Obergefell v. Hodges*, 135 U.S. 2584, 2621.

70 Den Otter, *In Defense of Plural Marriage*, 43, 189, 208; Rogozen, "Prioritizing Diversity," 137, 138. For similar formulations, see also Calhoun, "Who's Afraid of Polygamous Marriage?"; Faucon, "Polygamy after *Windsor*." Many of these arguments about polygamous unions turn on similar kinds of legal claims that could and have been made, and have been accepted by US courts, with regard to same-sex marriage. I will address the problems in the latter in the final section of the chapter. On contemporary popular representations of Mormons (both mainstream LDS and fundamentalists who continue to support plural marriage), including the ways they are positioned with regard to figurations of homosexuality and the closet, see Weber, *Latter-Day Scenes*. For a fascinating discussion of contemporary polygamy that notes its logistical differences from same-sex marriage and recommends the adoption of aspects of commercial partner law as part of legal regulation, see Davis, "Regulating Polygamy."

71 Rosenblum, "Democratic Sex," 71, 79; Den Otter, *In Defense of Plural Marriage*, 178; Rogozen, "Prioritizing Diversity," 139.

72 Den Otter, *In Defense of Plural Marriage*, 5, 28.

73 As Alexander Weheliye observes, "the benefits accrued through the juridical acknowledgment of racialized subjects as fully human often exacts a steep entry price, because inclusion hinges on accepting the codification of personhood as property, which is, in turn, based on the comparative distinction between groups" (*Habeas Viscus*, 77).

74 This formulation was offered by Justice Thomas Cooley in 1879 (Ziegler, *Beyond Abortion*, 19).

75 Warren and Brandeis, "The Right to Privacy," 207, 205.

76 On transformations in the legal and cultural understanding of marriage and family life from the late nineteenth century to the late twentieth century, see Chauncey, *Why Marriage?*; Coontz, *The Way We Never Were*; Cott, *Public Vows*; Montegary, *Familiar Perversions*; and Polikoff, *Beyond (Straight and Gay)*.

77 *Griswold v. Connecticut*, 381 U.S. 479 (1965), 481. On the background to the case, see Johnson, *Griswold v. Connecticut*.

78 *Griswold v. Connecticut*, 484–85.

79 *Griswold v. Connecticut*, 482, 486.

80 Stein, *Sexual Injustice*, 30.

81 *Griswold v. Connecticut*, 495–96.

82 See Coontz, *The Way We Never Were*; Fullilove, *Root Shock*; Lipsitz, *How Racism Takes Place*; Massey and Denton, *American Apartheid*; and Taylor, *Race for Profit*.

83 See *Buck v. Bell*, 274 U.S. 200 (1927); Carter, *The Heart of Whiteness*; Nelson, *Women of Color*; Ordover, *American Eugenics*; Roberts, *Killing the Black Body*; Samuels, *Fantasies of Identification*; and Threadcraft, *Intimate Justice*.

84 Minow, "We, the Family," 959.

85 *Eisenstadt v. Baird*, 405 U.S. 438 (1972), 453, 447, 453.

86 See Cott, *Public Vows*, 199; Johnson, *Griswold v. Connecticut*, 201–2, 222; and Stein, *Sexual Injustice*, 48.

87 The decisions and concurrences in *Griswold* and *Eisenstadt* also make clear that the liberty/privacy right they outline does not mean that other statutes criminalizing sexual behavior beyond the scope of heteromonogamy are thereby invalidated. See Johnson, *Griswold v. Connecticut*, 192–200; Stein, *Sexual Injustice*, 32–33, 50.

88 *Roe v. Wade*, 410 U.S. 113 (1973), 152–53 (ellipses in original), 155, 163. On the ways varied movements in the 1970s and 1980s sought to use *Roe* to expand the possibilities for what "privacy" legally might mean, see Ziegler, *Beyond Abortion*. For critiques of the framing of abortion rights in terms of "privacy," see Gurr, *Reproductive Justice*; Nelson, *Women of Color*; Roberts, *Killing the Black Body*; and Ross et al., *Radical Reproductive Justice*. *Roe v. Wade* was overruled by the Supreme Court's decision in *Dobbs v. Jackson* (2022), which raised significant questions about the right to privacy logic articulated from *Griswold* onwards, but I want to foreground the implications of the kinds of right to privacy frames/arguments that continue to proliferate as the principal public means of arguing for forms of reproductive justice.

89 *Planned Parenthood v. Casey*, 505 U.S. 833 (1992), 847–48, 851.

90 *Planned Parenthood v. Casey*, 851, 852, 853.

91 *Roe v. Wade*, 116; *Planned Parenthood v. Casey*, 887–94, 898.

92 Bridges, *The Poverty of Privacy Rights*, 98.

93 Here, I am implicitly drawing on Alexander Weheliye's understanding of racialization as an "assemblage" through which various social and political relations are transformed into qualities of the "flesh" (*Habeas Viscus*). See also Puar, *Terrorist Assemblages*.

94 *Dandridge v. Williams*, 397 U.S. 471 (1970), 486, 484, 484–85.

95 *Harris v. McRae*, 448 U.S. 297 (1980), 314–15.

96 Bridges, *The Poverty of Privacy Rights*, 11, 12. See also Kandaswamy, *Domestic Contradictions*; Mink, *Welfare's End*; and Ross, "Conceptualizing Reproductive Justice."

97 As Bridges observes of dominant ways of conceptualizing poor women, "her lack of autonomy in constituting and defining herself simply complements her lack of autonomy in supporting herself financially" (*The Poverty of Privacy Rights*, 198). Gwendolyn Mink refers to the attributions

of dependency, deviancy, and unworthiness that attach to public assistance, and attendant forms of state surveillance and intervention, as "the welfare police state" (*Welfare's End*, 4).

98 *Dandridge v. Williams*, 521; *Harris v. McRae*, 343. For Native women who currently seek medical treatment under the Indian Health Service, there is no access to abortion except under the provisions provided in the Hyde Amendment: rape, incest, and to save the life of the mother. See Gurr, *Reproductive Justice*, 128–30. On the role of family caps in current welfare policy (TANF), see Romero and Agénor, "The Welfare Family Cap."

99 *Loving v. Virginia*, 388 U.S. 1 (1967), 11. On the conservative implications of the *Loving* decision, see also Byrd, "*Loving* Unbecoming"; Pascoe, *What Comes Naturally*, 287–306; Reddy, *Freedom with Violence*, 182–218; and Somerville, "Queer *Loving*."

100 On the global context of what was couched as population control, see Murphy, *The Economization of Life*.

101 On narratives of worthiness and their relation to racializing attributions of criminality, even in the absence of the commission of an actual crime, see Cacho, *Social Death*; Dayan, *The Law Is a White Dog*; Spade, *Normal Life*; and Stallings, *Funk the Erotic*.

102 For background on the history of welfare in the United States, see Brown, "Ghettos"; Davis, *Battered Black Women*; Fording, "'Laboratories of Democracy'"; Hancock, *The Politics of Disgust*, 23–64; Kandaswamy, *Domestic Contradictions*; Lash, "*When the Welfare People Come*"; Levenstein, "Gendering Postwar Urban History"; Mink, *Welfare's End*; O'Connor, *Poverty Knowledge*; Roberts, *Killing the Black Body*; and Soss et al., "Introduction."

103 Sparks, "Queens, Teens, and Model Mothers," 178; Public Law 104–93, 110 Stat. 2110. For extended discussion of the shape of the legislation, the continuities and differences between PRWORA and previous legislation, and the ways the legislation presumes that marriage is the solution to poverty and promotes marriage *instead of* seeking to alleviate poverty, see Mink, *Welfare's End*. As Soss et al. argue, "Under TANF, agency workers have an expanded scope of discretion that includes when to divert would-be applicants, whether to grant exemptions from program rules, whom to sanction for what kinds of infractions, and which clients to inform about which available benefits and services" ("Introduction," 17–18). For an ethnographic discussion of this process, see Davis, *Battered Black Women*. The funding structure of the PRWORA also enables states to reduce welfare rolls while continuing to hold on to the fixed federal funds given them for welfare, mobilizing those funds toward other state expenses and thereby lowering taxes largely for the white middle class. See Brown, "Ghettos."

104 As Alice O'Connor suggests, "As used by poverty experts, the very concept of 'dependency' made receiving welfare a personal pathology, something that became harder to 'escape' the longer it went on, while

such descriptors as 'long-termer' and 'recidivism' virtually equated using welfare with a criminal offense" (*Poverty Knowledge*, 254). Such narratives also overlook the numerous forms of government support provided to white people from which people of color, particularly African Americans, historically have been excluded, including Social Security (when established attached to jobs other than those in which most people of color were employed and from which expenditures usually are much higher than what a given individual has contributed over their working life), tax deductions for local property taxes and mortgage interest (from which African Americans largely have been excluded due to ongoing forms of residential segregation), direction of federal and state funds toward supporting white-dominated municipalities (despite the fact that people of color tend to be charged relatively more for municipal and property taxes), provision of extensive government funds and credit for farming (from which Black people largely have been excluded), securing of government bonds through borrowing from white investment capitalists (often at the expense of Black people, both as taxpayers and in terms of prison construction), and construction and maintenance of highways and interstates that facilitate both white movement to the suburbs and relocation of businesses there. See Coontz, *The Way We Never Were*; Daniel, *Dispossession*; Gilmore, *Golden Gulag*; Lipsitz, *How Racism Takes Place*; Mink, *Welfare's End*; Rothstein, *The Color of Law*; and Taylor, *Race for Profit*.

105 I address these topics, as well as the Moynihan Report, at greater length in chapter 4.

106 Ibrahim, *Troubling the Family*, 52.

107 As Ibrahim notes of the Moynihan Report, "Just as *Loving* struck down the last vestiges of antimiscegenation in judicial review, the black family was highlighted as antithetical to the values of the state. Just as the nuclear family became the site where the races can now intermingle and amalgamate according to personalized discretion, the black family was rhetorically singled out for its unique inability to integrate the values of American society and achieve the recognizably healthy qualities that families should demonstrate" (*Troubling the Family*, 52). On the Moynihan Report, see also Coates, "The Black Family"; Ferguson, *Aberrations in Black*; Geary, *Beyond Civil Rights*; and Greenbaum, *Blaming the Poor*.

108 Davis, *Battered Black Women*, 33–34.

109 As Gwendolyn Mink argues, "We should not think of welfare as a subsidy for dependence; nor should we think of it as an income substitute for the wage earned by breadwinners.... Rather, we should reconceive welfare as the income *owed* to persons who work inside the home caring for, nurturing, and protecting children" (*Welfare's End*, 19), and such a position would acknowledge that welfare functions as "remuneration for real work" (31). On the increasing displacement of the labor of social reproduction to the "family," see Briggs, *How All Politics*.

110 Davis, *Battered Black Women*, 42. On the emergence of the image of the "welfare queen" and the work it performed during the debate over PRWORA, see Hancock, *The Politics of Disgust*. On the ways the figure relates to the nonheteronormativity of blackness, see Cohen, "Punks, Bulldaggers, and Welfare Queens"; Ferguson, *Aberrations in Black*; and Kandaswamy, *Domestic Contradictions*.

111 Such an association may help explain why there were many Black officials who also repudiated women on welfare, understanding welfare itself as a racialized status related but not reducible to its association with women of color. See Hancock, *The Politics of Disgust*, 88–116.

112 On the variability among states of numbers of persons of color on welfare prior to PRWORA and the possible effects of such differences on the pursuit of various kinds of waivers in those states (which helped shape the form that PRWORA eventually took), see Fording, "'Laboratories of Democracy.'"

113 Roberts, *Killing the Black Body*, 8, 19. On figurations of Black motherhood as monstrous, see also Sharpe, *Monstrous Intimacies*. On the long history of Lamarkianism in the United States (the belief that lived social circumstances and patterns become biologically encoded and transmitted through reproduction), as well as the racial politics of notions of malleability, see Schuller, *The Biopolitics of Feeling*; Schuller and Gill-Peterson, "The Biopolitics of Plasticity."

114 Ange-Marie Hancock addresses this process as the creation of "disgust" via forms of "public identity." See Hancock, *The Politics of Disgust*. Roberts further observes, "While poor single mothers must endure government surveillance for their paltry benefits, 'self-sufficient' traditional families receive huge public subsidies—Social Security, tax breaks, and government-backed mortgages, for example—without any loss of privacy" (*Killing the Black Body*, 226). See also Bridges, *The Poverty of Privacy Rights*; Mink, *Welfare's End*; and Sparks, "Queens, Teens, and Model Mothers."

115 Ordover, *American Eugenics*, 78–79, 134; Roberts, *Killing the Black Body*, 59–67; Silliman et al., *Undivided Rights*, 59. Roberts notes that "labeling a young woman feebleminded was often an excuse to punish her sexual immorality. Many women were sent to institutions to be sterilized solely because they were promiscuous or had become pregnant out of wedlock. A review of sterilizations in California found that three out of four of the sterilized women had been judged sexually delinquent prior to their institutional commitment" (*Killing the Black Body*, 69).

116 *Buck v. Bell*, 205–6, 207. The Court did limit the reach of sterilization laws in *Skinner v. Oklahoma*, 316 U.S. 535 (1942), but not by finding them to be a fundamental violation of personal rights. Instead, the decision merely argued for the need for "strict scrutiny" of the classifications used in involuntary sterilization laws (541), as well as distinguishing the Oklahoma law in this case from the Virginia law at issue in *Buck v. Bell*

by noting that the latter includes the possibility of judicial review of the sterilization determination in ways that preserved due process, which the Oklahoma law lacks.

117 On the connections (both ideological and organizational) between pre–World War II eugenics and postwar form(ul)ations, see Ordover, *American Eugenics*; Ross, "Trust Black Women."

118 Lawrence, "Indian Health Service," 404.

119 O'Sullivan, "Informing Red Power," 967–68; Ralstin-Lewis, "Continuing Struggle against Genocide," 75; Silliman et al., *Undivided Rights*, 14.

120 O'Sullivan, "Informing Red Power," 968. This figure can be contrasted with the estimated 70,000 people who were sterilized under eugenic laws from the early twentieth century (Silliman et al., *Undivided Rights*, 59).

121 See Lawrence, "Indian Health Service"; O'Sullivan, "Informing Red Power"; and Ralstin-Lewis, "Continuing Struggle against Genocide." On the colonial dynamics of the Indian Health Service, see also Gurr, *Reproductive Justice*.

122 The Committee for Abortion Rights and Against Sterilization Abuse (CARASA), founded in NYC in 1977, "saw a direct connection between decreasing federal funding for abortion and an increase in coerced sterilization. CARASA argued that 'in the absence of adequate income, birth control, childcare, and health care, we cannot assume that the rise in sterilization is a result of 'free choice'" (O'Sullivan, "Informing Red Power," 975). See also Roberts, *Killing the Black Body*, 97. For discussion of the lack of reproductive health options for Native women who depend on the Indian Health Service, which helps increase the number of people who choose tubal ligation as a form of birth control, see Gurr, *Reproductive Justice*.

123 On court cases and HEW regulations in the period, see Lawrence, "Indian Health Service"; O'Sullivan, "Informing Red Power"; Ralstin-Lewis, "Continuing Struggle against Genocide"; and Silliman et al., *Undivided Rights*.

124 Lawrence, "Indian Health Service," 410. See also O'Sullivan, "Informing Red Power"; Ralstin-Lewis, "Continuing Struggle against Genocide"; and Roberts, *Killing the Black Body*, 90–93. On the ways claims about habitual criminality were part of earlier eugenics discourses, including being used to justify state action against political dissidents, see Ordover, *American Eugenics*.

125 As Silliman et al. argue, "Reproductive justice is not difficult to define or remember. It has three primary values: 1) the right *not* to have a child; 2) the right to *have* a child; and 3) the right to parent children in safe and healthy environments" (*Undivided Rights*, vii). The concept of "reproductive justice" was first used by African American women meeting in Chicago in 1994 as part of a pro-choice conference and was revived almost a decade later at the SisterSong conference in Atlanta in November 2003. See Leonard, "Laying the Foundations." On the work of the concept of

reproductive justice, see also Gurr, *Reproductive Justice*; Nelson, *Women of Color*; Ross et al., *Radical Reproductive Justice*; and Stallings, *A Dirty South Manifesto*.

126 Roberts, *Killing the Black Body*, 201.
127 Stoler, *Race and the Education of Desire*, 99.
128 In the celebratory vein, see Frank, *Awakening*. For some touchstone arguments that foreground forms of racialization, see Byrd, "*Loving* Unbecoming"; Eng, *The Feeling of Kinship*; Reddy, *Freedom with Violence*; Rodríguez, *Sexual Futures*; and Somerville, "Queer *Loving*."
129 Franke, *Wedlocked*, 12, 13.
130 Puar, *Terrorist Assemblages*, 31, 35.
131 *Griswold v. Connecticut*, 485; *Planned Parenthood v. Casey*, 847–48.
132 Stoler, *Race and the Education of Desire*, 12.
133 Although, laws against fornication and adultery remain on the books in many jurisdictions throughout the United States, which could lead to prosecution for sexual activity outside of marriage or inside it. See Chambers, *Against Marriage*.
134 See Canaday, *The Straight State*; Chauncey, *Why Marriage?*; Frank, *Awakening*; Montegary, *Familiar Perversions*; Ordover, *American Eugenics*; Somerville, "Queer *Loving*"; and Weston, *Families We Choose*.
135 See Somerville, "Queer *Loving*"; Stein, *Sexual Injustice*.
136 See Cohen, "Punks, Bulldaggers, and Welfare Queens."
137 *Bowers v. Hardwick*, 478 U.S. 106 (1986), 190–91, 189, 204, 205.
138 *Lawrence v. Texas*, 567, 573–74.
139 See Eng, *The Feeling of Kinship*, 23–57; Puar, *Terrorist Assemblages*, 114–65; and Willse and Spade, "Freedom in a Regulatory State?"
140 *Obergefell v. Hodges*, 2593, 2594, 2602, 2608.
141 See Coontz, *Social Origins of Private Life*; Cott, *Public Vows*; Coviello, *Intimacy in America*; Merish, *Sentimental Materialism*; Nelson, *National Manhood*; and Perry, *Vexy Thing*.
142 See Povinelli, *The Empire of Love*.
143 Carter, *The Heart of Whiteness*, 3, 6. Liz Montegary has described these sets of assumptions as "racialized relational norms" (*Familiar Perversions*, 10).
144 Carter, *The Heart of Whiteness*, 154.
145 See Brandzel, "Queering Citizenship?"; Franke, *Wedlocked*; Reddy, *Freedom with Violence*, 182–218; and Somerville, "Queer *Loving*." On the erasure of Mildred Loving's Cherokee and Rappahannock ancestry in the case and the ways the case is remembered and mobilized, see also Byrd, "*Loving* Unbecoming." Also, as several scholars have noted, *Lawrence v. Texas* does not discuss the fact of Tyron Garner's blackness, which is particularly notable given that the reason the police were there in the first place was a call (likely by a jealous ex-lover) that there was a Black man "going crazy with a gun" (Eng, *The Feeling of Kinship*, 36). The criminalization of blackness, then, provided the backdrop against which the

possibility for recognizing intimate privacy emerged. On this dynamic, and the ways Garner himself ceased to be meaningful to gay publics after the case (as indicated by the inability to crowdsource sufficient funds for his burial three years after the decision), see Chamberlin, "Akinship."

146 On histories of criminalizing sexual and gendered conduct understood as marking forms of perverse identity, see Canaday, *The Straight State*; Chauncey, *Why Marriage?*; Ritchie, *Invisible No More*; Spade, *Normal Life*; and Stryker, *Transgender History*.

147 *Bowers v. Hardwick*, 195, 208, 213.

148 See Cohen, *A Body Worth Defending*; Harris, "Whiteness as Property"; and Macpherson, *Political Theory of Possessive Individualism*.

149 *Lawrence v. Texas*, 562, 578, 575. As Craig Willse and Dean Spade argue, "*Lawrence* does not challenge the mechanics of discipline itself, even if it shifts the terms of subjectification" ("Freedom in a Regulatory State?," 315–16). They further note, "a very small number of queer and trans people are incarcerated for sodomy, but a disproportionate number are incarcerated for crimes of poverty such as loitering, prostitution, and possession or sale of illegal drugs" (328). See also Ritchie, *Invisible No More*.

150 *Obergefell v. Hodges*, 2600.

151 *Lawrence v. Texas*, 578.

152 On blackness and criminality as the necessary context out of which "kinship" emerges, see Chamberlin, "Akinship."

153 See Cacho, *Social Death*; Ellison, "The Strangeness of Progress"; Hinton, *From the War on Poverty*; Manalansan, "Race, Violence"; Muhammad, *The Condemnation of Blackness*; Rodríguez, *Sexual Futures*; and Wacquant, *Punishing the Poor*. I will further address this dynamic, particularly with regard to African Americans, in chapter 4.

154 Manalansan, "Race, Violence," 146, 151.

155 On the ways discourses of safety are mobilized to protect gay and lesbian privacy and private property, see Ellison, "The Strangeness of Progress"; Hanhardt, *Safe Space*.

156 *Obergefell v. Hodges*, 2608.

157 As Jodi Byrd argues, these cases can be understood as "using equal protection [and due process] to expand the notion of individual rights over and against collective group rights" ("*Loving* Unbecoming," 208). On the ways these cases maintain the "special rights" of marriage, over and against policies that would benefit more LGBT people as well as others, see Polikoff, *Beyond (Straight and Gay)*.

158 *United States v. Windsor*, 570 U.S. 744 (2013), 796, 797. In a somewhat bizarre twist, Justice Roberts in his dissent in *Obergefell* argued that the Court's understanding of marriage rights for same-sex couples as a vital part of the "liberty" contained in the Fourteenth Amendment involves a "substantive due process" argument that is somehow akin to the denial of Congress's right to regulate slavery in the Territories in *Dred Scott v.*

	Sandford (1857). Thus, not only do gay and lesbian rights have nothing to do with the forms of racial remediation at issue in the Fourteenth Amendment, but the Court's endorsement of them is somehow continuous with its previous endorsement of slavery. See *Obergefell v. Hodges*, 2616–17.
159	See Byrd, "*Loving* Unbecoming."
160	This dynamic in the decisions seems particularly notable given that DOMA was passed in the same session with two other laws that both promoted marriage and distributed access to citizenship rights in racialized ways: PRWORA and the Illegal Immigration Reform and Immigrant Responsibility Act. See Brandzel, "Queering Citizenship?"; Montegary, *Familiar Perversions*, 50–51; and Polikoff, *Beyond (Straight and Gay)*, 90–92.
161	*United States v. Windsor*, 763; *Obergefell v. Hodges*, 2594.
162	*United States v. Windsor*, 763.
163	*Obergefell v. Hodges*, 2595, 2596. On the ways discourses of homosexual immutability take part in a eugenic imaginary that long has targeted (homo)sexual deviance for elimination, see Ordover, *American Eugenics*; Sedgwick, *Epistemology of the Closet*.
164	*Obergefell v. Hodges*, 2598, 2602.
165	*Obergefell v. Hodges*, 2596.
166	In his dissent, Justice Roberts did mark this dynamic in *Loving*, but in order to assert that striking down laws against interracial marriage did not affect its "core structure": "Removing racial barriers to marriage . . . did not change what a marriage was" (*Obergefell v. Hodges*, 2614, 2619).
167	See Bentley, "Marriage as Treason"; Cott, *Public Vows*; Franke, *Wedlocked*; Hartman, *Scenes of Subjection*; Hunter, *Bound in Wedlock*; Luibhéid, *Entry Denied*; Ngai, *Impossible Subjects*; Pascoe, *What Comes Naturally*; Rifkin, *When Did Indians Become Straight?*; and Shah, *Stranger Intimacy*.
168	*United States v. Windsor*, 766.
169	*Obergefell v. Hodges*, 2598, 2599, 2603.
170	*Loving v. Virginia*, 11.
171	Roberts, *Killing the Black Body*, 71.
172	Somerville, "Queer *Loving*," 357. See also Reddy, *Freedom with Violence*, 182–218; Stein, *Sexual Injustice*, 14, 44–46.
173	Although, some scholars have noted that a vastly disproportionate number of gay and lesbian families raising children are, in fact, headed by people of color and that marriage may function as a desirable goal in order to gain access to a range of rights with regard to parenting that would not otherwise be available, especially in states that otherwise do not have LGBT-friendly policies. See Briggs, *How All Politics*, 175–76; Montegary, *Familiar Perversions*, 8, 141. On the ways marriage largely fails to address the partnership and child-rearing concerns of same-sex couples, see Polikoff, *Beyond (Straight and Gay)*. On the use of marriage

as a way for Black same-sex couples to engage intraracial assumptions about sexuality and respectability, see Moore, "Marriage Equality."

174 Ross, "Beyond the Closet," 168, 173. See also Snorton, *Black on Both Sides*; Somerville, *Queering the Color Line*; Stoler, *Race and the Education of Desire*; Weheliye, *Habeas Viscus*; and Wynter, "Unsettling the Coloniality."

175 On homonormativity, see Duggan, *The Twilight of Equality?*; Puar, *Terrorist Assemblages*; Spade, *Normal Life*.

176 Simpson, *As We Have Always Done*, 23.

177 See Hancock, *Intersectionality*; Lorde, *Sister Outsider*; and Spade, *Normal Life*.

178 Carruthers, *Unapologetic*, 110.

179 Coviello, *Make Yourselves Gods*, 229.

Four. Blackness, Criminality, Governance

1 Lubiano, "Black Nationalism," 232, 233, 236.

2 Curley et al., "Decolonisation Is a Political Project"; Goeman, "Land as Life," 72, 73. See also Byrd, "Weather with You"; Byrd et al., "Predatory Value"; and Nichols, *Theft Is Property!*

3 Harris, "Of Blackness and Indigeneity," 220. On the ways Black bodies are presented/positioned as incapable of exerting sovereignty, and thus of being political subjects, see also Cordis, "Settler Unfreedoms."

4 Black political mappings have reconceptualized scale in ways that challenge the limits of the nation form, but they largely have done so at a scale envisioned as above or geographically exceeding that of the nation-state. For examples, see Bonilla, *Non-Sovereign Futures*; Edwards, *The Practice of Diaspora*; Getachew, *Worldmaking after Empire*; Higashida, *Black Internationalist Feminism*; Stephens, *Black Empire*; and Wilder, *Freedom Time*. For differently configured efforts to suggest the value of notions of sovereignty and/or nationhood for Black studies, see Lara, *Queer Freedom*; Sealey, *Creolizing the Nation*; and Singh, *Black Is a Country*.

5 Keeling, *The Witch's Flight*, 8, 46.

6 Keeling, *The Witch's Flight*, 138, 149.

7 Here I am thinking of the critique of the capitalist privatization of social reproduction. See Federici, *Patriarchy of the Wage*.

8 Harjo, *Spiral to the Stars*, 12, 40.

9 Byrd, "To Hear the Call," 342. This piece is a commentary on Roderick Ferguson's address as President of the American Studies Association, and Byrd here is praising Ferguson's engagement with such place-based epistemologies. See also Byrd, "Weather with You."

10 Byrd et al., "Predatory Value," 11.

11 For examples, see Cohen, "Punks, Bulldaggers, and Welfare Queens"; Ferguson, *Aberrations in Black*; Haley, *No Mercy Here*; Macharia, *Frottage*;

Nyong'o, *The Amalgamation Waltz*; Ross, "Beyond the Closet"; Stallings, *Funk the Erotic*; and Thomas, *Sexual Demon of Colonial Power*.

12 I will address the use of the concept of *kinship* in characterizing Black social formations, but on blackness as kinlessness, see Bentley, "The Fourth Dimension"; Chamberlin, "Akinship"; Hartman, *Lose Your Mother*; Sharpe, *Monstrous Intimacies*; Weheliye, *Habeas Viscus*; and Wynter, "Unsettling the Coloniality of Being."

13 Edwards, *Charisma*, xvii, 11.

14 See Kelley, *Freedom Dreams*.

15 See Moten, "The Subprime and the Beautiful."

16 On the politics of respectability within Black political discourses, see Carby, *Reconstructing Womanhood*; Cohen, *The Boundaries of Blackness*; duCille, *The Coupling Convention*; Ellison, "Black Femme Praxis"; Ferguson, *Aberrations in Black*; Green, *Love, Activism*; Jenkins, *Private Lives, Proper Relations*; Ladner, *Tomorrow's Tomorrow*; Macharia, *Frottage*; Nyong'o, *The Amalgamation Waltz*; Stallings, *Funk the Erotic*; and Thomas, *Sexual Demon of Colonial Power*. However, what has been termed *the politics of respectability* also cannot be understood simply as collusion with or assimilation to white norms. As Claudia Tate argues with regard to depictions of heteromarital domesticity in late nineteenth-century and early twentieth-century African American women's novels, such representations of respectability can be understood as "feminized black political desire" that function as a "gendered discourse of citizenship" in which "the appropriation of bourgeois gender conventions in general were fundamental to the emancipatory discourse of nineteenth-century African Americans" (*Domestic Allegories*, 24, 51, 56).

17 Wynter, "Unsettling the Coloniality," 260, 296. On Wynter's work, see McKittrick, *Sylvia Wynter*; Thomas, "*Marronnons*/Let's Maroon"; and Weheliye, *Habeas Viscus*.

18 See Spillers, "Mama's Baby, Papa's Maybe."

19 Weheliye, *Habeas Viscus*, 4, 77.

20 See also Hartman, *Scenes of Subjection*; King, "The Labor of (Re)reading"; and Snorton, *Black on Both Sides*.

21 Weheliye, *Habeas Viscus*, 42. See also Cohen, "Punks, Bulldaggers, and Welfare Queens"; Ellison, "Black Femme Praxis"; Ferguson, *Aberrations in Black*; Holland, *The Erotic Life*; Morgan, *Laboring Women*; Ross, "Beyond the Closet"; Snorton, *Black on Both Sides*; Spillers, "Mama's Baby, Papa's Maybe"; and Thomas, *Sexual Demon of Colonial Power*.

22 Weheliye, *Habeas Viscus*, 4, 8.

23 For varied articulations of this kind of argument, see Bonilla, *Non-Sovereign Futures*; Brand, *A Map to the Door*; Hartman, *Lose Your Mother*; McKittrick, "Rebellion/Invention/Groove"; Scott, *Conscripts of Modernity*; Sexton, "The Vel of Slavery"; and Wilderson, *Red, White, and Black*.

24 Weheliye, *Habeas Viscus*, 31.
25 Hartman, *Lose Your Mother*, 234.
26 Harney and Moten, *The Undercommons*, 61, 98, 20, 45.
27 Scott, *Conscripts of Modernity*, 4, 19.
28 See Rifkin, *Fictions of Land and Flesh*.
29 A counterpoint to this framing lies in Black discourses of marronage, which in the Caribbean and Latin America provide a language through which to talk about landed and self-governing Black collectivity. See Bilby, *True-Born Maroons*; Engle, *The Elusive Promise*; Escobar, *Territories of Difference*; French, *Legalizing Identities*; Gottlieb, *Mother of Us All*; Greene, "Introduction"; Ng'weno, "Can Ethnicity Replace Race?"; and Sharpe, *Ghosts of Slavery*, 1–43. The emphasis on such landedness, though, is in contrast to other associations of marronage, primarily in regard to fugitivity. See Bonilla, *Non-Sovereign Futures*; Rifkin, *Fictions of Land and Flesh*, 168–219; and Roberts, *Freedom as Marronage*.
30 Benjamin, "Black AfterLives Matter," 65. Rain Prud'homme-Cranford et al.'s notion of being "kinshipped" does similar work (*Louisiana Creole Peoplehood*, 5).
31 McKittrick, *Demonic Grounds*, viii, 4, 69. Jovan Scott Lewis observes that starting from a sense of Black "geographic emplacement can ... produce other narratives" (*Violent Utopia*, 198).
32 On the supposed errancy of Black bodies, see also Cervenak, *Wandering*.
33 Hartman, *Lose Your Mother*, 225, 234.
34 Carruthers, *Unapologetic*, 109, 110.
35 Simpson, *As We Have Always Done*, 230, 231; Barker, *Native Acts*, 223.
36 Cohen, "Deviance as Resistance," 31, 37, 38, 30.
37 Cohen, "Deviance as Resistance," 40. Such conscious mobilization is significant given the ways that the people cast as deviant may themselves identify with liberal ideals, even though their own actions and relationships do not conform to them. See Cohen, *Democracy Remixed*.
38 Cohen, "Deviance as Resistance," 31.
39 Alexander Weheliye suggests that "resistance and agency assume full, self-present, and coherent subjects working against something or someone," and he asks, "Why are formations of the oppressed deemed liberatory only if they resist hegemony and/or exhibit the full agency of the oppressed?" (*Habeas Viscus*, 2). For discussions of this issue within enslavement, see also Freeburg, *Counterlife*; Sharpe, *Ghosts of Slavery*. In this vein, I am pointing toward the conceptual and political possibilities opened by addressing certain "formations of the oppressed" as political orders, even in the absence of such subjects' conscious commitment to that project.
40 Edwards, *Charisma*, 3, 11, xv, 107.
41 Edwards, *Charisma*, 109, 118, 119. In this vein, Irvin J. Hunt addresses the ways that Black political movements often are discussed as a "wave-like

form" that "rises and falls" while "miss[ing] the time beneath the wave" (*Dreaming the Present*, 87).
42 Carruthers, *Unapologetic*, 8.
43 See Alexander, *The New Jim Crow*; Dayan, *The Law Is a White Dog*; Hartman, *Scenes of Subjection*; and Wagner, *Disturbing the Peace*.
44 Haley, *No Mercy Here*, 68, 251.
45 On the notion of "assemblages," see Puar, *Terrorist Assemblages*; Weheliye, *Habeas Viscus*.
46 See Foner, *Reconstruction*; Hahn, *Nation under Our Feet*; and Hunter, *To 'Joy My Freedom*.
47 Foner, *Reconstruction*, 405; Hahn, *Nation under Our Feet*, 247, 273, 328.
48 See also Hahn, *Nation under Our Feet*, 37; Hunter, *To 'Joy My Freedom*, 62, 67–68, 97; Jones, *Labor of Love*, 58, 65; and Penningroth, *The Claims of Kinsfolk*, 46, 77, 103.
49 I do not mean to diminish the importance of achieving the vote, the struggles over Black enfranchisement in the period, and the severity of white violence to prevent Black enfranchisement and to intimidate and block Black voters where and when such rights had been achieved officially. On these dynamics, see Du Bois, *Black Reconstruction*; Edwards, *Gendered Strife and Confusion*; Foner, *Reconstruction*; Hahn, *Nation under Our Feet*; Rosen, *Terror in the Heart*; and Woods, *Development Arrested*.
50 Hunter, *To 'Joy My Freedom*, 73.
51 Hahn, *Nation under Our Feet*, 17.
52 At various points Hahn offers the following formulations: "kinship held together and financed an assortment of 'societies,' 'associations,' and 'joint-stock companies' that formed with astonishing rapidity after emancipation"; "the unit of local league organizations comfortably meshed with the perimeters of reconstituted kinship groups that could span a number of plantations and farms"; the lists of people produced by the Republican Party to serve as registrars for elections "were men of mature age who were . . . at the intersection, if not the head of, dense kinship networks" and therefore "exercised local influence for quite some time"; and churches were "composed chiefly of interconnected families laboring on a single plantation or on adjacent plantations and farms" (*Nation under Our Feet*, 167, 183, 196, 232).
53 Harjo, *Spiral to the Stars*, 39. I'm invoking Indigenous formulations of peoplehood while recognizing the potential distinctions between modes of Black sociality and those of Indigenous peoplehood in their histories, aims, and trajectories, as well as recognizing the ways enslavement and post-emancipation Black freedom took place on territories from which Native nations were dispossessed. On Indian removal in what is now the US Southeast, see Garrison, *Legal Ideology*; Norgren, *The Cherokee Cases*. Despite the force of Indian Removal as a federal policy in the 1830s, Native peoples remain across the South. See Adams, *Who Belongs?*; Fin-

ger, *Cherokee Americans*; Klopotek, *Recognition Odysseys*; and Lowery, *Lumbee Indians*.

54 For examples, see Bell, *Claiming Freedom*, 64, 81; Berlin et al., "Afro-American Families," 89; Hahn, *Nation under Our Feet*, 18, 169; and Penningroth, *The Claims of Kinsfolk*, 87.

55 See Bell, *Claiming Freedom*; Bercaw, *Gendered Freedoms*; Berlin et al., "Afro-American Families"; Edwards, *Gendered Strife and Confusion*; Hahn, *Nation under Our Feet*; Hunter, *Bound in Wedlock*; Jones, *Labor of Love*; and Penningroth, *The Claims of Kinsfolk*.

56 Bercaw, *Gendered Freedoms*, 21, 23. See also Kaye, *Joining Places*. While these patterns of interdependence initially may have arisen out of the economies of enslavement, especially in terms of masters' consistent failure to provide sufficient provisions to sustain Black life (Hahn, *Nation under Our Feet*, 32; Penningroth, *The Claims of Kinsfolk*, 77), such shared practices and modes of relation are not simply reducible to the wasting exigencies of enchattelment or the deprivations of post-emancipation regimes of production.

57 Moreover, when formal institutions were targeted for assault and destruction by white supremacist organizations, often known collectively as the Ku Klux Klan, emplaced networks of relationality remained that could both rebirth such institutions and provide the principles and bonds that embodied and enabled rural Black projects of self-determination. On the Klan, see Du Bois, *Black Reconstruction*, 464–84, 503–8, 551; Foner, *Reconstruction*, 425–59; Hahn, *Nation under Our Feet*, 265–316; Howard, *Autobiography*, 374–89; and Rosen, *Terror in the Heart*, 179–242.

58 This resonates with Christopher Freeburg's analysis of the ways discussions of enslavement tend to totalize the effects of living within that institution and its ongoing legacies, mobilizing them toward particular political aims. See Freeburg, *Counterlife*. While I explicitly am arguing that Black social formations in the wake of emancipation can/should be seen as *political orders*, part of my point in doing so is that the practices and networks addressed do not need to become part of what looks like politics from within a liberal or state-focused frame, nor do they need to achieve a scale that can be characterized as *national*, in order to be valued as forms of collective worldmaking.

59 Justice, *Why Indigenous Literatures Matter*, 197. I should clarify that I am not so much speaking of something like the "Black Belt thesis" that emerged in the 1920s, in which African Americans in the rural South were conceptualized as a nation within a nation, as addressing the ways that localized constellations often named as kinship networks operated as matrices of political self-organization, without necessarily being coordinated or forming an integrated "nation." On the Black Belt thesis, see Higashida, *Black Internationalist Feminism*, 18; Kelley, *Freedom Dreams*, 49; and Young, *Soul Power*, 156–57. On the internal colony model used by

various intellectuals and groups in the mid-twentieth century to theorize antiblack oppression, see Boggs and Boggs, "The City"; Byrd, *The Transit of Empire*, 117–16; Higashida, *Black Internationalist Feminism*; Singh, *Black Is a Country*; Ture and Hamilton, *Black Power*; and Young, *Soul Power*.

60 Carruthers, *Unapologetic*, 74, 110. As Monica M. White notes, "[the] study of everyday forms of resistance misses activities that are not disruptive but rather constructive, in the sense that the aggrieved actively build alternatives to existing political and economic relationships" (*Freedom Farmers*, 6), and what I seek to highlight are the ways such alternatives of governance may not take institutionalized form and thus may end up being categorized as part of the "private sphere" through figurations of kinship.

61 Bell, *Claiming Freedom*, 42; Berlin et al., "Afro-American Families," 90–91; Foner, *Reconstruction*, 107; Hahn, *Nation under Our Feet*, 37, 50, 169–74; Hunter, *Bound in Wedlock*, 255; Jones, *Labor of Love*, 61; and Penningroth, *The Claims of Kinsfolk*, 117. Elsa Barkley Brown observes, "The proliferation of scholarly works centered on the flowering of black women's political activity in the late-nineteenth and early-twentieth centuries has perhaps left the impression that this was the inaugural moment or even height of black women's participation in politics" ("Negotiating and Transforming," 137). She, instead, draws attention to the tradition of Black women's active participation in mass meetings and various conventions in the wake of emancipation. Similarly, we might highlight the profound role of Black women in sustaining networks of governance that often are not understood as "political activity." For discussion of Black women's role in Black public spheres across the nineteenth century, see also Jones, *All Bound Up Together*.

62 Such networks were not always free of violence, particularly domestic abuse, for which there was often little remedy, especially given the economic and legal exigencies of having a man as part of the household. See Famer-Kaiser, *Freedwomen and the Freedmen's Bureau*, 141–66. Much of this violence may have been a function of increasing official efforts to position Black men as heads of household and as exerting a patriarchal authority over women and children, undermined and frustrated by white propertyholders and thus exercised through violence. On the extensive patterns of white sexual assault of Black women in the late nineteenth century, and the ways it illustrates the gendered dimensions of white supremacy, see Rosen, *Terror in the Heart*.

63 "Letter from the Secretary of War" (1866), 171.

64 "Message from the President" (1866), 181; "Letter of the Secretary of War" (1867), 57.

65 See Guha, "Prose of Counter-Insurgency."

66 In October 1865, Commissioner of the Freedmen's Bureau O. O. Howard issued a circular indicating, "Vagrant laws made for free people, and now

in force on the statue-books of the States embraced in the operations of this bureau, will be recognized and extended to the freedmen" ("Letter from the Secretary of War" [1866], 197–98). This acceptance meant that the bureau put itself in the business of enforcing significant aspects of the Black Codes passed by early Reconstruction governments in the South, in cases where the statutory language was race-neutral but the implications and enforcement were about directing African Americans back to slave-like arrangements of labor with white landowners. On the Black Codes, see Bercaw, *Gendered Freedoms*, 129–30; Du Bois, *Black Reconstruction*, 167–80; Edwards, *Gendered Strife and Confusion*, 38–39; and Foner, *Reconstruction*, 199–206. The Black Codes were superseded by the federal passage of the Civil Rights Act of 1866, which officially recognized African Americans' rights to engage in contracts, including marriage. See Famer-Kaiser, *Freedwomen and the Freedmen's Bureau*, 147; Foner, *Reconstruction*, 243–51; Hunter, *Bound in Wedlock*, 5, 241; and Stanley, *From Bondage to Contract*, 56–57. On President Johnson's executive implementation of Reconstruction prior to congressional intervention in 1867, see Du Bois, *Black Reconstruction*, 237–324; Foner, *Reconstruction*, 176–227; Howard, *Autobiography*, 277–92.

67 On the operation of the Freedmen's Bureau, see Du Bois, *Black Reconstruction*; Famer-Kaiser, *Freedwomen and the Freedmen's Bureau*; Foner, *Reconstruction*; Howard, *Autobiography*; and Oubre, *Forty Acres and a Mule*.

68 While addressing the ways formerly enslaved people constructed political orders in the wake of emancipation, I also should note that such activity was not separate from their ongoing demands that the US government provide food, shelter, and other resources for those who until recently had been held in bondage.

69 Howard, *Autobiography*, 164, 229. While many African Americans moved often during Reconstruction and afterwards, most of that movement remained within the same local area, enabling the maintenance of social networks of interdependence. When moving greater distances, many people moved in groups. See Bercaw, *Gendered Freedoms*; Edwards, *Gendered Strife and Confusion*; and Hahn, *Nation under Our Feet*.

70 In his second circular issued after being appointed commissioner of the Freedmen's Bureau, Howard informed agents that their primary job lay in making sure that Black people were put to work: "The demands for labor are sufficient to afford employment to nearly if not quite all the able-bodied refugees and freedmen," who needed to be disabused of the idea "that they can live without labor" and "the false pride which renders some of the refugees more willing to be supported in idleness than to support themselves." He further insisted, "the able-bodied should be encouraged, and if necessary, compelled to labor for their own support" ("Letter from the Secretary of War" [1866], 178).

71 Howard, *Autobiography*, 221.
72 Stanley, *From Bondage to Contract*, 37. Saidiya Hartman argues, "In this case, the family does not provide a barrier to the values of the marketplace; to the contrary, the domestic is valued because it is essential to managing laboring families, inculcating suitable ideas of settlement and stability, and nurturing responsible and rational individuals" (*Scenes of Subjection*, 156).
73 Fisk, *Plain Counsels for Freedmen*, 47, 54.
74 Hunter, *Bound in Wedlock*, 123. Hunter further observes, "Families were not eager to discard the eclectic configurations that had sustained them for generations and continued to be of service as they put pieces of their lives together. But for employers, particularly cotton landowners, a certain kind of family form was considered most suitable for inculcating stability and encouraging profit-making. Employers used the nuclear family to whittle down labor units to their most efficient figures, married couples and children" (257). On the adjudication of marriage, legitimacy, and inheritance among formerly enslaved people in the post-emancipation South, see Perrone, "Back into the Days."
75 See Bercaw, *Gendered Freedoms*; Edwards, *Gendered Strife and Confusion*; Famer-Kaiser, *Freedwomen and the Freedmen's Bureau*; Hunter, *Bound in Wedlock*; and Kandaswamy, *Domestic Contradictions*.
76 Bercaw, *Gendered Freedoms*, 120. Bercaw adds, "By 1866 labor contracts indicated that dependents were not welcome on plantations. Suddenly alternative household structures became an exception rather than the rule on plantations. Moreover, the contracts dramatically diminished independent ownership of livestock and control over garden plots" (123).
77 Penningroth, *The Claims of Kinsfolk*, 115; Famer-Kaiser, *Freedwomen and the Freedman's Bureau*, 26. Similarly, in 1863, one of the chief administrators in the War Department insisted, "My judgement is that one of the first things to be done with these people, to qualify them for citizenship, for self-protection and self-support is to impress upon them the family obligation" (Franke, *Wedlocked*, 125).
78 See Bercaw, *Gendered Freedoms*; duCille, "Blacks of the Marrying Kind"; Franke, *Wedlocked*; Hahn, *Nation under Our Feet*; Hunter, *Bound in Wedlock*; and Penningroth, *The Claims of Kinsfolk*.
79 "Letter from the Secretary of War" (1866), 93.
80 "Letter from the Secretary of War" (1866), 2–3. For very similar formulations from agents in other states, see "Letter from the Secretary of War" (1866), 59, 90.
81 "Letter from the Secretary of War" (1866), 92, 111.
82 In accounts by bureau agents, "taking up" served as a condensed way of figuring a range of relationships, such as cohabiting without sexual relations, temporary romantic connections without any intention of long-term commitment, serial monogamy due to one or both partners being

sold elsewhere, and marriage-like arrangements that had not been legally registered. For examples, see Bercaw, *Gendered Freedoms*, 164; Berlin et al., "Afro-American Families," 96–98; Fisk, *Plain Counsels for Freedmen*, 31; "Letter from the Secretary of War" (1866), 108–11, 155; "Letter of the Secretary of War" (1867), 123–24; and "Message from the President," 5. On the range of relationships among African Americans prior to and in the immediate wake of emancipation, including the variable use of terms such as "taking up" and "sweethearting," see Bercaw, *Gendered Freedoms*, 99–116; Franke, *Wedlocked*, 63–83; Hunter, *Bound in Wedlock*, 23–60, 196–232; and Perrone, "Back into the Days." Many African Americans saw the potential for legally recognized marriage as a significant mark of freedom and a vehicle for staging claims to autonomy from white control. Yet, federal laws passed during the Civil War and state laws in its wake often legalized the marriages of African Americans who would not otherwise have chosen to institutionalize those relationships, largely in an effort to provide a wide-ranging statutory fix for the problems of legally determining familial relations and inheritance given the absence of such legal concepts for the enslaved under slavery. As Katherine Franke notes, "The automaticity of the marriage laws meant that many couples found themselves legally married when they had never intended to be; many were unaware at all that they were legally wed" (*Wedlocked*, 133). For discussion of the array of statutes that shaped legal determinations of marriage, see also Hunter, *Bound in Wedlock*; Kandaswamy, *Domestic Contradictions*; and Perrone, "Back into the Days."

83 In a report from Mississippi in 1866, the agent asserts, "The State cannot and ought not to let any man lie about idle, without property, doing mischief. A vagrant law is right in principle. I cannot ask the civil officers to leave you idle, to beg or steal. If they find any of you without business and means of living, they will do right if they treat you as bad persons and take away your misused liberty" ("Message from the President," 36). Accusations of idleness, and thus potential vagrancy, were also made against Black women who were not working under contracts. See Berlin et al., "Afro-American Families," 111–13. The insistence on nuclear family homemaking for freedpeople, then, did not extend to insulating Black women from paid labor outside the home. See also Bercaw, *Gendered Freedoms*; Edwards, *Gendered Strife and Confusion*; Hartman, *Scenes of Subjection*; Hunter, *Bound in Wedlock*; and Kandaswamy, *Domestic Contradictions*.

84 Although Black men were understood in patriarchal terms as the ones with whom white landowners should negotiate for the labor of wives and children, "Vagrancy laws in some states, such as Mississippi, South Carolina, and Texas, penalized those same heads of households who 'abandon, neglect, or refuse to aid in the support of their families, and who may be complained of by their families'" (Hunter, *Bound in Wedlock*, 245). Mary Famer-Kaiser notes, "Like civil officials, the bureau regarded freedwomen

who stirred up trouble as vagrants," particularly unmarried women: "The bureau also threatened black women who gave their employers trouble or raucously refused to accept employment with prosecution as vagrants" (*Freedwomen and the Freedmen's Bureau*, 88). On white supremacist narratives of Black women as morally lax and sexually available, which justified forms of sexual assault, see Rosen, *Terror in the Heart*.

85 Edwards, *Gendered Strife and Confusion*, 55.

86 See Edwards, *Gendered Strife and Confusion*, 55; Franke, *Wedlocked*, 131–39; Hunter, *Bound in Wedlock*, 284; Perrone, "Back into the Days," 135; and Stanley, *From Bondage to Contract*, 46. Punishment for these kinds of profligacy also had consequences for political participation. If convicted of these felonies, men could be stripped of their right to vote. See Franke, *Wedlocked*, 139.

87 Moreover, while not part of the criminal law per se, statutes allowing for the "apprenticeship" of Black children (many of whom were not, in fact, any longer children) to white landowners—often their former masters—employed liberal ideologies of enfamilyment as a model against which to measure Black households. And if these households were found wanting—such as in cases where a woman or women lived without male partners or the parents were deemed immoral, vicious, or vagrant—the children could be bound out until adulthood. See Berlin et al., "Afro-American Families," 107–11; Edwards, *Gendered Strife and Confusion*, 39–59; Famer-Kaiser, *Freedwomen and the Freedman's Bureau*, 96–140; Franke, *Wedlocked*, 166–69; Hunter, *To 'Joy My Freedom*, 35–36; and "Letter from the Secretary of War" (1866), 60, 63, 94, 152, 197. Children living with single mothers were often categorized as if they were orphans. On the nexus later in the nineteenth century between charges of Black women's failure as mothers and their criminal prosecution and incarceration, see Haley, *No Mercy Here*.

88 Du Bois, *Black Reconstruction*, 71; Franke, *Repair*, 83–102; Hahn, *Nation under Our Feet*, 80–81; "Message from the President," 38–39; and Oubre, *Forty Acres and a Mule*, 17, 28, 168. For discussion of conditions in the Delta during and after the Civil War, see Bercaw, *Gendered Freedoms*; Kaye, *Joining Places*; and Woods, *Development Arrested*.

89 Sherman's later suggestion that the army might provide those families with mules is likely from where the phrase "forty acres and a mule" comes. See Foner, *Reconstruction*, 70; Howard, *Autobiography*, 191–92; and Oubre, *Forty Acres and a Mule*, 18–19, 46–71. As Karen Cook Bell observes, Sherman's actions were not largesse but were a response to the fact that he actively was under investigation by the War Department for cruelties against Black refugees who followed his troops (*Claiming Freedom*, 35–36). For discussion of patterns of collective self-organization in the area, see Bell, *Claiming Freedom*, 42; "Letter from the Secretary of War" (1866), 92; "Letter of the Secretary of War" (1867), 114. For discussion of

the legal status of land in the Sea Islands during and after the war, see also Franke, *Repair*, 19–82.

90 Famer-Kaiser, *Freedwomen and the Freedman's Bureau*, 21; Foner, *Reconstruction*, 158–59; Hahn, *Nation under Our Feet*, 129–30, 145–46; Howard, *Autobiography*, 202–3; and "Letter from the Secretary of War" (1866), 179–85.

91 In September of that year, the bureau issued orders countermanding its previous ones, instead indicating how Confederate lands were to be returned and that those formerly enslaved people living on those lands were to be removed after that year's crop was harvested. See Bell, *Claiming Freedom*, 36–44; Famer-Kaiser, *Freedwomen and the Freedman's Bureau*, 186; Foner, *Reconstruction*, 159–60; Howard, *Autobiography*, 229–44; and "Letter from the Secretary of War" (1866), 91, 193.

92 Bell, *Claiming Freedom*, 45–50; Famer-Kaiser, *Freedwomen and the Freedman's Bureau*, 68, 199; Foner, *Reconstruction*, 159–62; Hahn, *Nation under Our Feet*, 173; "Letter of the Secretary of War" (1867), 111; and "Message from the President," 22, 26, 38–39. Despite the federal commitment to affirm whites' control over their abandoned plantations, African Americans continued to circulate narratives of a coming redistribution of lands, which also led to ongoing resistance against accepting annual contracts to labor for whites on what the government had determined to be their property. See "Letter from the Secretary of War" (1866), 58, 95, 162, 198; "Letter of the Secretary of War" (1867), 50, 114; and "Message from the President," 23, 25.

As part of implementing a policy of forcing freedpeople back to the plantation through contracts backed by the threat of criminal prosecution, bureau agents repeatedly indicated the necessity of removing Black people from enclaves near cities, towns, and military depots. Numbering in the tens of thousands, they were ad hoc communities in impermanent shelters often called "free towns" or "freedman's towns." Such movements quite often involved groups that encompassed but significantly exceeded nuclear families, at times including large numbers of people who had resided with or near each other in enslavement and who had extensive and intensive social bonds that they understood as marking a kind of collective identity (they sometimes referred to themselves or were referred to by others as "families," even if they contained hundreds of people). See Bercaw, *Gendered Freedoms*, 19–21, 42; Du Bois, *Black Reconstruction*, 76; Farmer-Kaiser, *Freedwomen and the Freedman's Bureau*, 59; Foner, *Reconstruction*, 81–82; Hahn, *Nation under Our Feet*, 119; "Letter from the Secretary of War" (1866), 4, 58, 163; "Letter of the Secretary of War" (1867), 57, 100–101; "Message from the President," 4, 36; Penningroth, *The Claims of Kinsfolk*, 170; and Woods, *Development Arrested*, 7.

93 Kevin Bruyneel addresses the ways accounts of Reconstruction often leave out the matter of settlement, particularly the importance of the

availability of homesteads on public lands in the construction of whiteness and white supremacy (*Settler Memory*, 45–75). I'm also seeking to think the role of land and indigeneity in the period, but from a different angle, emphasizing the ways Black people constructed place-based networks of self-governance that can be made visible through Indigenous analytics and that, like Indigenous modes of peoplehood, were subject to state intervention in order to secure normative (white) modes of property and jurisdiction.

94 Penningroth, *The Claims of Kinsfolk*, 137.

95 "Letter from the Secretary of War" (1866), 64–65.

96 "Letter from the Secretary of War" (1866), 154; "Message from the President," 36.

97 While pursuing a policy of enforcing the need for contracts with white landholders, Howard did argue for the desirability of creating "colonies" of Black landowners under the Southern Homestead Act, although that may have been as much from an antiblack desire to segregate them as for their protection from white intervention. See Oubre, *Forty Acres and a Mule*, 91, 117.

98 Hartman, *Scenes of Subjection*, 146; Penningroth, *The Claims of Kinsfolk*, 143.

99 Bell, *Claiming Freedom*, 75–81; Franke, *Repair*, 41, 47, 53–54; Hahn, *Nation under Our Feet*, 454–59; Jones, *Labor of Love*, 49–50, 64, 81; "Letter from the Secretary of War" (1866), 5; "Letter of the Secretary of War" (1867), 57, 111; "Message from the President," 39; Oubre, *Forty Acres and a Mule*, 105, 106, 143, 167–69; Penningroth, *The Claims of Kinsfolk*, 158–60; and Purifoy, "North Carolina (Un)Incorporated," 55–58. On the operation of the Southern Homestead Act and the difficulties many African Americans had in accessing its potentials, see Edwards, "African Americans"; Oubre, *Forty Acres and a Mule*. On the continuing struggle for Black landedness in the South, see Franke, *Repair*, 133–38; Nathans, *A Mind to Stay*; Purifoy, "North Carolina (Un)Incorporated"; Stack, *Call to Home*; White, *Freedom Farmers*; and Woods, *Development Arrested*.

100 On the historical and ongoing limitations of municipalization as a strategy of Black empowerment, see Purifoy, "North Carolina (Un)Incorporated".

101 White, *Freedom Farmers*, 5, 6; Woods, *Development Arrested*, 7. On the political work of Black cooperatives, including how their formulation challenges many extant ways of thinking about the constitution and aims of Black political movements, see Hunt, *Dreaming the Present*.

102 In a summary report in 1869, Commissioner Howard noted, "The reports of murders, assaults, and outrages of every description were so numerous, and so full of horrible details, that at times one was inclined to believe the whole white population engaged in a war of extermination against the blacks" (*Autobiography*, 370). Clyde Woods observes with regard to white supremacist political violence in the 1880s, "There is no way to

estimate accurately the thousands upon thousands of African American community leaders and members who were murdered during this period," and similar statements can be made with regard to the 1860s (*Development Arrested*, 82).

103   As Nancy Bercaw argues, "Freedom, from their experience, came from building and sustaining as many connections as possible, enabling them to avoid the power of both employers and the government to regulate their actions" (*Gendered Freedoms*, 49).

104   Moynihan, *The Negro Family*, 48, vii. The report originally was issued as an intragovernmental document in March 1965, and it served as the basis for a speech by President Johnson in June, was leaked to reporters in July, and was published for a general audience that August. On Moynihan's background, the lead-up to the report, and debates over the report in the 1960s, including its citation as calling for the need for concerted national action to redress structural racism, see Coates, "The Black Family"; Geary, *Beyond Civil Rights*; and Greenbaum, *Blaming the Poor*. On the intellectual precedents for Moynihan's way of figuring Black pathology, see Muhammad, *The Condemnation of Blackness*; O'Connor, *Poverty Knowledge*. On the significant effects of the report, see Ferguson, *Aberrations in Black*; Franke, *Wedlocked*; Ibrahim, *Troubling the Family*; and O'Connor, *Poverty Knowledge*.

105   On the relation between the subjugated Black body and organizations of scale, see McKittrick, *Demonic Grounds*.

106   Stack, *All Our Kin*, 28, 23, 9. For studies published around the same time that had similar findings, see Aschenbrenner, *Lifelines*; Ladner, *Tomorrow's Tomorrow*.

107   Stack, *All Our Kin*, 29–30, 43, 44.

108   Stack, *All Our Kin*, 30, 46.

109   Moynihan, *The Negro Family*, 5, vii.

110   On the ways Black freedom is figured as a running form of unpayable debt to whites/whiteness, see Hartman, *Scenes of Subjection*. On the ways such notions of debt offer a way of rethinking blackness as a resource for sociality beyond property, see Harney and Moten, *The Undercommons*; Moten, "The Subprime and the Beautiful."

111   Moynihan, *The Negro Family*, 5, 38, 30, 19, 47. On the ways poverty knowledges from the 1950s onward understood impoverishment as a function of failures and deficiencies in individuals and privatized households, including drawing on Chicago School notions of social "disorganization" as part of processes through which populations are integrated into urban life, see O'Connor, *Poverty Knowledge*.

112   The report makes such claims despite its own description of the unemployment rate for African Americans as being "at disaster levels" for over three decades and of rates of educational segregation as continuing at pre-*Brown* levels (*The Negro Family*, 20, 45).

113 On the act and the work of the committee, see Goldstein, *Poverty in Common*, 115–30; Hinton, *From the War on Poverty*, 32–39; Moynihan, *Maximum Feasible Misunderstanding*, 61–74.

114 Committee on Juvenile Delinquency and Youth Crime, *Report to the President*, 4, 6–7.

115 The narrative that failed Black enfamilyment (and accompanying patterns of licentious immorality and excessive publicness) engendered criminal tendencies and behavior gained traction as a means of addressing increased Black presence in the North amid the first wave of the Great Migration. As Khalil Gibran Muhammad has shown, at the end of the nineteenth century "the statistical rhetoric of the 'Negro criminal' became proxy for a national discourse on black inferiority," serving as an "objective" index of the ingrained incapacities of Black people in the North to participate successfully in urban and industrial modernity (*The Condemnation of Blackness*, 8). The existence of neighborhoods of densely populated and almost exclusively Black areas in cities across the North and Midwest was due to large-scale Black flight from white violence in the South. From the 1890s to the 1930s over two million African Americans left the South for cities like Chicago, New York, and Philadelphia (Gregory, "The Second Great Migration," 20–21; Massey and Denton, *American Apartheid*, 29). The exponential increase in population density within areas that already were rather cramped was a result of extensive campaigns of white terror in the places to which they had fled, including numerous mob assaults to prevent African Americans from moving beyond areas understood as segmented off for Black inhabitance. See Balto, *Occupied Territory*; Hartman, *Wayward Lives, Beautiful Experiments*.

116 Hinton, *From the War on Poverty*, 56–57. On the uprisings, see Baldwin, "Report from Occupied Territory"; Camp, *Incarcerating the Crisis*; and Countryman, *Up South*, 154–60.

117 Hinton, *From the War on Poverty*, 81, 104; Simon, *Governing through Crime*, 89–94.

118 Commission on Law Enforcement, *The Challenge of Crime*, 68, 59, 61, 63, vi, 76. The 1967 report of the Commission on Law Enforcement and Administration of Justice (better known as the Crime Commission) insists, "Warring on poverty, inadequate housing and unemployment, is warring on crime," adding that "every effort to improve life in America's 'inner cities' is an effort against crime" (Commission on Law Enforcement, 6). Although recognizing that reporting procedures affect the administrative narration of the character and scope of "crime," the report repeatedly returns to arrest statistics as if they were a somewhat reliable index of the prevalence of "crime," rather than expressive of police practice and forms of administrative record-keeping. On the conflation of arrest rates with crime, see Balto, *Occupied Territory*, 45, 145–64; Hinton, *From the War on Poverty*, 6. The report speaks of "school segregation, and the housing

segregation that underlies it," later referencing "rigid barriers of residential segregation," resulting overcrowding, and significant discrimination in employment (Commission on Law Enforcement, vi, 57, 62, 71). Even when the ongoing modes of political violence that produced geographies of containment and impoverishment are noted, they fail to mean—to shift how such neighborhoods appeared within administrative and policy visions.

119 Moynihan, *The Negro Family*, vii.

120 Boggs and Boggs, "The City," 163; Taylor, *Race for Profit*, 115. On this rhetorical pattern, see Mays, *City of Dispossessions*, 122–30. James Baldwin also offers a more oblique reference, noting, "Occupied territory is occupied territory, even though it be found in that New World which the Europeans conquered" ("Report from Occupied Territory"). On Baldwin's invocation of Native peoples and histories of settlement, see Bruyneel, *Settler Memory*, 76–110.

121 On the reservation as racialized containment, see Denetdale, *Reclaiming Diné History*; Goeman, *Mark My Words*; Ostler, *The Plains Sioux*; Piatote, "The Indian/Agent Aporia"; Rand, *Kiowa Humanity*; and Rockwell, *Indian Affairs*.

122 While the centrality of the ongoing history of housing discrimination to African American poverty and the conditions faced by urban Black neighborhoods was well-known in the 1960s, the significance of such patterns largely was ignored within federal policy in favor of the crime paradigm, which actually helped fuel further segregation. Such an awareness/analysis appears quite clear in the report by the National Advisory Commission on Civil Disorders (commonly known as the Kerner Commission) issued in 1968, which sold over two million copies when it was published (Taylor, *From #BlackLivesMatter*, 47). See National Advisory Commission, *The Kerner Report*, 13, 247, 463–77.

123 Since the early twentieth century, states and municipalities had been passing zoning laws explicitly preventing African American residence in certain areas, as well as limiting building to single-family homes (which served the same end). These maneuvers were often backed or even encouraged by federal administrations, but with the creation of the Home Owners' Loan Corporation (HOLC) and the Federal Housing Administration (FHA) in the mid-1930s, the federal government became a driver of residential segregation across the country. As Keeanga-Yamahtta Taylor observes, "developing narratives concerning perceived domestic dysfunction within Black living spaces—whether nonnormative family structures or poverty or dilapidated living structures [due to previous patterns of segregation and structural disinvestment]—cast Black dwellings as incapable of achieving the status of *home*, thus reducing them to their base *exchange value*" (*Race for Profit*, 11). Beyond severely limiting options for African American mobility through policies that coded Black

neighborhoods as inherently unstable and as unworthy of investment, the federal government compounded this institutionalized valuelessness through massive allocations for what was alternately referred to as "urban renewal" and "slum clearance." The Housing Acts of 1949 and 1954 made possible, by 1973, the destruction of 2,500 neighborhoods in 993 cities, the majority of which had significant African American populations—leading to the well-known adage "Urban Renewal Means Negro Removal" (Fullilove, *Root Shock*, 4, 20). This pattern created distance between Black and white zones of residence, pushed Black residents away from downtown areas seen as targets for investment, and, perhaps most importantly, allowed for the construction of highways that facilitated white commuters' and consumers' access to the city while fortifying the process of suburbanization. Urban renewal went hand-in-glove with the funding of the interstate system by Congress in 1956, which itself made no provisions for the relocation of those who were displaced. In addition to dispossessing millions of people and destroying vital neighborhood networks that had sustained already impoverished communities, this massive subsidization of white flight vastly increased the housing crisis that already existed in remaining Black neighborhoods, into which people were locked due to the segregationist imperatives that shaped the federally managed and incentivized matrix of home financing. On the dynamics of residential segregation and their ramifying effects, see Balto, *Occupied Territory*; Fullilove, *Root Shock*; Hunter and Robinson, *Chocolate Cities*; Lipsitz, *How Racism Takes Place*; Massey and Denton, *American Apartheid*; Mays, *City of Dispossessions*; Pattillo, *Black on the Block*; Purifoy, "North Carolina (Un)Incorporated"; Rothstein, *The Color of Law*; Shabazz, *Spatializing Blackness*; and Taylor, *Race for Profit*.

124 Rothstein, *The Color of Law*, 173. This dynamic of limited housing options was also deeply gendered, given that landlords often would refuse to rent to single mothers, pushing them toward public housing. See Levenstein, "Gendering Postwar Urban History," 340.

125 As of 1938, median African American rent in Manhattan, for example, was 50 percent higher than median rent for whites, and by the mid-1960s, the median percentage of income paid for housing in major metro areas in the United States was 25 percent higher for African Americans than whites. See Rothstein, *The Color of Law*, 174; National Advisory Commission, *The Kerner Report*, 468. Banks and landlords further pointed to the ongoing threat of "urban renewal" as a reason to avoid investments and upkeep in the buildings they owned. The scope of the infrastructural problems of buildings in urban areas can be illustrated by the fact that in 1972, the Department of Commerce estimated that the cost of rebuilding dilapidated buildings and housing stock in cities across the country would be $191 billion *per year* for at least several years (Taylor, *Race for Profit*, 58).

126 The absence of loans meant that when African Americans did purchase homes, largely in neighborhoods that were being blockbusted and were adjacent to existing Black-majority areas, they had to pay much more for those homes (both as downpayment and in terms of the home's price) and often had to do so through "contract sales," in which payments were in installments but the homeowner did not receive equity along the way—a system that also prevented further movement except by foreclosure for a missed payment. In the wake of the uprisings of 1968, Congress passed a revised Housing and Urban Development (HUD) Act, which allowed for extensive forms of what Keeanga-Yamahtta Taylor calls "predatory inclusion." See Taylor, *Race for Profit*. States and cities also overassessed the value of Black homes for property tax purposes and underassessed white ones, creating an extractive tax imbalance—one that was not challenged by the federal government despite its awareness of it and that was made possible by federally backed financing of mortgages and urban development that created and maintained separate Black spaces (Rothstein, *The Color of Law*, 171). On intermunicipal competition for resources and how it produces Black poverty, as well as directly led to the Flint water crisis, see Michigan Civil Rights Commission, "The Flint Water Crisis."

127 Hunter and Robinson, *Chocolate Cities*, xiii, 124, 178. See also Hunter et al., "Black Placemaking." On the emergence of the phrase "chocolate city" in relation to Washington, DC, and the more recent citations of diversity as part of strategies for gentrifying and whitening the city, see Summers, *Black in Place*.

128 Fullilove, *Root Shock*, 27.

129 It would be possible to read such relations of unwaged care and support as supplementing, and thus enabling the maintenance and even intensification of, dynamics of capitalist extraction. To the extent that networks of sociality help capacitate Black life in the absence of additional state resources or corporate investment, those very networks may facilitate ongoing abandonment and the privatization of the costs and needs of social reproduction. See Federici, *Patriarchy of the Wage*. Even as this dynamic may be true, I still want to hold on to the idea of such networks as having effects and organizing dynamics that exceed the ways they may take shape within modes of extractivist structural violence, as representing potentials for social organization and governance not derived from or beholden to liberal frames. On the dangers of such potentially utopian investment in social forms adopted amid systemic abjection, see Povinelli, *Economies of Abandonment*. I will return to this issue in the coda.

130 Venkatesh, *American Project*, 31–32; Williams, *Politics of Public Housing*, 47–48.

131 Naples, *Grassroots Warriors*, 11.

132 Naples, *Grassroots Warriors*, 191, 12, 21, 110, 114, 124–25.

133 Naples, *Grassroots Warriors*, 111.
134 In this vein, Naples suggests, "I identified a broad-based notion of 'doing politics' that included any struggle to gain control over definitions of self and community, to augment personal and communal empowerment, to create alternative institutions and organizational processes, and to increase the power and resources of the community workers' defined community—although not all of these practices were viewed as 'politics' in the community worker's terminology" (*Grassroots Warriors*, 180).
135 Stack, *All Our Kin*, 28.
136 Stack, *All Our Kin*, 33. Stack further observes, "I learned that poverty creates a necessity for this exchange of goods and services. The needs of families living at bare subsistence are so large compared to their average daily income that it is impossible for families to provide independently for fixed expenses and daily needs" (29).
137 Venkatesh, *American Project*, 83–84.
138 Venkatesh, *American Project*, 88.
139 Stack, *All Our Kin*, 89.
140 Williams, *Politics of Public Housing*, 46.
141 Rhoda Williams observes, "From the beginning, public housing served as a base for organizing around subsistence and poor women's issues. In Baltimore and throughout the country, public housing tenants emerged as leaders, organizers, and participants in antipoverty efforts" (*Politics of Public Housing*, 212).
142 On forms of tenant self-organization and leadership in public housing, see Ladner, *Tomorrow's Tomorrow*; Vale, *After the Projects*; Venkatesh, *American Project*; and Williams, *Politics of Public Housing*.
143 Simpson, "The Place Where," 19.
144 Hunter and Robinson, *Chocolate Cities*, 59, 88. Such a privileging of Black networks also does not efface the horrific living conditions produced by the segregationist assemblages to which Black people and neighborhoods were subject, including the prevalence of levels of insects and vermin that proved directly hazardous to the health (and even lives) of people living in dilapidated and dangerous buildings. As Keenga-Yamahtta Taylor notes, a survey on housing in Harlem in the 1960s revealed that only 17 percent of the inhabitants said they would want to stay, and a poll after the uprisings in Detroit and Newark in 1967 indicated that "84 percent of Blacks believed that the ghetto should be 'torn down'" (*Race for Profit*, 78). However, the terrible living conditions and the desire for alternatives to them does not itself mean that those living in such neighborhoods wanted to get away from their everyday interpersonal networks and modes of community formation.
145 On continuing connections to the South in the wake of the Great Migration, see Aschenbrenner, *Lifelines*; Hunter and Robinson, *Chocolate Cities*; and Stack, *Call to Home*. On the ways the North, Midwest, and West

to which African Americans moved during the Great Migration, as well as the post-emancipation history of the South, can be conceptualized as a continuation of plantation logics/political economies, see Hunter and Robinson, *Chocolate Cities*; McKittrick, "Plantation Futures"; Purifoy, "North Carolina (Un)Incorporated"; and Woods, *Development Arrested*. On understanding Black placemaking in ways that challenge the plantation as an organizing trope, see Lewis, *Violent Utopia*; Slocum, *Black Towns, Black Futures*.

146   See Daniel, *Dispossession*; Hunt, *Dreaming the Present*, 136–92; White, *Freedom Farmers*; and Woods, *Development Arrested*. On Black land loss in the South over the twentieth century due to the legal dynamics of tenancy-in-common, see Goldstein, "On the Reproduction of Race," 47–49. On the continued presence of incorporated as well as legally unacknowledged Black towns across the South from the late nineteenth century through the present, see Purifoy, "North Carolina (Un)Incorporated."

147   Mindy Fullilove observes, "At the level of the community, the loss of the collective capacity to solve problems in order to make progress became a permanently crippling one," and she adds, "for the displaced citizens, urban renewal sapped resources and depleted strength in a manner that increased the vulnerability of the uprooted not simply for a few years, but for many decades to come" (*Root Shock*, 99).

148   Such problems and failures included the absence of play areas and play equipment for children, creating immense pressures on building infrastructure; the absence of working elevators; the failure to fix heating, cooling, water, and septic malfunctions; a failure to exterminate insects and vermin; and nonperformance of basic upkeep of the buildings' physical plant.

149   Elizabeth Hinton argues, "The War on Poverty is best understood not as an effort to broadly uplift communities or as a moral crusade to transform society by combating inequality or want, but as a manifestation of fear about urban disorder and about the behavior of young people, particularly young African Americans" (*From the War on Poverty*, 32). Similarly, Daniel Geary suggests, "Johnson wanted to fight poverty, but he wanted to do it on the cheap and without alienating economic elites" (*Beyond Civil Rights*, 30).

150   Goldstein, *Poverty in Common*, 25. He later adds that through the EOA "the Johnson administration supplied local communities with administrative forms intended to secure local participation in mainstream political norms": "Community was, in this sense, a means of acquiring the skills necessary to identify and pursue collective interests and to participate in the prevailing political and economic system" (*Poverty in Common*, 160). On the EOA and the CAPs, see also Moynihan, *Maximum Feasible Misunderstanding*; Naples, *Grassroots Warriors*; and O'Connor, *Poverty Knowledge*, 124–210.

151　By the end of 1965, federal rules had changed such that organizations receiving community action funds required approval from municipal authorities, and the legislation officially was amended in 1967 to reflect this policy.

152　Naples, *Grassroots Warriors*, 2–3.

153　Naples, *Grassroots Warriors*, 146; Williams, *Politics of Public Housing*, 164, 216.

154　Office of Economic Opportunity, *Workbook*, 13, 20, 24.

155　Office of Economic Opportunity, *Workbook*, 24, 27, 59.

156　Moynihan, *Maximum Feasible Misunderstanding*, 111.

157　Moynihan, *Maximum Feasible Misunderstanding*, 136–37, 182.

158　Naples, *Grassroots Warriors*, 39. See also Levenstein, "Gendering Postwar Urban History"; Williams, *Politics of Public Housing*.

159　Hinton, *From the War on Poverty*, 98–99, 119–20.

160　First used in an article in *Time* magazine in 1977, the notion of the "underclass" gained public policy force during the Reagan era, and by the 1990s, it was normalized as a referential frame through which to describe African American neighborhoods, without appearing directly to do so. On the figure of the "underclass," see Cacho, *Social Death*; Cohen, *Democracy Remixed*; Kelley, *Yo' Mama's Disfunktional!*; Macek, *Urban Nightmares*; Massey and Denton, *American Apartheid*; O'Connor, *Poverty Knowledge*; Taylor, *Race for Profit*; and Wilson, *When Work Disappears*.

161　Garza, *The Purpose of Power*, 41; Cox, *Shapeshifters*, 17, 57. On the ways seemingly conservative notions of racial pathology and the need for state intervention often follow from equally pathologizing liberal frameworks, see Greenbaum, *Blaming the Poor*; Hinton, *From the War on Poverty*; Kelley, *Yo' Mama's Disfunktional!*; Macek, *Urban Nightmares*; Murakawa, *The First Civil Right*; and O'Connor, *Poverty Knowledge*. As Lisa Marie Cacho argues, various populations "are not merely excluded from legal protection but criminalized as always already the object and target of law" (*Social Death*, 5), and she later adds that "race and racialized spaces are the signifiers that make an unsanctioned action legible as illicit and recognizable as a crime" (38). Similarly, Angela Davis notes that "programs for decriminalization will not only have to address specific activities that have been criminalized—such as drug use and sex work—but also criminalized populations and communities" (*Are Prisons Obsolete?*, 113).

162　As indicated in the report "The Economic State of Black America in 2020," "Across the 51 metropolitan areas in the United States with at least 1 million residents, the average segregation index was at still nearly 60—where 0 represents full integration and 100 represents complete separation of racial groups" (Joint Economic Committee, 15). As Patrick Sharkey indicates, "over 70 percent of African Americans who live in today's poorest, most racially segregated neighborhoods are from the same families that lived in the ghettos of the 1970s" (*Stuck in Place*, 9).

See also Pattillo, *Black on the Block*, 327; Peterson and Krivo, *Divergent Social Worlds*, 40, 63.

Massive cuts in federal funding for cities from the 1970s onward meant that state and municipal resources increasingly were strapped. The Reagan administration significantly cut federal support for cities and for all related policy initiatives, including items like public transportation, social service block grants (also converting more federal programs into such grants, facilitating states' diversion of resources from cities), economic development assistance, public service positions, and public works as well as specifically slashing federal funds available to support both public housing and AFDC (commonly known as welfare). On cuts under the Reagan administration, see Cohen, *The Boundaries of Blackness*; Greenbaum, *Blaming the Poor*; O'Connor, *Poverty Knowledge*; Wilson, *Cities and Race*; and Wilson, *When Work Disappears*. The public housing budget went from $55.7 billion in 1980 to $15.2 billion in 1987 (Kelley, *Yo' Mama's Disfunktional!*, 94), and eligibility for AFDC was reduced by about 50 percent due to the Reagan-initiated Omnibus Budget Reconciliation Act of 1981 (Wilson, *Cities and Race*, 32). Many cities closed hospitals, eliminated fire companies, and significantly reduced public sector jobs, which had provided the bulk of gains in African American employment over the 1960s and early 1970s. See also Lipsitz, "From *Plessy* to Ferguson"; Massey and Denton, *American Apartheid*; Michigan Civil Rights Commission, "The Flint Water Crisis"; Sharkey, *Stuck in Place*; and Smith, "Giuliani Time."

163 Mass incarceration also substantially skews statistical assessments of the status of Black communities, since incarcerated people are not included in community surveys, unemployment numbers, or any of the other means of collecting general data on the US population. See Alexander, *The New Jim Crow*, 229; Gottschalk, *Caught*, 255; and Pettit, *Invisible Men*.

164 Ta-Nehisi Coates refers to the unacknowledged evidence of such extraction as "the plunder everywhere around us," and he later notes, "Black life is cheap, but in America black bodies are a natural source of incomparable value" (*Between the World*, 21, 132).

165 On the dynamics of blackness and middle-class identification in this period, see Jenkins, *Black Bourgeois*.

166 On these dynamics, see Ferguson, *One-Dimensional Queer*, 81–113; Kinney, *Beautiful Wasteland*; Pattillo, *Black on the Block*; Quizar, "Land of Opportunity"; Smith, "Giuliani Time"; Stein, *Capital City*; Summers, *Black in Place*; Vale, *After the Projects*; Wilson, *Cities and Race*; and Woods, "Les Misérables." On the global dynamics of gentrification, see Smith, "New Globalism, New Urbanism." In addition, Black communities have been targeted for predatory lending (such as subprime home loans), leading to rampant foreclosures that have only increased dynamics

of abandonment, debt extraction, housing insecurity, and the collective neighborhood instabilities they generate. As of 2008, before the crash, predatory lending practices with regard to home loans had resulted in somewhere between $164 billion and $213 billion in losses for people of color, largely African Americans (Woods, "Les Misérables," 776). During the Great Recession starting in 2008, Black homeowners were 70 percent more likely to face foreclosure than white homeowners (Joint Economic Committee, "The Economic State," 14). Much of the targeting of Black neighborhoods for subprime loans involved persuading people to refinance from fixed-rate to subprime loans or to take out new subprime home equity loans in order to increase liquidity for other expenses/debts, leading to the loss of homes where the owners could sustain the prior mortgage or already had paid it off. See also Goldstein, "Finance and Foreclosure"; Lipsitz, *How Racism Takes Place*, 9, 106–7; Moten, "The Subprime and the Beautiful"; and Rothstein, *The Color of Law*, 110–13. For the historical precursor to this dynamic in FHA/HUD practices in the late 1960s and early 1970s, see Taylor, *Race for Profit*. As indicated in the report "The Economic State of Black America in 2020," "Homes in majority-Black neighborhoods are valued at $48,000 less on average than homes in neighborhoods with few or no Black residents, even when controlling for home quality and neighborhood amenities" (Joint Economic Committee, 15). See also Lipsitz, *How Racism Takes Place*, 58; Peterson and Krivo, *Divergent Social Worlds*, 28; and Taylor, *Race for Profit*, 262. Significantly lower rates of Black homeownership as well as depressed home values in Black neighborhoods, and the generational effects of both, provide a good bit of the differential in white and Black median household wealth, with white wealth being ten times greater (Joint Economic Committee, 1).

167 For examples of the use of this formulation in contemporary discourse, see Kinney, *Beautiful Wasteland*, 138; Lipstiz, *How Racism Takes Place*, 34, 111; Quizar, "Land of Opportunity"; and Taylor, *Race for Profit*, 115.

168 Clear, *Imprisoning Communities*, 89. Loïc Wacquant offers a similar formulation—"negative symbolic value" (Wacquant, *Punishing the Poor*, 204).

169 Jordan Camp argues that the growth of mass incarceration can be understood as a counterinsurgent response to the forms of revolutionary movement, particularly led by Black people, in the 1960s and onward. See Camp, *Incarcerating the Crisis*. However, while policies in the 1970s and 1980s certainly did emerge as a reaction to forms of mass protest, this characterization of late-twentieth-century policy seems to me to underplay the continuities with earlier eras as well as the ways state modes of extraction redeploy similar premises as previous modes of antiblack extraction, such as the durability of figurations of a nexus of Black deviance-criminality. By contrast, James Forman argues that the

system of mass incarceration arose as a result of a series of incremental, contingent, and localized decisions that accrued and gained momentum, often initially supported by Black people. This analysis seems to underplay both the structural role of discourses of Black criminality in legitimizing continuing segregationist dynamics and geographies and the kinds of changes that occurred in US political economy as a function of deindustrialization, on which Camp focuses, that contribute to the rendering of Black people as a surplus population in terms of existing patterns of labor exploitation. See Forman, *Locking Up Our Own*. As Forman documents, though, the role of criminal justice policy in systemic modes of asset stripping and collective assault against African American communities does not mean that there has not been Black support for increases in policing and sentencing, although such support might be understood largely as due to the absence of other readily available public policy options for addressing questions of community safety as well as the view that additional criminal justice sanctions are a means of trying to redress the historic disregard of the police for Black well-being.

170 Africans Americans are 33 percent of the prison population while only accounting for 13 percent of the US adult population. Moreover, Black people are six times more likely to be imprisoned than whites, which is down from seven times more likely a little over a decade ago. See Carson, "Prisoners in 2018"; Joint Economic Committee, "The Economic State," 19–20. These figures, though, actually significantly understate the size of criminal justice interventions in the United States. They only cover those currently in jail or prison rather than the additional millions of people who are under some manner of state control (including parole, probation, and community sanctions), who pass through jails each year, and who already have served sentences but carry the status of convicted felon and all that it entails. See Gottschalk, *Caught*; Schenwar and Law, *Prison by Any Other Name*; and Story, *Prison Land*.

171 Taylor, *From #BlackLivesMatter*, 122. For example, as Simon Balto observes, in 2010 the Chicago Police Department had 160,000 arrests, 72 percent of which were of African Americans (Balto, *Occupied Territory*, 256). On the use of criminal justice databases, see Alexander, *The New Jim Crow*, 136; Wacquant, *Punishing the Poor*, 135–46.

172 Thomas and Jin, "U.S. Crime Rates Dropped"; U.S. Department of Justice, "State and Local Government Expenditures," 1.

173 These extraordinary increases in criminal justice investments and allocations have little statistical relationship to crime rates of any kind, never mind a proportional connection that would indicate the efficacy of such policy measures—especially given the profound damage wrought by them, particularly in Black communities. It is also important to remember that "many accounts use *arrest records* as the evidentiary index, even

while rates of actual criminalized acts remain unknown or contested" (Story, *Prison Land*, 58).

174   Ruth Wilson Gilmore observes, "as a class, convicts are deindustrialized cities' working or workless poor," and she later adds, with regard to California from 1980–1994, "with two additional recessions, employment failed to keep up with the labor force and the number of prisoners goes off the charts" (*Golden Gulag*, 7, 72). As Marie Gottschalk notes, "incarceration rates tend to increase with rising unemployment rates, regardless of whether the crime rate is rising or falling" (*Caught*, 29), and Angela Davis observes, "The massive prison-building project that began in the 1980s created the means of concentrating and managing what the capitalist system had declared to be a human surplus" (*Are Prisons Obsolete?*, 91). In this sense, unemployed African Americans in urban areas function as, in Gilmore's terms, one among a number of surpluses—including underutilized lands, speculative capital, and government administrative capacities—that were, and are, absorbed through mass incarceration.

175   Balto, *Occupied Territory*, 260–61. Even with respect to speculative private investments in state projects, such funds could have generated interest if invested in schools, parks, or other social welfare building, if governments had prioritized such spending (Gilmore, *Golden Gulag*, 126). As Brett Story notes, "The myth of the state in retreat is belied by the money alone: in the United States, state expenditures at all scales (federal, state, and local) has increased as a percentage of GDP by approximately 10 percent... since the beginning of the nation's prison-building boom in the early 1970s" (Story, *Prison Land*, 17).

176   In 2012, $235 billion dollars were spent in the United States on criminal justice institutions and agencies, and approximately 1 in 8 state employees worked in corrections (Gottschalk, *Caught*, 32). In California and New York, the Department of Corrections has become the largest state agency (Gilmore, *Golden Gulag*, 15; Story, *Prison Land*, 111). Such funds could have been committed to "non-cage-based employment" if "public sector investment [were] maximized for social goods such as schools, parks, museums, and mass transport" (Gilmore, *Golden Gulag*, 246). Conversely, the presumption of criminality means that African Americans without a conviction often are hired at lower rates than white people with one. See Pager, *Marked*.

177   This phenomenon can be illustrated by reference to "million-dollar blocks," such as Brownsville in Brooklyn, New York: the concept "refers to the spatially concentrated urban origins of the nation's 2.2 million prisoners, a disproportionate number of whom come from just a handful of neighborhoods in the country's biggest cities. In many places the concentration is so dense that states are spending in excess of a million dollars a year to incarcerate the residents of single city blocks" (Story, *Prison Land*, 5). Patterns of carceral extraction also include the seizure of funds

and property from those arrested and imprisoned, the numerous fees leveled against those in prison as well as those on probation and parole, and the costs absorbed by the families of those who are imprisoned (such as for lawyers, phone calls, and commissary goods). See Alexander, *The New Jim Crow*; Clear, *Imprisoning Communities*; Coates, "The Black Family"; Schenwar and Law, *Prison by Any Other Name*; and Story, *Prison Land*.

178 See Greenbaum, *Blaming the Poor*, 107–9; Lipsitz, "From *Plessy* to Ferguson"; Ritchie, *Invisible No More*, 10; Story, *Prison Land*, 1–4; and Woods, "Les Misérables," 790. For example, New York City generates almost $1 billion annually from "quality of life" fines, overwhelmingly lodged against people of color (Taylor, *From #BlackLivesMatter*, 129).

Governmental asset stripping also has incentivized intensifying movement of capital outside Black neighborhoods by private entities, helping propel deindustrialization and attendant massive increases in unemployment while also creating conditions that enable private lenders to continue to redline such communities (although putatively on the basis of neutral determinations of value). See Woods, "Les Misérables." William Julius Wilson notes, "From 1967 to 1987, Philadelphia lost 64 percent of its manufacturing jobs; Chicago lost 60 percent; New York City, 58 percent; Detroit, 51 percent. In absolute numbers, these percentages represent the loss of 160,000 jobs in Philadelphia, 326,000 in Chicago, 520,000—over half a million—in New York, and 108,000 in Detroit" (*When Work Disappears*, 29–30). From 1978 to 1982, one in three manufacturing jobs were eliminated (Camp, *Incarcerating the Crisis*, 104), and during the 1980s, "the country lost 16 production, transportation, and laborer jobs per thousand of working-age population" (Wilson, *When Work Disappears*, 27). By the end of the 1970s, more than 50 percent of African American manufacturing laborers had lost their positions (Camp, *Incarcerating the Crisis*, 65). However, we should be wary of overstating the accessibility of access to manufacturing positions for African Americans given extensive racism in hiring and unionization. See Camp, *Incarcerating the Crisis*; Kinney, *Beautiful Wasteland*. Even during the peak of Black employment in manufacturing in 1970, only about 12 percent of Black men were employed in such positions (Gottschalk, *Caught*, 85).

179 Stein, *Capital City*, 64. These dynamics are part of what Fred Moten has described as the "disownership" imposed on Black people within existing systems of white-dominant propertyholding ("The Subprime and the Beautiful," 241). See also Harris, "Whiteness as Property."

180 See Balto, *Occupied Territory*; Smith, "Giuliani Time"; and Story, *Prison Land*.

181 Greenbaum, *Blaming the Poor*, 100.

182 Commenting on the police murders of Black people, such as Michael Brown and Eric Garner, Fred Moten suggests that they serve as "deadly manifestations of broken-windows policing": "What they made clear, is

that we *are* the broken windows. We constitute this threat to the already existing normative order" (quoted in Story, *Prison Land*, 178).

183   Wilson, *Thinking about Crime*, 76. His article "Broken Windows" was originally co-authored with George L. Kelling Jr. and is reprinted in *Thinking about Crime*.

184   Wilson argues, "The traditional function of the police—indeed, the purpose for which they were originally created about 150 years ago—was to maintain order in urban neighborhoods," and this function "assigns them an important part to be sure, in crime control, but an even more important part in the maintenance of orderly neighborhoods" (*Thinking about Crime*, 74). On "police power" as the local right to manage order, separate from the question of the police as a particular kind of government institution or set of agents, see Wagner.

185   Wilson, *Thinking about Crime*, 78–79.

186   Wilson also invokes the Indianizing figure of "urban frontiers" (*Thinking about Crime*, 87).

187   Wilson, *Thinking about Crime*, 36.

188   The role of racialized and racializing middle-class norms in driving police activity, as Andrea Ritchie argues, can be seen in arrests and harassment for perceived "failure to meet individual police officers' subjective expectations of gender appropriate behavior[,] . . . giving rise to a minimum of intensified scrutiny that often escalates to verbal and sexual harassment, detention, and citation or arrest": "They project narratives rooted in white supremacist heteropatriarchy onto our racially gendered bodies, then act on and enforce them through surveillance and suspicion, violence and violation" (*Invisible No More*, 135). See also Ellison, "Black Femme Praxis."

189   On neighborhood effects of impoverishment and criminalization, see also Pattillo, *Black on the Block*; Peterson and Krivo, *Divergent Social Worlds*; Pettit, *Invisible Men*; Sharkey, *Stuck in Place*; and Story, *Prison Land*. On the sense of police presence in Black neighborhoods as an occupation, including when conducted under the rubric of "community policing," see Coates, *Between the World*; Goffman, *On the Run*; Khan-Cullors and Bandele, *When They Call You*; and Schenwar and Law, *Prison by Any Other Name*. This monitoring of Black personhood for signs of excessive publicness and symptoms of deviant tendencies also shapes much of the contemporary provision of social services. See Alexander, *The New Jim Crow*; Beckett and Murakawa, "Mapping the Shadow"; Bridges, *Poverty of Privacy Rights*; Cox, *Shapeshifters*; Davis, *Battered Black Women*; Goffman, *On the Run*; Kelley, *Yo' Mama's Disfunktional!*; Lash, *"When the Welfare People Come"*; Richie, *Arrested Justice*; Roberts, *Shattered Bonds*; Schwenwar and Law, *Prison by Any Other Name*; Simon, *Governing through Crime*; Threadcraft, *Intimate Justice*; Wacquant, *Punishing the Poor*; and Wilson, *Cities and Race*.

190   While Black Lives Matter refers to a specific organization with its own history and priorities, it also powerfully signifies a range of organizations and activist efforts that have emerged in the last decade and that share many of the same principles with regard to their political philosophy and goals as well as the constituencies to whom they are committed. On the history of these organizations and the Black Lives Matter movement, see Carruthers, *Unapologetic*; Garza, *The Purpose of Power*; Garza et al., "A HerStory"; Khan-Cullors and Bandele, *When They Call You*; The Movement for Black Lives, "Vision for Black Lives," https://m4bl.org/policy-platforms/; Ransby, *Making All Black Lives*; and Taylor, *From #BlackLivesMatter*.

191   Garza, *The Purpose of Power*, 120.

192   Black Lives Matter, accessed November 10, 2020, https://blacklivesmatter.com/about/.

193   Carruthers, *Unapologetic*, 10, 11. Similarly, the platform of the Movement for Black Lives "elevate[s] the experiences and leadership of the most marginalized people": "We reject false solutions and believe we can achieve a complete transformation of the current systems, which place profit over people and make it impossible to breathe." Echoing the final words of Eric Garner, who was choked to death by police in New York City in July 2014, this statement of principles extends beyond the criminal justice system per se to indict the range of institutionalized forces that constrain possibilities for Black living, instead working toward modes of "Black self-determination and community control" that do not simply replicate the false promises offered by existing systems of governance. See the "Platform" section of Movement for Black Lives, "Vision for Black Lives" For background on BYP100 and the Movement for Black Lives (or M4BL), see Ransby, *Making All Black Lives*.

194   Ransby, *Making All Black Lives*, 2–3.

195   BYP100's 2014 Statement on Radical Inclusivity indicates that the organization "does not advocate 'respectability politics,' meaning we do not look to the middle class for examples for how Black people should dress or act," further noting that their approach to organizing focuses on "supporting/creating campaigns that focus on interlocking oppressions of marginalized peoples," with the understanding that "Black families do not have to look a certain way" (Carruthers, *Unapologetic*, 12).

196   Taylor, *From #BlackLivesMatter*, 79. Such de facto acceptance of existing power dynamics regularly includes support for criminal justice institutions, despite clearly racialized patterns of state intervention, assault, and incarceration. For discussion of this dynamic, specifically with regard to protests of police murders, see Ransby, *Making All Black Lives*, 81–95. On African American support for increased criminal justice measures, see Forman, *Locking Up Our Own*.

197   Cohen, *The Boundaries of Blackness*, 19.

198   The further marginalization of those already seen as deviant and degraded due to their blackness, though, itself functions as a response to histories of devaluation and state violence, since such Black "moral panics" are "based in the knowledge that the dominant society's labeling of certain behaviors by the marginal community as deviant and threatening has historically led to the greater regulation, surveillance, and repression of that community" (Cohen, *Democracy Remixed*, 39). Candice Jenkins refers to this investment in the potentially safety-creating powers of middle-class normativities as the "salvific wish" (*Private Lives, Proper Relations*).

199   Garza, *The Purpose of Power*, 116.

200   Garza, *The Purpose of Power*, 47, 56, 136.

201   Garza, *The Purpose of Power*, 273, 274, 275.

202   Garza, *The Purpose of Power*, 220.

203   Garza, *The Purpose of Power*, 158–59.

204   Carruthers, *Unapologetic*, 7, 139.

205   Carruthers, *Unapologetic*, 109, 89. Garza observes, "Organizations are a critical component of movements—they become the places where people can find community and learn about what's happening around them, why it's happening, who it benefits, and who it harms. Organizations are the places where we learn skills to take action and to organize to change the laws and change our culture" (*The Purpose of Power*, 142).

206   On the importance of kinds of Black political imagination that are not configured around permanent institutional transformation, see Hunt, *Dreaming the Present*.

207   Hunter and Robinson, *Chocolate Cities*, 178; Hunter et al., "Black Placemaking," 51.

208   As Cox argues, the young women in her study illustrate a sense of what she calls "critical entitlement," in which they explicitly recognize "the intrinsic value of all human life and the right to be protected and cared for" while also understanding the promises by social institutions to do so as actionable requirements—for example, "that schools and programs live up to their stated and official missions to provide services" for them (*Shapeshifters*, 67, 75).

209   Cox, *Shapeshifters*, 8, 30. The strong resonance between Cox's analysis of contemporary African American girls and that of Joyce A. Ladner in *Tomorrow's Tomorrow* (published in 1971) indicates the long-term persistence of the patterns Cox addresses. On the ways making Black men's experience of the criminal justice system paradigmatic effaces the role of the police in the lives of Black women, girls, and femmes as well as helping license the erasure of violence against them within Black communities, see also Davis, *Battered Black Women*; Harris-Perry, *Sister Citizen*; Richie, *Arrested Justice*; and Ritchie, *Invisible No More*.

210 In offering this narrative of vernacular Black governance as separate from institutions of the state and formal activist and mutual aid organizations, I'm trying to walk three lines simultaneously: between an engagement with care and a gendered presumption of its contours; between the presumed boundaries of intimate life and enforced publicness; and between a rejection of narratives of collective damage and a de facto celebration of conditions of structural abjection. As María Puig de la Bellacasa suggests, care can be thought of as the "concrete work of maintenance, with ethical and affective implications, and as a vital politics in interdependent worlds," and she later suggests, "Thinking of practices of everyday care as a necessary activity to the maintenance of every world makes them a collective affair," a set of interdependencies that generate "specific relational arrangements of caring" (*Matters of Care*, 5, 160, 61). I am attempting to think about such expansive networks, projects, processes, and principles of care, refusing to reduce them to a matter of individuated households and understanding them as constituting a sense of collectivity—albeit with porous, relationally constituted boundaries (as opposed to the reified borders of state jurisdictional grids). However, I am also mindful of the presumption that such care should fall to women, girls, and femmes: they often are subject to social sanction for failing to provide the kinds of care that is presumed to be their responsibility. Part of the impetus for my description of such networks as governance is to ungender such responsibility. I'm also trying to push against liberal notions of the presumed coherence and privatized insulation of the intimate sphere, but in doing so, I'm aware of the difficulties faced by Black people, particularly Black women, in withdrawing from intrusive, and potentially abusive, forms of publicness—in having spaces of autonomy. See Bridges, *Poverty of Privacy Rights*; Quashie, *The Sovereignty of Quiet*; Richie, *Arrested Justice*; and Threadcraft, *Intimate Justice*. Candace Jenkins argues that "the gendered opposition of racial politics and intimacy constitutes a major oversight in contemporary understandings of African American sociopolitical subjectivity, that in fact the 'political' and the 'intimate' may be mutually constitutive signs for the black subject" (*Private Lives, Proper Relations*, 33). In many ways, I seek to build on this insight, foregrounding how the spaces, relations, and affects taken to be part of "the intimate" are part of networks of interdependence that have their own organization and, thus, productively can be named as governance. While I do not have the space to do so here, exploring Kevin Quashie's analysis of "surrender" and "vulnerability" as modalities of Black collectivity might be helpful in further reformulating notions of publicness. See Quashie, *The Sovereignty of Quiet*.

211 Carruthers, *Unapologetic*, 108, 109, 91.

212 See Harjo, *Spiral to the Stars*.

213   Carruthers, *Unapologetic*, 46, 53. I would include projects of mutual aid that are not formally institutionalized within this description. On mutual aid, although formulated largely in terms of organizations, see Spade, *Mutual Aid*. I also would include, as discussed earlier, dynamics that often are narrated as part of an "informal," "alternative," or "underground" economy. For discussion of contemporary patterns of negotiation over resource distribution and placemaking in poor Black urban communities, see Venkatesh, *Off the Books*.

214   On the attempted strangulation of Indigenous political orders, see Simpson, *Mohawk Interruptus*.

215   Garza, *The Purpose of Power*, 229.

216   Garza, *The Purpose of Power*, 56, 254, 229.

217   See the "Platform" section in Movement for Black Lives, "Vision for Black Lives."

218   See the sections "End the War on Black People," "Economic Justice," and "Community Control" in Movement for Black Lives, "Vision for Black Lives."

219   Carruthers, *Unapologetic*, 46; Garza, *The Purpose of Power*, 90.

220   Cohen, *Democracy Remixed*, 53, 54. The norms that Cohen discusses have been characterized by Ta-Nehisi Coates as "the Dream," the impossible notion of Black access to supposed American ideals. See Coates, *Between the World*.

221   Garza, *The Purpose of Power*, 172.

222   Purifoy, "North Carolina (Un)Incorporated," 165, 168.

223   Simpson, *As We Have Always Done*, 23.

Coda: Inside/Outside State Forms

1   In the US code, Indian Country is defined as follows: "(a) all land within the limits of any Indian reservation under the jurisdiction of the United States Government, notwithstanding the issuance of any patent, and, including rights-of-way running through the reservation, (b) all dependent Indian communities within the borders of the United States whether within the original or subsequently acquired territory thereof, and whether within or without the limits of a state, and (c) all Indian allotments, the Indian titles to which have not been extinguished, including rights-of-way running through the same." "Indian Country Defined," 18 U.S. Code § 1151 (1948), https://www.law.cornell.edu/uscode/text/18/1151.

2   *Oklahoma v. Castro-Huerta*, 142 S. Ct. 2486 (2022), 8–9, 11.

3   See Deer and Richland, *Introduction to Tribal Legal Studies*; Duthu, *American Indians and the Law*; and Wilkins and Lomawaima, *Uneven Ground*.

4   In *Oklahoma v. Castro-Huerta*, that assertion is tied to a nebulous statement in an obscure case from 1962, *Organized Village of Kake v. Egan*, which the opinion references twice (*Oklahoma v. Castro-Huerta*, 12, 33).
5   *Oklahoma v. Castro-Huerta*, 8
6   *Oklahoma v. Castro-Huerta*, 35. This claim is itself utterly incoherent, given that the decision discusses the area in question as Indian Country, which only would be the case if the treaties that defined that area as Creek land were still in effect. The Five Tribes refers to those peoples who had been removed from the US Southeast in the 1830s—the Cherokees, Creeks, Choctaws, Chickasaws, and Seminoles—who historically were known as the "Five Civilized Tribes." On the treaties of 1866, see Burton, *Indian Territory*; Byrd, *The Transit of Empire*, 117–46; Chang, *Color of the Land*; Debo, *The Road to Disappearance*; Roberts, *I've Been Here*; and Saunt, *Black, White, and Indian*.
7   For examples of critique of the pursuit of state recognition by Indigenous peoples, see Barker, *Native Acts*; Coulthard, *Red Skin, White Masks*; Goeman, *Mark My Words*; Million, *Therapeutic Nations*; Simpson, *Mohawk Interruptus*; Simpson, *As We Have Always Done*; and Yazzie, "US Imperialism."
8   *Oklahoma v. Casto-Huerta*, 9.
9   See Biolsi, "Imagined Geographies"; Mackey, *Unsettled Expectations*; and Palmer, "Rendering Settler Sovereign Landscapes."
10 *Oklahoma v. Castro-Huerta*, 25–26.
11 *Oklahoma v. Castro-Huerta*, 26.
12 *Oklahoma v. Castro-Huerta*, 10.
13 Greenwood was its own town, founded on what had been Creek land, and it was annexed to the city of Tulsa in 1910. See Lewis, *Violent Utopia*, 12–13.
14 See Chang, *Color of the Land*, 194–97; Lewis, *Violent Utopia*, 21–54; and Roberts, *I've Been Here*, 128–32.
15 See Slocum, *Black Towns, Black Futures*.
16 On the enslavement of Black people by the Five Tribes, in addition to the sources in note 6, see Miles, *Ties That Bind*; Perdue, *Slavery and the Evolution*; and Snyder, *Slavery in Indian Country*.
17 From 1890 to 1907, for example, the Black population in Indian Territory rose from 19,000 to 80,000 (Chang, *Color of the Land*, 152).
18 Lewis, *Violent Utopia*, 175, 221.
19 On shifting patterns of white supremacy in Oklahoma after statehood in 1907, see Chang, *Color of the Land*, 175–204.
20 Lewis addresses the "repeated waves of structural assault" to which Black residents of North Tulsa have been subject, indicating that in 2019 a third of the city of Tulsa's budget was dedicated to policing (*Violent Utopia*, 60).
21 See Lewis, *Violent Utopia*; Slocum, *Black Towns, Black Futures*.
22 Povinelli, *Economies of Abandonment*, 128.
23 Amin, *Disturbing Attachments*, 8, 6.

24   On the limits of the drama of exposure as a critical frame, see Sedgwick, *Touching Feeling*, 123–52.
25   Such identification might be described as *cruel optimism*. See Berlant, *Cruel Optimism*.
26   On the critical possibilities of thinking *beside*, see Sedgwick, *Touching Feeling*.
27   Muñoz, *Disidentifications*, 7, 11–12.
28   Here I'm also thinking of Critical Race Theory's engagement with the quotidian dynamics of race in ways that highlight the importance of attending to the immediate exigencies of racialized persons and communities, even if such interventions do not fit the theoretical goal of being unimplicated in violent systems. In particular, see Williams, *Alchemy of Race and Rights*.
29   The following discussion draws on Chang, *Color of the Land*; Debo, *The Road to Disappearance*; Lewis, *Violent Utopia*; Roberts, *I've Been Here*; and Saunt, *Black, White, and Indian*.
30   Citizens of the Five Nations, including those who were once enslaved, were made citizens of the United States by congressional statute in 1901 (Chang, *Color of the Land*, 160).
31   On "moves to innocence," see Tuck and Yang, "Decolonization Is Not a Metaphor."
32   See Bailey, *Butch Queens*; Belcourt, "Can the Other of Native Studies"; Byrd, "What's Normative"; Federici, *Patriarchy of the Wage*; Richardson, *Queer Limit of Black Memory*; and Richie, *Arrested Justice*.
33   Maynard and Simpson, *Rehearsals for Living*, 10, 25, 93, 94.
34   See Byrd, *The Transit of Empire*; Guidotti-Hernández, *Unspeakable Violence*; Jackson, *Creole Indigeneity*; Mays, *City of Dispossessions*; and Quizar, "Land of Opportunity."

BIBLIOGRAPHY

Adams, David Wallace. *Education for Extinction: American Indians and the Boarding School Experience, 1875–1828*. Lawrence: University Press of Kansas, 1995.

Adams, Mikaëla M. *Who Belongs? Race, Resources, and Tribal Citizenship in the Native South*. New York: Oxford University Press, 2016.

Adoptive Couple v. Baby Girl. 570 U.S. 637, 133 S. Ct. 2552 (2013).

Ahmed, Sara. *The Cultural Politics of Emotion*. New York: Routledge, 2004.

Ahmed, Sara. *Queer Phenomenology: Orientations, Objects, Others*. Durham: Duke University Press, 2006.

Aikau, Hokulani K. *A Chosen People, A Promised Land: Mormonism and Race in Hawai'i*. Minneapolis: University of Minnesota Press, 2012.

Aikau, Hokulani K., Maile Arvin, Mishuana Goeman, and Scott Morgensen. "Indigenous Feminisms Roundtable." *Frontiers: A Journal of Women's Studies* 36, no. 3 (2015): 84–106.

Alexander, Michelle. *The New Jim Crow: Mass Incarceration in the Age of Colorblindness*. New York: New Press, 2010.

Amin, Kadji. *Disturbing Attachments: Genet, Modern Pederasty, and Queer History*. Durham: Duke University Press, 2017.

Andersen, Chris. *"Métis": Race, Recognition, and the Struggle for Indigenous Peoplehood*. Vancouver: UBC Press, 2014.

Andersen, Chris. "Urban Aboriginality as Distinctive Identity, in Twelve Parts." In *Indigenous in the City: Contemporary Identities and Cultural Innovation*, edited by Evelyn Peters and Chris Andersen, 46–68. Vancouver: UBC Press, 2013.

Anderson, Gary Clayton. *The Indian Southwest, 1580–1830: Ethnogenesis and Reinvention*. Norman: University of Oklahoma Press, 1999.

Anzaldúa, Gloria. *Borderlands/La Frontera: The New Mestiza*. 2nd ed. San Francisco: Aunt Lute Books, 1999.

Arvin, Maile. *Possessing Polynesians: The Science of Settler Colonial Whiteness in Hawai'i*. Durham: Duke University Press, 2019.

Aschenbrenner, Joyce. *Lifelines: Black Families in Chicago*. Prospect Heights, IL: Waveland Press, 1975.

Bailey, Marlon. *Butch Queens Up in Pumps: Gender, Performance, and Ballroom Culture in Detroit*. Ann Arbor: University of Michigan Press, 2013.

Baker, Lee D. *Anthropology and the Racial Politics of Culture*. Durham: Duke University Press, 2010.

Baldwin, James. "A Report from Occupied Territory." *The Nation*, July 11, 1966. https://www.thenation.com/article/archive/report-occupied-territory/.

Balibar, Etienne. "Is There a 'Neo-Racism'?" In *Race, Nation, Class: Ambiguous Identities*, edited by Etienne Balibar and Immanuel Wallerstein, translated by Chris Turner, 17–28. New York: Verso, 1991.

Balto, Simon. *Occupied Territory: Policing Black Chicago from Red Summer to Black Power*. Chapel Hill: University of North Carolina Press, 2019.

Barker, Joanne. "Confluence: Water as an Analytic of Indigenous Feminisms." *American Indian Culture and Research Journal* 43, no. 3 (2019): 1–40.

Barker, Joanne. *Native Acts: Law, Recognition, and Cultural Authenticity*. Durham: Duke University Press, 2011.

Barr, Juliana. *Peace Came in the Form of a Woman: Indians and Spaniards in the Texas Borderlands*. Chapel Hill: University of North Carolina Press, 2007.

Beardall, Theresa Rocha, and Frank Edwards. "Abolition, Settler Colonialism, and the Persistent Threat of Indian Welfare." *Columbia Journal of Race and Law* 11, no. 3 (2021): 533–73.

Beckett, Katherine, and Naomi Murakawa. "Mapping the Shadow Carceral State: Toward an Institutionally Capacious Approach to Punishment." *Theoretical Criminology* 16, no. 2 (2012): 221–44.

Belcourt, Billy-Ray. "Can the Other of Native Studies Speak?" *Decolonization: Indigeneity, Education and Society*, February 1, 2016, https://decolonization.wordpress.com/2016/02/01/can-the-other-of-native-studies-speak/.

Bell, Duncan. "What Is Liberalism?" *Political Theory* 42, no. 6 (2014): 682–715.

Bell, Karen Cook. *Claiming Freedom: Race, Kinship, and Land in Nineteenth-Century Georgia*. Columbia: University of South Carolina Press, 2018.

Beltrán, Cristina. *Cruelty as Citizenship: How Migrant Suffering Sustains White Democracy*. Minneapolis: University of Minnesota Press, 2020.

Benhabib, Seyla. *The Claims of Culture: Equality and Diversity in the Global Era*. Princeton: Princeton University Press, 2002.

Benjamin, Ruha. "Black AfterLives Matter: Cultivating Kinfulness as Reproductive Justice." In *Making Kin Not Population*, edited by Adele E. Clarke and Donna Haraway, 41–66. Chicago: Prickly Paradigm Press, 2018.

Bentley, Nancy. "The Fourth Dimension: Kinlessness and African American Narrative." *Critical Inquiry* 35, no. 1 (2009): 270–92.

Bentley, Nancy. "Marriage as Treason: Polygamy, Nation, and the Novel." In *The Futures of American Studies*, edited by Robyn Wiegman and Donald E. Pease, 341–79. Durham: Duke University Press, 2002.

Ben-Zvi, Yael. "Where Did Red Go? Lewis Henry Morgan's Evolutionary Inheritance and U.S. Racial Imagination." *CR: The New Centennial Review* 7, no. 2 (2007): 201–29.

Bercaw, Nancy D. *Gendered Freedoms: Race, Rights, and the Politics of Household in the Delta, 1861–1875*. Gainesville: University Press of Florida, 2003.

Berger, Bethany R. "Indian Policy and the Imagined Indian Woman." *Kansas Journal of Law and Public Policy* 14 (2004): 103–15.

Berger, Bethany R. "In the Name of the Child: Race, Gender, and Economics in *Adoptive Couple v. Baby Girl*." *Florida Law Review* 67 (2015): 295–362.

Berger, Bethany R. "'Power over This Unfortunate Race': Race, Politics, and Indian Law in *United States v. Rogers*." *William and Mary Law Review* 45 (2004): 1957–2052.

Berger, Bethany R. *Tribal Constitutionalism: States, Tribes, and the Governance of Membership*. New York: Oxford University Press, 2010.

Berlant, Lauren. *Cruel Optimism*. Durham: Duke University Press, 2011.

Berlant, Lauren. *The Female Complaint: The Unfinished Business of Sentimentality in American Culture*. Durham: Duke University Press, 2008.

Berlant, Lauren, and Michael Warner. "Sex in Public." *Critical Inquiry* 24, no. 2 (1998): 548–66.

Berlin, Ira, Steven F. Miller, and Leslie S. Rowland. "Afro-American Families in the Transition from Slavery to Freedom." *Radical History Review* 42 (1988): 89–121.

Berman, Jacob Rama. *American Arabesque: Arabs and Islam in the Long Nineteenth Century*. New York: New York University Press, 2012.

Bey, Marquis. *Them Goon Rules: Fugitive Essays on Radical Black Feminism*. Tucson: University of Arizona Press, 2019.

Bilby, Kenneth M. *True-Born Maroons*. Gainesville: University Press of Florida, 2005.

Biolsi, Thomas. "Imagined Geographies: Sovereignty, Indigenous Space, and American Indian Struggle." *American Ethnologist* 32, no. 2 (2005): 239–59.

Biolsi, Thomas. *Organizing the Lakota: The Political Economy of the New Deal on the Pine Ridge and Rosebud Reservations*. Tucson: University of Arizona Press, 1992.

Blackhawk, Ned. *Violence over the Land: Indians and Empires in the Early American West*. Cambridge: Harvard University Press, 2006.

Blackwell, Maylei, Floridalma Boj Lopez, and Luis Urrieta Jr. "Introduction: Critical Latinx Indigeneities." *Latino Studies* 15, no. 2 (2017): 126–37.

Blumin, Stuart M. *The Emergence of the Middle Class: Social Experience in the American City, 1760–1900*. New York: Cambridge University Press, 1989.

Boggis, Terry, Debanuj Das Gupta, Joseph Nicholas DeFillipis, Lisa Duggan, Amber L. Hollibaugh, Nancy Polikoff, and Ignacio G. Rivera. "The *Beyond Same-Sex Marriage* Statement Ten Years Later." In *Queer Families and Relationships after Marriage Equality*, edited by Michael W. Yarbrough, Angela Jones, and Joseph Nicholas DeFillipis, 118–32. New York: Routledge, 2018.

Boggs, James, and Grace Lee Boggs. "The City Is the Black Man's Land." In *Pages from a Black Radical's Notebook: A James Boggs Reader*, edited by Stephen M. Ward, 162–70. Detroit: Wayne State University Press, 2011. First published 1966 in *Monthly Review*.

Bonilla, Yarimar. *Non-Sovereign Futures: French Caribbean Politics in the Wake of Disenchantment*. Chicago: University of Chicago Press, 2015.

Bowers v. Hardwick. 478 U.S. 106 (1986).

Boydston, Jeanne. *Home and Work: Housework, Wages, and the Ideology of Labor in the Early Republic*. New York: Oxford University Press, 1990.

Bradway, Teagan, and Elizabeth Freeman. "Introduction: Kincoherence/Kinaesthetics/Kinematics." In *Queer Kinship: Race, Sex, Belonging, Form*, edited by Teagan Bradway and Elizabeth Freeman, 1–24. Durham: Duke University Press, 2022.

Bradway, Teagan, and Elizabeth Freeman, eds. *Queer Kinship: Race, Sex, Belonging, Form*. Durham: Duke University Press, 2022.

Brady, Mary Pat. *Scales of Captivity: Racial Capitalism and the Latinx Child*. Durham: Duke University Press, 2022.

Brand, Dionne. *A Map to the Door of No Return: Notes to Belonging*. Toronto: Vintage Canada, 2001.

Brandzel, Amy. "Queering Citizenship? Same-Sex Marriage and the State." *GLQ* 11, no. 2 (2005): 171–204.

Bridges, Khiara M. *The Poverty of Privacy Rights*. Stanford: Stanford University Press, 2017.

Briggs, Laura. *How All Politics Became Reproductive Politics: From Welfare Reform to Foreclosure to Trump*. Oakland: University of California Press, 2017.

Briggs, Laura. *Taking Children: A History of American Terror*. Oakland: University of California Press, 2020.

Brooks, James F. *Captives and Cousins: Slavery, Kinship, and Community in the Southwest Borderlands*. Chapel Hill: University of North Carolina Press, 2002.

Brooks, Lisa. *Our Beloved Kin: A New History of King Philip's War*. New Haven: Yale University Press, 2018.

Brown, Elsa Barkley. "Negotiating and Transforming the Public Sphere: African American Political Life in the Transition from Slavery to Freedom." *Public Culture* 7, no. 1 (1994): 107–46.

Brown, Michael K. "Ghettos, Fiscal Federalism, and Welfare Reform." In *Race and the Politics of Welfare Reform*, edited by Sanford F. Schram, Joe Soss, and Richard C. Fording, 47–71. Ann Arbor: University of Michigan Press, 2003.

Brown v. Buhman. 947 F.2d 1170 (10th Cir. 2013).

Brownwell, Margo S. "Who Is an Indian? Searching for an Answer to the Question at the Core of Federal Indian Law." *University of Michigan Journal of Law Reform* 34 (2000–2001): 275–320.

Bruyneel, Kevin. *Settler Memory: The Disavowal of Indigeneity and the Politics of Race in the United States*. Chapel Hill: University of North Carolina Press, 2021.

Bruyneel, Kevin. *The Third Space of Sovereignty: The Postcolonial Politics of U.S.-Indigenous Relations*. Minneapolis: University of Minnesota Press, 2007.

Buck v. Bell, 274 U.S. 200 (1927).

Burton, Jeffrey. *Indian Territory and the United States, 1866–1906*. Norman: University of Oklahoma Press, 1995.

Butler, Judith. *Antigone's Claim: Kinship between Life and Death*. New York: Columbia University Press, 2000.

Byrd, Jodi. "*Loving* Unbecoming: The Queer Politics of the Transition Narrative." In *Critically Sovereign: Indigenous Gender, Sexuality, and Feminist Studies*, edited by Joanne Barker, 207–28. Durham: Duke University Press, 2017.

Byrd, Jodi. "To Hear the Call and Respond: Grounded Relationalities and the Spaces of Emergence." *American Quarterly* 71, no. 2 (2019): 337–42.

Byrd, Jodi. *The Transit of Empire: Indigenous Critiques of Colonialism*. Minneapolis: University of Minnesota Press, 2011.

Byrd, Jodi. "Weather with You: Settler Colonialism, Antiblackness, and the Grounded Relationalities of Resistance." *Critical Ethnic Studies* 5, no. 1–2 (2019): 207–14.

Byrd, Jodi. "What's Normative Got to Do With It? Toward Indigenous Queer Relationality." *Social Text* 38, no. 4 (2020): 105–23.

Byrd, Jodi, Alyosha Goldstein, Jodi Melamed, and Chandan Reddy. "Predatory Value: Economies of Dispossession and Disturbed Relationalities." *Social Text* 26, no. 2 (2018): 1–18.

Cacho, Lisa Marie. *Social Death: Racialized Rightlessness and the Criminalization of the Unprotected*. New York: New York University Press, 2012.

Calhoun, Cheshire. "Who's Afraid of Polygamous Marriage? Lessons for Same-Sex Marriage Advocacy from the History of Polygamy." *San Diego Law Review* 42 (2005): 1023–42.

Camp, Jordan T. *Incarcerating the Crisis: Freedom Struggles and the Rise of the Neoliberal State*. Oakland: University of California Press, 2016.

Canaday, Margot. *The Straight State: Sexuality and Citizenship in Twentieth-Century America*. Princeton: Princeton University Press, 2009.

Cannon, Martin J. *Men, Masculinity, and the Indian Act*. Vancouver: UBC Press, 2019.

Carby, Hazel. *Reconstructing Womanhood: The Emergence of the Afro-American Woman Novelist*. New York: Oxford University Press, 1987.

Carroll, Clint. *Roots of Our Renewal: Ethnobotany and Cherokee Environmental Governance*. Minneapolis: University of Minnesota Press, 2015.

Carruthers, Charlene A. *Unapologetic: A Black, Queer, and Feminist Mandate for Radical Movements*. Boston: Beacon Press, 2018.

Carson, E. Ann. "Prisoners in 2018." Washington, DC: Bureau of Justice Statistics, U.S. Department of Justice, 2020. https://bjs.ojp.gov/library/publications/prisoners-2018.

Carsten, Janet. *After Kinship*. New York: Cambridge University Press, 2004.

Carter, Julian B. *The Heart of Whiteness: Normal Sexuality and Race in America, 1880–1940*. Durham: Duke University Press, 2007.

Castile, George Pierre. *To Show Heart: Native American Self-Determination and Federal Indian Policy, 1960–1975*. Tucson: University of Arizona Press, 1998.

Cattelino, Jessica. *High Stakes: Florida Seminole Gaming and Sovereignty*. Durham: Duke University Press, 2008.

Cervenak, Sarah Jane. *Wandering: Philosophical Performances of Racial and Sexual Freedom*. Durham: Duke University Press, 2014.

Chakrabarty, Dipesh. *Provincializing Europe: Postcolonial Thought and Historical Difference*. Princeton: Princeton University Press, 2000.

Chamberlin, Christopher. "Akinship." In *Queer Kinship: Race, Sex, Belonging, Form*, edited by Teagan Bradway and Elizabeth Freeman, 203–26. Durham: Duke University Press, 2022.

Chambers, Clare. *Against Marriage: An Egalitarian Defence of the Marriage-Free State*. New York: Oxford University Press, 2017.

Chambers-Letson, Joshua. *After the Party: A Manifesto for Queer of Color Life*. New York: New York University Press, 2018.

Chang, David A. *The Color of the Land: Race, Nation, and the Politics of Land Ownership in Oklahoma, 1832–1929*. Chapel Hill: University of North Carolina Press, 2010.

Chang, David A. *The World and All the Things upon It: Native Hawaiian Geographies of Exploration*. Minneapolis: University of Minnesota Press, 2016.

Chauncey, George. *Why Marriage? The History Shaping Today's Debate over Gay Equality*. 2nd ed. Basic Books: New York, 2005.

Cherokee Nation v. Georgia. 30 U.S. 1 (1831).

Cheyfitz, Eric. "The (Post)Colonial Construction of Indian Country: U.S. American Indian Literatures and Federal Indian Law." In *The Columbia Guide to American Indian Literatures of the United States since 1945*, edited by Eric Cheyfitz, 1–124. New York: Columbia University Press, 2006.

Chow, Rey. *The Protestant Ethnic and the Spirit of Capitalism*. New York: Columbia University Press, 2002.

Clarke, Adele E. "Introducing *Making Kin Not Population*." In *Making Kin Not Population*, edited by Adele E. Clarke and Donna Haraway, 1–40. Chicago: Prickly Paradigm Press, 2018.

Clear, Todd R. *Imprisoning Communities: How Mass Incarceration Makes Disadvantaged Neighborhoods Worse*. New York: Oxford University Press, 2007.

Cleveland v. United States, 329 U.S. 14 (1946).

Coates, Ta-Nehisi. *Between the World and Me*. New York: Spiegel and Grau, 2015.

Coates, Ta-Nehisi. "The Black Family in the Age of Mass Incarceration." *Atlantic*, October 2015, https://www.theatlantic.com/magazine/archive/2015/10/the-black-family-in-the-age-of-mass-incarceration/403246/.

Coffey, Wallace, and Rebecca Tsosie. "Rethinking the Tribal Sovereignty Doctrine: Cultural Sovereignty and the Collective Future of Indian Nations." *Stanford Law and Policy Review* 12 (2001): 191–210.

Cohen, Cathy J. *The Boundaries of Blackness: AIDS and the Breakdown of Black Politics*. Chicago: University of Chicago Press, 1999.

Cohen, Cathy J. *Democracy Remixed: Black Youth and the Future of American Politics*. New York: Oxford University Press, 2010.

Cohen, Cathy J. "Deviance as Resistance: A New Research Agenda for the Study of Black Politics." *Du Bois Review* 1, no. 1 (2004): 27–45.

Cohen, Cathy J. "Punks, Bulldaggers, and Welfare Queens: The Radical Potential of Queer Politics?" *GLQ* 3, no. 4 (1997): 437–65.

Cohen, Ed. *A Body Worth Defending: Immunity, Biopolitics, and the Apotheosis of the Modern Body*. Durham: Duke University Press, 2009.

Cohen, Felix S. *On the Drafting of Tribal Constitutions*. Vol. 1, American Indian Law and Policy Series. Edited by David E. Wilkins. Norman: University of Oklahoma Press, 2006.

Commission on Law Enforcement and Administration of Justice. *The Challenge of Crime in a Free Society*. Washington, DC: Government Printing Office, 1967.

Committee on Juvenile Delinquency and Youth Crime. *Report to the President*. Washington, DC: Government Printing Office, 1962.

Coontz, Stephanie. *The Social Origins of Private Life: A History of American Families 1600–1900*. New York: Verso, 1988.

Coontz, Stephanie. *The Way We Never Were: American Families and the Nostalgia Trap*. Rev. ed. New York: Basic Books, 2016.

Cordis, Shanya. "Settler Unfreedoms." *American Indian Culture and Research Journal* 43, no. 2 (2019): 9–23.

Cotera, María Eugenia. *Native Speakers: Ella Deloria, Zora Neale Hurston, Jovita González, and the Poetics of Culture*. Austin: University of Texas Press, 2008.

Cott, Nancy F. *Public Vows: A History of Marriage and the Nation*. Cambridge: Harvard University Press, 2000.

Coulthard, Glen Sean. *Red Skin, White Masks: Rejecting the Colonial Politics of Recognition*. Minneapolis: University of Minnesota Press, 2014.

Countryman, Matthew J. *Up South: Civil Rights and Black Power in Philadelphia*. Philadelphia: University of Pennsylvania Press, 2006.

Coviello, Peter. *Intimacy in America: Dreams of Affiliation in Antebellum Literature*. Minneapolis: University of Minnesota Press, 2005.

Coviello, Peter. *Make Yourselves Gods: Mormons and the Unfinished Business of American Secularism*. Chicago: University of Chicago Press, 2019.

Cox, Aimee Meredith. *Shapeshifters: Black Girls and the Choreography of Citizenship*. Durham: Duke University Press, 2015.

Cross, Terry L., and Robert J. Miller. "The Indian Child Welfare Act of 1978 and Its Impact on Tribal Sovereignty and Governance." In *Facing the Future: The Indian Child Welfare Act at 30*, edited by Matthew L. M. Fletcher, Wenone T. Singel, and Kathryn E. Fort, 13–28. East Lansing: Michigan State University, 2008.

Curley, Andrew, Pallavi Gupta, Lara Lookabaugh, Christopher Neubert, and Sara Smith. "Decolonisation Is a Political Project: Overcoming Impasses between Indigenous Sovereignty and Abolition." *Antipode* 54, no. 4 (2022): 1043–62.

Curry, Lucy A. "A Closer Look at *Santa Clara Pueblo v. Martinez*: Membership by Sex, by Race, and by Tribal Tradition." *Wisconsin Women's Law Journal* 16 (2001): 161–214.

Dandridge v. Williams, 397 U.S. 471 (1970).

Daniel, Pete. *Dispossession: Discrimination against African American Farmers in the Age of Civil Rights*. Chapel Hill: University of North Carolina Press, 2013.

Danziger, Edmund Jefferson, Jr. *Survival and Regeneration: Detroit's American Indian Community*. Detroit: Wayne State University Press, 1991.

Das Gupta, Monisha. *Unruly Immigrants: Rights, Activism, and Transnational South Asian Politics in the United States*. Durham: Duke University Press, 2006.

Davis, Adrienne D. "Regulating Polygamy: Intimacy, Default Rules, and Bargaining for Equality." *Columbia Law Review* 110 (2010): 1955–2046.

Davis, Angela Y. *Are Prisons Obsolete?* New York: Seven Stories Press, 2003.

Davis, Dána-Ain. *Battered Black Women and Welfare Reform: Between a Rock and a Hard Place*. Albany: State University of New York Press, 2006.

Davis v. Beason, 133 U.S. 333 (1890).

Day, Iyko. *Alien Capital: Asian Racialization and the Logic of Settler Colonial Capitalism*. Durham: Duke University Press, 2016.

Dayan, Colin. *The Law Is a White Dog: How Legal Rituals Make and Unmake Persons*. Princeton: Princeton University Press, 2011.

Debo, Angie. *The Road to Disappearance: A History of the Creek Indians*. Norman: University of Oklahoma Press, 1941.

Deer, Sarah. "Native People and Violent Crime: Gendered Violence and Tribal Jurisdiction." *Du Bois Review* 15, no. 1 (2018): 89–106.

Deer, Sarah, and Justin Richland. *Introduction to Tribal Legal Studies*. New York: Rowman and Littlefield, 2015.

DeFilippis, Joseph Nicholas. "Introduction." In *Queer Activism after Marriage Equality*, edited by Joseph Nicholas DeFilippis, Michael W. Yarbrough, and Angela Jones, 1–13. New York: Routledge, 2018.

Delano, Sterling F. *Brook Farm: The Dark Side of Utopia*. Cambridge: Harvard University Press, 2004.

Deloria, Ella. *Speaking of Indians*. Lincoln: University of Nebraska Press, 1998. First published 1944.

Deloria, Philip J. *Indians in Unexpected Places*. Lawrence: University of Kansas Press, 2004.

Deloria, Philip J. *Playing Indian*. New Haven: Yale University Press, 1998.

Deloria, Vine, Jr., and Clifford M. Lytle. *The Nations Within: The Past and Future of American Indian Sovereignty*. Austin: University of Texas Press, 1984.

DeMallie, Raymond J. "Kinship and Biology in Sioux Culture." In *North American Indian Anthropology: Essays on Society and Culture*, edited by Raymond J. DeMallie and Alfonso Ortiz, 125–46. Norman: University of Oklahoma Press, 1994.

D'Emilio, John, and Estelle B. Freedman. *Intimate Matters: A History of Sexuality in America*. 2nd ed. Chicago: University of Chicago Press, 1997.

Denetdale, Jennifer Nez. "Chairmen, Presidents, and Princesses: The Navajo Nation, Gender, and the Politics of Tradition." *Wicazo Sa Review* 21, no. 1 (2006): 9–28.

Denetdale, Jennifer Nez. *Reclaiming Diné History: The Legacies of Navajo Chief Manuelito and Juanita*. Tucson: University of Arizona Press, 2007.

Denetdale, Jennifer Nez. "Return to 'The Uprising at Beautiful Mountain in 1913': Marriage and Sexuality in the Making of the Modern Navajo Nation." In *Critically Sovereign: Indigenous Gender, Sexuality, and Feminist Studies*, edited by Joanne Barker, 69–98. Durham: Duke University Press, 2017.

Denial, Catherine J. *Making Marriage: Husbands, Wives, and the American State in Dakota and Ojibwe Country*. Minneapolis: Minnesota Historical Society, 2013.

Denike, Margaret. "The Racialization of White Man's Polygamy." *Hypatia* 25, no. 4 (2010): 852–74.

Dennison, Jean. *Colonial Entanglement: Constituting a Twenty-First Century Osage Nation*. Chapel Hill: University of North Carolina Press, 2012.

Den Otter, Ronald C. *In Defense of Plural Marriage*. New York: Cambridge University Press, 2015.

Den Ouden, Amy E., and Jean O'Brien, eds. *Recognition, Sovereignty Struggles, and Indigenous Rights in the United States: A Sourcebook*. Chapel Hill: University of North Carolina Press, 2013.

Dhillon, Jaskiran. *Prairie Rising: Indigenous Youth, Decolonization, and the Politics of Intervention*. Toronto: University of Toronto Press, 2017.

Dillon, Elizabeth Maddock. *The Gender of Freedom: Fictions of Liberalism and the Literary Public Sphere*. Stanford: Stanford University Press, 2004.

Dillon, Stephen. *Fugitive Life: The Queer Politics of the Prison State*. Durham: Duke University Press, 2018.

Doerfler, Jill. *Those Who Belong: Identity, Family, Blood, and Citizenship among the White Earth Anishinaabeg*. East Lansing: Michigan State University Press, 2015.

Doxtator, Deborah. "What Happened to the Iroquois Clans? A Study of Clans in Three Nineteenth Century Rotinonhysonni Communities." PhD diss., University of Western Ontario, 1996.

Dred Scott v. Sandford. 60 U.S. 393 (1857).

Duarte, Marisa Elena. *Network Sovereignty: Building the Internet across Indian Country*. Seattle: University of Washington Press, 2017.

Du Bois, W. E. B. *Black Reconstruction in America, 1860–1880*. New York: Simon Schuster, 1992. First published 1935 by Harcourt, Brace, and Howe.

duCille, Ann. "Blacks of the Marrying Kind: Marriage Rites and the Right to Marry in the Tie of Slavery." *Differences* 29, no. 2 (2018): 21–67.

duCille, Ann. *The Coupling Convention: Sex, Text, and Tradition in Black Women's Fiction*. New York: Oxford University Press, 1993.

Duggan, Lisa. *The Twilight of Equality? Neoliberalism, Cultural Politics, and the Attack on Democracy*. Boston: Beacon Press, 2004.

Duthu, N. Bruce. *American Indians and the Law*. New York: Penguin Books, 2009.

Duthu, N. Bruce. *Shadow Nations: Tribal Sovereignty and the Limits of Legal Pluralism*. New York: Oxford University Press, 2013.

Edwards, Brent. *The Practice of Diaspora: Literature, Translation, and the Rise of Black Internationalism*. Cambridge: Harvard University Press, 2003.

Edwards, Erica R. *Charisma and the Fictions of Black Leadership*. Minneapolis: University of Minnesota Press, 2012.

Edwards, Laura F. *Gendered Strife and Confusion: The Political Culture of Reconstruction*. Urbana: University of Illinois Press, 1997.

Edwards, Richard. "African Americans and the Southern Homestead Act." *Great Plains Quarterly* 39, no. 2 (2019): 103–29.

Eisenstadt v. Baird, 405 U.S. 438 (1972).

Ellis, Nadia. *Territories of the Soul: Queered Belonging in the Black Diaspora*. Durham: Duke University Press, 2015.

Ellison, Treva. "Black Femme Praxis and the Promise of Black Gender." *Black Scholar* 49, no. 1 (2019): 6–16.

Ellison, Treva. "The Strangeness of Progress and the Uncertainty of Blackness." In *No Tea, No Shade: New Writings in Black Queer Studies*, edited by E. Patrick Johnson, 323–45. Durham: Duke University Press, 2016.

Eng, David L. *The Feeling of Kinship: Queer Liberalism and the Racialization of Intimacy*. Durham: Duke University Press, 2010.

Eng, David L., and Jasbir K. Puar. "Introduction: Left of Queer." *Social Text* 145 (2020): 1–24.

Engle, Karen. *The Elusive Promise of Indigenous Development: Rights, Culture, Strategy*. Durham: Duke University Press, 2010.

Ertman, Martha M. "Race Treason: The Untold Story of America's Ban on Polygamy." *Columbia Journal of Gender and Law* 19 (2010): 287–366.

Escobar, Arturo. *Territories of Difference: Place, Movements, Life, Redes*. Durham: Duke University Press, 2008.

Estes, Nick. *Our History Is Our Future: Standing Rock versus the Dakota Access Pipeline and the Long Tradition of Indigenous Resistance*. New York: Verso, 2019.

Fabian, Johannes. *Time and the Other: How Anthropology Makes Its Object* (1983). New York: Columbia University Press, 2002. First published 1983 by Columbia University Press.

Famer-Kaiser, Mary. *Freedwomen and the Freedmen's Bureau: Race, Gender, and Public Policy in the Age of Emancipation*. New York: Fordham University Press, 2010.

Faucon, Casey E. "Polygamy after *Windsor*: What's Religion Got to Do with It?" *Harvard Law and Policy Review* 9 (2015): 471–528.

Federici, Silvia. *Patriarchy of the Wage: Notes on Marx, Gender, and Feminism*. Oakland, CA: PM Press, 2021.

Feinberg, Richard. "Introduction: Schneider's Cultural Analysis of Kinship and Its Implications for Anthropological Relativism." In *The Cultural Analysis of Kinship: The Legacy of David M. Schneider*, edited by Richard Feinberg and Martin Ottenheimer, 1–32. Urbana: University of Illinois Press, 2001.

Ferguson, Roderick A. *Aberrations in Black: Toward a Queer of Color Critique*. Minneapolis: University of Minnesota Press, 2004.

Ferguson, Roderick A. *One-Dimensional Queer*. Medford, MA: Polity Press, 2019.

Ferguson, Roderick A. *The Reorder of Things: The University and Its Pedagogies of Minority Difference*. Minneapolis: University of Minnesota Press, 2012.

Field, Les W. (with the Muwekema Ohlone Tribe). "Unacknowledged Tribes, Dangerous Knowledge: The Muwekema Ohlone and How Indian Identities Are 'Known.'" *Wicazo Sa Review* 18, no. 2 (2003): 79–94.

Fielder, Brigitte. *Relative Races: Genealogies of Interracial Kinship in Nineteenth-Century America*. Durham: Duke University Press, 2020.

Finger, John R. *Cherokee Americans: The Eastern Band of Cherokees in the Twentieth Century*. Lincoln: University of Nebraska Press, 1991.

Fisk, Clinton B. *Plain Counsels for Freedmen: In Sixteen Brief Lectures*. Boston: American Tract Society, 1866.

Fixico, Donald L. *Termination and Relocation: Federal Indian Policy, 1945–1960*. Albuquerque: University of New Mexico Press, 1986.

Fixico, Donald L. *The Urban Indian Experience in America*. Albuquerque: University of New Mexico Press, 2000.

Fletcher, Matthew L. M. "ICWA and the Commerce Clause." In *Facing the Future: The Indian Child Welfare Act at 30*, edited by Matthew L. M. Fletcher, Wenone T. Singel, and Kathryn E. Fort, 28–49. East Lansing: Michigan State University, 2008.

Foner, Eric. *Reconstruction: America's Unfinished Revolution, 1863–1877*. Rev. ed. New York: Harper Perennial, 2014.

Fording, Richard C. "'Laboratories of Democracy' or Symbolic Politics? The Racial Origins of Welfare Reform." In *Race and the Politics of Welfare Reform*, edited by Sanford F. Schram, Joe Soss, and Richard C. Fording, 72–97. Ann Arbor: University of Michigan Press, 2003.

Forman, James, Jr. *Locking Up Our Own: Crime and Punishment in Black America*. New York: Farrar, Straus, and Giroux, 2017.

Forrester, Katrina. *In the Shadow of Justice: Postwar Liberalism and the Remaking of Political Philosophy*. Princeton: Princeton University Press, 2019.

Fortes, Meyer. *Kinship and the Social Order: The Legacy of Lewis Henry Morgan* (1969). New Brunswick: Aldine Transaction Publishers, 2006. First published 1969 by Aldine.

Foucault, Michel. "Governmentality." In *Power: Essential Works of Foucault, 1954–1984*, vol. 3, *Power*, edited by James D. Faubion, translated by Robert Hurley et al., 201–22. New York: New Press, 2000.

Foucault, Michel. *The History of Sexuality*. Vol. I, *An Introduction*. Translated by Robert Hurley. New York: Vintage Books, 1990. First published 1976 by Allen Lane.

Foucault, Michel. *"Society Must Be Defended": Lectures at the Collège de France 1975–1976*. Translated by David Macey. New York: Picador, 2003.

Frank, Nathaniel. *Awakening: How Gays and Lesbians Brought Marriage Equality to America*. Cambridge: Harvard University Press, 2017.

Franke, Katherine. *Repair: Redeeming the Promise of Abolition*. Rev. ed. Chicago: Haymarket Books, 2022.

Franke, Katherine. *Wedlocked: The Perils of Marriage Equality*. New York: New York University Press, 2015.

Franklin, Sarah. *Biological Relatives: IVF, Stem Cells, and the Future of Kinship*. Durham: Duke University Press, 2013.

Franklin, Sarah, and Susan McKinnon. "Introduction." In *Relative Values: Reconfiguring Kinship Studies*, edited by Sarah Franklin and Susan McKinnon, 1–28. Durham: Duke University Press, 2001.

Freeburg, Christopher. *Counterlife: Slavery after Resistance and Social Death.* Durham: Duke University Press, 2021.

Freeman, Elizabeth. *The Wedding Complex: Forms of Belonging in Modern American Culture.* Durham: Duke University Press, 2002.

French, Jan Hoffman. *Legalizing Identities: Becoming Black or Indian in Brazil's Northeast.* Chapel Hill: University of North Carolina Press, 2009.

Frickey, Philip P. "A Common Law for Our Age of Colonialism: The Judicial Divestiture of Indian Tribal Authority over Nonmembers." *Yale Law Journal* 109 (1999): 1–85.

Frickey, Philip P. "(Native) American Exceptionalism in Federal Public Law." *Harvard Law Review* 119 (2005): 431–90.

Fullilove, Mindy Thompson. *Root Shock: How Tearing Up City Neighborhoods Hurts America, and What We Can Do about It.* New York: New Village Press, 2016. First published 2004 by Ballantine.

Furlan, Laura M. *Indigenous Cities: Urban Indian Fiction and the Histories of Relocation.* Lincoln: University of Nebraska Press, 2017.

Gale, Leanne, and Kelly McClure. "Commandeering Confrontation: A Novel Threat to the Indian Child Welfare Act and Tribal Sovereignty." *Yale Law and Policy Review* 39 (2020): 292–346.

Gardner, Susan. "Speaking of Ella Deloria: Conversations with Joyzelle Gingway Godfrey, 1998–2000, Lower Brule Community College, South Dakota." *American Indian Quarterly* 24, no. 3 (2000): 456–81.

Garrison, Tim Alan. *The Legal Ideology of Removal: The Southern Judiciary and the Sovereignty of Native American Nations.* Athens: University of Georgia Press, 2002.

Garza, Alicia. *The Purpose of Power: How We Come Together when We Fall Apart.* New York: Random House, 2020.

Garza, Alicia, Opal Tometi, and Patrisse Cullors. "A HerStory of the #BlackLivesMatter Movement." http://blacklivesmatter.com. Accessed February 25, 2017.

Geary, Daniel. *Beyond Civil Rights: The Moynihan Report and Its Legacy.* Philadelphia: University of Pennsylvania Press, 2015.

Genetin-Pilawa, C. Joseph. *Crooked Paths to Allotment: The Fight over Federal Indian Policy after the Civil War.* Chapel Hill: University of North Carolina Press, 2012.

Getachew, Adom. *Worldmaking after Empire: The Rise and Fall of Self-Determination.* Princeton: Princeton University Press, 2020.

Gilmore, Ruth Wilson. *Golden Gulag: Prisons, Surplus, Crisis, and Opposition in Globalizing California.* Berkeley: University of California Press, 2007.

Goddard, Victoria. "Appropriate Kinship, Legitimate Nationhood: Shifting Registers of Gender and State." In *Reconnecting State and Kinship*, edited by Tatjana Thelen and Erdmute Alber, 108–29. Philadelphia: University of Pennsylvania Press, 2018.

Goeman, Mishuana. "Land as Life: Unsettling the Logics of Containment." In *Native Studies Keywords*, edited by Stephanie Nohelani Teves, Andrea Smith, and Michelle Raheja, 71–89. Tucson: University of Arizona Press, 2015.

Goeman, Mishuana. *Mark My Words: Native Women Mapping Our Nations.* Minneapolis: University of Minnesota Press, 2013.

Goeman, Mishuana. "Ongoing Storms and Struggles: Gendered Violence and Resource Exploitation." In *Critically Sovereign: Indigenous Gender, Sexuality, and Feminist Studies*, edited by Joanne Barker, 99–126. Durham: Duke University Press, 2017.

Goffman, Alice. *On the Run: Fugitive Life in an American City.* Chicago: University of Chicago Press, 2014.

Goldberg, Carole. "Members Only? Designing Citizenship Requirements for Indian Nations." *Kansas Law Review* 50 (2002): 437–71.

Goldberg-Ambrose, Carole. *Planting Tail Feathers: Tribal Survival and Public Law 280.* Los Angeles: American Indian Studies Center, University of California, 1997.

Goldstein, Alyosha. "Finance and Foreclosure in the Colonial Present." *Radical History Review* 118 (2014): 42–63.

Goldstein, Alyosha. "On the Reproduction of Race, Capitalism, and Settler Colonialism." In *Race and Capitalism: Global Territories, Transnational Histories*, 42–51. Los Angeles: Institute on Inequality and Democracy, UCLA, 2017.

Goldstein, Alyosha. *Poverty in Common: The Politics of Community Action during the American Century.* Durham: Duke University Press, 2012.

Goody, Jack. *The Development of the Family and Marriage in Europe.* New York: Cambridge University Press, 1983.

Gopinath, Gayatri. *Impossible Desires: Queer Diasporas and South Asian Public Cultures.* Durham: Duke University Press, 2005.

Gopinath, Gayatri. *Unruly Visions: The Aesthetic Practice of Queer Diaspora.* Durham: Duke University Press, 2018.

Gordon, Sarah Barringer. *The Mormon Question: Polygamy and Constitutional Conflict in Nineteenth-Century America.* Chapel Hill: University of North Carolina Press, 2002.

Gottlieb, Karla. *The Mother of Us All: A History of Queen Nanny, Leader of the Windward Jamaican Maroons.* Trenton, NJ: Africa World Press, 2000.

Gottschalk, Marie. *Caught: The Prison State and the Lockdown of American Politics.* Princeton: Princeton University Press, 2015.

Gover, Kirsty. "Genealogy as Continuity: Explaining the Growing Tribal Preference for Descent Rules in Membership Governance in the United States." *American Indian Law Review* 33 (2008–2009): 243–309.

Graham, Lorie M. "Reparations, Self-Determination, and the Seventh Generation." In *Facing the Future: The Indian Child Welfare Act at 30*, edited by Matthew L. M. Fletcher, Wenone T. Singel, and Kathryn E. Fort, 50–110. East Lansing: Michigan State University, 2008.

Green, Tara T. *Love, Activism, and the Respectable Life of Alice Dunbar-Nelson.* New York: Bloomsbury Academic, 2022.

Greenbaum, Susan D. *Blaming the Poor: The Long Shadow of the Moynihan Report on Cruel Images about Poverty.* New Brunswick: Rutgers University Press, 2015.

Greene, Shane. "Introduction: One Race, Roots/Routes, and Sovereignty in Latin America's Afro-Indigenous Multiculturalisms." *Journal of Latin American and Caribbean Anthropology* 12, no. 2 (2007): 329–55.

Gregory, James N. "The Second Great Migration: A Historical Overview." In *African American Urban History since World War II*, edited by Kenneth L. Kushner and Joe W. Trotter, 19–38. Chicago: University of Chicago Press, 2009.

Griswold v. Connecticut. 381 U.S. 479 (1965).

Grossberg, Michael. *Governing the Hearth: Law and the Family in Nineteenth-Century America*. Chapel Hill: University of North Carolina Press, 1985.

Guarneri, Carl J. *The Utopian Alternative: Fourierism in Nineteenth-Century America*. Ithaca: Cornell University Press, 1991.

Guha, Ranajit. "The Prose of Counter-Insurgency." In *Selected Subaltern Studies*, edited by Ranajit Guha and Gayatri Chakravorty Spivak, 45–86. New York: Oxford University Press, 1988.

Guidotti-Hernández, Nicole M. *Unspeakable Violence: Remapping U.S. and Mexican National Imaginaries*. Durham: Duke University Press, 2011.

Gunter, Dan. "The Technology of Tribalism: The Lemhi Indians, Federal Recognition, and the Creation of Tribal Identity." *Idaho Law Review* 35 (1998): 85–123.

Gurr, Barbara. *Reproductive Justice: The Politics of Health Care for Native American Women*. New Brunswick: Rutgers University Press, 2015.

Hahn, Steven. *A Nation under Our Feet: Black Political Struggles in the Rural South from Slavery to the Great Migration*. Cambridge: Harvard University Press, 2003.

Haley, Sarah. *No Mercy Here: Gender, Punishment, and the Making of Jim Crow Modernity*. Chapel Hill: University of North Carolina Press, 2016.

Hancock, Ange-Marie. *Intersectionality: An Intellectual History*. New York: Oxford University Press, 2016.

Hancock, Ange-Marie. *The Politics of Disgust: The Public Identity of the Welfare Queen*. New York: New York University Press, 2004.

Haney López, Ian F. *White by Law: The Legal Construction of Race*. New York: New York University Press, 1996.

Hanhardt, Christina B. *Safe Space: Gay Neighborhood History and the Politics of Violence*. Durham: Duke University Press, 2013.

Harjo, Laura. *Spiral to the Stars: Mvskoke Tools of Futurity*. Tucson: University of Arizona Press, 2019.

Harmon, Alexandra. *Indians in the Making: Ethnic Relations and Indian Identities around Puget Sound*. Berkeley: University of California Press, 1998.

Harmon, Alexandra, ed. *The Power of Promises: Rethinking Indian Treaties in the Pacific Northwest*. Seattle: University of Washington Press, 2008.

Harney, Stefano, and Fred Moten. *The Undercommons: Fugitive Planning and Black Study*. Minor Composition: New York, 2013.

Harring, Sidney L. *Crow Dog's Case: American Indian Sovereignty, Tribal Law, and United States Law in the Nineteenth Century*. New York: Cambridge University Press, 1994.

Harris, Cheryl I. "Of Blackness and Indigeneity: Comments on Jodi A. Byrd's 'Weather with You: Settler Colonialism, Antiblackness, and the Grounded Relationalities of Resistance.'" *Critical Ethnic Studies* 5, no. 1–2 (2019): 215–28.

Harris, Cheryl I. "Whiteness as Property." *Harvard Law Review* 106, no. 8 (1993): 1707–91.

Harris v. McRae. 448 U.S. 297 (1980).

Harris-Perry, Melissa V. *Sister Citizen: Shame, Stereotypes, and Black Women in America*. New Haven: Yale University Press, 2011.

Hartman, Saidiya V. *Lose Your Mother: A Journey along the Atlantic Slave Route*. New York: Farrar, Straus and Giroux, 2007.

Hartman, Saidiya V. *Scenes of Subjection: Terror, Slavery, and Self-Making in Nineteenth-Century America*. New York: Oxford University Press, 1997.

Hartman, Saidiya V. *Wayward Lives, Beautiful Experiments: Intimate Histories of Social Upheaval*. New York: W. W. Norton and Company, 2019.

Hauptman, Laurence M. *Conspiracy of Interests: Iroquois Dispossession and the Rise of New York State*. Syracuse: Syracuse University Press, 1999.

Hernández, Kelly Lytle. *City of Inmates: Conquest, Rebellion, and the Rise of Human Caging in Los Angeles, 1771–1965*. Chapel Hill: University of North Carolina Press, 2017.

Hickman, Jared. "*The Book of Mormon* as Amerindian Apocalypse." *American Literature* 86, no. 3 (2014): 429–62.

Higashida, Cheryl. *Black Internationalist Feminism: Women Writers of the Black Left, 1945–1995*. Urbana: University of Illinois Press, 2011.

Hill, Susan M. *The Clay We Are Made Of: Haudenosaunee Land Tenure on the Grand River*. Winnipeg: University of Manitoba Press, 2017.

Hinton, Elizabeth. *From the War on Poverty to the War on Crime: The Making of Mass Incarceration in America*. Cambridge: Harvard University Press, 2016.

Holland, Sharon. *The Erotic Life of Racism*. Durham: Duke University Press, 2012.

Hong, Grace Kyungwon. *Death beyond Disavowal: The Impossible Politics of Difference*. Minneapolis: University of Minnesota Press, 2015.

Howard, Oliver Otis. *Autobiography of Oliver Otis Howard*. Vol. 2. New York: Baker and Taylor Company, 1908.

Hoxie, Frederick E. *A Final Promise: The Campaign to Assimilate the Indians, 1880–1920*. Cambridge: Cambridge University Press, 1992. First published 1984 by University of Nebraska Press.

Hunt, Irvin J. *Dreaming the Present: Time, Aesthetics, and the Black Cooperative Movement*. Chapel Hill: University of North Carolina Press, 2022.

Hunter, Marcus Anthony, and Zandria F. Robinson. *Chocolate Cities: The Black Map of American Life*. Oakland: University of California Press, 2018.

Hunter, Marcus Anthony, Mary Pattillo, Zandria F. Robinson, and Keeanga-Yamahtta Taylor. "Black Placemaking: Celebration, Play, and Poetry." *Theory, Culture, and Society* 33, no. 7–8 (2016): 31–56.

Hunter, Tera W. *Bound in Wedlock: Slave and Free Black Marriage in the Nineteenth Century*. Cambridge: Harvard University Press, 2017.

Hunter, Tera W. *To 'Joy My Freedom: Southern Black Women's Lives and Labors after the Civil War*. Cambridge: Harvard University Press, 1997.
Hyde, Anne F. *Empires, Nations, and Families: A New History of the North American West, 1800–1860*. New York: Harper Collins, 2011.
Ibrahim, Habiba. *Troubling the Family: The Promise of Personhood and the Rise of Multiculturalism*. Minneapolis: University of Minnesota Press, 2012.
Innes, Robert Alexander. *Elder Brother and the Law of the People: Contemporary Kinship and Cowessess First Nation*. Winnipeg: University of Manitoba Press, 2013.
Iversen, Joan. *The Antipolygamy Controversy in U.S. Women's Movements, 1880–1925: A Debate on the American Home*. New York: Garland Publishing, 1997.
Jackson, Deborah Davis. *Our Elders Lived It: American Indian Identity in the City*. Dekalb: Northern Illinois University Press, 2002.
Jackson, Shona. *Creole Indigeneity: Between Myth and Nation in the Caribbean*. Minneapolis: University of Minnesota Press, 2012.
Jacobs, Margaret D. *A Generation Removed: The Fostering and Adoption of Indigenous Children in the Postwar World*. Lincoln: University of Nebraska Press, 2014.
Jaffke, Cheyanna L. "The 'Existing Indian Family' Exception to the Indian Child Welfare Act: The States' Attempt to Slaughter Tribal Interests in Indian Children." *Louisiana Law Review* 66 (2006): 733–61.
Jakobsen, Janet R. "Queer Is? Queer Does? Normativity and the Problem of Resistance." *GLQ* 4, no. 4 (1998): 511–36.
Jenkins, Candice M. *Black Bourgeois: Class and Sex in the Flesh*. Minneapolis: University of Minnesota Press, 2019.
Jenkins, Candice M. *Private Lives, Proper Relations: Regulating Black Intimacy*. Minneapolis: University of Minnesota Press, 2007.
Jenkins, Destin, and Justin Leroy, eds. *Histories of Racial Capitalism*. New York: Columbia University Press, 2021.
Johnson, Jessica Marie. *Wicked Flesh: Black Women, Intimacy, and Freedom in the Atlantic World*. Philadelphia: University of Pennsylvania Press, 2020.
Johnson, John W. *Griswold v. Connecticut: Birth Control and the Constitutional Right of Privacy*. Lawrence: University Press of Kansas, 2005.
Joint Economic Committee. "The Economic State of Black America in 2020." https://www.jec.senate.gov/public/_cache/files/ccf4dbe2-810a-44f8-b3e7-14f7e5143ba6/economic-state-of-black-america-2020.pdf.
Jones, Jacqueline. *Labor of Love, Labor of Sorrow: Black Women, Work, and the Family from Slavery to the Present*. Rev. ed. New York: Basic Books, 2010.
Jones, Martha S. *All Bound Up Together: The Woman Question in African American Public Culture, 1830–1900*. Chapel Hill: University of North Carolina Press, 2007.
Justice, Daniel Heath. "'Go Away, Water!': Kinship Criticism and the Decolonization Imperative." In *Reasoning Together*. The Native Critics Collective, edited by Janie Acoose et al., 147–68. Norman: University of Oklahoma Press, 2008.

Justice, Daniel Heath. "Notes toward a Theory of Anomaly." *GLQ* 16, no. 1–2 (2010): 207–42.

Justice, Daniel Heath. *Why Indigenous Literatures Matter.* Waterloo, Ontario: Wilfred Laurier University Press, 2018.

Kameʻeleihiwa, Lilikalā. *Native Land and Foreign Desires: How Shall We Live in Harmony?* Honolulu: Bishop Museum Press, 1992.

Kandaswamy, Priya. *Domestic Contradictions: Race and Gendered Citizenship from Reconstruction to Welfare Reform.* Durham: Duke University Press, 2021.

Kaplan, Amy. *The Anarchy of Empire in the Making of U.S. Culture.* Cambridge, MA: Harvard University Press, 2002.

Kauanui, J. Kēhaulani. *Hawaiian Blood: Colonialism and the Politics of Sovereignty and Indigeneity.* Durham: Duke University Press, 2008.

Kauanui, J. Kēhaulani. *Paradoxes of Hawaiian Sovereignty: Land, Sex, and the Colonial Politics of State Nationalism.* Durham: Duke University Press, 2018.

Kaye, Anthony E. *Joining Places: Slave Neighborhoods in the Old South.* Chapel Hill: University of North Carolina Press, 2007.

Kazanjian, David. *The Colonizing Trick: National Culture and Imperial Citizenship in Early America.* Minneapolis: University of Minnesota Press, 2003.

Keeling, Kara. *The Witch's Flight: The Cinematic, the Black Femme, and the Image of Common Sense.* Durham: Duke University Press, 2007.

Kelley, Robin D. G. *Freedom Dreams: The Black Radical Imagination.* Boston: Beacon Press, 2002.

Kelley, Robin D. G. *Yo' Mama's Disfunctional! Fighting the Culture Wars in Urban America.* Boston: Beacon Press, 2008. First published 1997.

Kelly, Lawrence C. *The Assault on Assimilation: John Collier and the Origins of Indian Policy Reform.* Albuquerque: University of New Mexico Press, 1983.

Khan-Cullors, Patrisse, and Asha Bandele. *When They Call You a Terrorist: A Black Lives Matter Memoir.* New York: St. Martin's Press, 2018.

Kim, Jodi. *Ends of Empire: Asian American Critique and the Cold War.* Minneapolis: University of Minnesota Press, 2010.

Kim, Jodi. *Settler Garrison: Debt, Imperialism, Militarism, and Transpacific Imaginaries.* Durham: Duke University Press, 2022.

King, Tiffany Lethabo. "The Labor of (Re)reading Plantation Landscapes Fugible(ly)." *Antipode* 48, no. 4 (2016): 1–18.

Kinney, Rebecca J. *Beautiful Wasteland: The Rise of Detroit as America's Postindustrial Frontier.* Minneapolis: University of Minnesota Press, 2016.

Klopotek, Brian. *Recognition Odysseys: Indigeneity, Race, and Federal Tribal Recognition Policy in Three Louisiana Indian Communities.* Durham: Duke University Press, 2011.

Konkle, Maureen. *Writing Indian Nations: Native Intellectuals and the Politics of Historiography, 1827–1863.* Chapel Hill: University of North Carolina Press, 2004.

Kuper, Adam. *The Reinvention of Primitive Society: Transformations of a Myth.* London: Routledge, 1997. First published 1988.

Kymlicka, Will. *Multicultural Odysseys: Navigating the New International Politics of Diversity*. New York: Oxford University Press, 2007.

Ladner, Joyce A. *Tomorrow's Tomorrow: The Black Woman*. Lincoln: University of Nebraska Press, 1995. First published 1971 by Doubleday.

Lara, Ana-Maurine. *Queer Freedom: Black Sovereignty*. Albany: SUNY Press, 2020.

Lash, Don. *"When the Welfare People Come": Race and Class in the U.S. Child Protection System*. Chicago: Haymarket Books, 2017.

The Late Corporation of the Church of Jesus Christ of Latter-Day Saints v. United States. 136 U.S. 1 (1890).

Latour, Bruno. *Reassembling the Social: An Introduction to Actor-Network Theory*. New York: Oxford University Press, 2017.

Lawrence, Bonita. *"Real" Indians and Others: Mixed-Blood Urban Native Peoples and Indigenous Nationhood*. Lincoln: University of Nebraska Press, 2004.

Lawrence, Jane. "The Indian Health Service and the Sterilization of Native American Women." *American Indian Quarterly* 24, no. 3 (2000): 400–419.

Lawrence v. Texas. 539 U.S. 558 (2003).

Le, Quynh Nhu. *Unsettled Solidarities: Asian and Indigenous Cross-Representations in the Américas*. Philadelphia: Temple University Press, 2019.

Lee, James Kyung-Jin. *Urban Triage: Race and the Fictions of Multiculturalism*. Minneapolis: University of Minnesota Press, 2004.

Leonard, Toni M. Bond. "Laying the Foundations for a Reproductive Justice Movement." In *Radical Reproductive Justice: Foundations, Theory, Practice, Critique*, edited by Loretta J. Ross, Lynn Roberts, Erika Derkas, Whitney Peoples, and Pamela Bridgewater Toure, 39–49. New York: Feminist Press, 2017.

Letter from the Secretary of War, In Answer To, A resolution of the House of March 8, transmitting a report by the Commissioner of the Freedman's Bureau, of all orders issued by him or any assistant commissioner. H. Exec. Doc. 70. 39th Cong., 1st Sess. (1866).

Letter of the Secretary of War, Communicating, In compliance with a resolution of the Senate of December 17, 1866, reports of the assistant commissioners of freedmen, and a synopsis of laws respecting persons of color in the late slave States. S. Exec. Doc. 6. 39th Cong., 1st Sess. (1867).

Levenstein, Lisa. "Gendering Postwar Urban History: African American Women, Welfare, and Poverty in Philadelphia." In *African American Urban History since World War II*, edited by Kenneth L. Kusmer and Joe W. Trotter, 337–55. Chicago: University of Chicago Press, 2009.

Lew-Williams, Beth. *The Chinese Must Go: Violence, Exclusion, and the Making of the Alien in America*. Cambridge, MA: Harvard University Press, 2018.

Lewis, Brian L. "Do You Know What You Are? You Are What You Is; You Is What You Am: Indian Status for the Purpose of Federal Criminal Jurisdiction and the Current Split in the Court of Appeals." *Harvard Journal on Racial and Ethnic Justice* 26 (2010): 241–85.

Lewis, Jovan Scott. *Violent Utopia: Dispossession and Black Restoration in Tulsa*. Durham: Duke University Press, 2022.

Lipsitz, George. "From *Plessy* to Ferguson." *Cultural Critique* 90 (2015): 119–39.
Lipsitz, George. *How Racism Takes Place*. Philadelphia: Temple University Press, 2011.
Lobo, Susan. "Urban Clan Mothers: Key Households in Cities." *American Indian Quarterly* 27, no. 3–4 (2003): 505–22.
Lorde, Audre. *Sister Outsider: Essays and Speeches*. Freedom, CA: Crossing Press, 1984.
Loving v. Virginia. 388 U.S. 1 (1967).
Lowe, Lisa. *Immigrant Acts: On Asian American Cultural Politics*. Durham: Duke University Press, 1996.
Lowe, Lisa. *The Intimacies of Four Continents*. Durham: Duke University Press, 2015.
Lowery, Malinda Maynor. *Lumbee Indians in the Jim Crow South: Race, Identity, and the Making of a Nation*. Chapel Hill: University of North Carolina Press, 2010.
Lubiano, Wahneema. "Black Nationalism and Black Common Sense: Policing Ourselves and Others." In *The House That Race Built*, edited by Wahneema Lubiano, 232–52. New York: Vintage Books, 1998.
Luciano, Dana. *Arranging Grief: Sacred Time and the Body in Nineteenth-Century America*. New York: New York University Press, 2007.
Luibhéid, Eithne. *Entry Denied: Controlling Sexuality at the Border*. Minneapolis: University of Minnesota Press, 2002.
Lyons, Scott Richard. *X-marks: Native Signatures of Assent*. Minneapolis: University of Minnesota Press, 2010.
Macek, Steve. *Urban Nightmares: The Media, the Right, and the Moral Panic over the City*. Minneapolis: University of Minnesota Press, 2006.
Macharia, Keguro. *Frottage: Frictions of Intimacy across the Black Diaspora*. New York: New York University Press, 2019.
Mackey, Eva. *Unsettled Expectations: Uncertainty, Land and Settler Decolonization*. Halifax: Fernwood Publishing, 2016.
Macpherson, C. B. *The Political Theory of Possessive Individualism: Hobbes to Locke*. New York: Oxford University Press, 1962.
Mall, Lorinda. "Keeping It in the Family: The Legal and Social Evolution of ICWA in State and Tribal Jurisprudence." In *Facing the Future: The Indian Child Welfare Act at 30*, edited by Matthew L. M. Fletcher, Wenone T. Singel, and Kathryn E. Fort, 164–220. East Lansing: Michigan State University, 2008.
Manalansan, Martin F., IV. "Race, Violence, and Neoliberal Spatial Politics in the Global City." *Social Text* 84–85, no. 3–4 (2005): 141–55.
Mandell, Daniel R. *Tribe, Race, History: Native Americans in Southern New England, 1780–1880*. Baltimore: Johns Hopkins University Press, 2008.
Martinez, George A. "Mexican Americans and Whiteness." In *Critical Race Theory: The Cutting Edge*, 2nd ed., edited by Richard Delgado and Jean Stefancic, 379–83. Philadelphia: Temple University Press, 2000.
Massey, Doreen. *Space, Place, and Gender*. Minneapolis: University of Minnesota Press, 1994.
Massey, Douglass S., and Denton, Nancy A. *American Apartheid: Segregation and the Making of the Underclass*. Cambridge: Harvard University Press, 1993.

Maynard, Robyn, and Leanne Betasamosake Simpson. *Rehearsals for Living*. Chicago: Haymarket Books, 2022.

Mays, Kyle T. *City of Dispossessions: Indigenous Peoples, African Americans, and the Creation of Modern Detroit*. Philadelphia: University of Pennsylvania Press, 2022.

Mbembe, Achille. "Necropolitics." Translated by Libby Meintjes. *Public Culture* 15, no. 1 (2003): 11–40.

McCarthy, Theresa. *In Divided Unity: Haudenosaunee Reclamation at Grand River*. Tucson: University of Arizona Press, 2016.

McClintock, Anne. *Imperial Leather: Race, Gender and Sexuality in the Colonial Contest*. New York: Routledge, 1995.

McCulloch, Anne Merline, and David E. Wilkins. "'Constructing' Nations within States: The Quest for Federal Recognition by the Catawba and Lumbee Tribes." *American Indian Quarterly* 19, no. 3 (1995): 361–88.

McDonnell, Janet A. *The Dispossession of the American Indian, 1887–1934*. Bloomington: Indiana University Press, 1991.

McGirt v. Oklahoma. 591 U. S. ____ (2020).

McKinnon, Susan. "The Economies in Kinship and the Paternity of Culture: Origin Stories in Kinship Theory." In *Relative Values: Reconfiguring Kinship Studies*, edited by Sarah Franklin and Susan McKinnon, 302–28. Durham: Duke University Press, 2001.

McKittrick, Katherine. *Demonic Grounds: Black Women and the Cartographies of Struggle*. Minneapolis: University of Minnesota Press, 2006.

McKittrick, Katherine. "Plantation Futures." *Small Axe* 17, no. 3 (2013): 1–15.

McKittrick, Katherine. "Rebellion/Invention/Groove." *Small Axe* 49 (2016): 79–91.

McKittrick, Katherine, ed. *Sylvia Wynter: On Being Human as Praxis*. Durham: Duke University Press, 2015.

Mehta, Uday Singh. *Liberalism and Empire: A Study in Nineteenth-Century British Liberal Thought*. Chicago: University of Chicago Press, 1999.

Melamed, Jodi. "Racial Capitalism." *Critical Ethnic Studies* 1, no. 1 (2015): 76–85.

Melamed, Jodi. *Represent and Destroy: Rationalizing Violence in the New Racial Capitalism*. Minneapolis: University of Minnesota Press, 2011.

Merish, Lori. *Sentimental Materialism: Gender, Commodity Culture, and Nineteenth-Century American Literature*. Durham: Duke University Press, 2002.

Message from the President of the United States, Communicating, In compliance with a resolution of the Senate of the 27th of February last, a communication from the Secretary of War, together with the reports of the assistant commissioners of the Freedmen's Bureau made since December 1, 1865. S. Exec. Doc. 27. 39th Cong., 1st Sess. (1866).

Michaelsen, Scott. *The Limits of Multiculturalism: Interrogating the Origins of American Anthropology*. Minneapolis: University of Minnesota Press, 1999.

Michigan Civil Rights Commission. "The Flint Water Crisis: Systemic Racism through the Lens of Flint: Report of the Michigan Civil Rights Commission," 2017, https://www.michigan.gov/documents/mdcr/VFlintCrisisRep-F-Edited3-13-17_554317_7.pdf.

Milczarek-Desai, Shefali. "(Re)Locating Other/Third World Women: An Alternative Approach to *Santa Clara Pueblo v. Martinez*'s Construction of Gender, Culture and Identity." UCLA *Women's Law Journal* 13 (2005): 235–91.

Miles, Tiya. *Ties That Bind: The Story of an Afro-Cherokee Family in Slavery and Freedom*. Berkeley: University of California Press, 2005.

Miles, Tiya, and Sharon Holland, eds. *Crossing Waters, Crossing Worlds: The African Diaspora in Indian Country*. Durham: Duke University Press, 2006.

Miller, Douglas K. *Indians on the Move: Native American Mobility and Urbanization in the Twentieth Century*. Chapel Hill: University of North Carolina Press, 2019.

Miller, Mark Edwin. *Forgotten Tribes: Unrecognized Indians and the Federal Acknowledgment Process*. Lincoln: University of Nebraska Press, 2004.

Million, Dian. *Therapeutic Nations: Healing in an Age of Indigenous Human Rights*. Tucson: University of Arizona Press, 2013.

Mills, Charles W. *Black Rights/White Wrongs: The Critique of Racial Liberalism*. New York: Oxford University Press, 2017.

Mink, Gwendolyn. *Welfare's End*. Rev. ed. Ithaca: Cornell University Press, 2002.

Minow, Martha. "We, the Family: Constitutional Rights and American Families." *Journal of American History* 74, no. 3 (1987): 959–83.

Mississippi Band of Choctaw Indians v. Holyfield. 490 U.S. 30 (1989).

Mohrman, K. *Exceptionally Queer: Mormon Peculiarity and U.S. Nationalism*. Minneapolis: University of Minnesota Press, 2022.

Molina, Natalia. *How Race Is Made in America: Immigration, Citizenship, and the Historical Power of Racial Scripts*. Oakland: University of California Press, 2013.

Montegary, Liz. *Familiar Perversions: The Racial, Sexual, and Economic Politics of LGBT Families*. New Brunswick: Rutgers University Press, 2018.

Moore, Mignon R. "Marriage Equality and the African American Case: Intersections of Race and LGBT Sexuality." *differences* 29, no. 2 (2018): 196–203.

Moraga, Cherríe L. *Loving in the War Years: Lo Que Nunca Paso Por Sus Labios*. 2nd rev. ed. Boston: South End Press, 2000.

Moreton-Robinson, Aileen. *The White Possessive: Property, Power, and Indigenous Sovereignty*. Minneapolis: University of Minnesota Press, 2015.

Morgan, Jennifer L. *Laboring Women: Reproduction and Gender in New World Slavery*. Philadelphia: University of Pennsylvania Press, 2004.

Morgan, Jennifer L. *Reckoning with Slavery: Gender, Kinship, and Capitalism in the Early Black Atlantic*. Durham: Duke University Press, 2021.

Morgan, Lewis Henry. *Ancient Society, or Researches in the Lines of Human Progress from Savagery through Barbarism to Civilization*. New York: Gordon Press, 1977. First published 1877 by Henry Holt and Company.

Morgan, Lewis Henry. *League of the Iroquois*. Edited by Willian N. Fenton. New York: Corinth Books, 1962. First published 1851 by Sage and Brother.

Morgensen, Scott L. "The Biopolitics of Settler Colonialism: Right Here, Right Now." *Settler Colonial Studies* 1, no. 1 (2011): 52–76.

Morgensen, Scott L. *Spaces between Us: Queer Settler Colonialism and Indigenous Decolonization*. Minneapolis: University of Minnesota Press, 2011.

Morton v. Mancari. 417 U.S. 535 (1974).

Moten, Fred. "The Subprime and the Beautiful." *African Identities* 11, no. 2 (2013): 237–45.

Moynihan, Daniel. *Maximum Feasible Misunderstanding: Community Action in the War on Poverty*. New York: Free Press, 1969.

Moynihan, Daniel. *The Moynihan Report: The Negro Family—the Case for National Action*. New York: Cosimo Reports, 2018. First published 1965 by U.S. Department of Labor.

Mueller, Max Perry. *Race and the Making of the Mormon People*. Chapel Hill: University of North Carolina Press, 2018.

Muhammad, Khalil Gibran. *The Condemnation of Blackness: Race, Crime, and the Making of Modern Urban America*. Cambridge: Harvard University Press, 2010.

Muñoz, José Esteban. *Cruising Utopia: The Then and There of Queer Futurity*. New York: New York University Press, 2009.

Muñoz, José Esteban. *Disidentifications: Queers of Color and the Performance of Politics*. Minneapolis: University of Minnesota Press, 1999.

Murakawa, Naomi. *The First Civil Right: How Liberals Built Prison America*. New York: Oxford University Press, 2014.

Murphy, Michelle. "Against Population, Towards Alterlife." In *Making Kin Not Population*, edited by Adele E. Clarke and Donna Haraway, 101–24. Chicago: Prickly Paradigm Press, 2018.

Murphy, Michelle. *The Economization of Life*. Durham: Duke University Press, 2017.

Naples, Nancy A. *Grassroots Warriors: Activist Mothering, Community Work, and the War on Poverty*. New York: Routledge, 1998.

Nathans, Sydney. *A Mind to Stay: White Plantation, Black Household*. Cambridge: Harvard University Press, 2017.

National Advisory Commission on Civil Disorders. *The Kerner Report*. Introduction by Julian E. Zelizer. Princeton: Princeton University Press, 2016. First published 1968.

Nelson, Dana. *National Manhood: Capitalist Citizenship and the Imagined Fraternity of White Men*. Durham: Duke University Press, 1998.

Nelson, Jennifer. *Women of Color and the Reproductive Rights Movement*. New York: New York University Press, 2003.

Ngai, Mae M. *Impossible Subjects: Illegal Aliens and the Making of Modern America*. Princeton: Princeton University Press, 2004.

Nguyen, Mimi Thi. *The Gift of Freedom: War, Debt, and Other Refugee Passages*. Durham: Duke University Press, 2012.

Ng'weno, Bettina. "Can Ethnicity Replace Race? Afro-Colombians, Indigeneity and the Colombian Multicultural State." *Journal of Latin American and Caribbean Anthropology* 12, no. 2 (2007): 414–40.

Nichols, Robert. "Contract and Usurpation: Enfranchisement and Racial Governance in Settler-Colonial Contexts." In *Theorizing Native Studies*, edited by Audra Simpson and Andrea Smith, 99–121. Durham: Duke University Press, 2014.

Nichols, Robert. *Theft Is Property! Dispossession and Critical Theory*. Durham: Duke University Press, 2019.

Norgren, Jill. *The Cherokee Cases: The Confrontation of Law and Politics*. New York: McGraw Hill, 1996.

Nyong'o, Tavia. *The Amalgamation Waltz: Race, Performance, and the Ruses of Memory*. Minneapolis: University of Minnesota Press, 2009.

Oakley, Katharine C. "Defining Indian Status for the Purpose of Federal Criminal Jurisdiction," *American Indian Law Review* 35 (2010): 177–209.

Obergefell v. Hodges. 135 U.S. 2584 (2015).

O'Brien, Jean. *Firsting and Lasting: Writing Indians Out of Existence in New England*. Minneapolis: University of Minnesota Press, 2010.

O'Connor, Alice. *Poverty Knowledge: Social Science, Social Policy, and the Poor in Twentieth-Century U.S. History*. Princeton: Princeton University Press, 2001.

Office of Economic Opportunity. *Workbook: Community Action Program*. Washington, DC: Government Printing Office, 1965.

Ogle, Kasey D. "Why Try to Change Me Now? The Basis for the 2016 Indian Child Welfare Act Regulations." *Nebraska Law Review* 96 (2018): 1007–32.

Oklahoma v. Castro-Huerta. 2022 U.S. LEXIS 3222.

Oliphant v. Schlie. 544 F.2d 1007 (9th Cir. 1976).

Oliphant v. Suquamish. 435 U.S. 191 (1978).

Oman, Nathan B. "Natural Law and the Rhetoric of Empire: *Reynolds v. United States*, Polygamy, and Imperialism." *Washington University Law Review* 88 (2011): 662–706.

Opinions of the Solicitor of the Department of the Interior Relating to Indian Affairs 1917–1974. Vol. 1. Washington, DC: Government Printing Office, 1979.

Ordover, Nancy. *American Eugenics: Race, Queer Anatomy, and the Science of Nationalism*. Minneapolis: University of Minnesota Press, 2003.

Organick, Aliza G. "Holding Back the Tide: The Existing Indian Family Doctrine and Its Continued Denial of the Right to Culture for Indigenous Children." In *Facing the Future: The Indian Child Welfare Act at 30*, edited by Matthew L. M. Fletcher, Wenone T. Singel, and Kathryn E. Fort, 221–34. East Lansing: Michigan State University, 2008.

Osorio, Jamaica Heolimeleikalani. *Remembering Our Intimacies: Moʻolelo, Aloha, ʻĀina, and Ea*. Minneapolis: University of Minnesota Press, 2021.

Ostler, Jeffrey. *The Plains Sioux and U.S. Colonialism from Lewis and Clark to Wounded Knee*. New York: Cambridge University Press, 2004.

O'Sullivan, Megan Devlin. "Informing Red Power and Transforming the Second Wave: Native American Women and the Struggle against Coerced Sterilization in the 1970s." *Women's History Review* 25, no. 6 (2016): 965–82.

Oubre, Claude F. *Forty Acres and a Mule: The Freedmen's Bureau and Black Land Ownership*. Baton Rouge: Louisiana State University Press, 2012. First published 1978.

Pacheco, Amanda M. K. "Broken Traditions: Overcoming the Jurisdictional Maze to Protect Native American Women from Sexual Violence." *University of San Francisco Journal of Law and Social Challenges* 11 (2009): 1–42.

Pager, Devah. *Marked: Race, Crime, and Finding Work in the Era of Mass Incarceration*. Chicago: University of Chicago Press, 2009.

Palmer, Meredith Alberta. "Rendering Settler Sovereign Landscapes: Race and Property in the Empire State." *Environment and Planning D: Society and Space* 38, no. 5 (2020): 793–810.

Pascoe, Peggy. *What Comes Naturally: Miscegenation Law and the Making of Race in America*. New York: Oxford University Press, 2009.

Pasternak, Shiri. *Grounded Authority: The Algonquins of Barriere Lake against the State*. Minneapolis: University of Minnesota Press, 2019.

Pattillo, Mary. *Black on the Block: The Politics of Race and Class in the City*. Chicago: University of Chicago Press, 2007.

Pearsall, Sarah M. S. *Polygamy: An Early American History*. New Haven: Yale University Press, 2019.

Pegues, Juliana Hu. *Space-Time Colonialism: Alaska's Indigenous and Asian Entanglements*. Chapel Hill: University of North Carolina Press, 2021.

Penningroth, Dylan C. *The Claims of Kinsfolk: African American Property and Community in the Nineteenth-Century South*. Chapel Hill: University of North Carolina Press, 2003.

Perdue, Theda. *Cherokee Women: Gender and Cultural Change, 1700–1835*. Lincoln: University of Nebraska Press, 1998.

Perdue, Theda. *Slavery and the Evolution of Cherokee Society, 1540–1866*. Knoxville: University of Tennessee Press, 1979.

Perrone, Giuliana. "'Back into the Days of Slavery': Freedom, Citizenship, and the Black Family in the Reconstruction-Era Courtroom." *Law and History Review* 37, no. 1 (2019): 125–61.

Perry, Imani. *Vexy Thing: On Gender and Liberation*. Durham: Duke University Press, 2018.

Peters, Evelyn, and Chris Andersen, eds. *Indigenous in the City: Contemporary Identities and Cultural Innovation*. Vancouver: UBC Press, 2013.

Peterson, Ruth D., and Lauren J. Krivo. *Divergent Social Worlds: Neighborhood Crime and the Racial-Spatial Divide*. New York: Russell Sage Foundation, 2010.

Pettit, Becky. *Invisible Men: Mass Incarceration and the Myth of Black Progress*. New York: Russell Sage Foundation, 2012.

Pexa, Christopher. *Translated Nation: Rewriting the Dakota Oyáte*. Minneapolis: University of Minnesota Press, 2019.

Pfister, Joel. *Individuality Incorporated: Indians and the Multicultural Modern*. Durham: Duke University Press, 2004.

Philp, Kenneth R. *Termination Revisited: American Indians on the Trail to Self-Determination, 1933–1953.* Lincoln: University of Nebraska Press, 1999.

Phipps, Kelly Elizabeth. "Marriage and Redemption: Mormon Polygamy in the Congressional Imagination, 1862–1887." *Virginia Law Review* 95 (2009): 435–87.

Piatote, Beth H. *Domestic Subjects: Gender, Citizenship, and Law in Native American Literature.* New Haven: Yale University Press, 2013.

Piatote, Beth H. "The Indian/Agent Aporia." *American Indian Quarterly* 37, no. 3 (2013): 45–62.

Pierce, Joseph. "In Good Relations: Native Adoption, Kinstillations, and the Grounding of Memory." In *Queer Kinship: Race, Sex, Belonging, Form*, edited by Teagan Bradway and Elizabeth Freeman, 95–118. Durham: Duke University Press, 2022.

Pinto, Samantha. *Difficult Diasporas: The Transnational Feminist Aesthetic of the Black Atlantic.* New York: New York University Press, 2013.

Pisarello, Laura E. "Lawless by Design: Jurisdiction, Gender, and Justice in Indian Country," *Emory Law Journal* 59 (2010): 1515–52.

Plane, Ann Marie. *Colonial Intimacies: Indian Marriage in Early New England.* Ithaca: Cornell University Press, 2000.

Planned Parenthood v. Casey. 505 U.S. 833 (1992).

Polikoff, Nancy D. *Beyond (Straight and Gay) Marriage: Valuing All Families under the Law.* Boston: Beacon Press, 2008.

Povinelli, Elizabeth A. *The Cunning of Recognition: Indigenous Alterities and the Making of Australian Multiculturalism.* Durham: Duke University Press, 2002.

Povinelli, Elizabeth A. *Economies of Abandonment: Social Belonging and Endurance in Late Liberalism.* Durham: Duke University Press, 2011.

Povinelli, Elizabeth A. *The Empire of Love.* Durham: Duke University Press, 2006.

Povinelli, Elizabeth A. "The Governance of the Prior." *interventions* 13, no. 1 (2011): 13–30.

Powell, Dana. *Landscapes of Power: Politics of Energy in the Navajo Nation.* Durham: Duke University Press, 2018.

Prucha, Francis Paul, ed. *Documents of United States Indian Policy.* 3rd ed. Lincoln: University of Nebraska Press, 2000.

Prud'homme-Cranford, Rain, Darryl Barthé, and Andrew J. Jolivette, eds. *Louisiana Creole Peoplehood: Afro-Indigeneity and Community.* Seattle: University of Washington Press, 2022.

Puar, Jasbir K. *Terrorist Assemblages: Homonationalism in Queer Times.* Durham: Duke University Press, 2007.

Puig de la Bellacasa, María. *Matters of Care: Speculative Ethics in More Than Human Worlds.* Minneapolis: University of Minnesota Press, 2017.

Purifoy, Danielle M. "North Carolina (Un)Incorporated: Place, Race, and Local Environmental Inequity." PhD diss., Duke University, 2018.

Quashie, Kevin. *The Sovereignty of Quiet: Beyond Resistance in Black Culture.* New Brunswick: Rutgers University Press, 2012.

Quasius, Marie. "Native American Rape Victims: Desperately Seeking an Oliphant-Fix," *Minnesota Law Review* 93 (2009): 1902–40.

Quizar, Jessi. "Land of Opportunity: Anti-Black and Settler Logics in the Gentrification of Detroit." *American Indian Culture and Research Journal* 43, no. 2 (2019): 113–33.

Quong, Jonathan. *Liberalism without Perfection*. Oxford: Oxford University Press, 2011.

Ralstin-Lewis, D. Marie. "The Continuing Struggle against Genocide: Indigenous Women's Reproductive Rights." *Wicazo Sa Review* 20, no. 1 (2005): 71–95.

Ramirez, Renya K. *Native Hubs: Culture, Community, and Belonging in Silicon Valley and Beyond*. Durham: Duke University Press, 2007.

Rand, Jacki Thompson. *Kiowa Humanity and the Invasion of the State*. Lincoln: University of Nebraska Press, 2008.

Ransby, Barbara. *Making All Black Lives Matter: Reimagining Freedom in the 21st Century*. Oakland: University of California Press, 2018.

Rawls, John. *Political Liberalism*. Expanded ed. New York: Columbia University Press, 2005.

Razack, Sherene H. *Dying from Improvement: Inquest and Inquiries into Indigenous Deaths in Custody*. Toronto: University of Toronto Press, 2015.

Reddy, Chandan. *Freedom with Violence: Race, Sexuality, and the US State*. Durham: Duke University Press, 2011.

Reynolds v. United States. 98 U.S. 145 (1879).

Richardson, Matt. *The Queer Limit of Black Memory: Black Lesbian Literature and Irresolution*. Columbus: Ohio State University, 2013.

Richie, Beth. *Arrested Justice: Black Women, Violence, and America's Prison Nation*. New York: New York University Press, 2012.

Richotte, Keith. *Claiming Turtle Mountain's Constitution: The History, Legacy, and Future of a Tribal Nation's Founding Documents*. Chapel Hill: University of North Carolina Press, 2017.

Rifkin, Mark. "Around 1978: Family, Culture, and Race in the Federal Production of Indianness." In *Critically Sovereign: Indigenous Gender, Sexuality, and Feminist Studies*, edited by Joanne Barker, 169–206. Durham: Duke University Press, 2017.

Rifkin, Mark. "Beyond Family: Kinship's Past, Queer Worldmaking, and the Question of Governance." In *Queer Kinship: Race, Sex, Belonging, Form*, edited by Elizabeth Freeman and Teagan Bradway, 138–158. Durham: Duke University Press, 2022.

Rifkin, Mark. *Beyond Settler Time: Temporal Sovereignty and Indigenous Self-Determination*. Durham: Duke University Press, 2017.

Rifkin, Mark. *Fictions of Land and Flesh: Blackness, Indigeneity, Speculation*. Durham: Duke University Press, 2019.

Rifkin, Mark. "Indigenizing Agamben: Rethinking Sovereignty in Light of the 'Peculiar' Status of Native Peoples," *Cultural Critique* 72 (Fall 2009): 88–124.

Rifkin, Mark. "Making Peoples into Populations: The Racial Limits of Tribal Sovereignty." In *Theorizing Native Studies*, edited by Audra Simpson and Andrea Smith, 149–87. Durham: Duke University Press, 2014.

Rifkin, Mark. *Manifesting America: The Imperial Construction of U.S. National Space*. New York: Oxford University Press, 2009.

Rifkin, Mark. *Settler Common Sense: Queerness and Everyday Colonialism in the American Renaissance*. Minneapolis: University of Minnesota Press, 2014.

Rifkin, Mark. *When Did Indians Become Straight? Kinship, the History of Sexuality, and Native Sovereignty*. New York: Oxford University Press, 2011.

Riley, Angela. "Good (Native) Governance." *Columbia Law Review* 107 (2007): 1049–125.

Riley, Angela. "(Tribal) Sovereignty and Illiberalism." *California Law Review* 95 (2007): 799–848.

Ritchie, Andrea J. *Invisible No More: Police Violence against Black Women and Women of Color*. Boston: Beacon Press, 2017.

Roberts, Alaina A. *I've Been Here All the While: Black Freedom on Native Land*. Philadelphia: University of Pennsylvania Press, 2021.

Roberts, Dorothy. *Killing the Black Body: Race, Reproduction, and the Meaning of Liberty*. New York: Random House, 1997.

Roberts, Dorothy. *Shattered Bonds: The Color of Child Welfare*. New York: Basic Civitas Books, 2002.

Roberts, Neil. *Freedom as Marronage*. Chicago: University of Chicago Press, 2015.

Robinson, Cedric J. *Black Marxism: The Making of the Black Radical Tradition*. 3rd rev. ed. Chapel Hill: University of North Carolina Press, 2021.

Rockwell, Stephen J. *Indian Affairs and the Administrative State in the Nineteenth Century*. New York: Cambridge University Press, 2010.

Rodríguez, Juana María. *Sexual Futures, Queer Gestures, and Other Latina Longings*. New York: New York University Press, 2014.

Rodríguez, Richard T. *Next of Kin: The Family in Chicano/a Cultural Politics*. Durham: Duke University Press, 2009.

Roe v. Wade. 410 U.S. 113 (1973).

Rogers, Brent M. *Unpopular Sovereignty: Mormons and the Federal Management of Early Utah Territory*. Lincoln: University of Nebraska Press, 2017.

Rogozen, Sarah. "Prioritizing Diversity and Autonomy in the Polygamy Legalization Debate." UCLA *Women's Law Journal* 24 (2017): 107–49.

Romero, Diana, and Madina Agénor. "The Welfare Family Cap: Reproductive Rights, Control, and Poverty Prevention." In *Radical Reproductive Justice: Foundations, Theory, Practice, Critique*, edited by Loretta J. Ross, Lynn Roberts, Erika Derkas, Whitney Peoples, and Pamela Bridgewater Toure, 381–96. New York: Feminist Press, 2017.

Rosen, Hannah. *Terror in the Heart of Freedom: Citizenship, Sexual Violence, and the Meaning of Race in the Postemancipation South*. Chapel Hill: University of North Carolina Press, 2009.

Rosenblum, Nancy L. "Democratic Sex: *Reynolds v. U.S.*, Sexual Relations, and Community." In *Sex, Preference, and Family: Essays on Law and Nature*, edited by David M. Estlund and Martha C. Nussbaum, 63–85. New York: Oxford University Press, 1998.

Ross, Loretta J. "Conceptualizing Reproductive Justice Theory: A Manifesto for Activism." In *Radical Reproductive Justice: Foundations, Theory, Practice, Critique*, edited by Loretta J. Ross, Lynn Roberts, Erika Derkas, Whitney Peoples, and Pamela Bridgewater Toure, 170–232. New York: Feminist Press, 2017.

Ross, Loretta J. "Trust Black Women: Reproductive Justice and Eugenics." In *Radical Reproductive Justice: Foundations, Theory, Practice, Critique*, edited by Loretta J. Ross, Lynn Roberts, Erika Derkas, Whitney Peoples, and Pamela Bridgewater Toure, 58–85. New York: Feminist Press, 2017.

Ross, Loretta J., Lynn Roberts, Erika Derkas, Whitney Peoples, and Pamela Bridgewater Toure, eds. *Radical Reproductive Justice: Foundations, Theory, Practice, Critique*. New York: Feminist Press, 2017.

Ross, Marlon B. "Beyond the Closet as Raceless Paradigm." In *Black Queer Studies: A Critical Anthology*, edited by E. Patrick Johnson and Mae G. Henderson, 161–89. Durham: Duke University Press, 2005.

Rothstein, Richard. *The Color of Law: A Forgotten History of How Our Government Segregated America*. New York: W. W. Norton and Co., 2017.

Ruppel, Kristin T. *Unearthing Indian Land: Living with the Legacies of Allotment*. Tucson: University of Arizona Press, 2008.

Rusco, Elmer. *A Fateful Time: The Background and Legislative History of the Indian Reorganization Act*. Reno: University of Nevada Press, 2000.

Russell, Steve. "Making Peace with Crow Dog's Ghost: Racialized Prosecution in Federal Indian Law," *Wicazo Sa Review* 21, no. 1 (2006): 61–76.

Sahlins, Marshall. *What Kinship Is—and Is Not*. Chicago: University of Chicago Press, 2013.

Saldaña-Portillo, María Josefina. *The Revolutionary Imagination in the Americas and the Age of Development*. Durham: Duke University Press, 1993.

Samuels, Ellen. *Fantasies of Identification: Disability, Gender, Race*. New York: New York University Press, 2014.

Santa Clara Pueblo v. Martinez. 436 U.S. 49 (1978).

Saranillio, Dean Itsuji. *Unsustainable Empire: Alternative Histories of Hawai'i Statehood*. Durham: Duke University Press, 2018.

Saunt, Claudio. *Black, White, and Indian: Race and the Unmaking of an American Family*. New York: Oxford University Press, 2005.

Schaeffer, Kaitlyn. "Answering Constitutional Challenges to the Tribal VAWA Provisions." *NYU Journal of Legislation and Public Policy* 21 (2018/2019): 993–1031.

Schenwar, Maya, and Victoria Law. *Prison by Any Other Name: The Harmful Consequences of Popular Reforms*. New York: New Press, 2020.

Schneider, David M. *A Critique of the Study of Kinship*. Ann Arbor: University of Michigan Press, 1984.

Schuller, Kyla. *The Biopolitics of Feeling: Race, Sex, and Science in the Nineteenth Century*. Durham: Duke University Press, 2018.

Schuller, Kyla, and Julian Gill-Peterson, eds. "The Biopolitics of Plasticity," *Social Text* 38, no. 2 (2020).

Scott, David. *Conscripts of Modernity: The Tragedy of Colonial Enlightenment*. Durham: Duke University Press, 2004.

Scott, James C. *The Art of Not Being Governed: An Anarchist History of Upland Southeast Asia*. New Haven: Yale University Press, 2009.

Sealey, Kris F. *Creolizing the Nation*. Evanston, IL: Northwestern University Press, 2020.

Sedgwick, Eve Kosofsky. *Epistemology of the Closet*. Berkeley: University of California Press, 1990.

Sedgwick, Eve Kosofsky. *Touching Feeling: Affect, Pedagogy, Performativity*. Durham: Duke University Press, 2003.

Sellers, Charles. *The Market Revolution: Jacksonian America, 1815–1846*. New York: Oxford University Press, 1991.

Sexton, Jared. *Amalgamation Schemes: Antiblackness and the Critique of Multiracialism*. Minneapolis: University of Minnesota Press, 2008.

Sexton, Jared. "The Vel of Slavery: Tracking the Figure of the Unsovereign." *Critical Sociology* 42, no. 4–5 (December 2014): 1–15.

Shabazz, Rashad. *Spatializing Blackness: Architectures of Confinement and Black Masculinity in Chicago*. Urbana: University of Illinois Press, 2015.

Shah, Nayan. *Stranger Intimacy: Contesting Race, Sexuality, and Law in the North American West*. Berkeley: University of California Press, 2012.

Shammas, Carole. *A History of Household Government in America*. Charlottesville: University of Virginia Press, 2002.

Sharkey, Patrick. *Stuck in Place: Urban Neighborhoods and the End of Progress toward Racial Equality*. Chicago: University of Chicago Press, 2013.

Sharma, Nitasha. *Hawaiʻi Is My Haven: Race and Indigeneity in the Black Pacific*. Durham: Duke University Press, 2021.

Sharpe, Christina. *Monstrous Intimacies: Making Post-Slavery Subjects*. Durham: Duke University Press, 2010.

Sharpe, Jenny. *Ghosts of Slavery: A Literary Archaeology of Black Women's Lives*. Minneapolis: University of Minnesota Press, 2003.

Shepherd, Jeffrey P. *We Are an Indian Nation: A History of the Hualapai People*. Tucson: University of Arizona Press, 2010.

Silliman, Jael, Marlene Berger Fried, Loretta Ross, and Elena R. Gutiérrez. *Undivided Rights: Women of Color Organize for Reproductive Justice*. 2nd ed. Chicago: Haymarket Books, 2016.

Simon, Jonathan. *Governing through Crime: How the War on Crime Transformed American Democracy and Created a Culture of Fear*. New York: Oxford University Press, 2007.

Simpson, Audra. *Mohawk Interruptus: Political Life across the Borders of Settler States*. Durham: Duke University Press, 2014.

Simpson, Audra. "The State Is a Man: Theresa Spence, Loretta Saunders and the Gender of Settler Sovereignty." *Theory and Event* 19, no. 4 (2016). https://muse.jhu.edu/article/633280.

Simpson, Leanne Betasamosake. *As We Have Always Done: Indigenous Freedom through Radical Resistance*. Minneapolis: University of Minnesota Press, 2017.

Simpson, Leanne Betasamosake. "The Place Where We All Live and Work Together: A Gendered Analysis of 'Sovereignty.'" In *Native Studies Keywords*, edited by Stephanie Nohelani Teves, Andrea Smith, and Michelle H. Raheja, 18–24. Tucson: University of Arizona Press, 2015.

Singh, Nikhil Pal. *Black Is a Country: Race and the Unfinished Struggle for Democracy*. Cambridge: Harvard University Press, 2004.

Skinner v. Oklahoma. 316 U.S. 535 (1942).

Slagle, Allogan. "Unfinished Justice: Completing the Restoration and Acknowledgement of California Indian Tribes." *American Indian Quarterly* 13, no. 4 (1989): 325–45.

Sleeper-Smith, Susan. *Indian Women and French Men: Rethinking Cultural Encounter in the Western Great Lakes*. Amherst: University of Massachusetts Press, 2001.

Slocum, Karla. *Black Towns, Black Futures: The Enduring Allure of a Black Place in the American West*. Chapel Hill: University of North Carolina Press, 2019.

Smith, Neil. "Giuliani Time: The Revanchist 1990s." *Social Text* 57 (1998): 1–20.

Smith, Neil. "New Globalism, New Urbanism: Gentrification as Global Urban Strategy." *Antipode* 34, no. 3 (2002): 427–50.

Smoak, Gregory E. *Ghost Dances and Identity: Prophetic Religion and American Indian Ethnogenesis in the Nineteenth Century*. Berkeley: University of California Press, 2006.

Snorton, C. Riley. *Black on Both Sides: A Racial History of Trans Identity*. Minneapolis: University of Minnesota Press, 2017.

Snyder, Christina. *Slavery in Indian Country: The Changing Face of Captivity in Early America*. Cambridge: Harvard University Press, 2010.

Somerville, Siobhan B. "Queer Loving." *GLQ* 11, no. 3 (2005): 335–70.

Somerville, Siobhan B. *Queering the Color Line: Race and the Invention of Homosexuality in American Culture*. Durham: Duke University Press, 2000.

Spade, Dean. *Mutual Aid: Building Solidarity during This Crisis (and the Next)*. New York: Verso, 2020.

Spade, Dean. *Normal Life: Administrative Violence, Critical Trans Politics, and the Limits of Law*. Rev. ed. Durham: Duke University Press, 2015.

Sparks, Holloway. "Queens, Teens, and Model Mothers: Race, Gender, and the Discourse of Welfare Reform." In *Race and the Politics of Welfare Reform*, edited by Sanford F. Schram, Joe Soss, and Richard C. Fording, 171–95. Ann Arbor: University of Michigan Press, 2003.

Speed, Shannon. *Incarcerated Stories: Indigenous Women Migrants and Violence in the Settler-Capitalist State*. Chapel Hill: University of North Carolina Press, 2019.

Spillers, Hortense J. "Mama's Baby, Papa's Maybe: An American Grammar Book." In *Black, White, and in Color: Essays on American Literature and Culture*, edited by Hortense J. Spillers, 203–29. Chicago: University of Chicago Press, 2003. First published 1987 in *Diacritics*.

Spruhan, Paul. "A Legal History of Blood Quantum in Federal Indian Law to 1935." *South Dakota Law Review* 51 (2006): 1–50.

Spurlock, John C. *Free Love: Marriage and Middle-Class Radicalism in America, 1825–1860*. New York: New York University Press, 1988.

Stack, Carol. *All Our Kin*. New York: Basic Books, 1997. First published 1974 by Harper and Row.

Stack, Carol. *Call to Home: African Americans Reclaim the Rural South*. New York: Basic Books, 1996.

Stallings, L. H. *A Dirty South Manifesto: Sexual Resistance and Imagination in the New South*. Oakland: University of California Press, 2020.

Stallings, L. H. *Funk the Erotic: Transaesthetics and Black Sexual Cultures*. Urbana: University of Illinois Press, 2015.

Stanley, Amy Dru. *From Bondage to Contract: Wage Labor, Marriage, and the Market in the Age of Slave Emancipation*. New York: Cambridge University Press, 1998.

Stein, Marc. *Sexual Injustice: Supreme Court Decisions from* Griswold *to* Roe. Chapel Hill: University of North Carolina Press, 2010.

Stein, Samuel. *Capital City: Gentrification and the Real Estate State*. New York: Verso, 2019.

Stephens, Michelle Ann. *Black Empire: The Masculine Global Imaginary of Caribbean Intellectuals in the United States, 1914–1962*. Durham: Duke University Press, 2005.

Stevens, Jacqueline. *Reproducing the State*. Princeton: Princeton University Press, 1999.

Stoler, Ann Laura. *Race and the Education of Desire: Foucault's History of Sexuality and the Colonial Order of Things*. Durham: Duke University Press, 1995.

Story, Brett. *Prison Land: Mapping Carceral Power across Neoliberal America*. Minneapolis: University of Minnesota Press, 2019.

Strathern, Marilyn. *Kinship, Law and the Unexpected: Relatives Are Always a Surprise*. New York: Cambridge University Press, 2005.

Stremlau, Rose. *Sustaining the Cherokee Family: Kinship and the Allotment of an Indigenous Nation*. Chapel Hill: University of North Carolina Press, 2011.

Strong, Pauline Turner. *Captive Selves, Captivating Others: The Politics and Poetics of Colonial American Captivity Narratives*. Boulder: Westview Press, 1999.

Strong, Pauline Turner. "What Is an Indian Family? The Indian Child Welfare Act and the Renascence of Tribal Sovereignty." *American Studies* 46, no. 3–4 (2005): 205–31.

Stryker, Susan. *Transgender History: The Roots of Today's Revolution*. 2nd ed. New York: Seal Press, 2017.

Sturm, Circe. *Blood Politics: Race, Culture, and Identity in the Cherokee Nation of Oklahoma*. Berkeley: University of California Press, 2002.

Sturm, Circe, ed. "Rethinking Blackness and Indigeneity in the Light of Settler Colonial Theory." *American Indian Culture and Research Journal* 43, no. 2 (2019): 1–156.

Summers, Brandi Thompson. *Black in Place: The Spatial Aesthetics of Race in a Post-Chocolate City*. Chapel Hill: University of North Carolina Press, 2019.

Suzack, Cheryl. *Indigenous Women's Writing and the Cultural Study of Law*. Toronto: University of Toronto Press, 2017.

Talbot, Christine. *A Foreign Kingdom: Mormons and Polygamy in American Political Culture, 1852–1890*. Urbana: University of Illinois Press, 2013.

TallBear, Kim. "Making Love and Relations beyond Settler Sex and Family." In *Making Kin Not Population*, edited by Adele E. Clarke and Donna Haraway, 145–66. Chicago: Prickly Paradigm Press, 2018.

TallBear, Kim. *Native American DNA: Tribal Belonging and the False Promise of Genetic Science*. Minneapolis: University of Minnesota Press, 2013.

Tapper, Melbourne. "Blood/Kinship, Governmentality, and Cultures of Order in Colonial Africa." In *Relative Values: Reconfiguring Kinship Studies*, edited by Sarah Franklin and Susan McKinnon, 329–54. Durham: Duke University Press, 2001.

Tate, Claudia. *Domestic Allegories of Political Desire: The Black Heroine's Text at the Turn of the Century*. New York: Oxford University Press, 1992.

Tawil, Ezra. *The Making of Racial Sentiment: Slavery and the Birth of the Frontier Romance*. New York: Cambridge University Press, 2006.

Taylor, Graham D. *The New Deal and American Indian Tribalism: The Administration of the Indian Reorganization Act, 1934–45*. Lincoln: University of Nebraska Press, 1980.

Taylor, Keeanga-Yamahtta. *From #BlackLivesMatter to Black Liberation*. Chicago: Haymarket Books, 2016.

Taylor, Keeanga-Yamahtta. *Race for Profit: How Banks and the Real Estate Industry Undermined Black Homeownership*. Chapel Hill: University of North Carolina Press, 2019.

Thelan, Tatjana, and Erdmute Alber. "Reconnecting State and Kinship: Temporalities, Scales, Classifications." In *Reconnecting State and Kinship*, edited by Tatjana Thelen and Erdmute Alber, 1–38. Philadelphia: University of Pennsylvania Press, 2018.

Thomas, Greg. "*Marronnons*/Let's Maroon: Sylvia Wynter's 'Black Metamorphosis' as a Species of Marroonage." *Small Axe* 49 (2016): 62–78.

Thomas, Greg. *The Sexual Demon of Colonial Power: Pan-African Embodiment and Erotic Schemes of Empire*. Bloomington: University of Indiana Press, 2007.

Thomas, Taylor Miller, and Beatrice Jin. "As U.S. Crime Rates Dropped, Local Police Spending Soared." *Politico*, July 19, 2020, https://www.politico.com/interactives/2020/police-budget-spending-george-floyd-defund/.

Thompson, Alvin O. *Flight to Freedom: African Runaways and Maroons in the Americas*. Kingston: University of the West Indies Press, 2006.

Threadcraft, Shatema. *Intimate Justice: The Black Female Body and the Body Politic*. New York: Oxford University Press, 2016.

Thrush, Coll. *Native Seattle: Histories from the Crossing-Over Place*. Seattle: University of Washington Press, 2007.

Towle, Evan B., and Lynn M. Morgan. "Romancing the Transgender Native: Rethinking the Use of the 'Third Gender' Concept." *GLQ* 8, no. 4 (2002): 469–97.

Trask, Haunani-Kay. *From a Native Daughter: Colonialism and Sovereignty in Hawai'i*. Rev. ed. Honolulu: University of Hawai'i Press, 1999.

Trautmann, Thomas R. *Lewis Henry Morgan and the Invention of Kinship*. Berkeley: University of California Press, 1987.

Trujillo, Simón Ventura. *Land Uprising: Native Story Power and the Insurgent Horizons of Latinx Indigeneity*. Tucson: University of Arizona Press, 2020.

Tuck, Eve, and K. Wayne Yang. "Decolonization Is Not a Metaphor." *Decolonization: Indigeneity, Education and Society* 1, no. 1 (2012): 1–40.

Ture, Kwame, and Charles V. Hamilton. *Black Power: The Politics of Liberation*. New York: Vintage Books, 1992. First published 1967 by Vintage Books.

Turner, Dale. *This Is Not a Peace Pipe: Towards a Critical Indigenous Philosophy*. Toronto: University of Toronto Press, 2006.

United States v. Antelope. 430 U.S. 641 (1977).

United States v. Kagama. 118 U.S. 375 (1886).

United States v. Wheeler. 435 U.S. 313 (1978).

United States v. Windsor. 570 U.S. 744 (2013).

U.S. Department of Health and Human Services. "The AFCARS Report." Washington, DC: Administration on Children, Youth, and Families, 2019.

U.S. Department of Justice. "State and Local Government Expenditures on Police Protection in the U.S., 2000–2017." Bureau of Justice Statistics, July 2020, https://www.bjs.gov/content/pub/pdf/slgeppus0017.pdf.

Vale, Lawrence J. *After the Projects: Public Housing Redevelopment and the Governance of the Poorest Americans*. New York: Oxford University Press, 2019.

Venkatesh, Sudhir Alladi. *American Project: The Rise and Fall of a Modern Ghetto*. Cambridge: Harvard University Press, 2000.

Venkatesh, Sudhir Alladi. *Off the Books: The Underground Economy of the Urban Poor*. Cambridge: Harvard University Press, 2006.

Villazor, Rose Cuison. "Blood Quantum Land Laws and the Race Versus Political Identity Dilemma," *California Law Review* 96 (2008): 801–37.

Visweswaran, Kamala. *Un/common Cultures: Racism and the Rearticulation of Cultural Difference*. Durham: Duke University Press, 2010.

Wacquant, Loïc. *Punishing the Poor: The Neoliberal Government of Social Insecurity*. Durham: Duke University Press, 2009.

Wagner, Bryan. *Disturbing the Peace: Black Culture and the Police Power after Slavery*. Cambridge, MA: Harvard University Press, 2009.

Warner, Michael. *The Trouble with Normal: Sex, Politics, and the Ethics of Queer Life*. New York: Free Press, 1999.

Warren, Samuel D., and Louis D. Brandeis. "The Right to Privacy." *Harvard Law Review* 4, no. 5 (1890): 193–220.

Waszak, Susan. "Contemporary Hurdles in the Application of the Indian Child Welfare Act." *American Indian Culture and Research* Journal 34, no. 1 (2010): 124–27.

Weber, Brenda R. *Latter-Day Scenes: Gender, Sexuality, and Mediated Mormonism*. Durham: Duke University Press, 2019.

Weheliye, Alexander G. *Habeas Viscus: Racializing Assemblages, Biopolitics, and Black Feminist Theories of the Human*. Durham: Duke University Press, 2014.

Weinbaum, Alys Eve. *Wayward Reproduction: Genealogies of Race and Nation in Transatlantic Modern Thought*. Durham: Duke University Press, 2004.

Weston, Kath. *Families We Choose: Lesbians, Gays, Kinship*. New York: Columbia University Press, 1991.

White, Monica W. *Freedom Farmers: Agricultural Resistance and the Black Freedom Movement*. Chapel Hill: University of North Carolina Press, 2018.

Wilder, Gary. *Freedom Time: Negritude, Decolonization, and the Future of the World*. Durham: Duke University Press, 2015.

Wilderson, Frank B., III. *Red, White, and Black: Cinema and the Structure of U.S. Antagonisms*. Durham: Duke University Press, 2010.

Wilkins, David E. *American Indian Sovereignty and the U.S. Supreme Court: The Masking of Justice*. Austin: University of Texas Press, 1997.

Wilkins, David E., and K. Tsianina Lomawaima. *Uneven Ground: American Indian Sovereignty and Federal Law*. Norman: University of Oklahoma Press, 2001.

Williams, Brackette F. "Classification Systems Revisited: Kinship, Caste, Race, and Nationality as the Flow of Blood and Spread of Rights." In *Naturalizing Power: Essays in Feminist Cultural Analysis*, edited by Sylvia Yangisako and Carol Delaney, 201–38. New York: Routledge, 1995.

Williams, Patricia J. *Alchemy of Race and Rights: Diary of a Law Professor*. Cambridge: Harvard University Press, 1992.

Williams, Patricia J. "Intimacy and the Untouchable: Marriage and the Traumatic History of 'In-law' and 'Outlaw' Family." *differences* 29, no. 2 (2018): 191–95.

Williams, Rhonda Y. *The Politics of Public Housing: Black Women's Struggles against Urban Inequality*. New York: Oxford University Press, 2004.

Williams, Robert A., Jr. *The American Indian in Western Legal Thought: The Discourses of Conquest*. New York: Oxford University Press, 1992.

Williams, Robert A., Jr. *Like a Loaded Weapon: The Rehnquist Court, Indian Rights, and the Legal History of Racism in America*. Minneapolis: University of Minnesota Press, 2005.

Willse, Craig, and Dean Spade. "Freedom in a Regulatory State? *Lawrence*, Marriage, and Biopolitics." *Widener Law Review* 11 (2005): 309–29.

Wilson, David. *Cities and Race: America's New Black Ghetto*. Routledge: New York, 2007.

Wilson, James Q. *Thinking about Crime*. Rev. ed. New York: Vintage Books, 1985.

Wilson, William Julius. *When Work Disappears: The World of the New Urban Poor.* New York: Vintage Books, 1996.

Wilson-Hokuwhitu, Nālani, ed. *The Past before Us: Moʻokūʻauhau as Methodology.* Honolulu: University of Hawaiʻi Press, 2019.

Witgen, Michael, *An Infinity of Nations: How the Native New World Shaped Early North America.* Philadelphia: University of Pennsylvania Press, 2012.

Wong, Edlie L. *Racial Reconstruction: Black Inclusion, Chinese Exclusion, and the Fictions of Citizenship.* New York: New York University Press, 2015.

Woods, Clyde. *Development Arrested: The Blues and Plantation Power in the Mississippi Delta.* New York: Verso, 2017. First published 1998.

Woods, Clyde. "Les Misérables of New Orleans: Trap Economics and the Asset Stripping Blues, Part 1." *American Quarterly* 61, no. 3 (2009): 769–96.

Wynter, Sylvia. "Unsettling the Coloniality of Being/Power/Truth/Freedom: Towards the Human, after Man, Its Overrepresentation—An Argument." CR: *The New Centennial Review* 3, no. 3 (2003): 257–337.

Yanagisako, Sylvia, and Carol Delaney. "Naturalizing Power." In *Naturalizing Power: Essays in Feminist Cultural Analysis*, edited by Sylvia Yangisako and Carol Delaney, 1–24. New York: Routledge, 1995.

Yanagisako, Sylvia Junko, and Jane Fishburne Collier. "Toward a Unified Analysis of Gender and Kinship." In *Gender and Kinship: Essays toward a Unified Analysis*, edited by Jane Fishburne Collier and Sylvia Junko Yanagisako, 14–52. Stanford: Stanford University Press, 1987.

Yazzie, Melanie. "Decolonizing Development in Diné Bikeyah." *Environment and Society* 9 (2018): 25–39.

Yazzie, Melanie. "US Imperialism and the Problem of 'Culture' in Indigenous Politics: Towards Indigenous Internationalist Feminism." *American Indian Culture and Research Journal* 40, no. 3 (2019): 95–117.

Young, Cynthia A. *Soul Power: Culture, Radicalism, and the Making of a U.S. Third World Left.* Durham: Duke University Press, 2006.

Young, Iris Marion. *Justice and the Politics of Difference.* Princeton: Princeton University Press, 2011. First published 1990.

Young, Robert J. C. *Colonial Desire: Hybridity in Theory, Culture, and Race.* New York: Routledge, 1995.

Ziegler, Mary. *Beyond Abortion:* Roe v. Wade *and the Battle for Privacy.* Cambridge: Harvard University Press, 2018.

INDEX

abortion: federal funding restrictions and, 172, 304n98, 307n122; privacy and, 169–70, 303n88

activist mothering, 234

Adoptive Couple v. Baby Girl (2013), 122, 125, 190, 293n87, 293n89

affect, political orders and, 16–25

Ahmed, Sara, 44, 49–50, 64, 68–69, 81, 105–6

Aid for Dependent Children (ADC), 175

Aid to Families with Dependent Children (AFDC) program, 175–81

Alito, Samuel (Justice), 125

allotment policy: ending of, 117, 128; Indigenous property rights and, 74–88, 262, 266–67, 285n98; Mormonism and, 160

All Our Kin (Stack), 227–28

aloha āina (Hawaiian love of the land), 134

American Freedmen's Inquiry Commission, 221

American Indian Movement, 179

Amin, Kadji, 263

Ancient Society (Morgan), 48–49, 148–49

Andersen, Chris, 139

anthropological discourse, Indigenous governance, 78–79

anti-miscegenation statutes, marriage laws and, 193–95, 305n107

artificial unity, in families, 44

Asia: alienness of, 167; immigration barriers for women from, 192–93; Mormon linkage with, 159–61

Baldwin, James, 325n120

Barker, Joanne, 210, 296n133

Belgrade, Daniel B., 105

Bellacasa, Puig de la, 339n210

belonging: clan belonging, Native feminist reframing of, 129–30; governance and exclusion of, 23; Indian Child Welfare Act and, 118–19; Indigenous concepts of, 16, 37–38, 79–82, 98–99, 114–16; kinship and, 45–47, 54–56, 73, 86–91; political orders and, 73–91, 102–7; racialization of, 103–16; sexuality and, 9; sovereignty and, 29; urbanization impact on, 138–40; zones of queerness and, 61–72

Benhabib, Seyla, 20–21, 275n46

Benjamin, Ruha, 208

Bentley, Nancy, 155, 299n37

Bercaw, Nancy, 216, 220, 323n103

Berlant, Lauren, 62, 273n26

"Beyond Same-Sex Marriage" statement, 70

Bill of Rights, privacy in, 165–66

biopolitics: of racialization, 10, 26, 273n21; tribal jurisdiction of, 94–98

Black Americans: incarceration rates for, 244–53; Indigenous tribal sovereignty and, 258–69; networks created by, 13–14, 204–12, 214–27, 315n57, 339n210; welfare policies and, 174–81, 304nn103–4. *See also* Blackness

Black Belt thesis, 315n59

Black Codes, 316n66

Black elected officials, Black activism and, 247–48

Black Lives Matter Global Network, 246

Black Lives Matter movement, 246–53, 337n190, 337n193

Blackmun, Harry, 183, 187

Black nationalism, 199–201

Blackness: aberrance and deviance linked to, 77–78; criminality and, 39–40, 202–4; deviance and dependency linked to, 175–81, 304–5n104, 305n107, 305n109; emancipation carceration after slavery and, 212–27; fornication and adultery linked to, 222–23; home and family and, 39–40; juvenile delinquency linked to, 230–31; land ownership and, 29–30; Moynihan report pathologization of, 227–42; policing and police violence linked to, 245–53, 335n182; political orders and, 200–204; ungovernability linked to, 204–12; welfare policy and, 174–81, 193–95, 305n107, 305n109. *See also* Black Americans

Black Panthers, 179

Black women: Black Lives Matter and, 247; Black nationalism and, 201; care ethics and, 339n210; Community Action Programs and, 240–41; family structure for, 13–14; forced sterilization of, 177–81, 202–3, 306nn114–16; networks developed by, 234–35, 316n62, 339n210; post-emancipation criminalization of, 213–14; rejection of failed domesticity by, 250–53, 338n208; reproductive justice movement and, 307n125; respectability politics and, 247–48, 312n16; shelter research on, 242–43; welfare policies targeting, 176–81, 193–95, 305n107, 304nn103–4, 305n109, 306nn111–15

Black Youth Project, 77–78

blood relationship: Black Creek people and, 266–69; kinship based on, 49–53; tribal determination of, 93–94, 114–16, 123–27. *See also* consanguinity; tiospaye (Dakota larger family group)

Boas, Franz, 78

bodies: Black bodies, governance of, 203; forced sterilization impact on, 179–81, 306nn113–16; Native feminist reframing of, 133–34; political orders and, 3–4, 73–91, 203; privacy rights and, 181–95

Boggs, Grace Lee, 232

Boggs, James, 232

bourgeois household model, Indigenous kinship concepts and, 48–49

Bowers v. Hardwick (1986), 181, 183, 186

Brandeis, Louis, 165–66

Bridges, Khiara M., 173, 303n97

Bridget, In re, 294n90

Briggs, Laura, 282n62

broken windows policing, 245, 335n182

Brown, Michael, 245, 335n182

Brown v. Board of Education, 229

Brown v. Buhman (2013), 162–64, 301n65, 301n68, 302n69

Bruyneel, Kevin, 321n93

Buchanan, James, 149–52

Buck v. Bell, 178, 306n116

Bureau of Indian Affairs (BIA), 102

Bureau of Refugees, Freedmen, and Abandoned Lands. *See* Freedmen's Bureau

Butler, Judith, 283n67

Buxton, C. Lee, 166

BYP100, 247, 337n195

Byrd, Jodi, 22–23, 202, 309n157

Camp, Jordan, 332n169

care ethics, Black governance and, 339n210

Carey v. Population Services (1977), 170, 187–88

Carruthers, Charlene A., 72, 84, 88, 90, 198, 209–12, 216–17, 247, 249, 251–53

Carsten, Janet, 280n28, 281n39

Carter, Julian, 185

Castro-Huerta, Victor Manuel, 258–64

Cherokee Nation v. Georgia, 289n28

children of Indigenous families: existing Indian family exception for, 294n90; Indian Child Welfare Act and, 117–27, 290n42; statistics on separation of, 1–2

Church of Jesus Christ of Latter-day Saints. *See* Mormonism

citizenship: Indigenous personhood and, 22–23, 108–16, 125–27, 290n42; marriage and, 193, 310n160

civilization, Mormon polygamy as threat to, 161

Civil Rights Act of 1964, 229

clan system of governance, 17–18

Clarke, Adele E., 45

Clear, Todd, 244
Cleveland, Grover, 156
Clinton, Bill, 175
Coates, Ta-Nehisi, 331n164, 340n220
Cohen, Cathy, 77, 210–11, 253, 340n220
collective activism: in Black neighborhoods, 234–35, 239–42; Freedmen's Bureau administration of, 217–18; governance and, 197–98, 210–12, 268–69; Moynihan report criticism of, 227, 233–34; Native feminist reframing of, 131–40; political orders and, 16–17, 20–25, 210–12, 268–69, 274n39
colonialism: Black personhood and, 206–12; families and, 1–3, 9–14, 55–61; heteronormativity and, 74–75; heteropatriarchal imposition under, 14–15; Indigenous family structure and, 75–78, 83–88, 274n39, 279n11, 279n17; kinship and, 52–61; Native feminist reframing of, 130–40; primitive accumulation and, 26–35; property ownership and, 200–201; settler concepts of Indianness and, 15–16
Commission on Public Growth, 178
Committee for Abortion Rights and Against Sterilization Abuse (CARASA), 307n122
Committee on Juvenile Delinquency and Youth Crimes, 230
Committee on Population and Family Planning, 178
commons: Black governance and, 207; governance and, 26–27. *See also* undercommons, Harney and Moten concept of
community: Black formation of, 234–38; Black political power and, 248–49; foreclosure of Black formation of, 223–27; Indian Child Welfare Act framework of, 119–27; Native feminist reframing of, 131–40; policing and police violence impact on, 245–46; urban migration and making of, 140
Community Action Programs (CAPS), 239–42, 330n151
Congress: Indian Child Welfare Act impact on, 117, 121–27; Mormon polygamy and, 152–64, 300nn46–47; tribal sovereignty and, 108–16, 142, 289n28, 293n74

consanguinuity, kinship and, 49–53. *See also* blood relationship
contraception: privacy rights and, 166–72; reproductive justice and, 307n125. *See also* reproduction
contract system for Black labor: Freedmen's Bureau creation of, 218–27, 318n72, 318n74, 318n76; property ownership and, 224–27
Coontz, Stephanie, 296n5
Coulthard, Glen, 26–28
couplehood: kinship and role of, 49–54; in queer scholarship, 66–73
Coviello, Peter, 159–60, 198, 299n45
Cox, Aimee Meredith, 242–43, 250–51, 338n208
Creek Freedmen, 267
Creek Nation, tribal sovereignty of, 258–69
creolization, 274n36
Crime Commission (Commission on Law Enforcement and Administration of Justice), 231–32, 324n118
criminality: Blackness linked to, 202–4, 218–19, 223–27, 233–42, 324n118, 330n161, 332–33n169; emancipation carceration and, 212–27; law enforcement funding increases and, 244–53; Moynihan report framework of, 227–42; privacy and, 171–72; race and, 171–72, 308n145; sexuality and, 186–95; tribal law and, 94–98, 290n31, 290n37, 290n39, 291n49, 292n70
Critical Race Theory, 342n28
Cullors, Patrisse, 246
culture: Black activism and, 252–53; Indian Child Welfare Act framework of, 117, 119–27; Indigenous sovereignty and, 74–88, 107–16, 291n57; kinship and, 46–48; political orders, 20–25; tribal jurisdiction and, 95–98
Cumming, Alfred, 152
Curry, Lucy A., 114
Curtis Act of 1898, 266

Dakota people, governance and kinship structures of, 75–80, 81–88
Dandridge v. Williams (1970), 172–74, 304n98

Davis, Angela, 201, 330n161
Davis, Dána-Ain, 176–77
Davis Bend, Mississippi, 223
Davis v. Beason (1890), 150, 155–56
Dawes Act (General Allotment Act) (1887), 128, 160
Dawes Commission, 266
Defense of Marriage Act (DOMA), 184, 189–91, 310n160
Deloria, Ella, 78–83, 86, 156, 285n98
Dennison, Jean, 83–88, 132
dependency rhetoric, welfare policy and, 175–81, 202–3, 303nn103–4, 305n107, 305n109
Deseret (Mormon state), 151
deviance: Blackness linked to, 203–4, 218–19, 223–27, 338n198; institutionalized ideologies of, 242–53; Moynihan Report framework of, 230–42; as resistance, 210–11, 316n60
Dillon, Elizabeth Maddock, 7
disidentification, patterns of, 265–69
"Doctrine of the Genealogical Unity of Mankind" (Schneider), 52
Douglas, William O. (Justice), 166
Dred Scott v. Sanford, 152, 309n158
due process, same-sex marriage and, 184–85, 190–91, 193–94
Duggan, Lisa, 70–71
Duthu, N. Bruce, 99, 104–5

Economic Opportunity Act (EOA), 239–42, 329n150
Edmunds Act (1882), 153, 156
Edmunds-Tucker Act, 154, 156, 158
Edwards, Erica, 204, 211–12, 214, 247
Eisenstadt v. Baird (1972), 168–69, 171, 186, 303n87
employment patterns for Black Americans, 323n112, 335n178
enfamilyment: Blackness and, 39–40, 66; defined, 2; Indigenous refusal of, 73–88; kinship concepts and, 48–49, 59–61; Moynihan report pathologization of, 227–42, 324n115; Native feminist reframing of, 130–40; political orders and, 3–4, 147–49; post-emancipation imposition of, 217–18; privacy and, 165; queer scholarship rejection of, 70–73; race-making and, 8–14; racialization of, 107–16; selfhood and, 60–61; tribal jurisdiction and, 94–98, 260–69; underclass ecology linked to failure of, 242; welfare policy and, 179–81
Eng, David, 32–33, 60–61, 67–68, 90–91
equal protection: Indigenous citizenship and, 108; privacy rights and, 169; same-sex marriage and, 184–85
erotic maroonage, marriage and families and, 66
Ertman, Martha M., 300n47
ethics of relation, Indigenous governance in context of, 74–88
eugenics, forced sterilization and, 167–68, 177–79
exchange systems, Black urban neighborhoods' use of, 235–37
Ex Parte Crow Dog (1883), 101–2

family: Blackness and, 39–40, 203–4; characteristics of, 2; Freedmen's Bureau policies concerning, 217–27; immigration policies and concepts of, 32–35; Indian Child Welfare Act framework of, 116–27, 292n73, 293n74; Indigenous concepts of, 48–61, 78–88, 108–27; institutionalization of, 5–6; kinship and, 44–48, 70–73; marriage and, 193; Mormon polygamy and, 150–64; Moynihan report pathologization of, 227–42; Native feminist remapping of, 127–40; normative ideology of, 145–49; nuclear family model, 66–73, 81–88, 145–46; privacy and personhood and, 146–49, 167–81; queer concepts of, 62–73, 88–91; racialization of, 6–14, 41, 81–88; state framework for, 12, 39, 164, 273n19, 296n5; welfare policies and role of, 175–81
Family Planning Act (1970), 178
Federal Housing Administration (FHA), 232–33, 238–39, 325n123
federal law and policy: funding policies and, 172–81, 238–39, 330n162; Indianness in,

382 · INDEX

37–38, 259; law enforcement spending and, 244–53; Mormon polygamy and, 149–64, 196, 300nn46–47; Moynihan report impact on, 227–42; pathologization of Blackness in, 233–42; racialized narrative of family and reproduction in, 137–40; residential segregation and, 243–53, 325n122; state governance and, 297n6; tribal jurisdiction and governance vs., 108–16, 258–69; welfare policy and, 177–81, 304nn103–4
Feinberg, Richard, 278n6
feminist politics and scholarship: Black Lives Matter and, 247; families and, 32–33, 272n13; on kinship, 44–48, 63; Mormon proto-feminisms and, 299n37; Native family reframing and, 127–40, 143–44; political orders and, 34–35
Ferguson, Roderick, 34, 77–78
Fifth Amendment: Indigenous citizenship and, 108; privacy rights and, 184–85, 189–90
First Amendment, religious freedom under, 154–55, 163–64, 298n29
Fisk, Clinton B., 219
Five Tribes treaties, slavery and, 262, 341n6
Floyd, John B., 157
forced sterilization: abortion funding and, 307n122; eugenics and, 167–68, 177–81, 306nn114–16; statistics on, 307n120
Forman, James, 332n169
Foucault, Michel, 9–10, 145, 272n14, 273n19
Fourteenth Amendment, privacy rights and, 165–66, 184–85, 189–90, 309n158
Fourth Amendment, privacy protections in, 171
Franke, Katherine, 181, 282n63
Frazier, E. Franklin, 227
Freeburg, Christopher, 315n58
Freedmen's Bureau, 204, 217–27, 316n66, 317n70, 318n72, 318n74, 318n76, 318n82, 321n91; in Oklahoma, 260, 266–67
Frickey, Philip, 99, 289n18
Fullilove, Mindy Thompson, 233

Galton, Francis (Sir), 177–78
Garfield, James, 157–58

Garner, Eric, 335n182, 337n193
Garner, Tyron, 308n145
Garza, Alicia, 242, 246–49, 252–54, 338n205
gender: Blackness and, 211; housing policies and, 326n124; political orders and violence based on, 14; tribal sovereignty and, 108–16
genealogy: culture and, 75; Indigenous governance and rejection of, 78–79, 141–44; kinship and, 44–48, 215–27; selfhood and, 60–61
General Allotment Act. *See* Dawes Act (General Allotment Act) (1887)
gens, Morgan's concept of, 53–56, 215
gentrification: queer space and, 281n49; residential segregation and, 243–53, 331n166
ghettos, Moynihan report framework of, 227, 233, 235–36, 328n144
Goeman, Mishuana, 78, 81, 136, 138, 200
Goldberg, Arthur (Justice), 167
Goldstein, Alyosha, 202, 240
Gopinath, Gayatri, 32, 277n76
governance: activist organizing and, 250–53; Black networks of, 204–12, 235–42, 339n210; bourgeois homemaking and, 7–8; collectivity as, 17–18; family and, 147–49, 273n19; Freedmen's Bureau role in, 218–27; funding policies and, 172–81, 238–39; Indian Child Welfare Act and, 116–17; Indigenous political orders and, 4, 38, 55–61, 73–88, 107–16, 237–38; kinship and, 54–61, 90–91, 215–27; liberalism view of, 18–25; Mormonism as threat to, 159–64; Moynihan Report framework of, 235–42; nationalism and, 199–200; Native feminist reframing of, 129–40; privacy and, 197–98; in queer scholarship, 32–33, 72–73; racialization and, 30–35, 272n18; tribal jurisdiction and, 3, 55–66, 93–98, 258–69
Government Accountability Office, 179
Grand Order of the Iroquois, 48
Grant, Ulysses S., 223
Grassley, Chuck, 93–94
Great Migration, urban community formation and, 238–39, 324n115, 328n145

Griswold, Estelle T., 166
Griswold v. Connecticut (1965), 166–81, 186, 303n87
Gunter, Dan, 113

Hahn, Steven, 214–15, 314n52
Haley, Sarah, 213
Hancock, Ange-Marie, 306n114
Harjo, Laura, 16, 133, 135, 139, 201, 215, 251
Harney, Stefano, 207, 209
Harris, Cheryl, 200
Harris v. McRae (1980), 172–74
Hartman, Saidiya, 206–7, 209, 318n72
Haudenosaunee life and governance: kinship in, 48–61; Native feminist reframing of, 129–31
Hawai'i, pre-annexation culture of, 131–34
Health Research Group, 179
heteronormativity: Blackness and, 39–40, 203; colonial framework for, 22–25; Indigenous reframing of, 74–88, 114–16; marriage laws and, 185–86; policing and police violence linked to, 246; queer scholarship on kinship and, 62–73; racial reproduction and, 106–7; same-sex marriage and, 181
heteropatriarchy: Indigenous displacement and, 14–15; kinship and, 47–48; nationalist investment in, 31–32; Native feminist reframing of, 129–40; queer scholarship on limits of, 66–73; tribal jurisdiction and, 104–7
Holmes, Oliver Wendell, 178
homeownership: decline in Black homeownership, 232–33, 327n126; gentrification and predatory lending and, 243–53, 331n166; Moynihan Report claims of Black failure in, 231–32; racialization of, 167, 227–28. *See also* land use and ownership; property
Home Owners' Loan Corporation, 325n123
Homestead Act, 153
homosexuality, privacy and, 182–95, 310n163
Hong, Grace K., 34
House of Kings (Creek legislature), 266
House of Warriors (Creek legislature), 266

Housing Act of 1949 and 1954, 325n123
Housing and Urban Development (HUD) Act, 327n126
housing projects and programs: broken windows policing and, 245; collective institutions and, 234–37; costs of, 326n125; gender and, 326n124; pathologization of Blackness and, 232–42, 325n122. *See also* residential segregation
Howard, O. O., 219, 316n66, 317n70, 322n97, 322n102
hub-genesis, 139–40
Hunter, Marcus Anthony, 237, 250, 318n74
Hunter, Tera, 214–15, 220
Hyde, Anne F., 12–14, 273n24
Hyde Amendment, 173–74, 304n98

Ibrahim, Habiba, 176
Illegal Immigration Reform and Immigrant Responsibility Act, 310n160
immigration, US anxiety over, 160–61
Immigration and Nationality Act of 1965, 32
imperialism: jurisdiction and, 12; kinship and, 43–44; manifest domesticity and, 272n12; Morgan on, 57–58; Mormonism and examples of, 157–63, 167, 191, 298nn27–29, 299n38, 301n63; political orders and, 10, 14, 16
imperium in imperio, Mormon polygamy and, 157, 196
implicit divestiture doctrine, tribal sovereignty and, 99
incarceration: Black American rates of, 244, 331n163, 333n170; economic conditions linked to, 334n174; emancipation and, 212–27; government spending on, 334nn175–77; growth of, 332n169; public spending on, 244–45
Indian Act (1876), 129
Indian Child Welfare Act (ICWA), 38, 116–27, 130, 135, 141, 190, 294n90
Indian Civil Rights Act (ICRA), 108–9, 292n70
Indian Country, legal definition of, 95, 287n2
Indian Health Service, 179, 304n98

Indianness: colonial concepts of, 15–16; in federal law and policy, 37–38, 94–98, 112–16, 140–44, 259, 288n11; Indian Child Welfare Act and concepts of, 119–27; Native feminist reframing of, 133–40; racialization of, 107–16, 259–60; tribal governance and jurisdiction and, 98–107, 115–16; urban migration impact on, 138–40

Indian Reorganization Act (IRA) (1934), 102, 108, 128–29, 132–40

Indigenous people: Black Americans and, 276n56, 314n53; family structure and, 48–61, 78–88, 116–27, 147–49, 167; kinship in culture of, 44–61, 73–88; land use among, 200–201; marriage laws and, 192; Mormonism and, 160–64, 300n56; Native feminist remapping and, 127–40; political orders and, 3–6, 12–14, 17–25, 73–91, 203; primitive accumulation and, 25–35; property rights and, 276n58; racialization of bodies of, 15–16; reframing of kinship by, 74–88; sexual assault and domestic violence and, 93–94, 287n5; sovereignty of, 94–98, 232, 237–38; state intervention in lives of, 37–38, 116–27; tribal governance and jurisdiction and, 3, 55–61, 93–94, 98–107, 258–69

Indigenous women: forced sterilization of, 179; murder of, 3–4; reproductive rights restrictions for, 304n98

individualism, right to privacy and, 165

inhabitance, queer scholarship on norms of, 68–73

internal colonialism, 29

interracial marriage, 174, 193–95

intimacy: colonial framework for, 146; Indigenous governance and, 74–88; Indigenous governance and role of, 73–74; kinship and, 13–14; networks and, 339n210; politics of, 273n26; privacy rights and, 166–67, 183–95; queer scholarship on, 62–73

Isaac, Calvin, 124

Jefferson, Thomas, 154
Jenkins, Candace, 339n210
Jessin v. County of Shasta, 178

Johnson, Andrew, 223
Johnson, Jessica Marie, 13–14
Johnson, Lyndon B., 178, 231, 234
jurisdiction: family structure and, 47, 54, 71–72, 78; federal polygamy laws and, 150–64; Indigenous kinship structures and, 74–75, 79–84, 88–91; liberal governance and, 39, 58, 81–84, 258–69; political orders and, 56; of state, 10, 12, 15, 17–38, 75–76, 258–69; tribal jurisdiction, 3, 55–61, 93–94, 98–107, 258–69

Justice, Daniel Heath, 79, 85–87

juvenile delinquency, Moynihan Report focus on, 230

Juvenile Delinquency and Youth Offenses Control Act (1961), 230

Kanaka ʻŌiwi (Native Hawaiian) governance, 131–34, 294n100
Kaplan, Amy, 272nn12–13
Katz v. United States (1967), 171
Kauanui, Kēhaulani, J., 84, 131–32
Kazanjian, David, 272n18
Keeling, Kara, 200–201, 205
Kelling, George L., 245
Kennedy, John F., 230
kinship: Black criminality in frame of, 213–27; Black networks and, 215–17, 224–27, 254–55, 314n52; defined, 2–3, 43–48; family and, 8–9, 12–14; genealogy of, 36–37; Indian Child Welfare Act framework of, 119–27; Indigenous governance and, 48–61, 73–88; institutionalization of, 5–6; marriage and, 193; Mormon polygamy and, 163–64; Native feminist remapping of, 127–40, 156; networks and, 2–3, 56–73, 228, 235–42; political orders and, 4, 48–49, 54–61, 73–88, 197–98, 216–27; racialization of, 12–14, 114–16, 203–4, 263–69, 272n13; same-sex marriage, 61–62; sovereignty and, 215–27; state framing of, 54–61, 156, 283n67; tribal jurisdiction and, 94–98, 114–16; twentieth-century theories of, 280n28; urbanization impact on, 138–40; zones of queerness and, 60–73

Ku Klux Klan, 315n57
Kyl, John, 93

labor: apprenticeship of Black children into, 320n87; Freedmen's Bureau contract system for, 217–20
Lamarkianism, 306n113
land use and ownership: Black dispossession in rural South from, 238–39, 315n59, 321nn91–92, 329n146; boundary treaties and, 260–69, 340n1; colonial dispossession and, 27–35, 138–40, 296n133; in Hawaii, 131–34; nationalism and, 200–201; Native feminist reframing of, 136–37; post-emancipation Black claims of, 223–27, 391nn91–93; religious institutions and, 300n45; in Tulsa, Oklahoma, 262–63. *See also* property
Late Corporation of the Church of Jesus Christ of the Latter-Day Saints v. United States, The, 150, 158–59, 161–62, 300n49
Latin America, Indigeneity and migration from, 277n69
law enforcement: arrest rates for Black Americans and, 244–53, 331n163, 333n170; Black organization against police violence and, 243–53; Black population and violence by, 232, 330n161, 335n182, 336n184, 336n188; federal spending on, 244–53, 333n173, 334nn175–77
Law Enforcement Assistance Act, 231
Lawrence v. Texas (2003), 163, 184, 186–88, 308n145, 308n149
League of the Ho-dé-no-sau-nee, or Iroquois (Morgan), 48
Lewis, Brian L., 103, 290n31
Lewis, Jovan Scott, 29, 262, 341n20
LGBT people: kinship and, 67–73; marriage equality for, 70–73, 152, 309n158, 310n173; normative home and family and, 60–61
liberalism: forced sterilization and, 180–81; Indigenous governance in context of, 74–88; kinship and, 58–61, 80–88; marriage and privacy and, 184–95; normative foundation of, 297n10; nuclear family ideology and, 145–49; political orders as alternative to, 14–25, 264–69; polygamy and privacy under, 159–64; privacy protections and, 171–72; queer models of enfamilyment and, 67–73; race and, 275n50
Lieber, Francis, 157, 160, 299n38
lifeworlds, Hunter and Robinson's concept of, 250–51
Lorde, Audre, 277n66
Loving, Mildred, 308n145
Loving v. Virginia, 174, 186, 192–95, 308n145, 310n166
Lowe, Lisa, 146
Lubiano, Wahneema, 199–201
Lyon, Caleb, 161

Major Crimes Act (1885), 102–3, 290n31
Manalansan, Martin, 188
manifest domesticity, 272nn12–13
marriage: Freedmen's Bureau contracts for, 219–23, 318n74, 318n76, 318n82; Indigenous concepts of, 48–61, 78–88, 279n17; interracial marriage and, 174, 308n145; Mormon polygamy and, 150–64; Native feminist reframing of, 129–40; political orders and monogamy in, 155–56, 197–98, 299n38; privacy rights and, 166–68, 174, 181–95; in queer scholarship, 66–73, 282nn62–63, 309n157; same-sex marriage, 61–73, 181–95; state framework for, 39, 128–29
marronage, 66, 313n29
Marshall, Thurgood, 109–12, 174, 288n11
Martin, Trayvon, 246
Martinez, Audrey, 108–9
Marx, Karl, 26–27
McCarthy, Theresa, 129–30
McClintock, Anne, 279n11
McGirt v. Oklahoma, 260–61
McKean, James, 157
McKittrick, Katherine, 208
Medicaid, 179
Mehta, Uday, 18–19, 147, 180
Melamed, Jodi, 202
Michi Saagiig Nishnaabeg self-determination, 80
migrancy, racialization and, 32

Mills, Charles, 275n50
Mink, Gwendolyn, 303n97, 305n109
minority nationalism, 31
Minow, Martha, 168
Mississippi Band of Choctaw Indians v. Holyfield (1989), 122–25
modernity, family as core of, 49
Moreton-Robinson, Aileen, 276n58
Morgan, Jennifer, 273n27
Morgan, Lewis Henry: on aberrance and unfitness, 186; on colonialism, 130; enfamilyment and work of, 147; gens concept of, 53–54, 215; on Indianness and non-Indianness, 37–38; on jurisdiction, 101; on kinship, 46–61, 71, 84, 86, 89, 280n21; on marriage, 82; normativity and work of, 161; on political orders, 96, 199–200
Morgensen, Scott, 273n21
Mormonism: contemporary representations of, 302n70; federal assault on, 149–64, 196, 300nn46–47; homonationalism and, 198; Indigenous peoples and, 160–64, 299n45; polygamy and, 186. *See also* polygamy
Morrill, Justin, 299n41
Morrill Act (1862), 153–54, 298n27, 298n33, 299n41
Morton v. Mancari (1974), 102–3, 113, 118, 140–41, 289n24, 289n28
Moten, Fred, 207, 209, 335n182
mothers' clubs, Black neighborhoods' development of, 234–35
Moynihan, Daniel Patrick, 227, 323n104
Moynihan Report. See *Negro Family: The Case for National Action, The* (Moynihan Report)
Muhammad, Khalil Gibran, 324n115
Muñoz, José Esteban, 65, 265–66
Murphy, Michelle, 87, 272n18
mutual aid, Black governance and, 339n210, 340n213. *See also* networks
Mvskoke people, political orders and, 16–17, 133, 135. *See also* Creek Nation

Naples, Nancy A., 234–35, 240–42, 328n134
National Advisory Commission on Civil Disorders (Kerner Commission), 325n122

nationalism, governance and, 199–200. *See also* Black nationalism
Navajo Nation, political culture of, 136–37
Negro Family: The Case for National Action, The (Moynihan Report): Community Action Programs criticism in, 241–42; criminality of Blackness and, 204; economic and employment data in, 323n112; kinship discussed in, 228–29; origins of, 323n104; pathologization of Black families in, 227–42, 254–56; welfare policies and, 176, 305n107
neighborhoods: Black collective self-organization in, 234–42, 315nn57–58; destruction of Black neighborhoods, 232–33, 323n112, 335n178; exchange systems in Black neighborhoods, 235–37; federal disinvestment in, 243–53; kinship and, 216–17, 315n56; Moynihan Report pathologization of, 240–42; policing and police violence in Black neighborhoods, 245–53
neoliberalism, kinship valorization and, 67–73
networks: biological connection and, 53–55; Black Americans' use of, 13–14, 204–12, 214–27, 315n57, 339n210; Black Lives Matter Global Network, 246–47; Black neighborhood exchange systems and, 234–37, 328n144; capitalist extraction enabled by, 327n129; governance and alternative forms of, 11–12, 40–41, 88–89, 197–98, 208–12, 339n210; imperialism and role of, 146; Indigenous use of, 12–13, 16–17, 21–24, 75–88, 207; institutionalization and codification of Black networks, 214–15; kinship and, 2–3, 56–73, 228; labor and role of, 201; political orders and, 34–35, 203–4, 207–12; privacy and, 197; queer scholarship on, 32–33; racialization and dismantling of, 29–30; tribal governance and, 128–40; urbanization's impact on, 140–44; violence in, 316n62. *See also* mutual aid
Nichols, Robert, 23, 27–28
Nixon, Richard, 178

non-Indianness: colonial concepts of, 15–16; in federal law and Indian policy, 37–38, 94–98, 112–16, 288n11, 290n32, 290n35, 290n37; tribal jurisdiction and, 98–107, 258–69, 287n3
nonnuclear families, Indigenous concepts of, 75–78
nuclear family model: Black criminality in frame of, 213–27; Freedmen's Bureau use of, 219–23, 319n83; liberal ideology and, 145–46; Moynihan Report use of, 229–30; polygamy as threat to, 145–49; privacy and, 167, 171–81; in queer scholarship, 66–73; racialization and, 81–88; welfare policies and, 175–81

Obergefell v. Hodges (2015), 181, 184–85, 188, 190–95, 302n69, 309n158
O'Connor, Alice, 304n104
Oklahoma v. Castro-Huerta, 36, 258–69, 341n4, 341n6
Oliphant, Mark David, 98–107
Oliphant v. Schlie, 288n17, 289n19
Oliphant v. Suquamish, 38, 94–107, 110–12, 119, 121, 126–27, 135, 142, 258–59, 287n3, 288n16, 289nn19–20, 290n35, 290n37
Orientalism, Mormonism and, 160–61, 163
Osorio, Jamaica Heolimeleikalani, 134–35
O'Sullivan, Megan Devlin, 178–79

Pacific Railroad Act, 153
Parker, Ely S., 48
Pasternak, Shiri, 84
patriarchy: Mormon polygamy and, 157–59; Native feminist reframing of, 129–30; racialization and, 7–8; tribal tradition of, 112–16
Pattillo, Mary, 250
Pearsall, Sarah M. S., 160
penal capital, 244
Penningroth, Dylan, 224
Perry, Imani, 7–8, 272n13
Personal Responsibility and Work Opportunity Reconciliation Act (PWORA), 175, 304n103, 306n112, 310n160
personhood: Blackness and, 205–12; family and, 146–49; forced sterilization and, 180–81; kinship and, 281n39; Native feminist reframing of, 131–40; privacy rights in framework of, 170–81, 187–95; racialization and, 206–12, 302n73; same-sex marriage, 184–95; state enfamilyment policies and, 78
Pexa, Christopher, 83
Phipps, Kelly Elizabeth, 300n47
Piatote, Beth, 137
pilina (Hawaiian ties or relationships), 134
Plaine Counsels for Freedmen (Fisk), 219
Plane, Ann Marie, 279n17
Planned Parenthood League, 166
Planned Parenthood v. Casey (1992), 169–70, 184
Poland Act (1874), 153
political orders: alternative reconfiguration of, 14–25, 257–69; Black activism and, 250–53; Blackness and concepts of, 199–205, 208–12; collective activity and, 16–17, 20–25, 210–12, 268–69, 274n39; culture and, 20–25; emancipation carceration after slavery and, 212–27, 317n68; families and, 3–4; Indigenous governance and, 3–6, 17–25; kinship concepts and, 4, 48–49, 54–61, 73–91, 214–27; monogamy linked to, 155–56; Mormonism as threat to, 149–64; Native feminist remapping of, 127–40; polygamy as threat to, 155–64; primitive accumulation and, 27–35; property ownership and, 223–27; queer scholarship on kinship and, 69–73, 90–91; racialization and, 41, 140–44; tribal jurisdiction and, 96–98, 112–16, 260–69
polygamy: decriminalization arguments for, 162–64; family and, 145–47; federal assault on, 149–64, 196, 299n37, 300nn46–47, 301n68, 301n70; marriage laws and, 186; monogamy infrastructure and, 297n10
popular sovereignty, 152
Population Council, 178
Port Madison Indian Reservation, 98
poverty: increased concentrations of, 243–53, 330n162; juvenile delinquency linked to, 230; privacy protections and, 172–73, 303n97; public narratives of, 228, 323n111; welfare policies and, 176–78, 304nn103–4

Povinelli, Elizabeth, 59–60, 75, 185, 263, 274n39
power, Black self-determination and dynamics of, 248–53
"Powers of Indian Tribes," 128
pregnancy, privacy rights and, 166–81
Presidential Task Force on Urban Renewal, 232
primitive accumulation, racialization as, 25–35, 147–49, 263–69
Prince v. Massachusetts (1944), 170
priorness, Indigenous peoples' assertion of, 28–35
privacy: criminality and protection of, 171–72; family and, 146–49; forced sterilization and, 176–81, 306nn113–16; individual rights and, 165–66; Mormon polygamy and, 150–64; normative foundations of, 297n10; poverty and absence of, 172–73, 303n97; queer scholarship on kinship and, 62–73; racialization and right to, 165–81; same-sex marriage and, 181–95; state framework for, 39; welfare policy and, 172–74
problem-space: defined, 5; networks and, 207–8
property: Black American ownership of, 205–12, 262–63; family structure and rules of, 56–61, 274n42; Freedmen's Bureau control of, 223–271; Indigenous concepts of, 74–88, 262–63, 276n58, 285n98; nationalism and, 200–201; post-emancipation claims involving, 217–18; settler dispossession and transformation into, 27–35. *See also* land use and ownership
Puar, Jasbir, 32–33, 181, 194
public housing: federal policies and funding for, 238–39, 328n136, 328n141; Moynihan Report pathologization of, 235–37
Public Law 280, 118
public space: colonial framing of, 137–40; queer scholarship on role of, 63–73
Purifoy, Danielle, 254

Quashie, Kevin, 339n210
queer scholarship: Black Lives Matter and, 247, 251–53; families and, 32–33, 272n13, 282nn61–63; intimacy and, 60–61; on kinship, 44–48, 60–73, 89–90, 281n45; racialization in, 77–78; state framework for, 34–39
Quong, Jonathan, 274n42, 275n45

racialization and race: criminality and, 39–40, 308n145; families and, 1–3, 6–14, 55–61, 66–73, 75–78, 272n13; grounded relationalities and, 202; heteronormativity and, 74–88; homeownership and, 167; Indian Child Welfare Act framework of, 117–27; Indigenous peoplehood and, 4–5, 23–25, 75–78, 107–16, 259–60; interracial marriage and, 174; kinship and, 43–48, 52–61, 66–73, 272n13; marriage laws and, 181–95; Mormonism and, 160–64; Native feminist remapping of, 127–40, 143–44; personhood and, 302n73, 303n93; political orders and, 14–25; as primitive accumulation, 25–35, 147–49, 263–69; privacy rights and, 148–49, 165–66, 172–81; same-sex marriage and, 181–82, 189–95, 310n173; state policy and, 39, 142–44; tribal jurisdiction and, 94–98, 104–7; welfare benefits and, 174–81
Ramirez, Renya, 139
Rawls, John, 18–20, 274n42, 298n31
Reagan, Ronald, 330n162
Reconstruction era: Black relocation during, 317n69; Black social networks in, 213–15; post-emancipation carceration during, 212–27
Reddy, Chandan, 32, 202
redescription, defined, 5–6
Reed, Adolph Jr., 238
Rehnquist, William (Justice), 98, 101–2, 105–6, 288n17, 289n23
religious freedom, polygamy and, 154–55
Relocation Program, 138–40
reproduction: heteronormativity and racialization of, 106–7; kinship and role of, 50–52; nonnormative patterns of, 77; post-emancipation criminalization of, 213–14; privacy rights and, 166–81, 303n88; reproductive justice and, 307n125; welfare policy and, 177–78. *See also* contraception; forced sterilization

reservation ideology, US Indian policy and, 137–40
residential segregation: blockbusting and, 327n126; federal policies of, 243–53, 325n123; gentrification and, 243–53, 331n166; Moynihan report normalization of, 227, 232–42; persistence of, 330n162; state and municipal laws enforcing, 325n123; Tulsa Race Massacre and, 262–63
respectability politics, Black rejection of, 247–53, 312n16
Reynolds, George, 298n27
Reynolds v. United States (1879), 150, 154–55, 157–63, 167, 191, 298nn27–29, 299n38, 301n63
"Right to Privacy, The" (Warren and Brandeis), 165
Roberts, Dorothy, 177, 180, 306n115
Roberts, John, 190–91, 302n69, 306nn114–15, 309n158, 310n166
Robert Taylor Homes, 236
Robinson, Cedric, 211, 250
Robinson, Zandria F., 237
Rockefeller, Nelson, 178
Rodríguez, Juana María, 44, 63, 67–68, 77, 84, 285n106
Roe v. Wade (1973), 169–71, 186, 303n88
Rogers, Brent, 151
Rosenblum, Nancy, 300n47
Ross, Marlon, 195

Safe Streets and Crime Control Act (1967), 231
Sahlins, Marshall, 44–45, 278n6
Said, Edward, 163
same-sex marriage: federal law and, 181–95, 302nn69–70, 309n158, 310n173; kinship and, 61–73
Santa Clara Pueblo v. Martinez, 38, 97–98, 107–16, 118–19, 121, 130, 132, 135, 141
scale, rule-making and modes of, 6–7
"Scheme of Life That Worked, A" (Deloria), 79
Schneider, David, 45–46, 50–52, 89, 276n6
Scott, David, 5, 207

Scott, James C., 32–33
Sea Islands, Black settlement of, 223
Sealey, Kris, 274n36
self-determination and governance: Black urban self-organization and, 238–42, 250–53; federal law on, 137–40; Indian Child Welfare Act and, 116–17; Indian Reorganization Act and, 128–29; Native feminist reframing of, 131–40; organization against police violence and, 243–53; racialization and, 205–12, 267–69; tribal jurisdiction and, 96–98
selfhood: enfamilyment and, 60–61; in queer scholarship, 66–73
settler framework: heteronormativity in, 22–25; Indianness concepts in, 15–16
sexual assault of Indigenous women, tribal jurisdiction and, 3, 93–98
sexuality: Blackness and, 203; kinship and, 44; marriage and, 195–96, 308n133; privacy rights and, 181–95; queer scholarship on, 62–73; racialization and, 9–14
Shelby County v. Holder, 190
Sherman, William Tecumseh (General), 223, 320n89
Sherman Reservation (Mississippi), 223
Shoah, eugenics and, 178
Simpson, Audra, 3, 14–16, 74–75
Simpson, Leanne, 14–15, 21, 80, 88, 197, 203, 210, 237, 285n107
Sister Wives (reality television show), 162–63
Six Nations of Grand River, 129
Skinner v. Oklahoma, 306n116
slavery: Black personhood and, 206–12; emancipation carceration after, 212–27; Five Tribes treaties ending, 262; Indigenous involvement in, 266–69; kinship and, 14; LGBTQ rights linked to, 309n158; networks during, 217–27, 315nn56–58; objectification and, 273n27; polygamy and, 149–53
Smith, Joseph, 150–51
Southern Homestead Act, 322n97
sovereignty: belonging and, 29, 115–16; family formation and, 197–98; Indian Child Welfare Act and concepts of, 117–27;

Indigenous concepts of, 15–16, 22–25; kinship and, 215–27; Native feminist reframing of, 131–40; polygamy as threat to, 152–64; privacy and, 148–49; racial delineation of, 107–16; state policy and, 39; tribal jurisdiction and, 94–98, 109–16; vernacular sovereignties, 139, 251–52, 255, 266, 339n210
Special Field Order No. 15, 223
Spillers, Hortense, 41, 205
Stack, Carol, 227–28, 328n136
Stallings, L. H., 63, 65–66
Stanley, Amy Dru, 219–20
state: assault on Mormonism by, 149–64; enfamilyment policies of, 12, 39, 78, 164, 273n19, 296n5; federal law and power of, 257–64, 297n6; governance and institutions of, 210–12; jurisdiction of, 4, 7, 10, 12, 15, 17–38, 97–98; juvenile delinquency and role of, 230; kinship and organization of, 54–61, 283n67; marriage and family in framework of, 39, 181–95; nationalism and, 199–200; political orders and role of, 34–35, 257–58; primitive accumulation and racialization by, 25–35; racialization and, 40–41; tribal jurisdiction and governance in relation to, 75–78, 80–88, 98–116, 258–69, 287n3
Stoler, Ann Laura, 8–14, 161, 181–82
stranger sociality, 47
strict scrutiny standard, forced sterilization and, 306n116
Supreme Court (US), 257–63, 297n6
Suzack, Cheryl, 132

Talbot, Christine, 150, 156–57, 299n37
TallBear, Kim, 75–78, 84, 164
Tate, Claudia, 312n16
Taylor, Keeanga-Yamahtta, 247, 250, 328n144
Temporary Assistance for Needy Families (TANF), 175, 304n103
territoriality: Indian Child Welfare Act and, 124–27; Indigenous tribal governance and, 55–56, 98–107; Mormon polygamy and, 150–51, 159–64; primitive accumulation and, 27–35; slavery and, 152–53
Thirteenth Amendment, 212–27

tiospaye (Dakota larger family group), 82, 130–31
Tometi, Opal, 246
Treaty of Guadalupe Hidalgo, 151
tribal governance and jurisdiction: blood relationship determination and, 93–94, 114–16, 123–27; Indian Child Welfare Act and, 116–27; kinship structures and, 74–75, 79–84, 88–91; Mormon polygamy and, 151–52; Native feminist remapping of, 127–40; non-Indianness and, 98–107, 258–69, 287n3; self-governance and, 107–16; sexual assault and violence against women and, 3, 93–98; sovereignty and, 98–116, 259–60, 287n3
Tucker, John Randolph, 160
Tulsa Race Massacre, 262–63

underclass ecology, Black deviance linked to, 242, 330n160
undercommons, Harney and Moten concept of, 207, 209
ungovernability, Blackness and, 204–12
United States: immigration policies in, 32; Indigenous land seizure in, 33; Indigenous policies in, 38–39; marriage and family law in, 39; tribal jurisdiction in, 95–98
United States Housing Authority, 237
United States v. Windsor (2013), 184, 189–95, 309n158
urbanization: funding policies and, 172–81, 238–39, 330n162; Great Migration and, 238–39, 324n115; juvenile delinquency linked to, 230; law enforcement and police violence and, 245–53; Moynihan Report pathologization of, 230–42; Native people targeted for, 138–40; residential segregation and, 243–53, 325n123, 326n125, 329nn147–48; welfare policies and, 175–81
U.S. v. Antelope, 102–3, 289n24
U.S. v. Kagama, 109, 122, 289–90n28
U.S. v. Nice, 122
U.S. v. Rogers, 290n39
U.S. v. Wheeler, 111, 291n49
Utah territory, Mormon community in, 150–54

vagrancy, criminalization of Black Americans based on, 213, 218, 222–27, 319n84
Venkatesh, Sudhir Alladi, 236–37
vernacular sovereignties: for Black Americans, 251–52, 255, 339n210; Indigenous nations and, 139, 261, 266
village, Black community formation as, 238
violence: Black organization against police violence, 243–53; against women, tribal jurisdiction and, 3, 93–98
Violence Against Women Act (VAWA), reauthorization of, 93–95, 286n1, 287n5, 287n7
voting rights: polygamy and, 155–56, 299n37; violence and prevention of, 314n49
Voting Rights Act (1965), 190

Warner, Michael, 62
War on Poverty, 234, 239, 242, 329n149
Warren, Samuel D., 165–66
Weheliye, Alexander, 205–8, 272n13, 302n73, 303n93, 313n39
welfare policy: forced sterilization and, 177–81, 306nn113–16; privacy rights and reform of, 172–74, 304nn103–4; racialization of, 174–81

White, Monica M., 226
whiteness: anti-miscegenation statutes and, 193–95; family structure and role of, 167–68; governance and, 10; Mormonism linked to, 159–61; post-emancipation political economy of, 218–23; privacy rights and, 174–75
Williams, Rhonda, 240
Wilson, James Q., 245–46, 336n184
women: Indigenous women, violence and assault of, 93–94, 287n5; marriage laws and role of, 191–95; privacy rights for, 166–81; sexuality in scholarship on, 63; tribal traditions and role of, 112–16
Woods, Clyde, 226, 322n102
Worcester v. Georgia, 288n17
Workbook (Office of Economic Opportunity), 240–41
Wynter, Sylvia, 205–6, 212

Yazzie, Melanie, 85, 136–37
Young, Brigham, 151–52, 298n27

Zimmerman, George, 246
zones of queerness, kinship and, 61–73

www.ingramcontent.com/pod-product-compliance
Lightning Source LLC
Chambersburg PA
CBHW031721230426
43669CB00007B/201